# Bird- house

D1368445

SLG Publishing      San Jose, California

AGN
BIR

6-10
KK

**Written and Illustrated by**
Vernon White

Published by
SLG Publishing
P.O. Box 26427
San Jose, CA 95159
www.slgcomic.com

President and Publisher
Dan Vado

Editor-in-Chief
Jennifer de Guzman

First Printing: February 2010
ISBN: 1-59362-185-X
ISBN-13: 978-1-59362-185-8

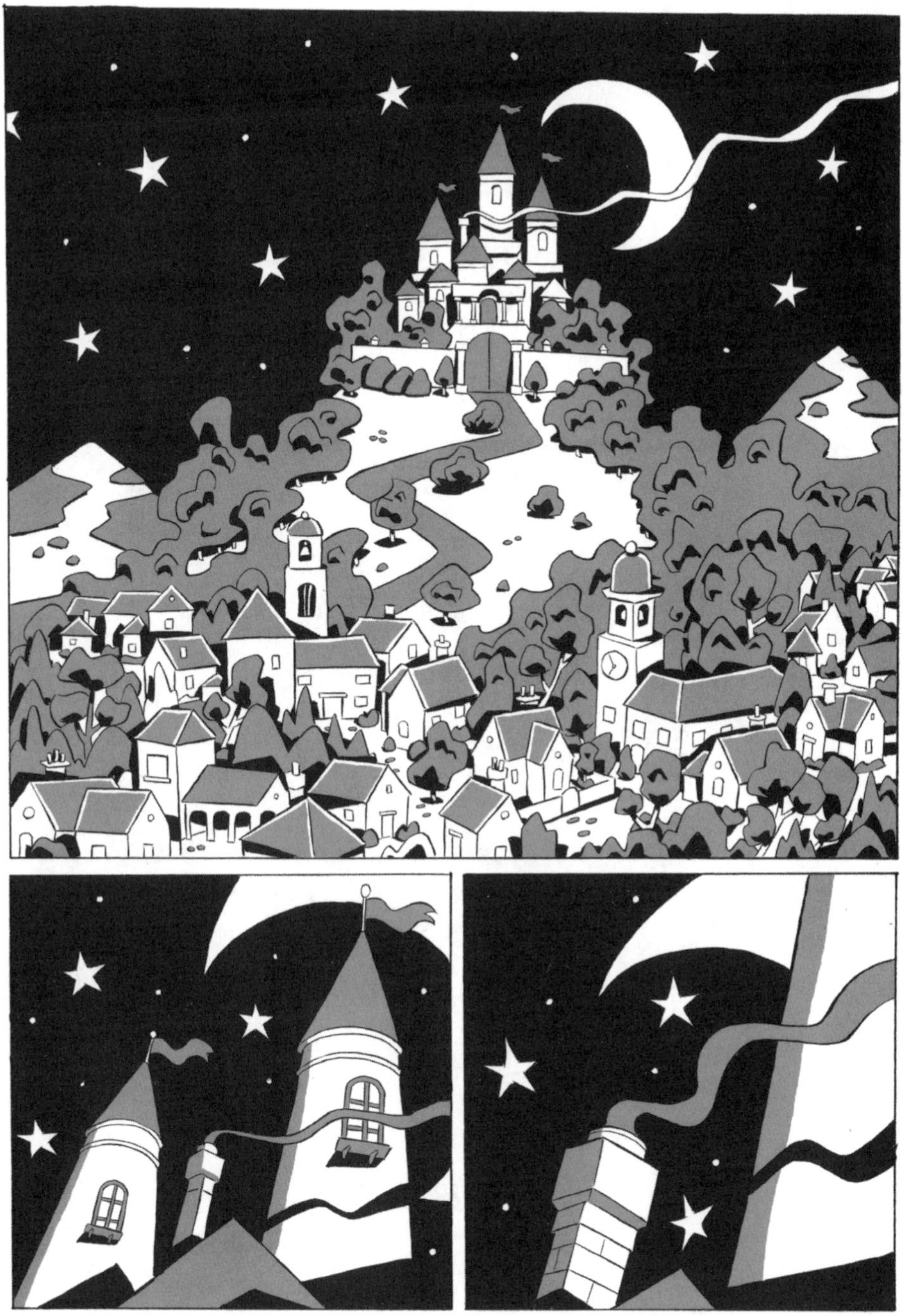

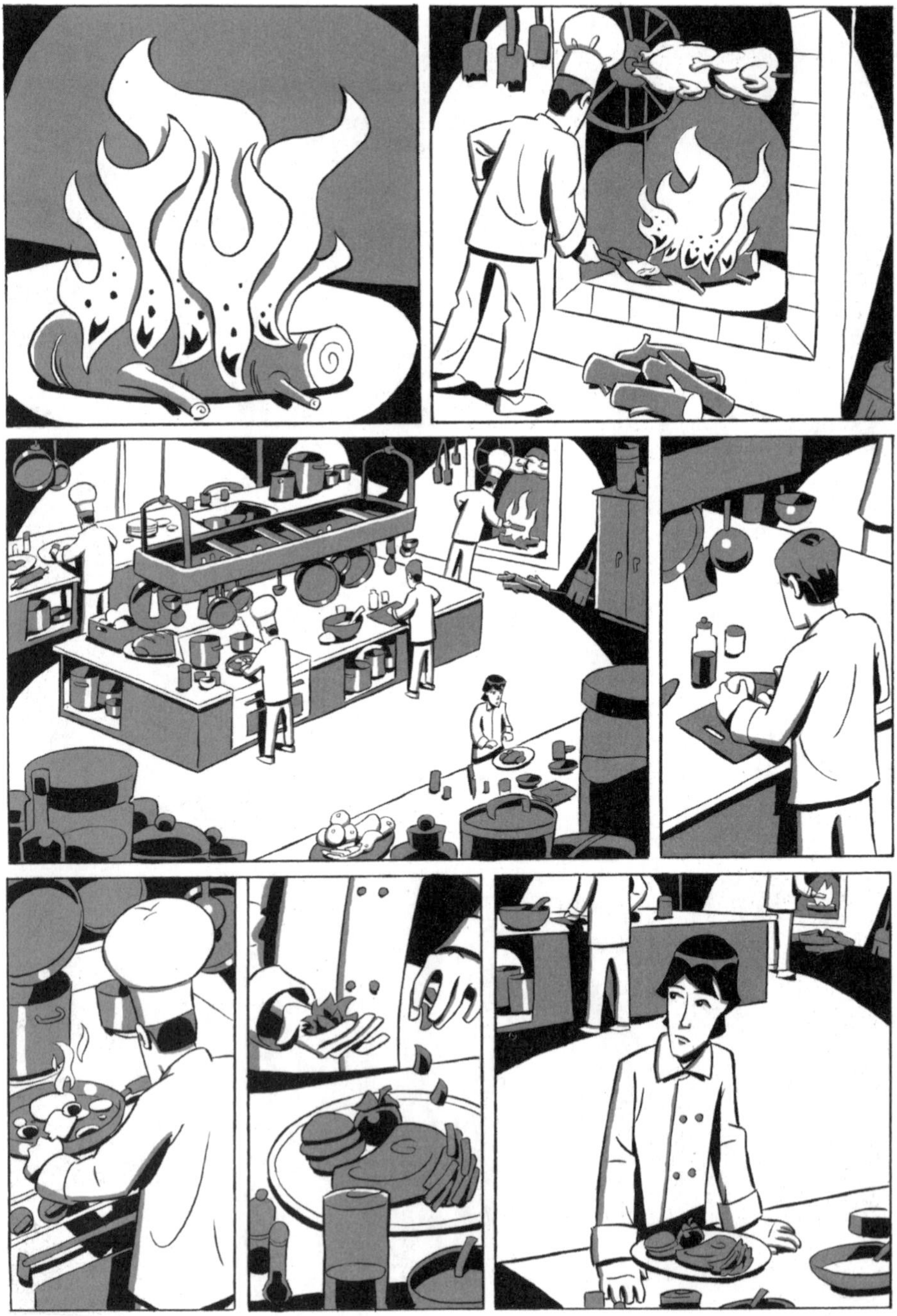

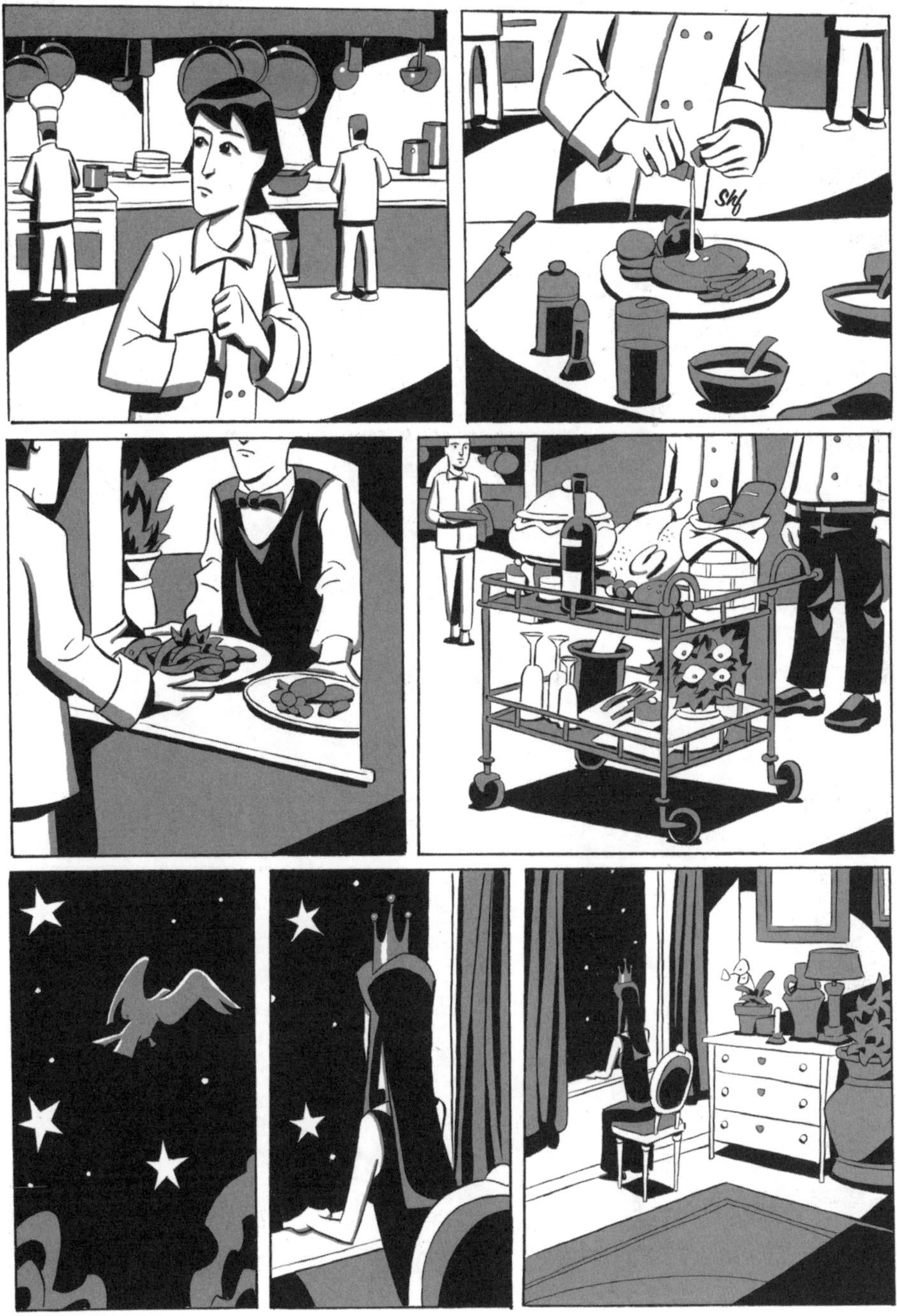

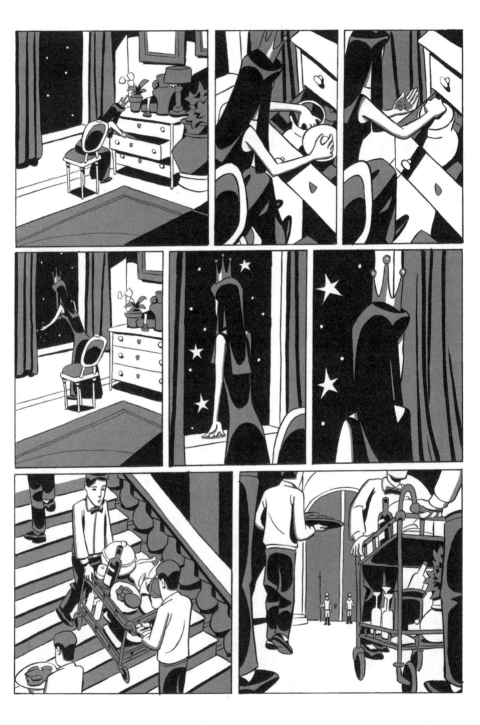

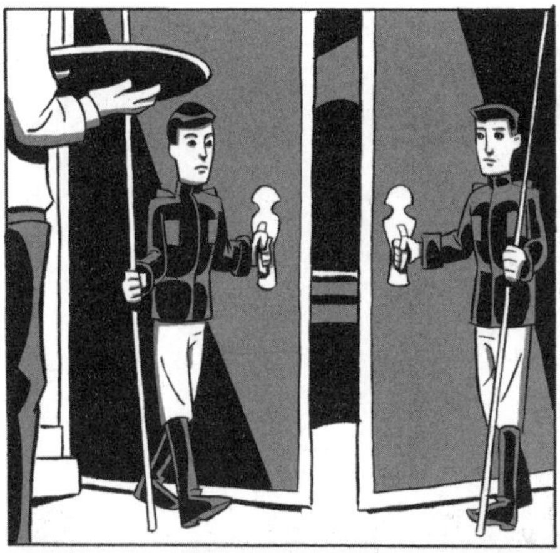
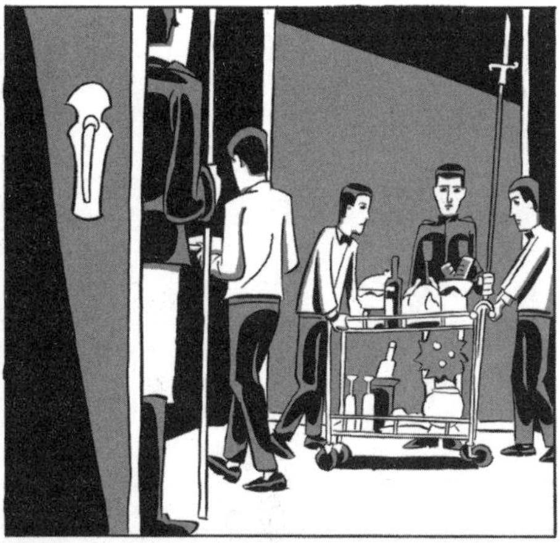
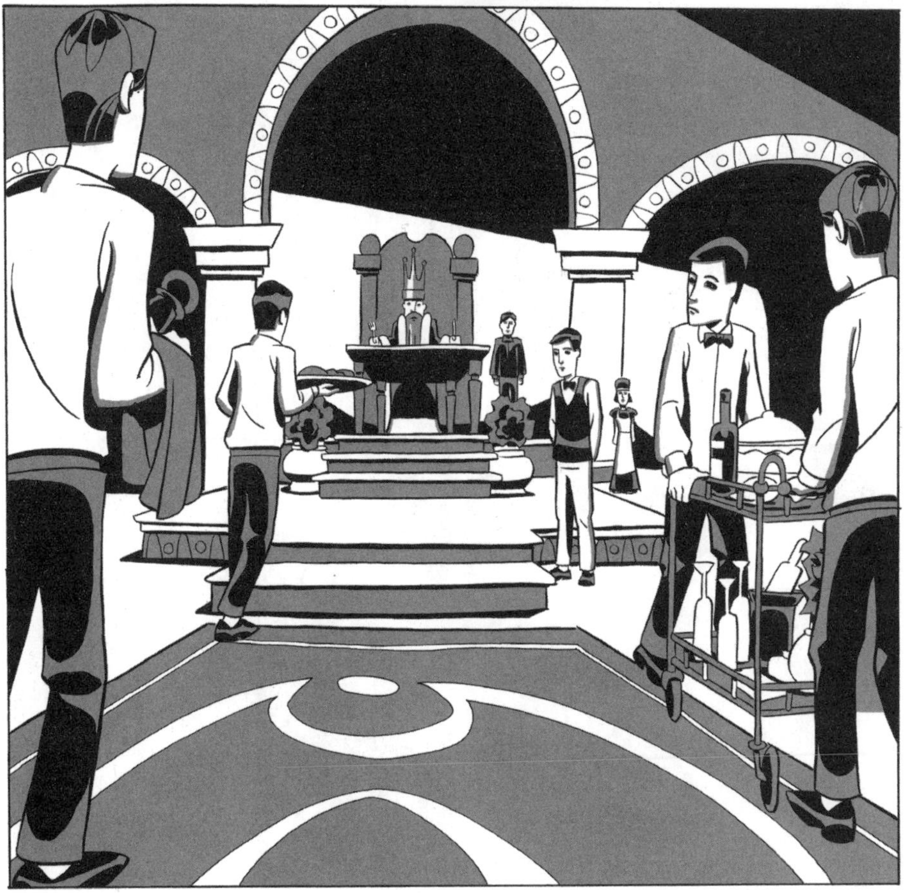

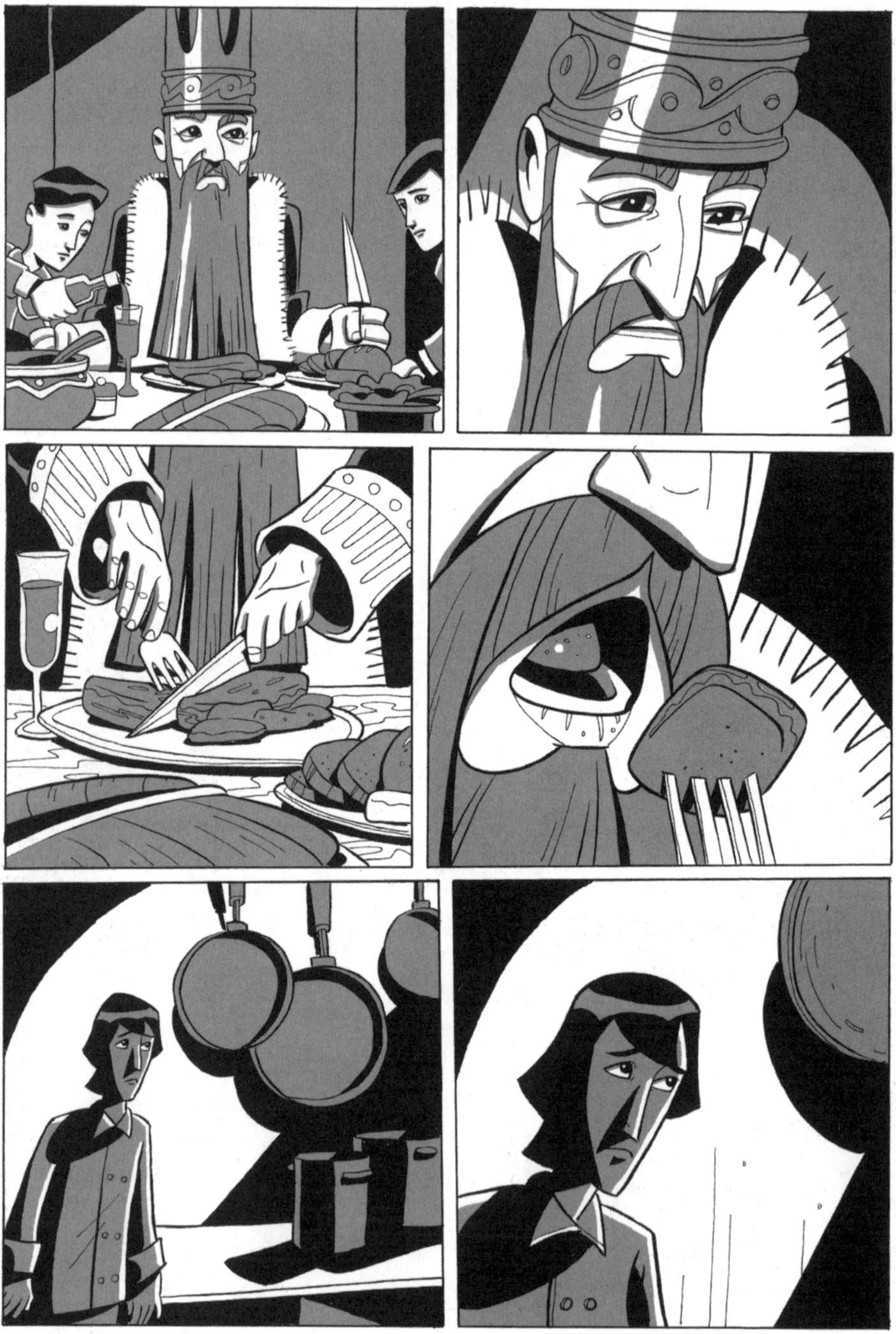

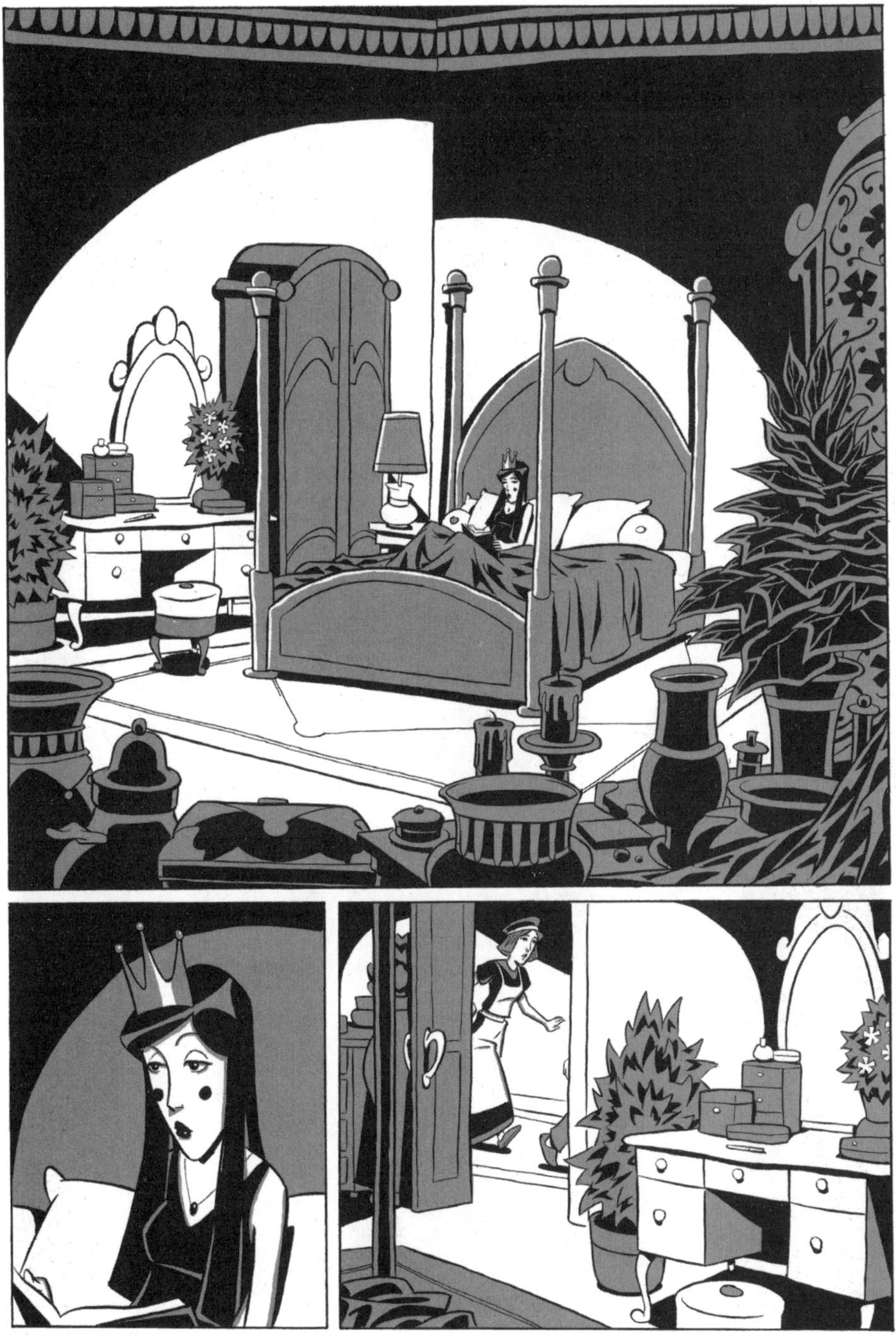

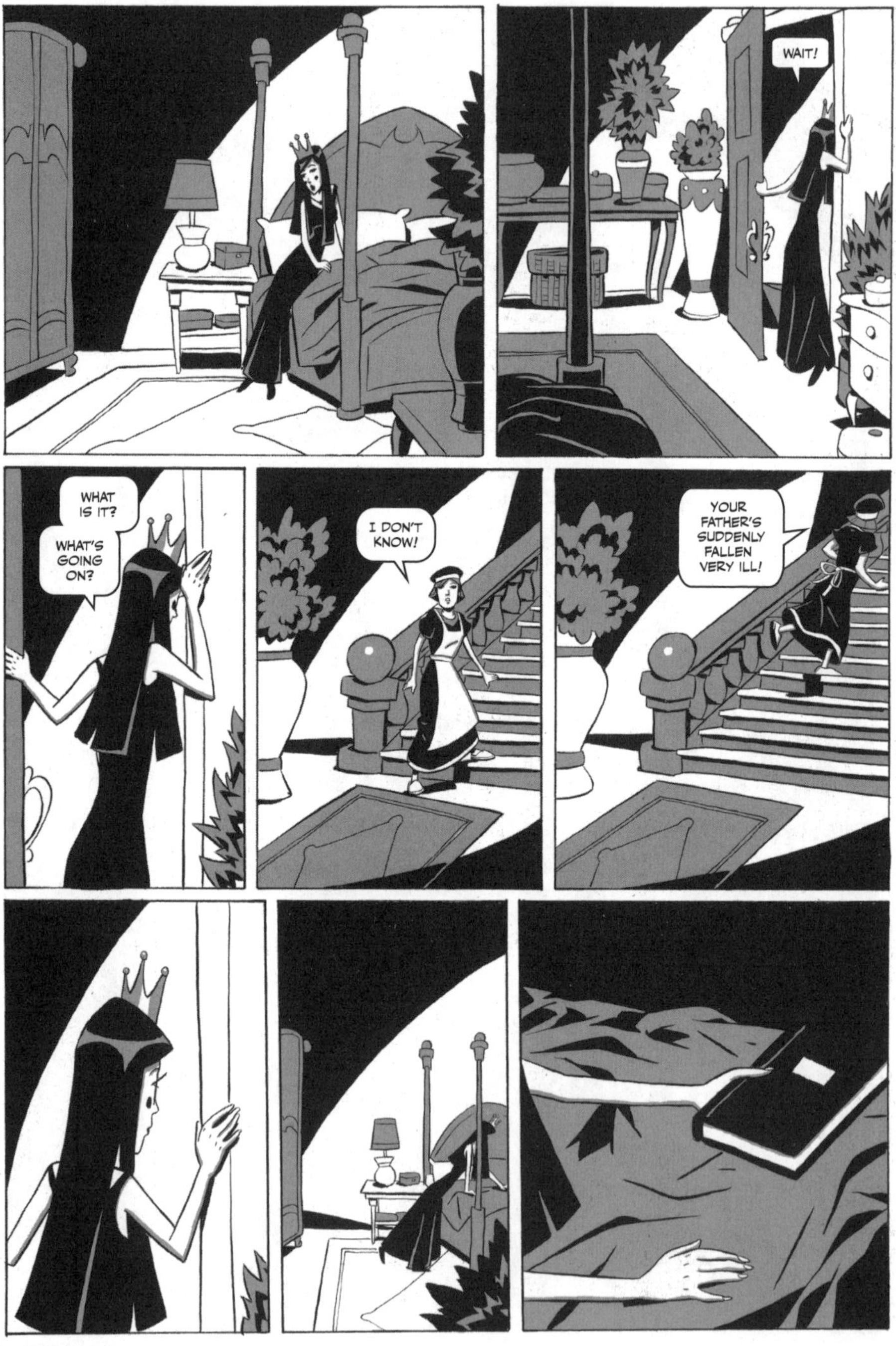
WAIT!
WHAT IS IT?
WHAT'S GOING ON?
I DON'T KNOW!
YOUR FATHER'S SUDDENLY FALLEN VERY ILL!

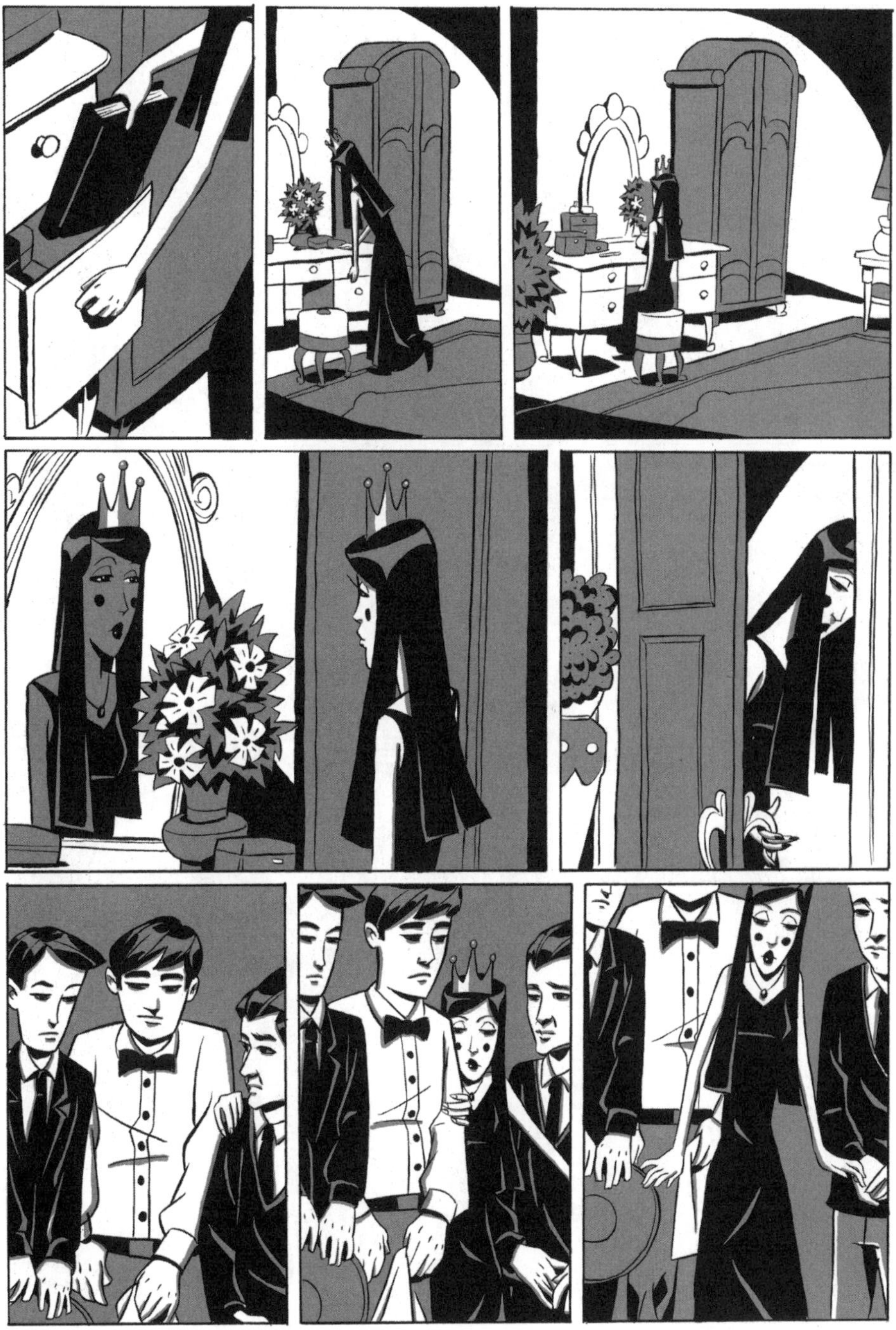

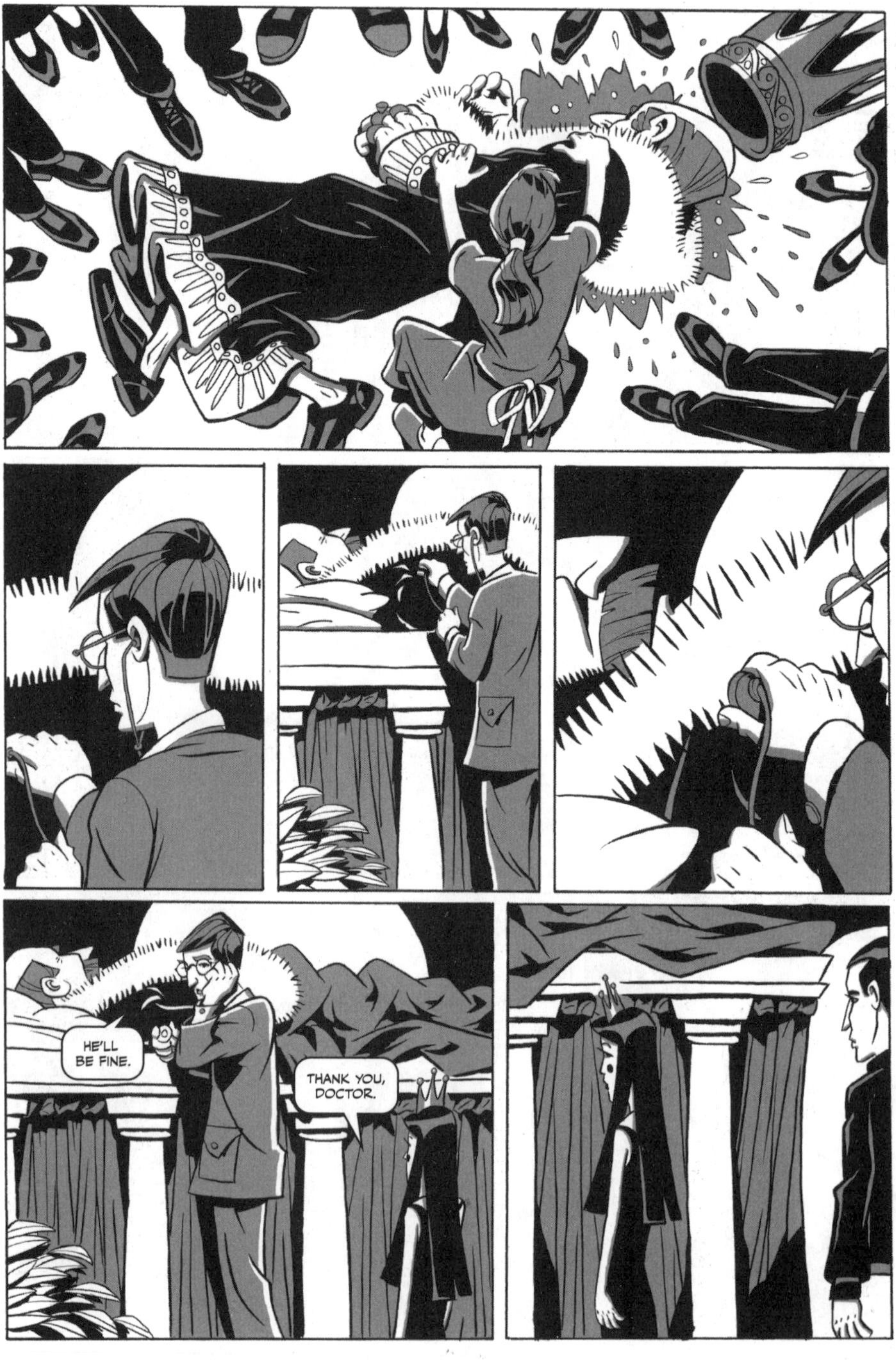
HE'LL BE FINE.
THANK YOU, DOCTOR.

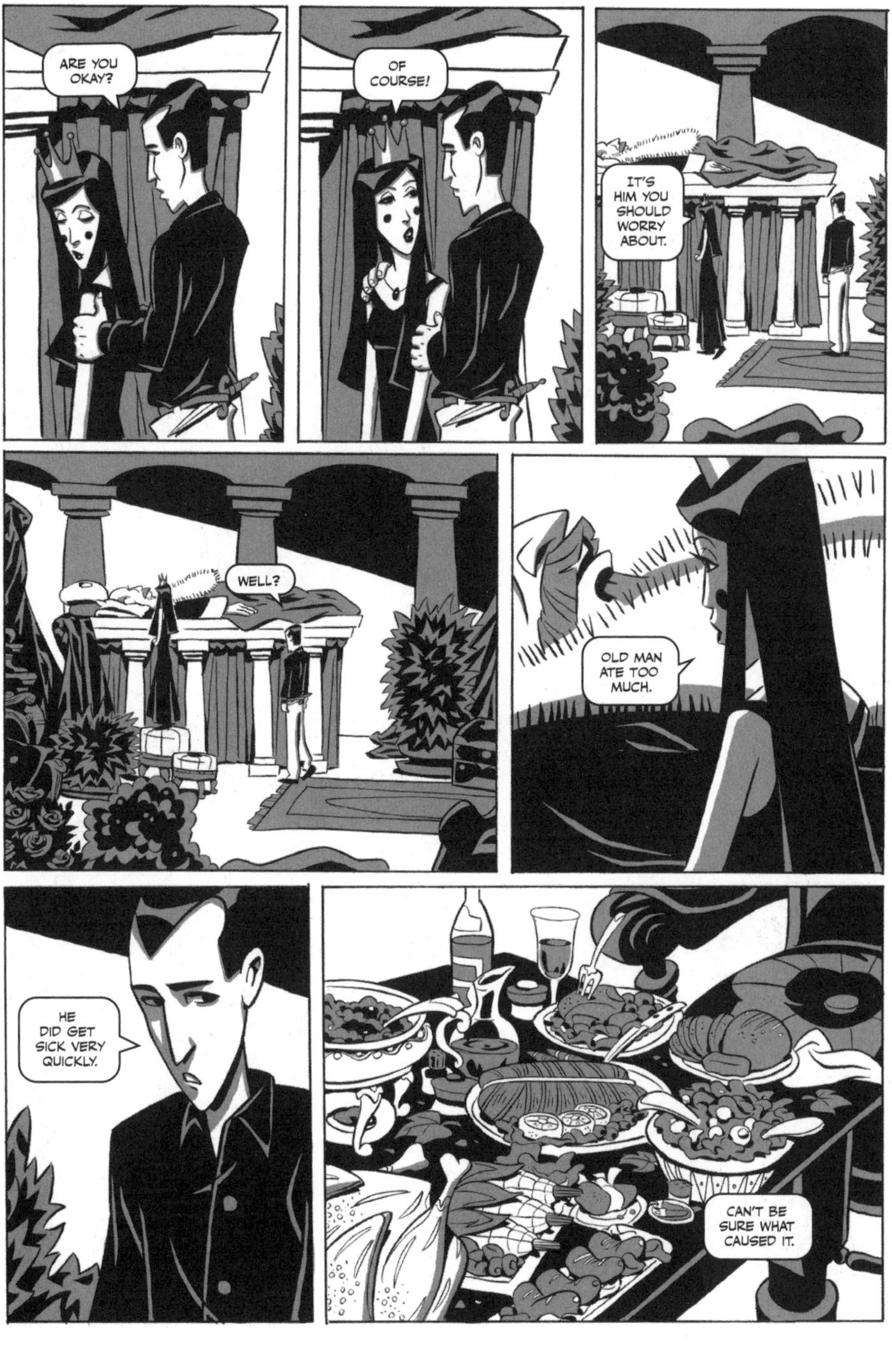
ARE YOU OKAY?
OF COURSE!
IT'S HIM YOU SHOULD WORRY ABOUT.
WELL?
OLD MAN ATE TOO MUCH.
HE DID GET SICK VERY QUICKLY.
CAN'T BE SURE WHAT CAUSED IT.

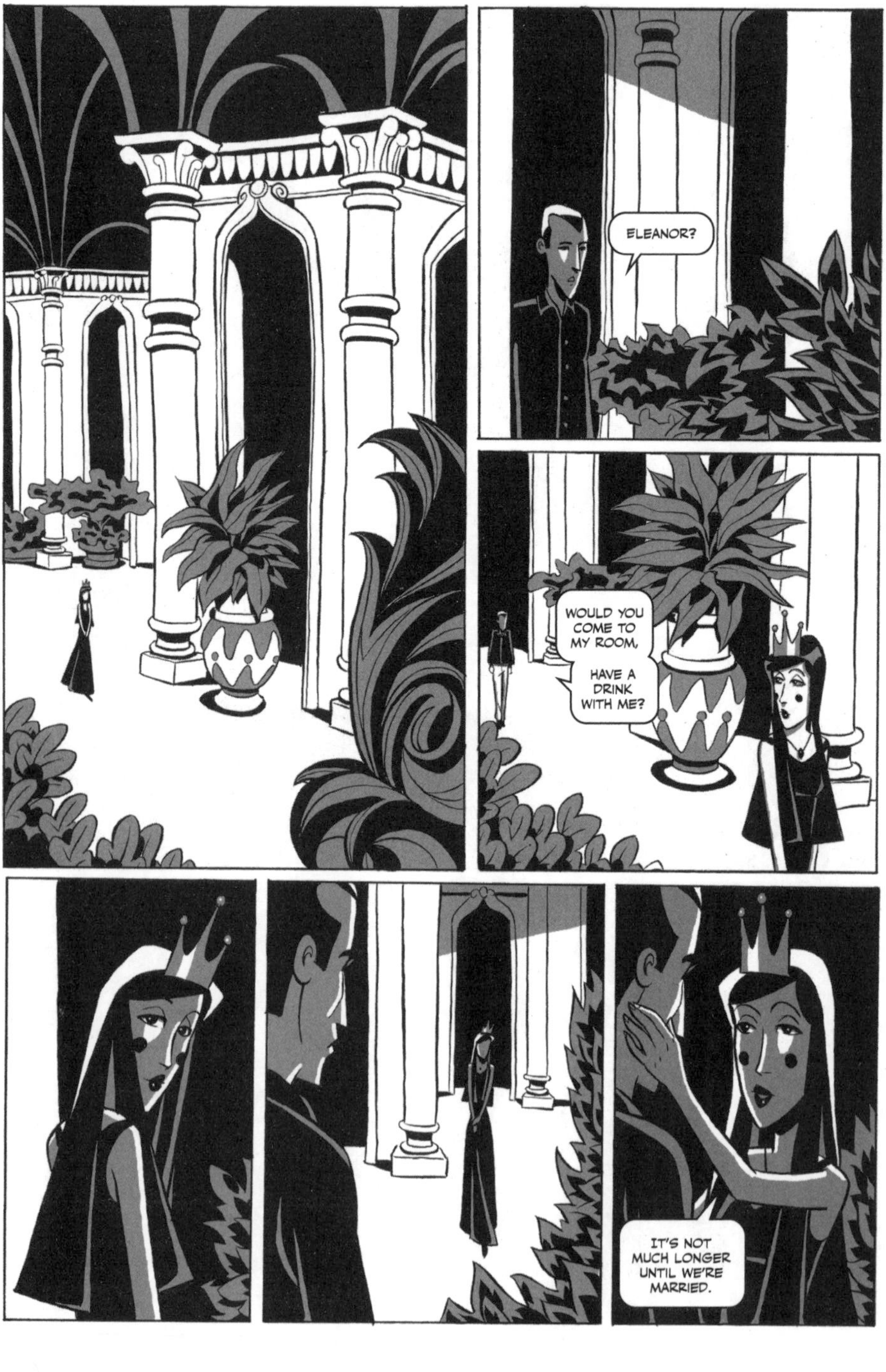
ELEANOR?
WOULD YOU COME TO MY ROOM,
HAVE A DRINK WITH ME?
IT'S NOT MUCH LONGER UNTIL WE'RE MARRIED.

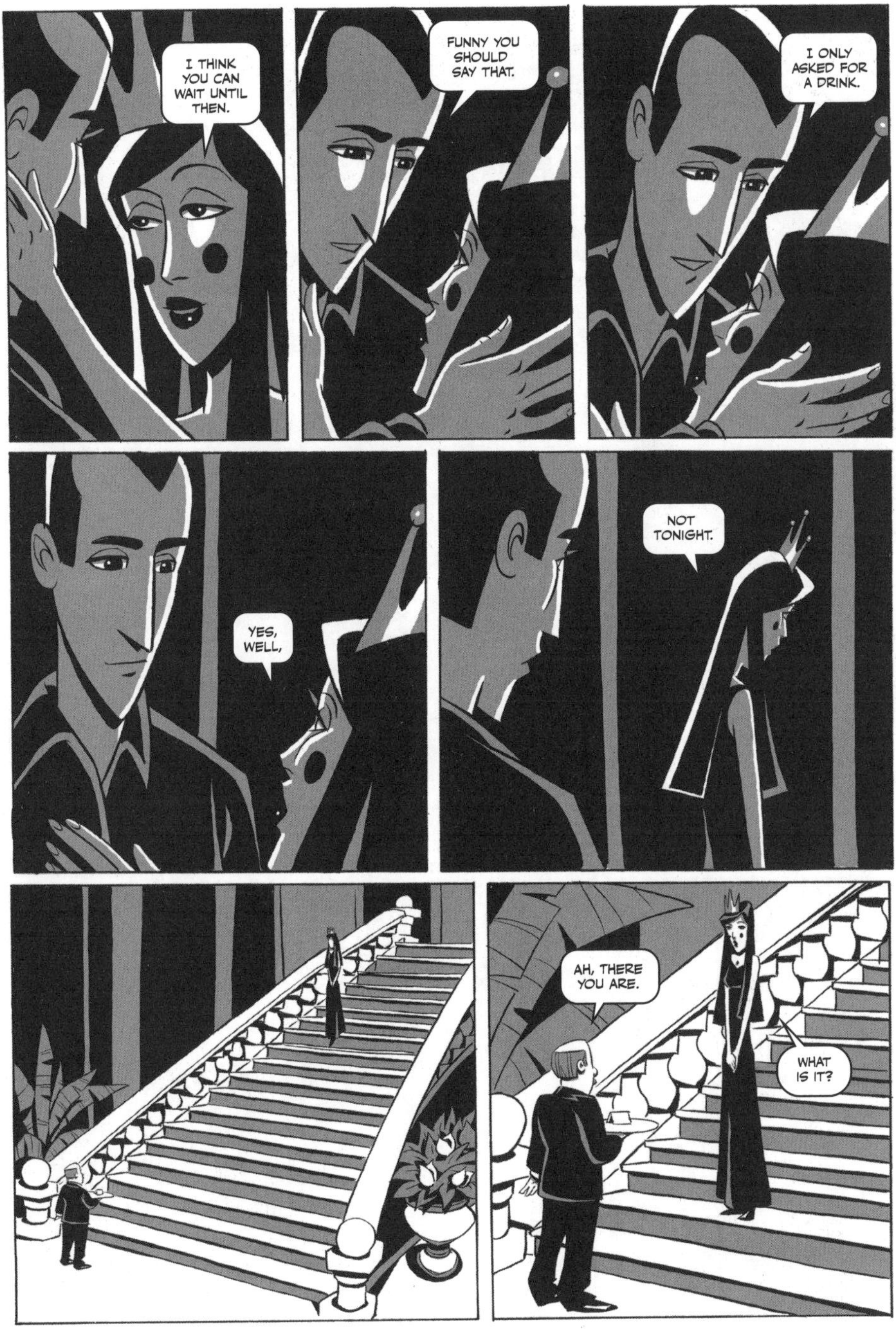
I THINK YOU CAN WAIT UNTIL THEN.
FUNNY YOU SHOULD SAY THAT.
I ONLY ASKED FOR A DRINK.
YES, WELL,
NOT TONIGHT.
AH, THERE YOU ARE.
WHAT IS IT?

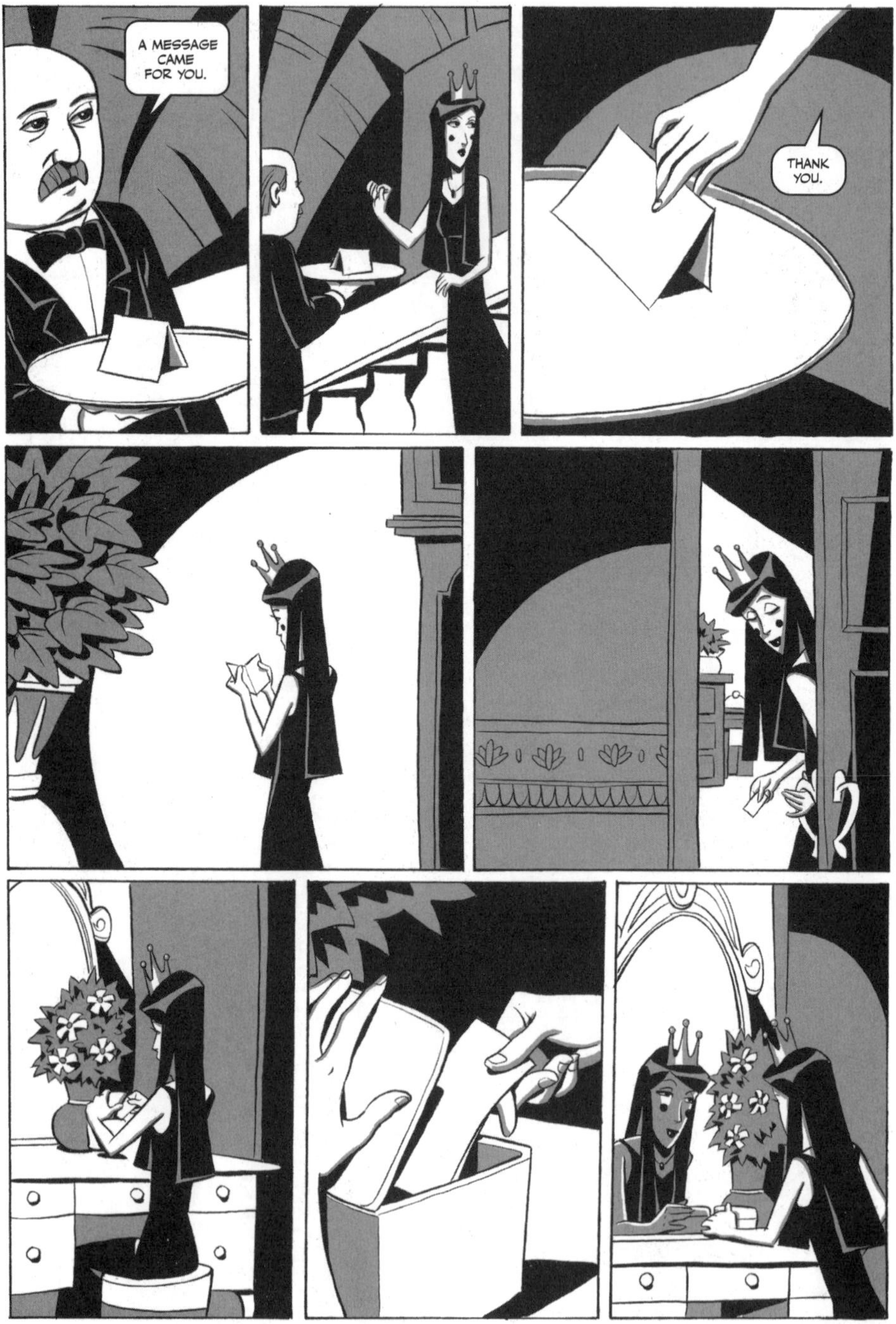
A MESSAGE CAME FOR YOU.
THANK YOU.

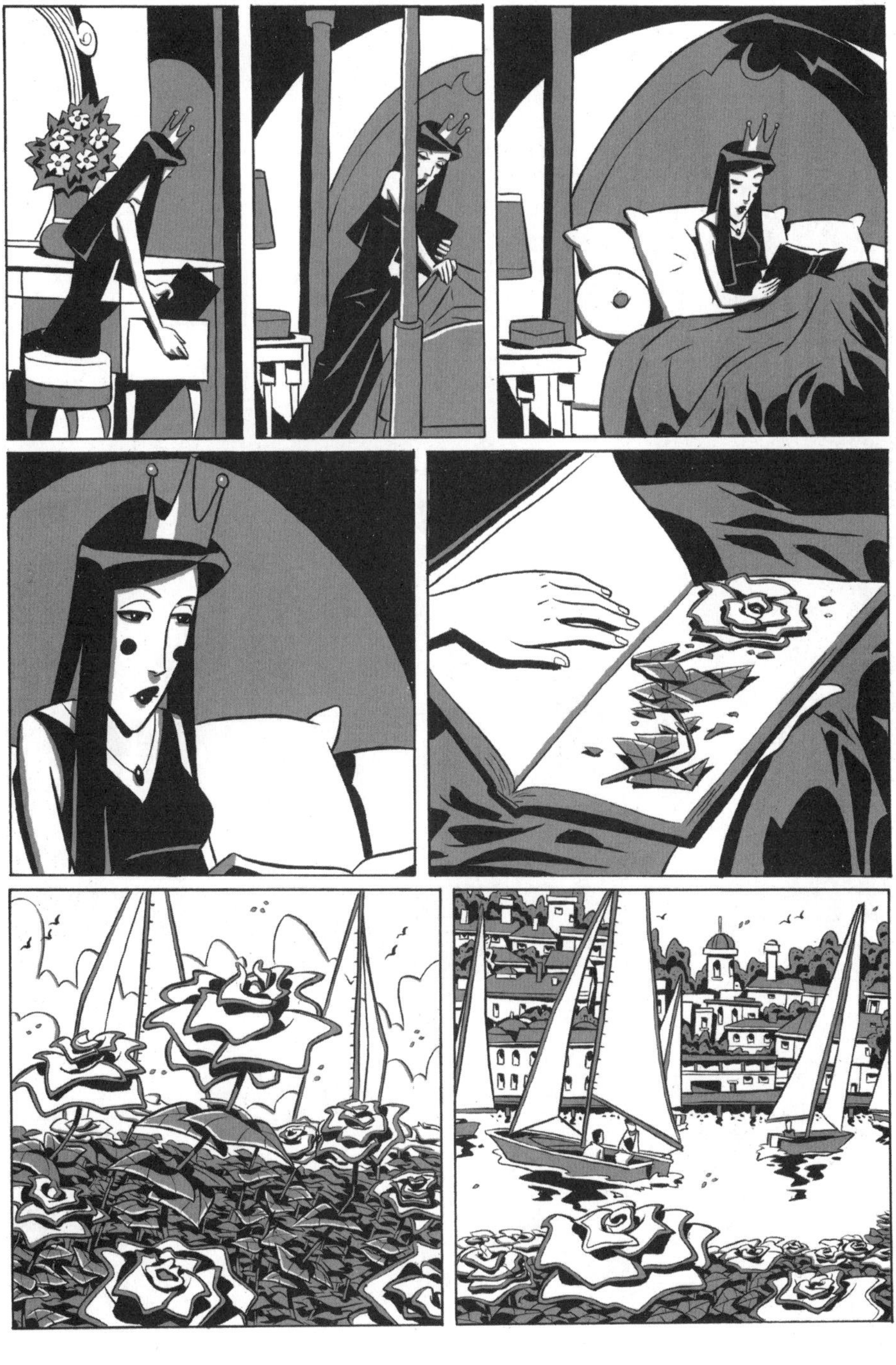

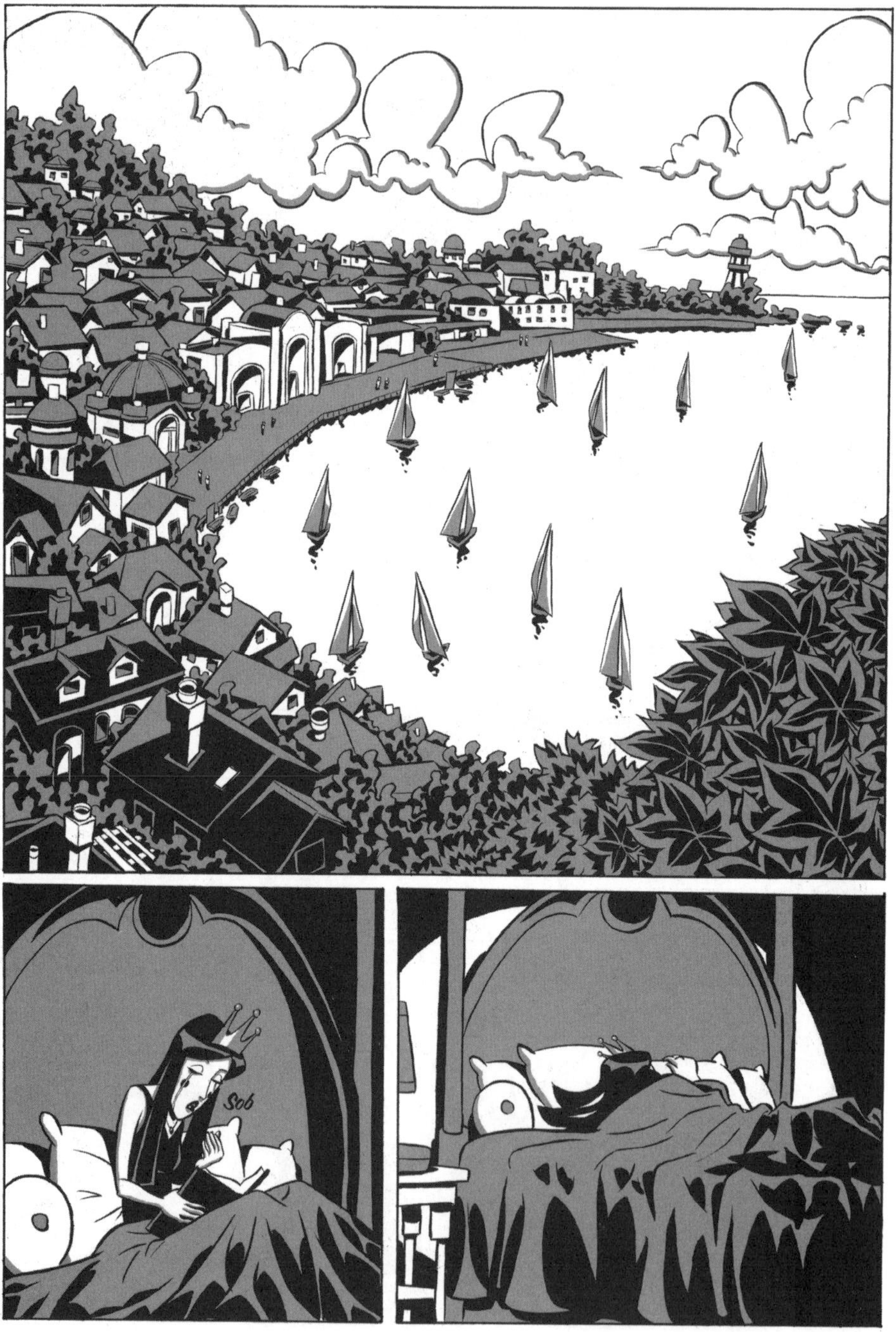
Sob

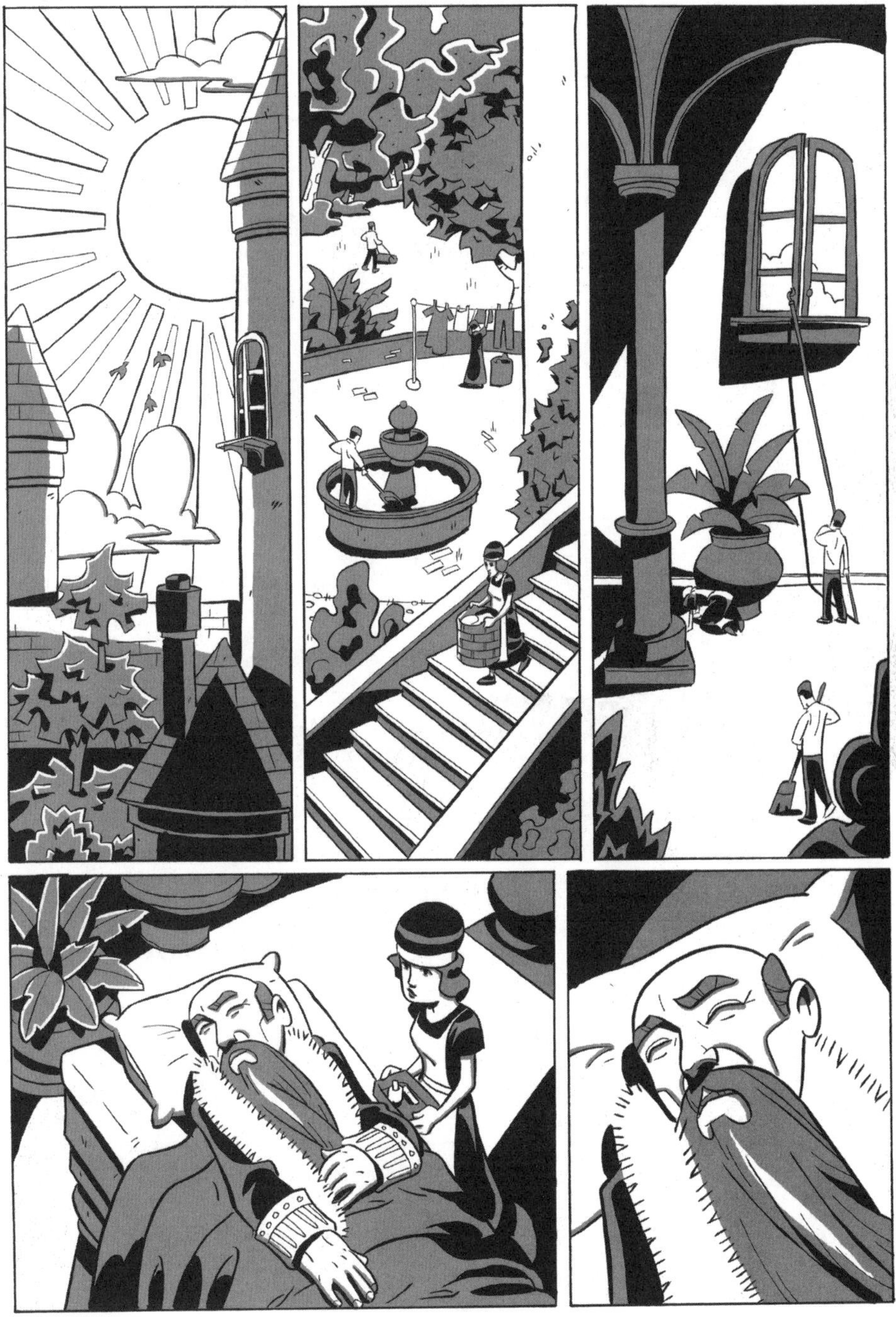

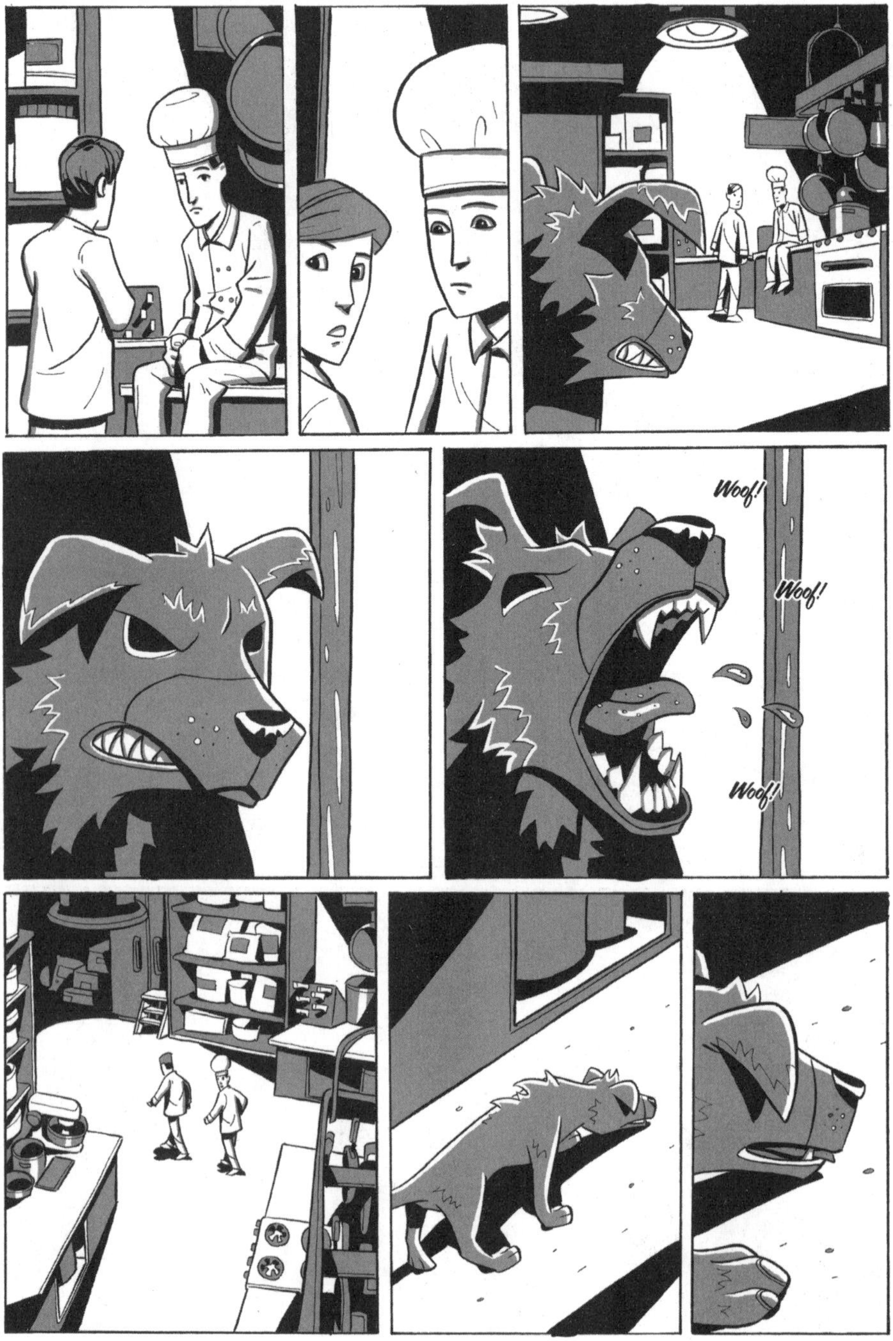
Woof!
Woof!
Woof!

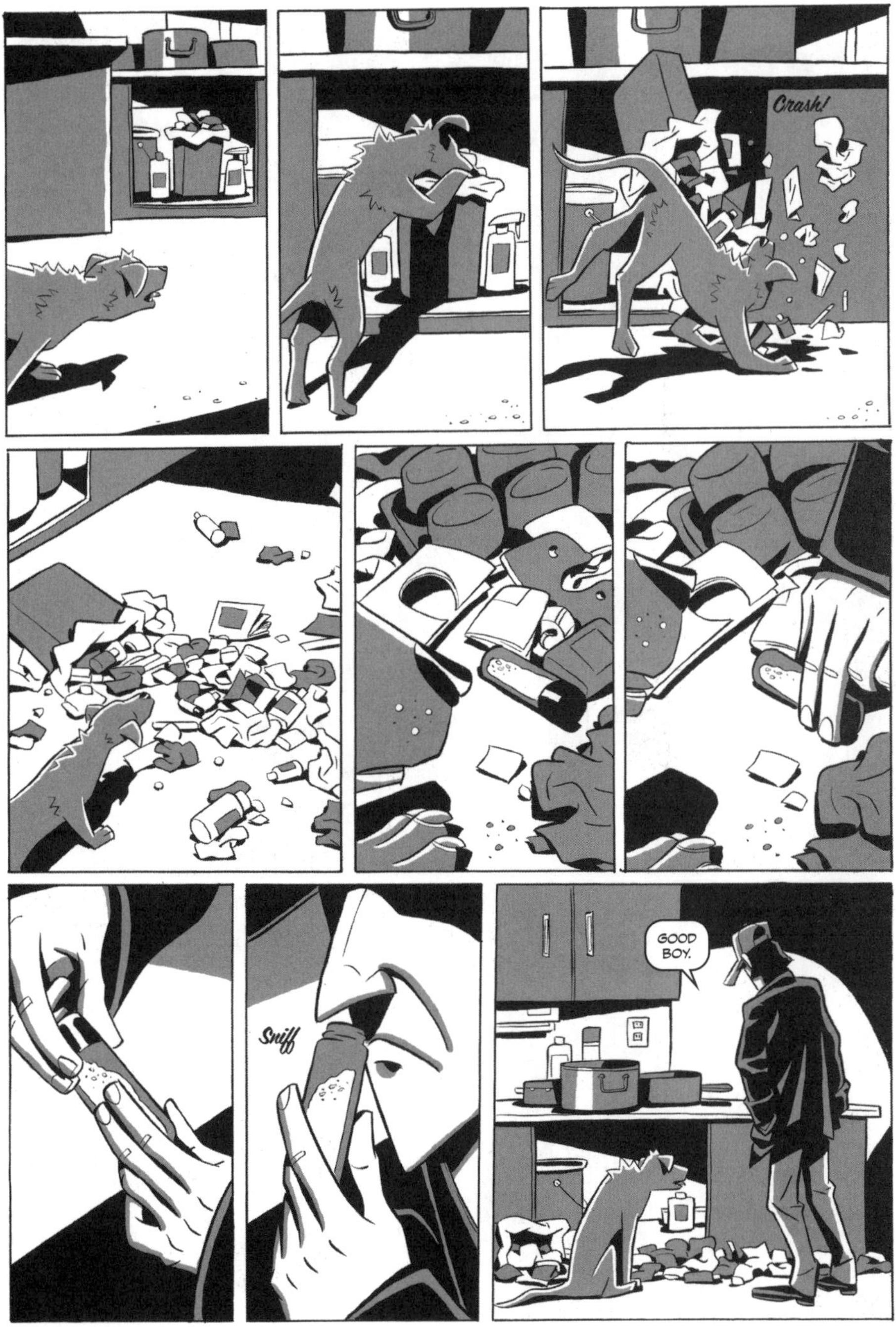
Crash!
Sniff
GOOD BOY.

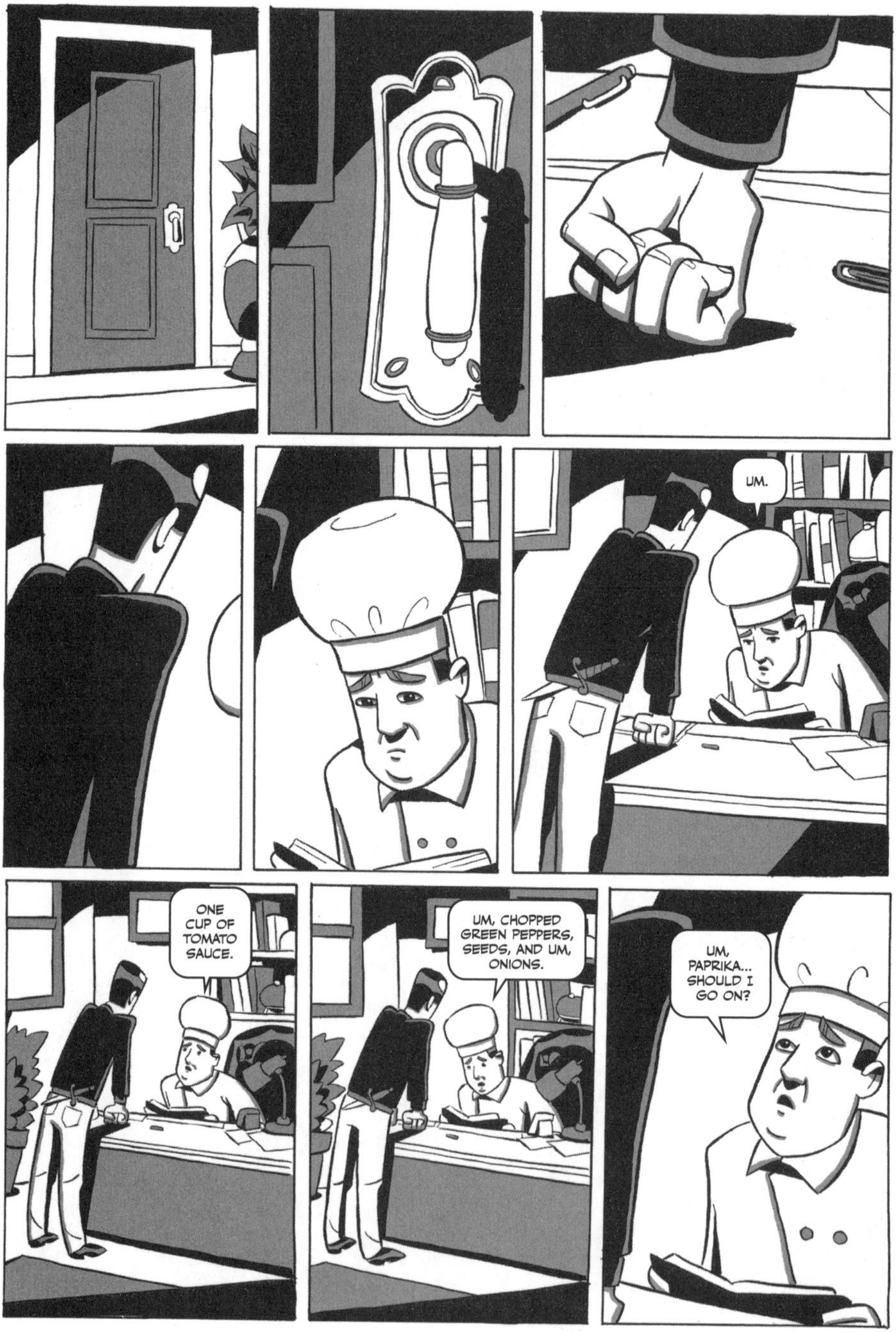
UM.
ONE CUP OF TOMATO SAUCE.
UM, CHOPPED GREEN PEPPERS, SEEDS, AND UM, ONIONS.
UM, PAPRIKA... SHOULD I GO ON?

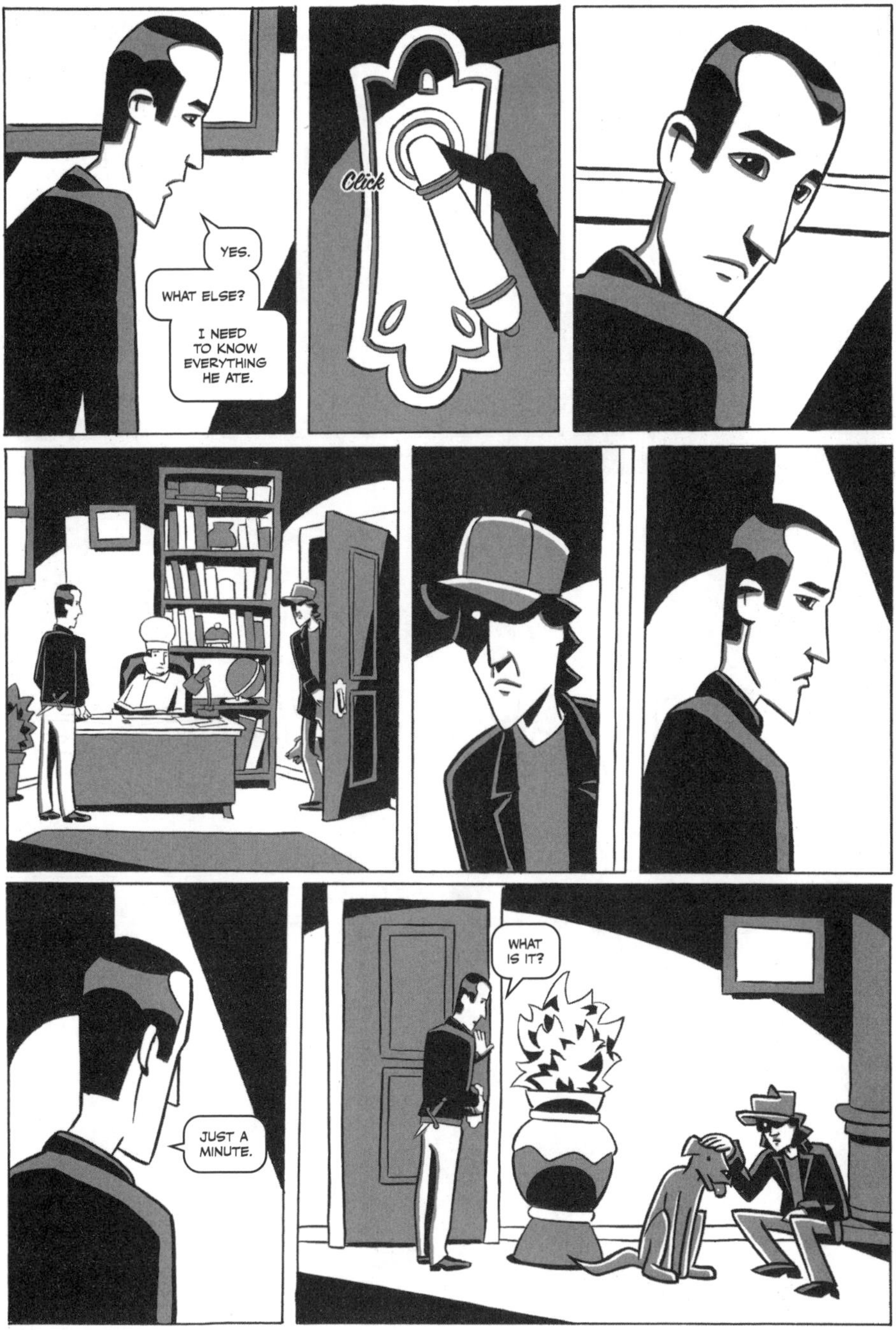
YES.
WHAT ELSE?
I NEED TO KNOW EVERYTHING HE ATE.
Click
JUST A MINUTE.
WHAT IS IT?

I FOUND THIS IN THE KITCHEN.

WHERE WAS IT?

SOMEONE THREW IT INTO THE GARBAGE.

COME ON.

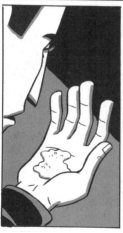

IT'S POISON.

I'LL TELL THE KING.

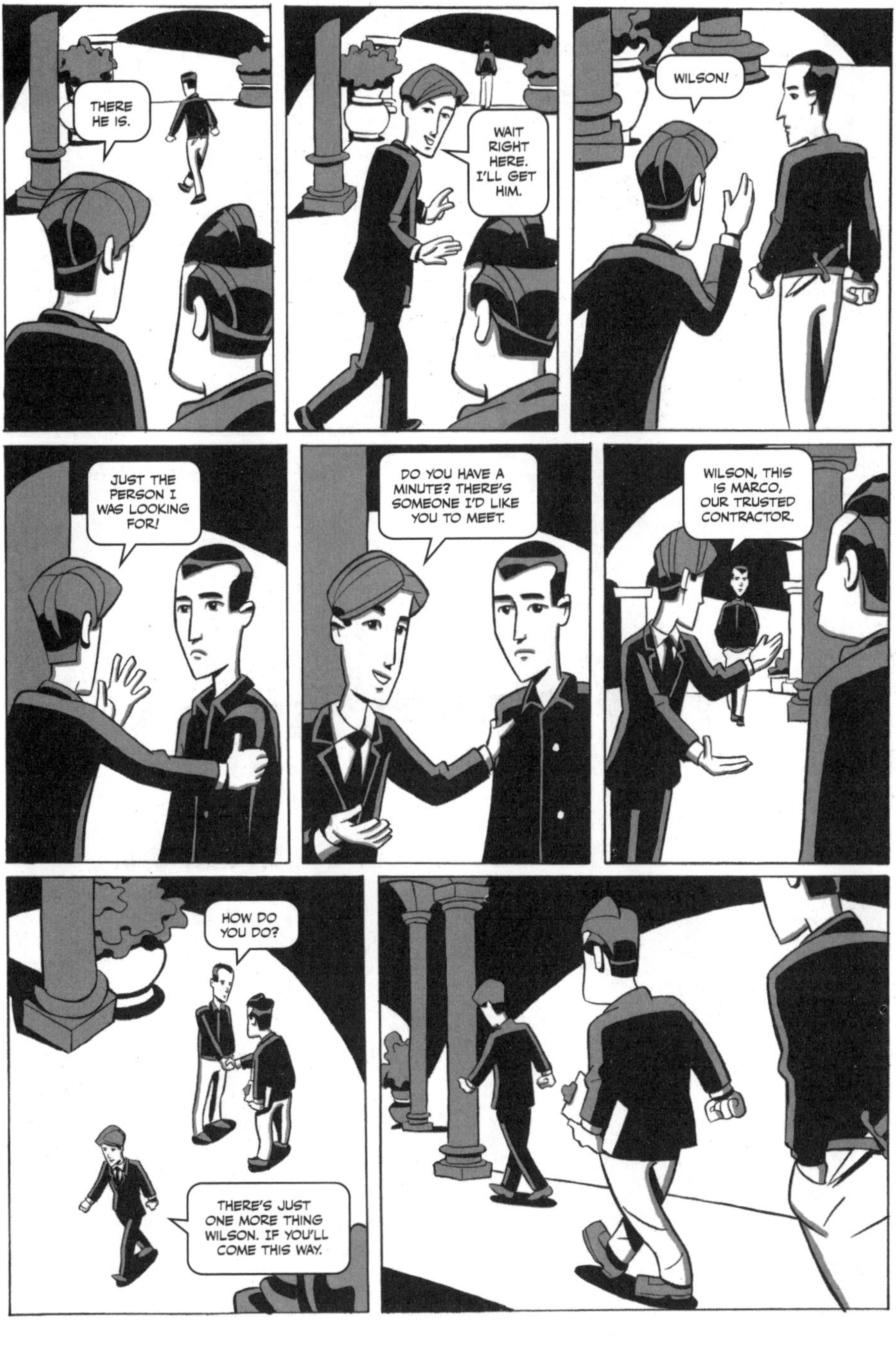

THERE HE IS.
WAIT RIGHT HERE. I'LL GET HIM.
WILSON!
JUST THE PERSON I WAS LOOKING FOR!
DO YOU HAVE A MINUTE? THERE'S SOMEONE I'D LIKE YOU TO MEET.
WILSON, THIS IS MARCO, OUR TRUSTED CONTRACTOR.
HOW DO YOU DO?
THERE'S JUST ONE MORE THING WILSON. IF YOU'LL COME THIS WAY.

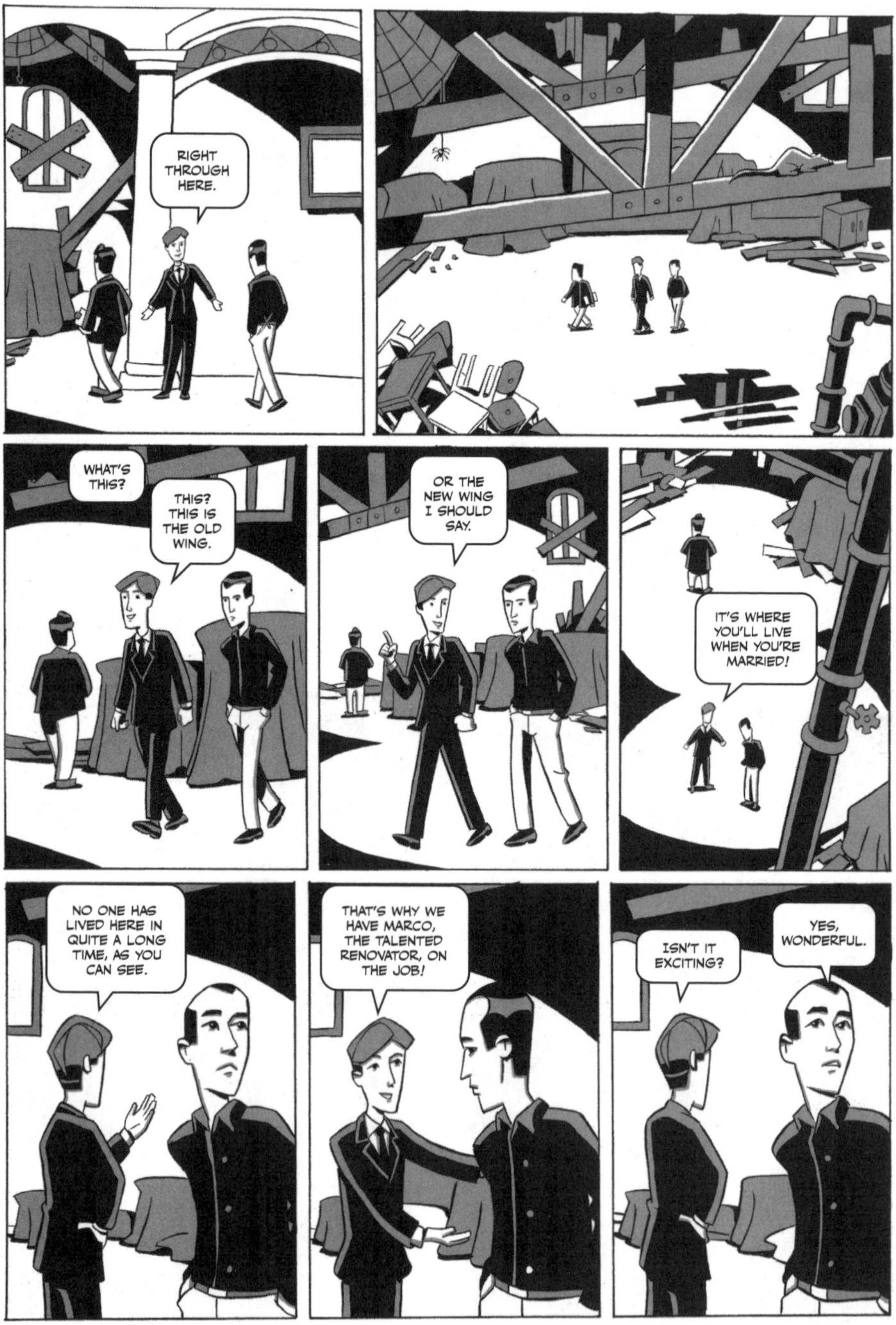
RIGHT THROUGH HERE.
WHAT'S THIS?
THIS? THIS IS THE OLD WING.
OR THE NEW WING I SHOULD SAY.
IT'S WHERE YOU'LL LIVE WHEN YOU'RE MARRIED!
NO ONE HAS LIVED HERE IN QUITE A LONG TIME, AS YOU CAN SEE.
THAT'S WHY WE HAVE MARCO, THE TALENTED RENOVATOR, ON THE JOB!
ISN'T IT EXCITING?
YES, WONDERFUL.

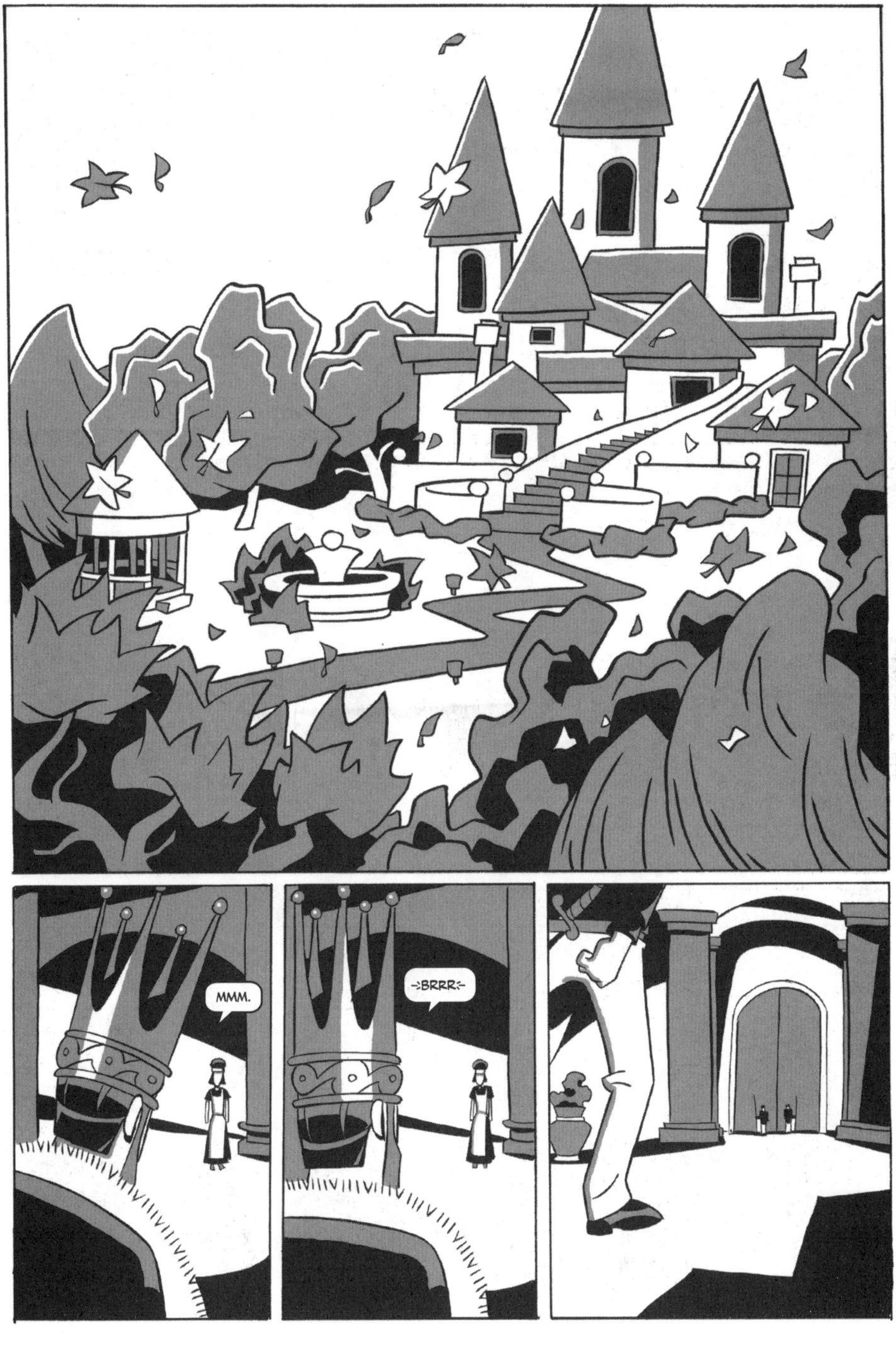
MMM.
-BRRR-

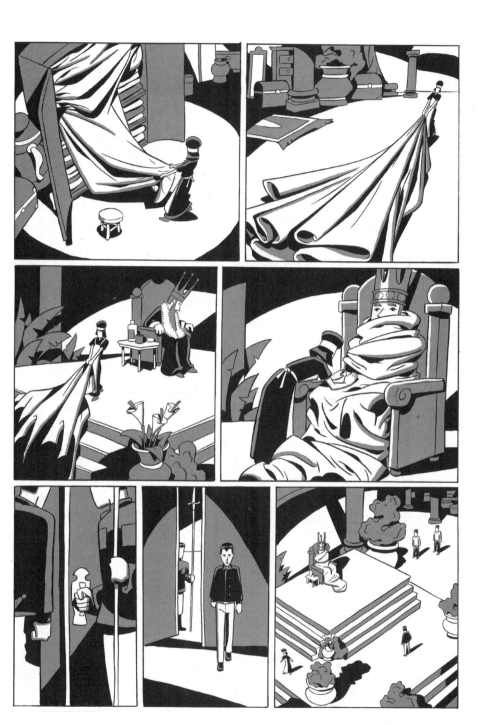

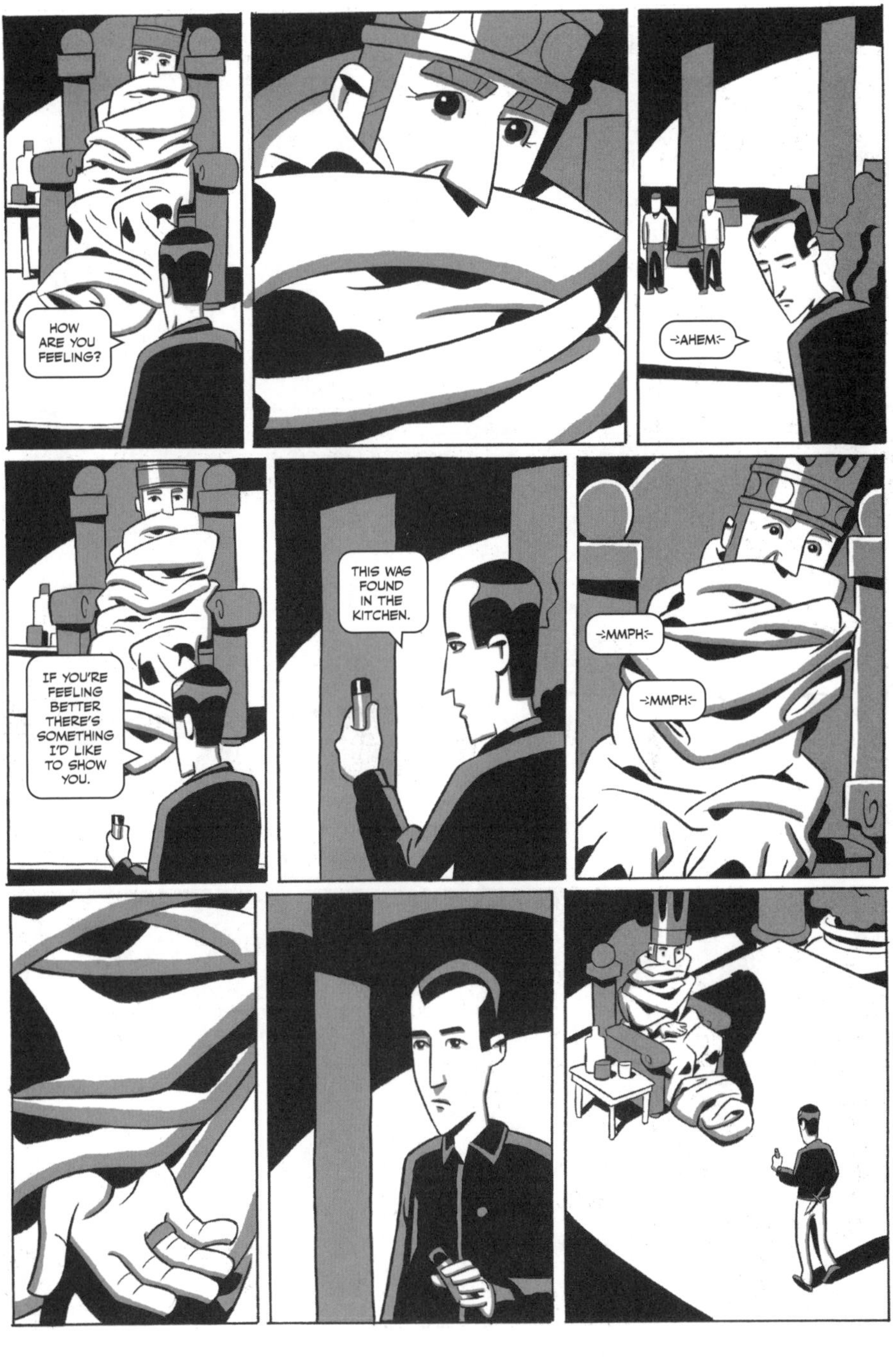
HOW ARE YOU FEELING?
-AHEM-
IF YOU'RE FEELING BETTER THERE'S SOMETHING I'D LIKE TO SHOW YOU.
THIS WAS FOUND IN THE KITCHEN.
-MMPH-
-MMPH-

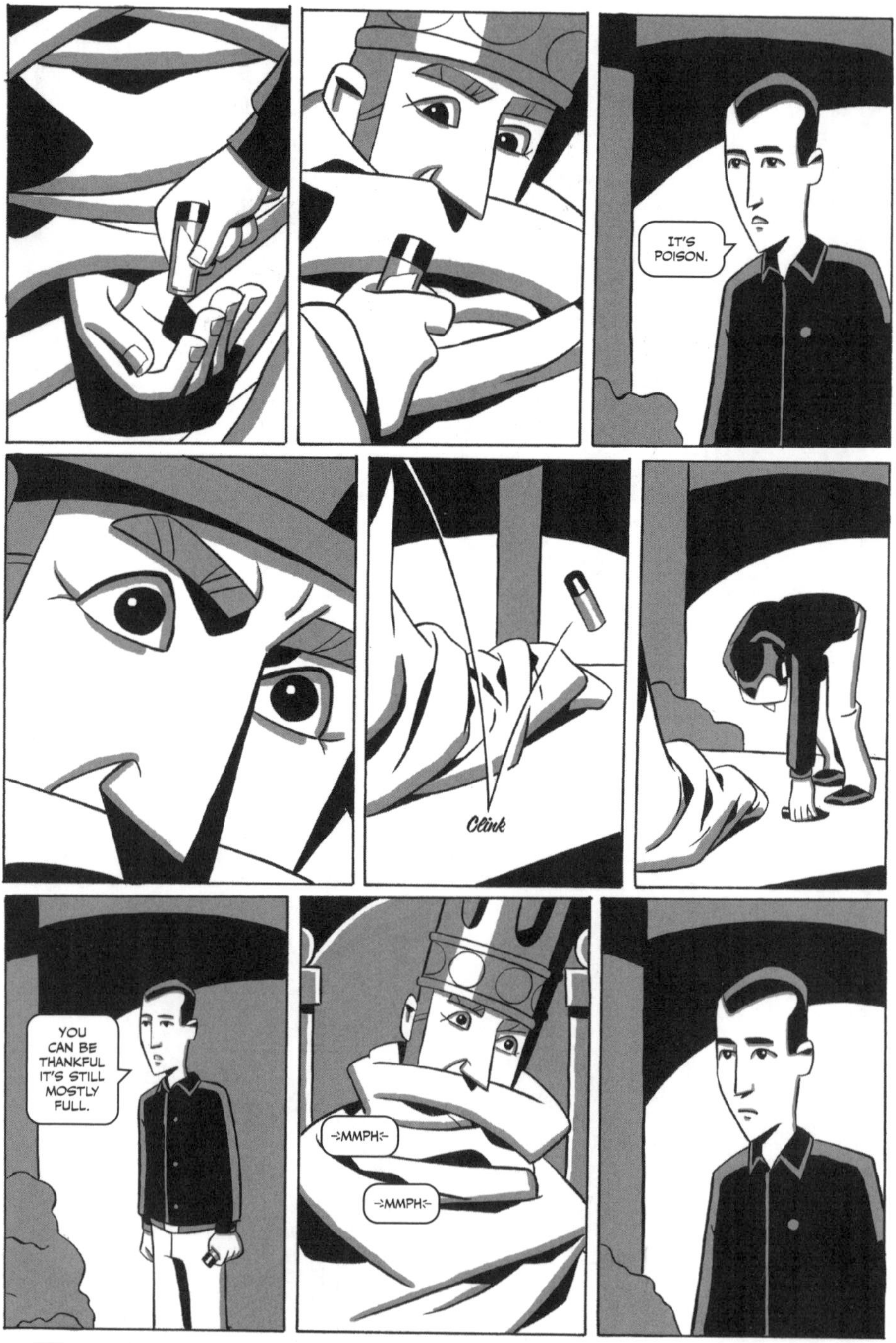
IT'S POISON.
Clink
YOU CAN BE THANKFUL IT'S STILL MOSTLY FULL.
~MMPH~
~MMPH~

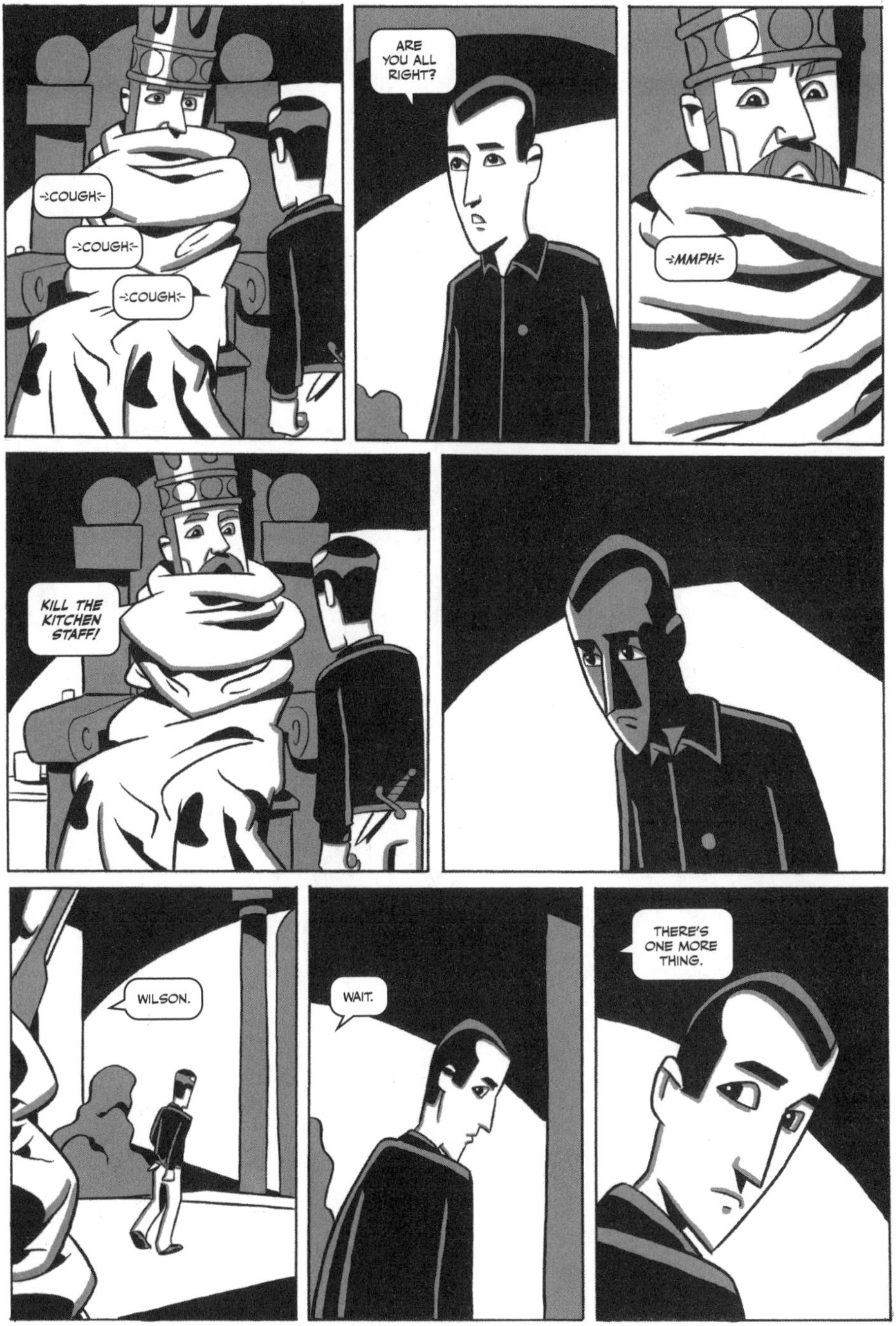
COUGH
COUGH
COUGH
ARE YOU ALL RIGHT?
MMPH
KILL THE KITCHEN STAFF!
WILSON.
WAIT.
THERE'S ONE MORE THING.

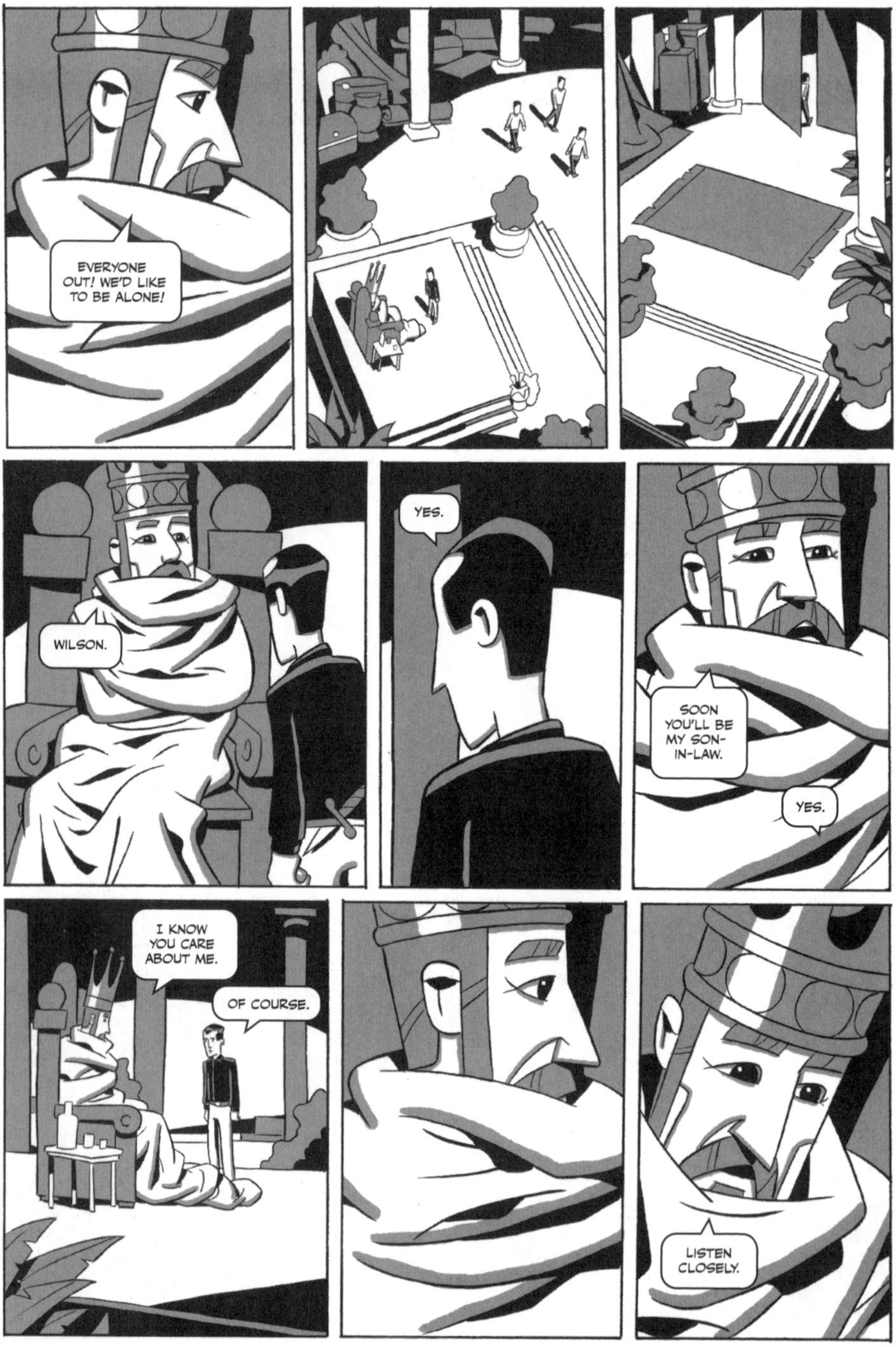
EVERYONE OUT! WE'D LIKE TO BE ALONE!
WILSON.
YES.
SOON YOU'LL BE MY SON-IN-LAW.
YES.
I KNOW YOU CARE ABOUT ME.
OF COURSE.
LISTEN CLOSELY.

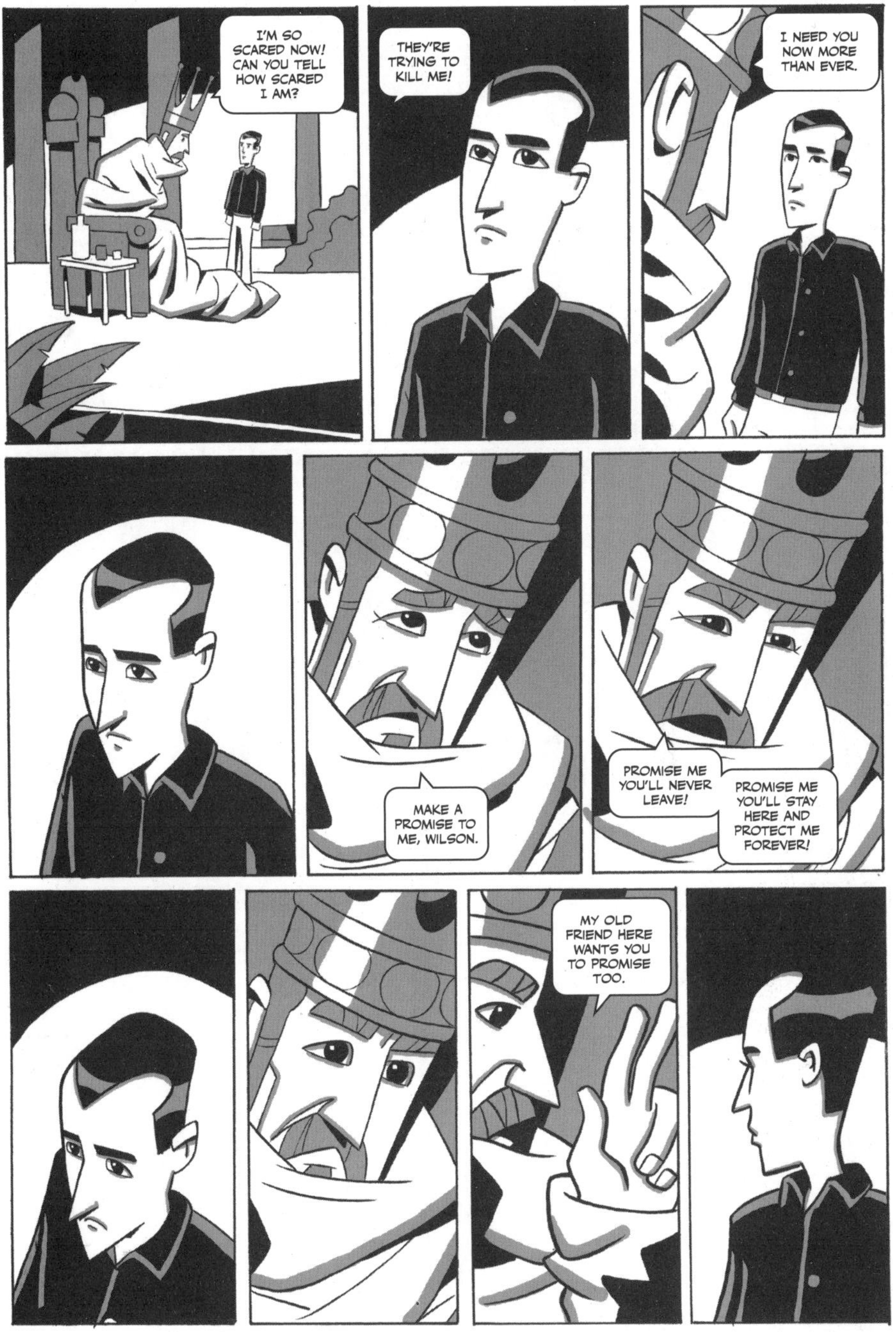
I'M SO SCARED NOW! CAN YOU TELL HOW SCARED I AM?
THEY'RE TRYING TO KILL ME!
I NEED YOU NOW MORE THAN EVER.
MAKE A PROMISE TO ME, WILSON.
PROMISE ME YOU'LL NEVER LEAVE!
PROMISE ME YOU'LL STAY HERE AND PROTECT ME FOREVER!
MY OLD FRIEND HERE WANTS YOU TO PROMISE TOO.

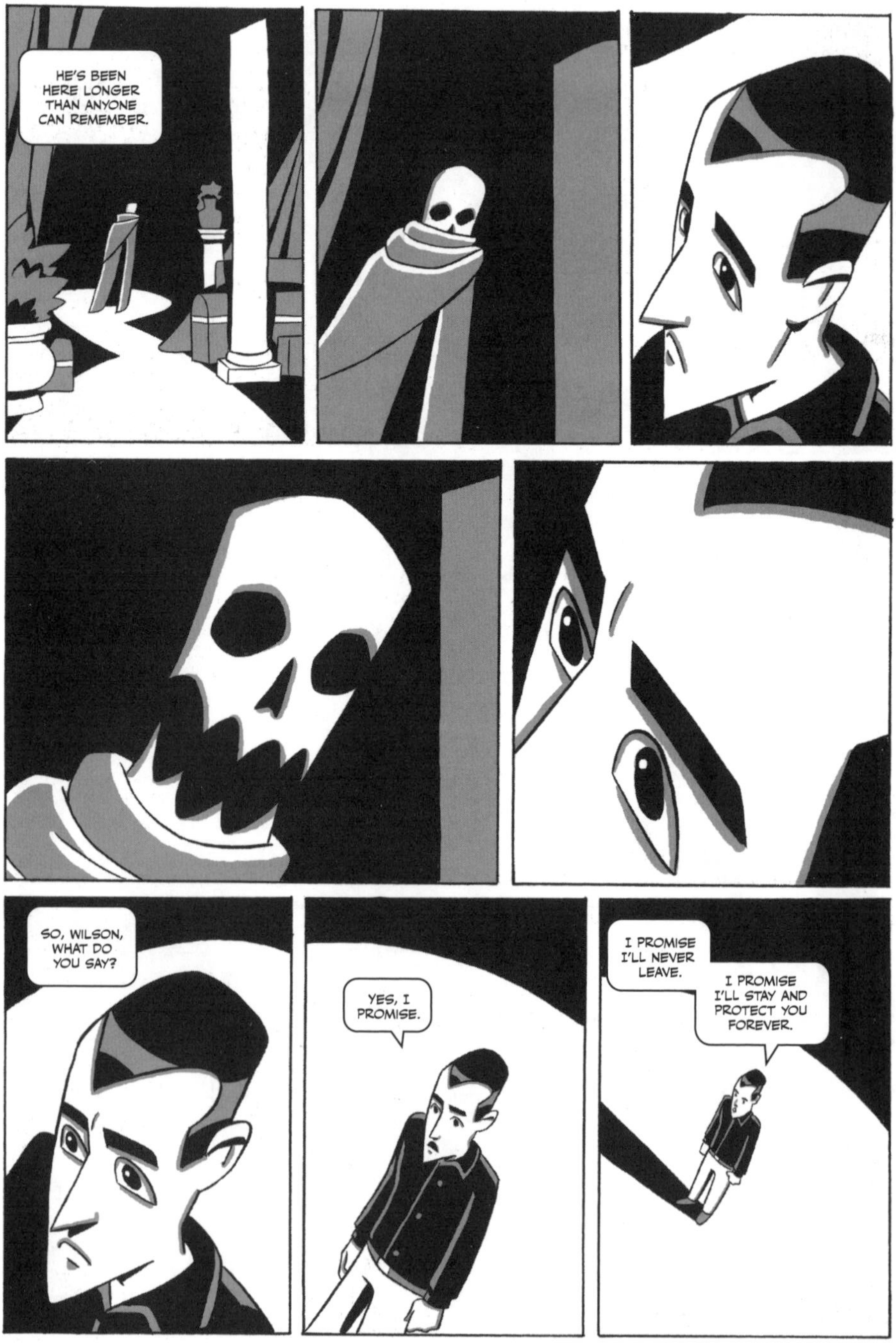
HE'S BEEN HERE LONGER THAN ANYONE CAN REMEMBER.
SO, WILSON, WHAT DO YOU SAY?
YES, I PROMISE.
I PROMISE I'LL NEVER LEAVE.
I PROMISE I'LL STAY AND PROTECT YOU FOREVER.

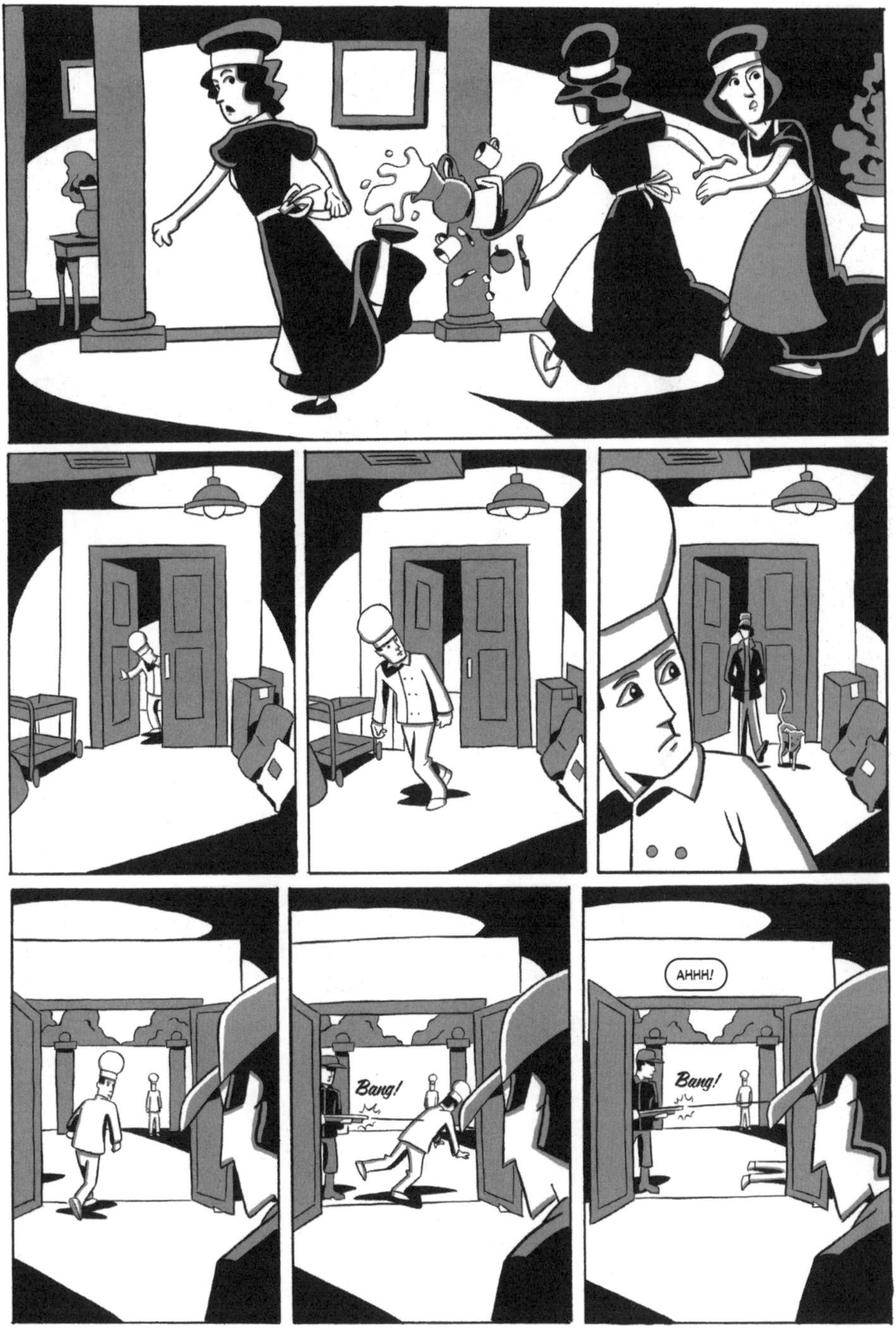
Bang!
Bang!
AHHH!

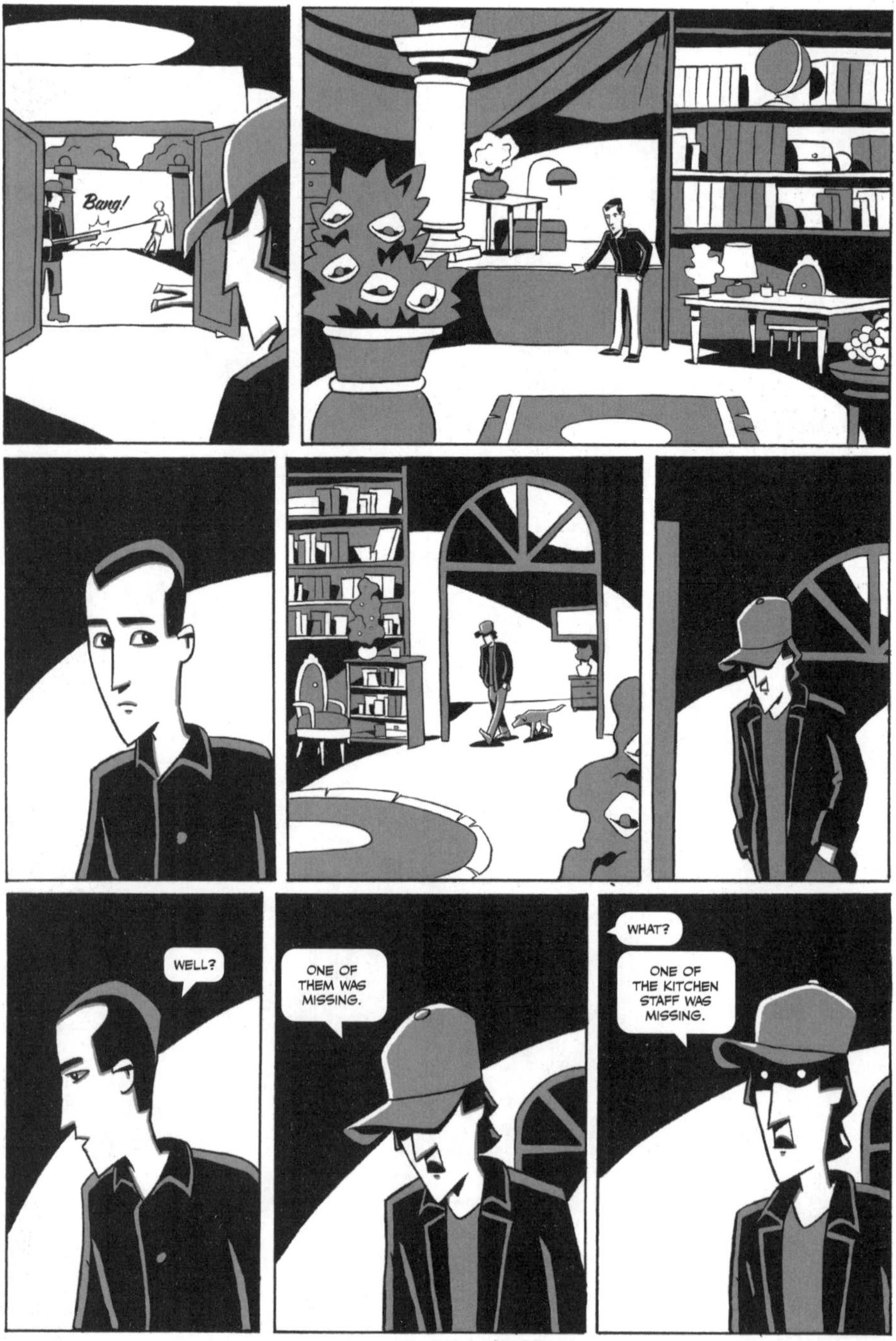
Bang!
WELL?
ONE OF THEM WAS MISSING.
WHAT?
ONE OF THE KITCHEN STAFF WAS MISSING.

WE HAVE TO FIND HIM.

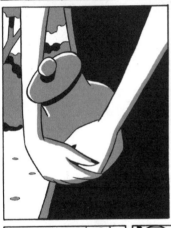

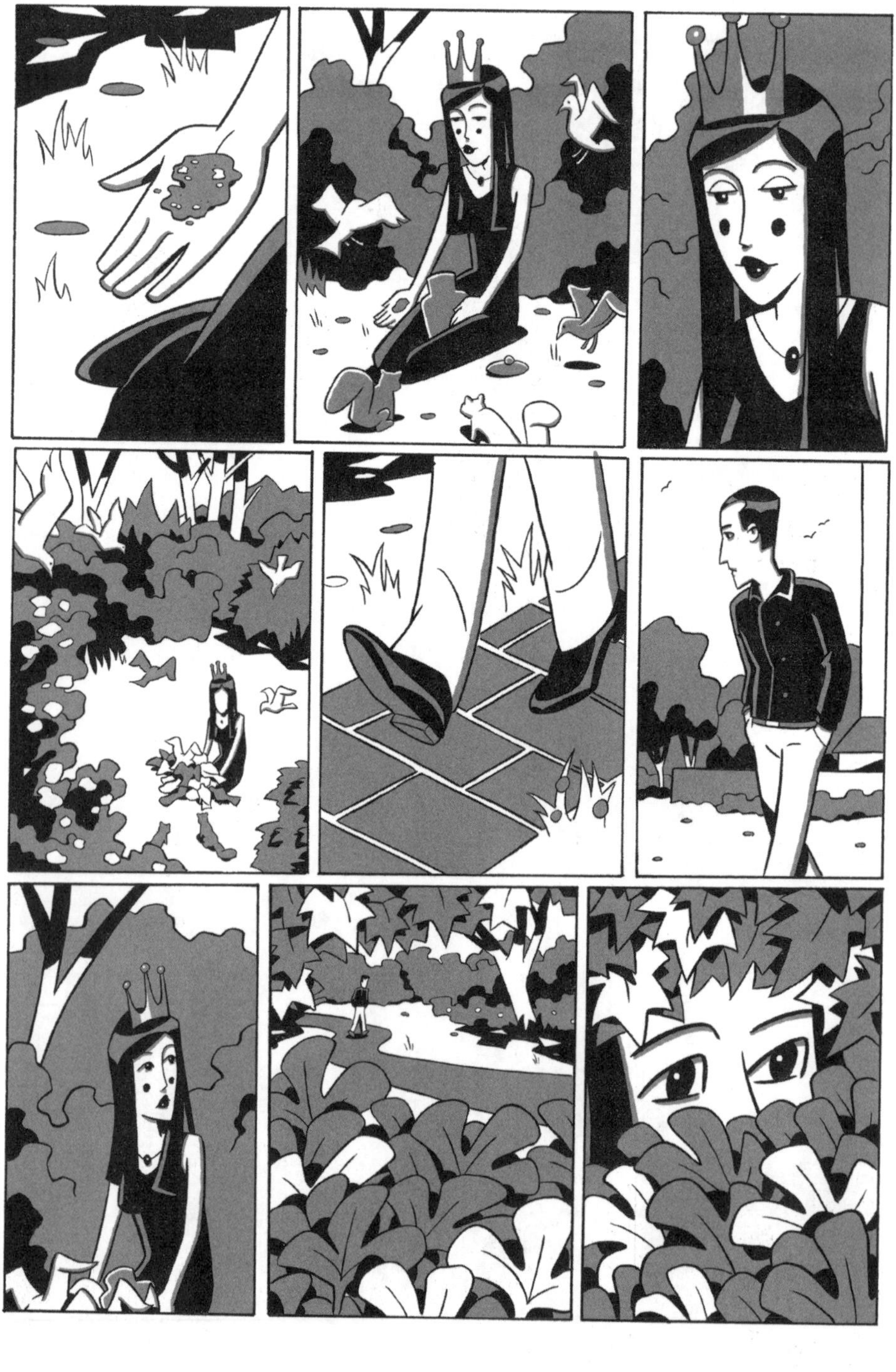

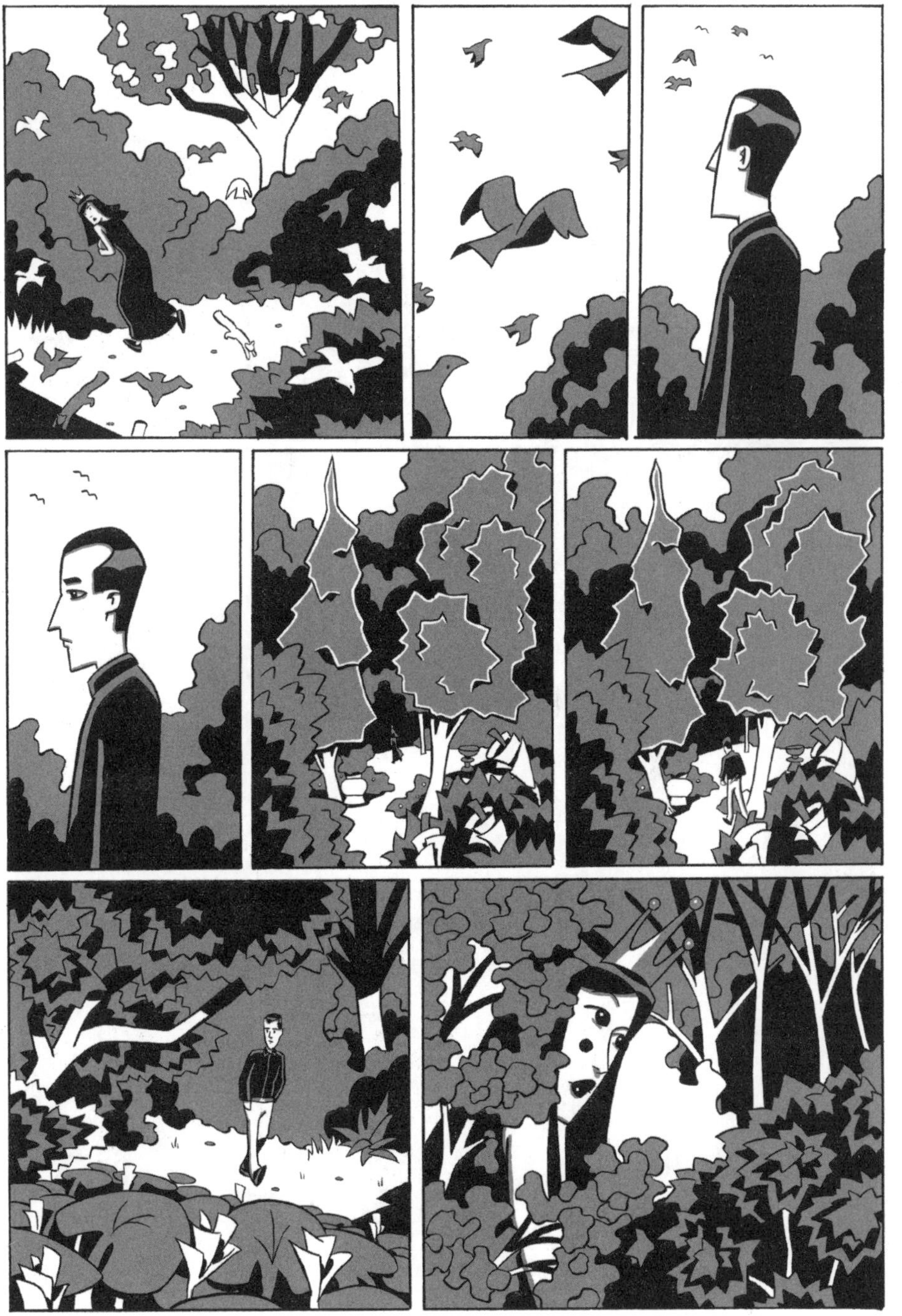

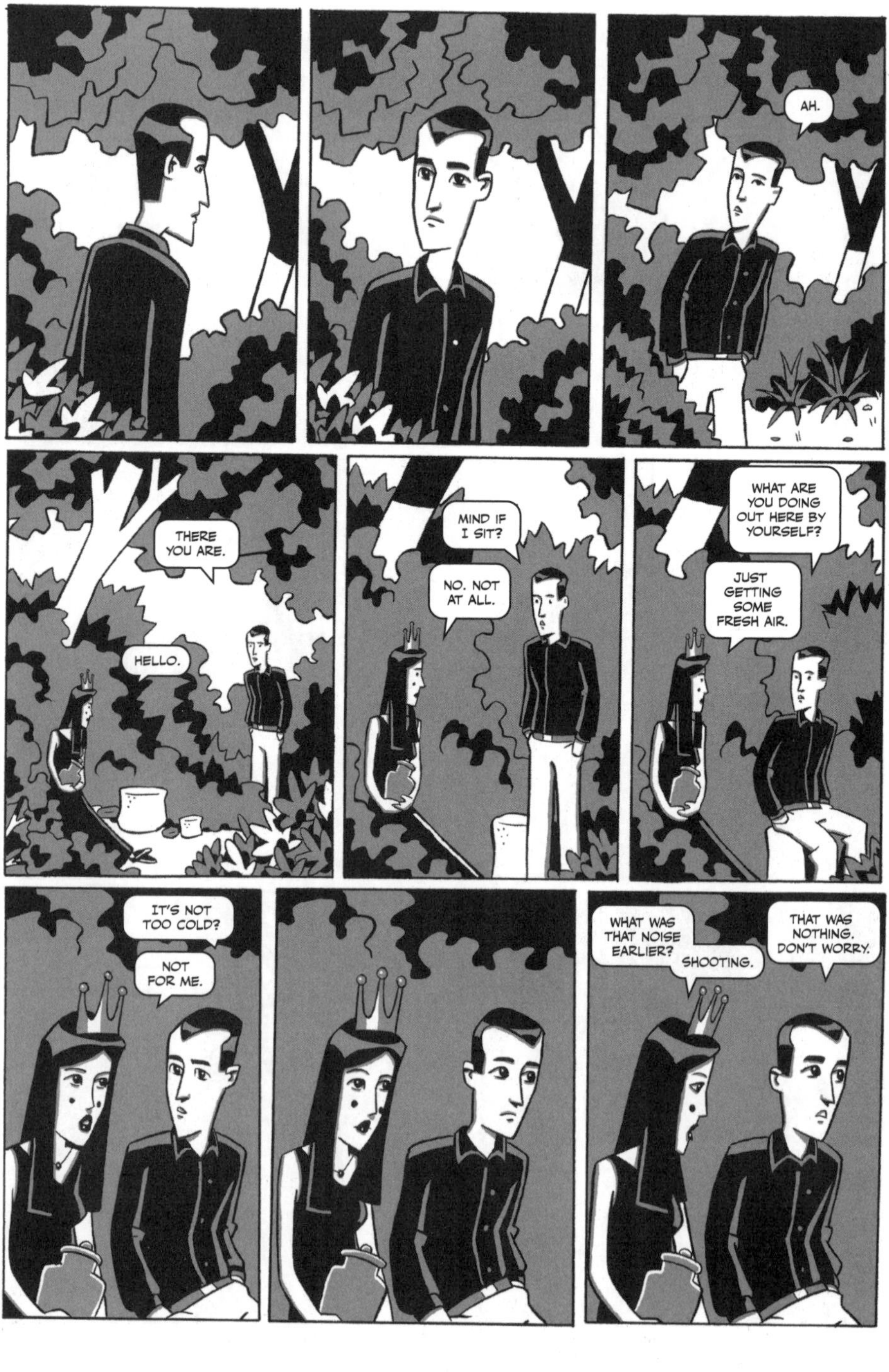
AH.
THERE YOU ARE.
HELLO.
MIND IF I SIT?
NO. NOT AT ALL.
WHAT ARE YOU DOING OUT HERE BY YOURSELF?
JUST GETTING SOME FRESH AIR.
IT'S NOT TOO COLD?
NOT FOR ME.
WHAT WAS THAT NOISE EARLIER?
SHOOTING.
THAT WAS NOTHING. DON'T WORRY.

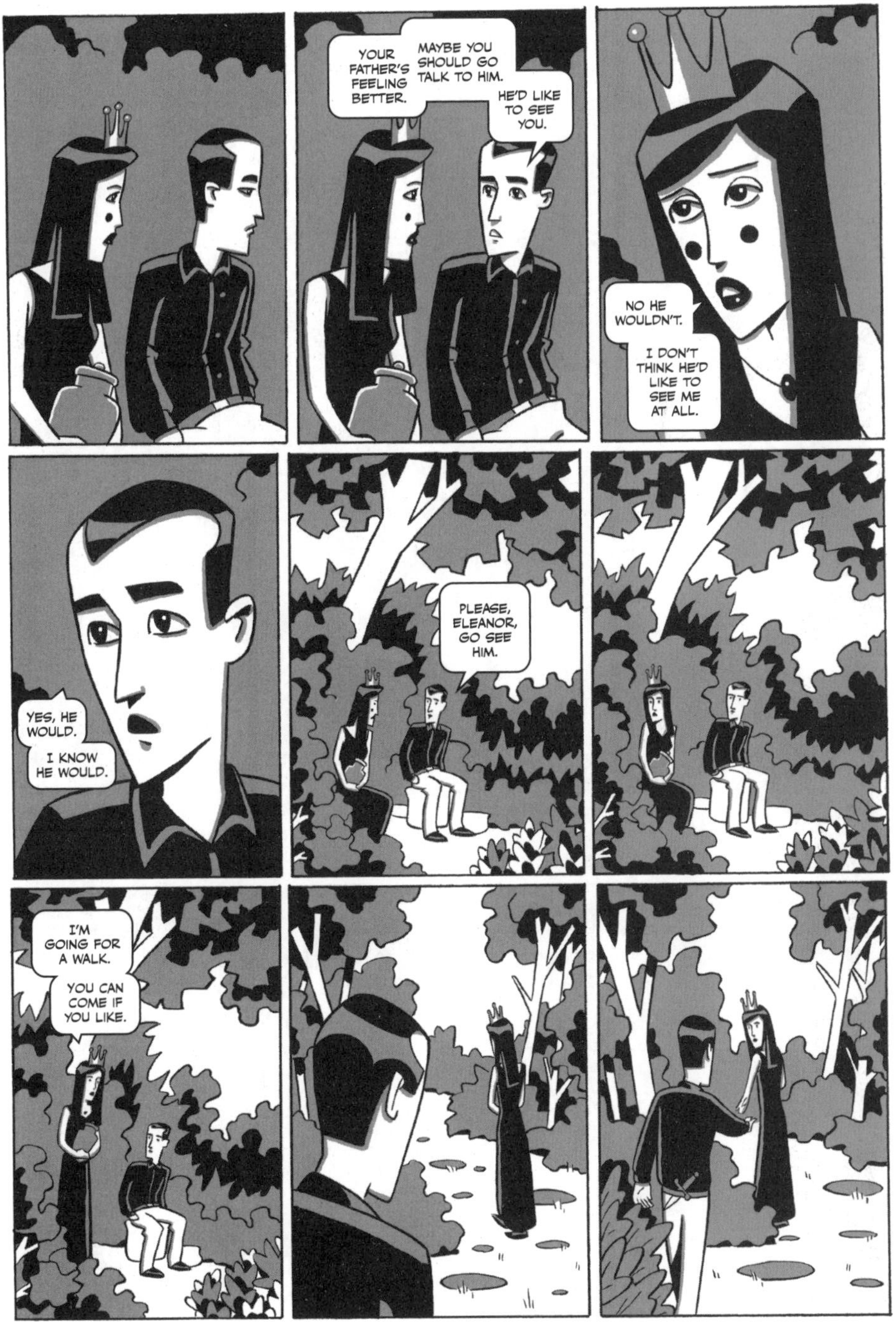
YOUR FATHER'S FEELING BETTER.
MAYBE YOU SHOULD GO TALK TO HIM.
HE'D LIKE TO SEE YOU.
NO HE WOULDN'T.
I DON'T THINK HE'D LIKE TO SEE ME AT ALL.
YES, HE WOULD.
I KNOW HE WOULD.
PLEASE, ELEANOR, GO SEE HIM.
I'M GOING FOR A WALK.
YOU CAN COME IF YOU LIKE.

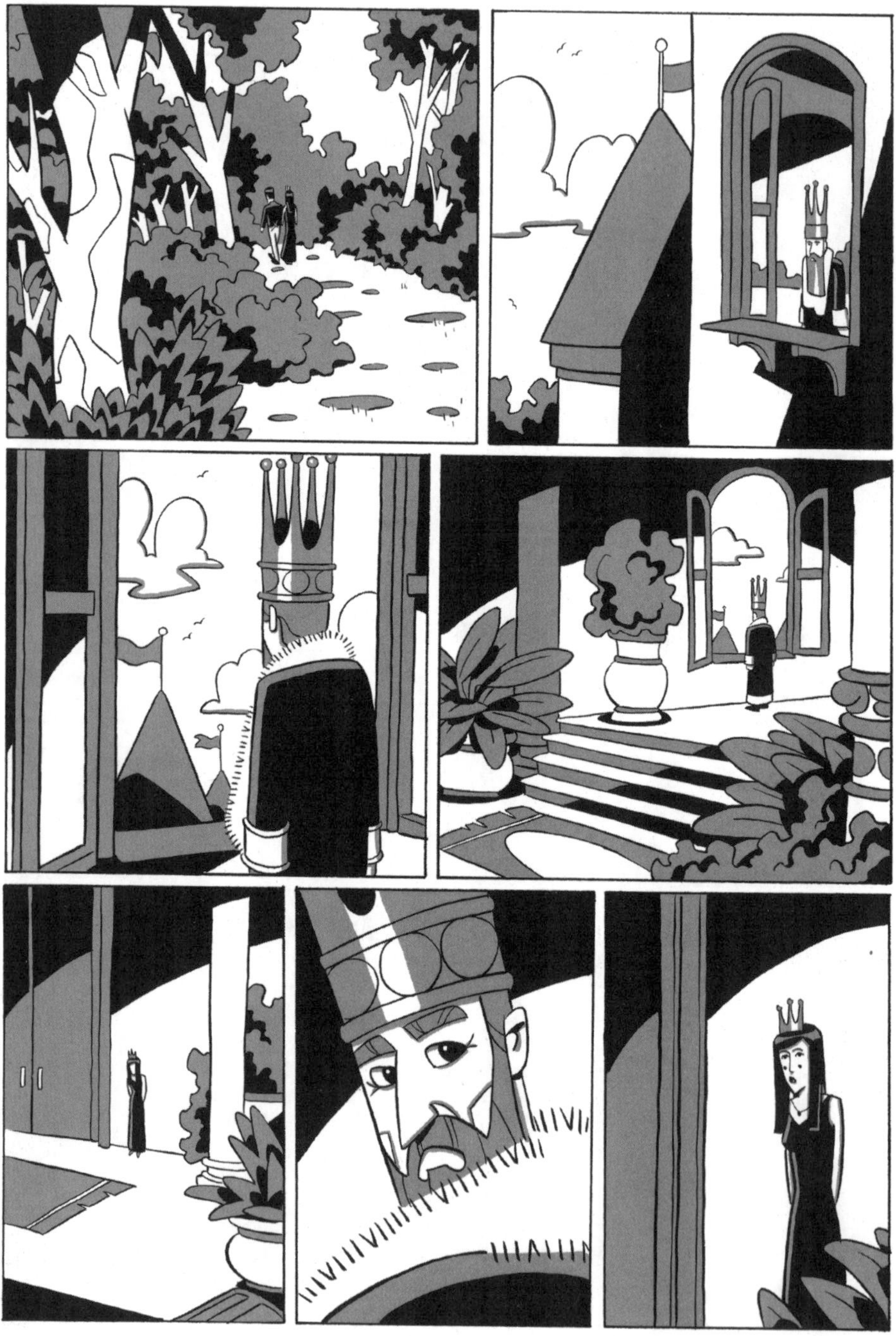

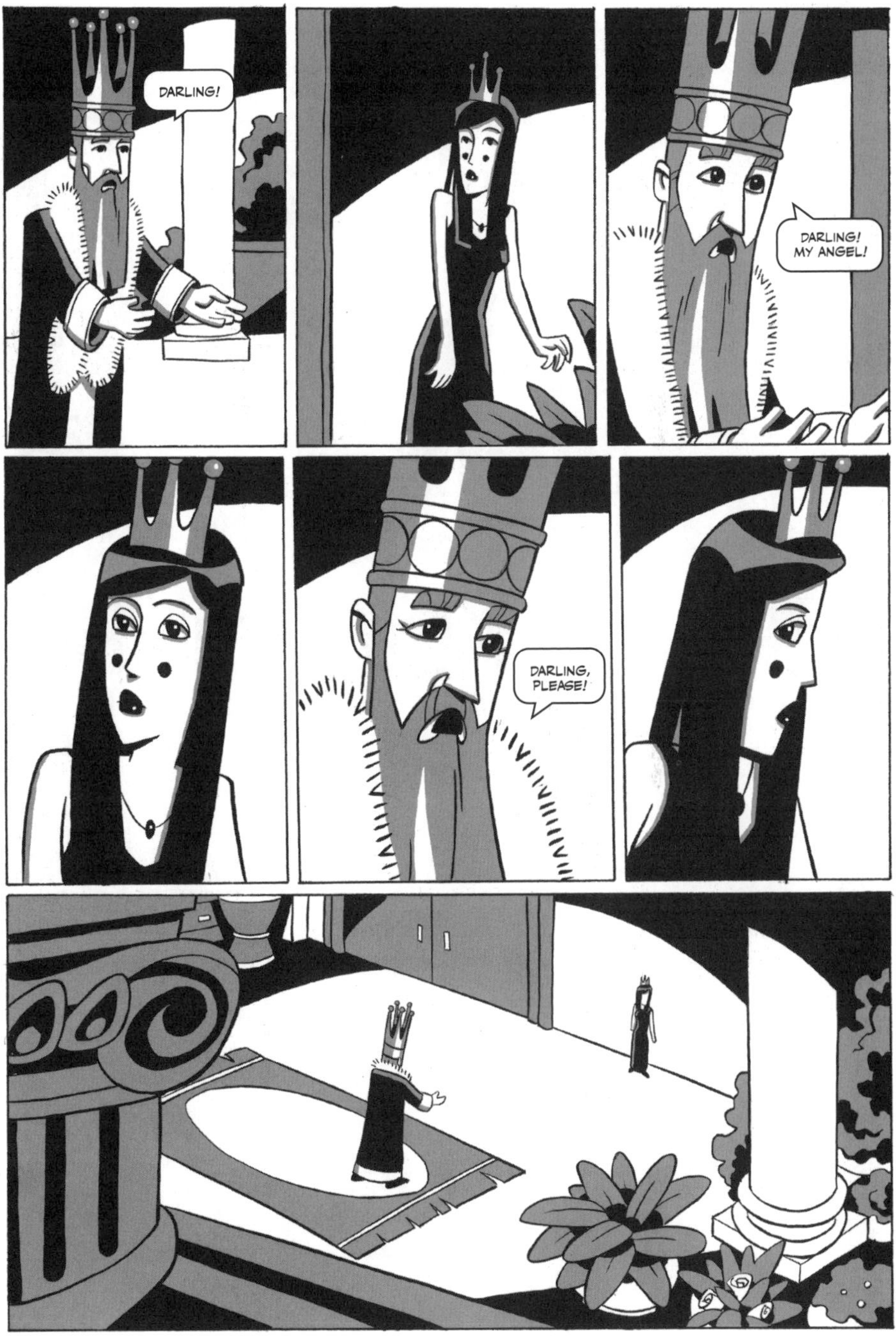
DARLING!
DARLING! MY ANGEL!
DARLING, PLEASE!

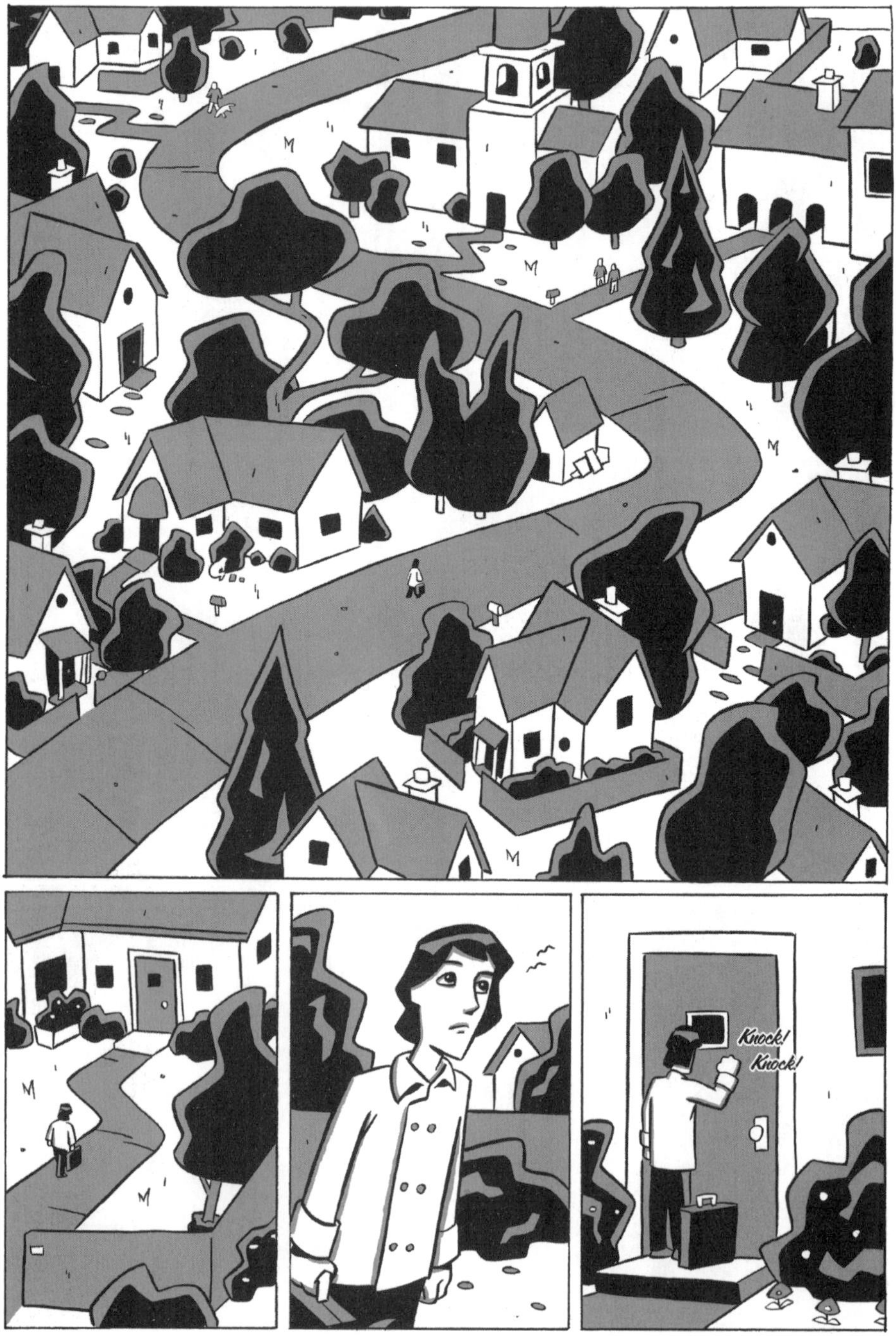
Knock!
Knock!

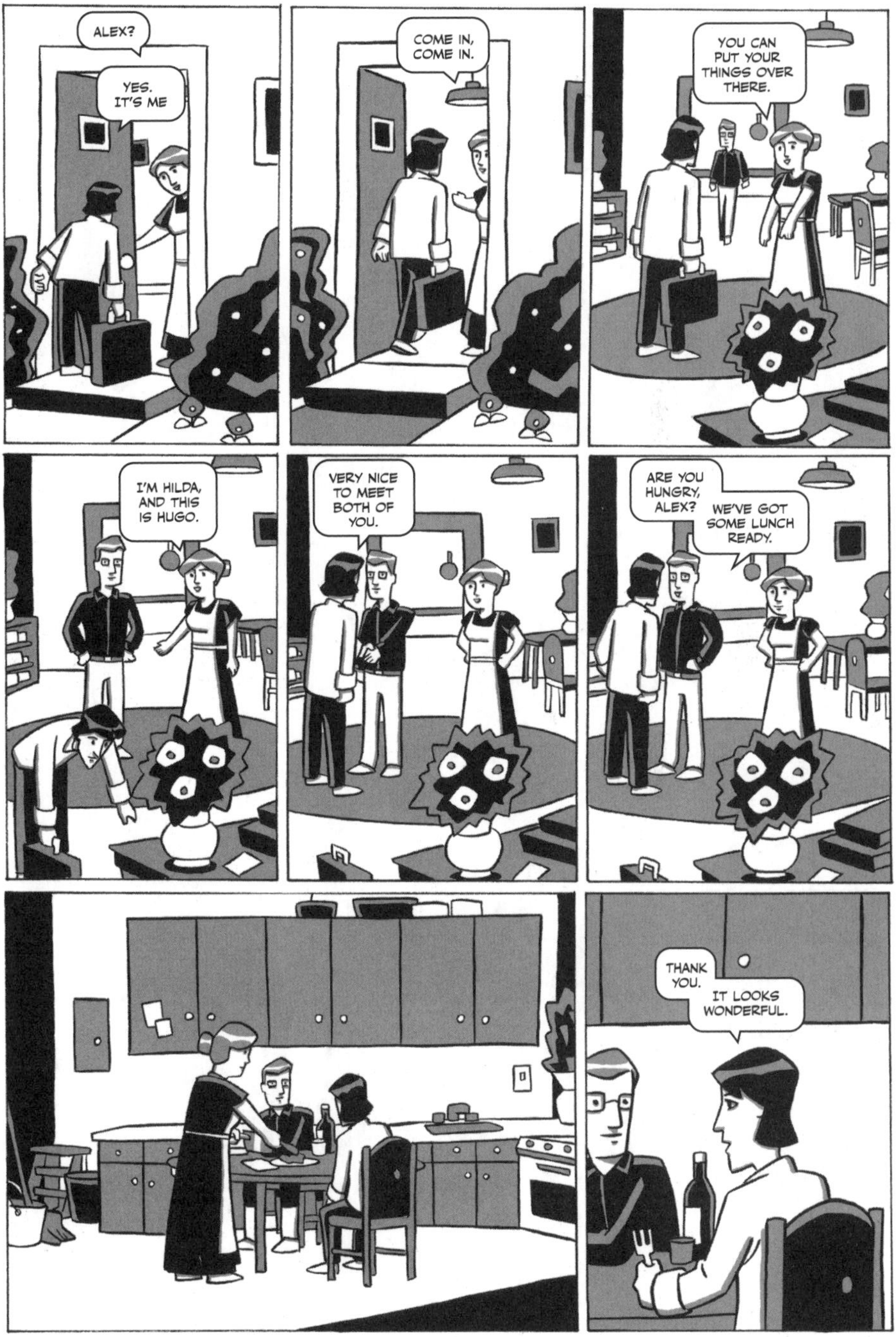
ALEX?
YES. IT'S ME
COME IN, COME IN.
YOU CAN PUT YOUR THINGS OVER THERE.
I'M HILDA, AND THIS IS HUGO.
VERY NICE TO MEET BOTH OF YOU.
ARE YOU HUNGRY, ALEX?
WE'VE GOT SOME LUNCH READY.
THANK YOU.
IT LOOKS WONDERFUL.

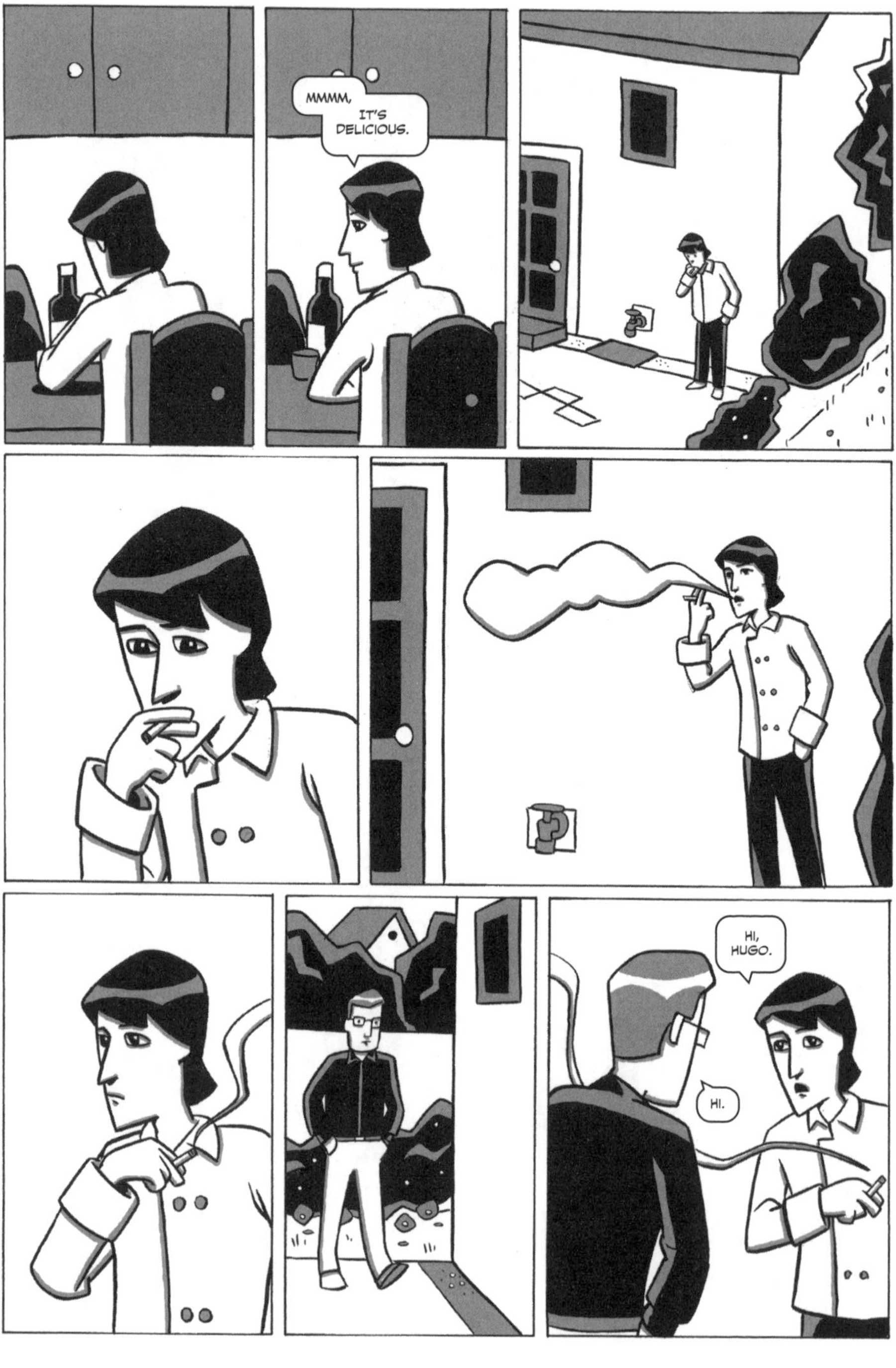
MMMM, IT'S DELICIOUS.
HI, HUGO.
HI.

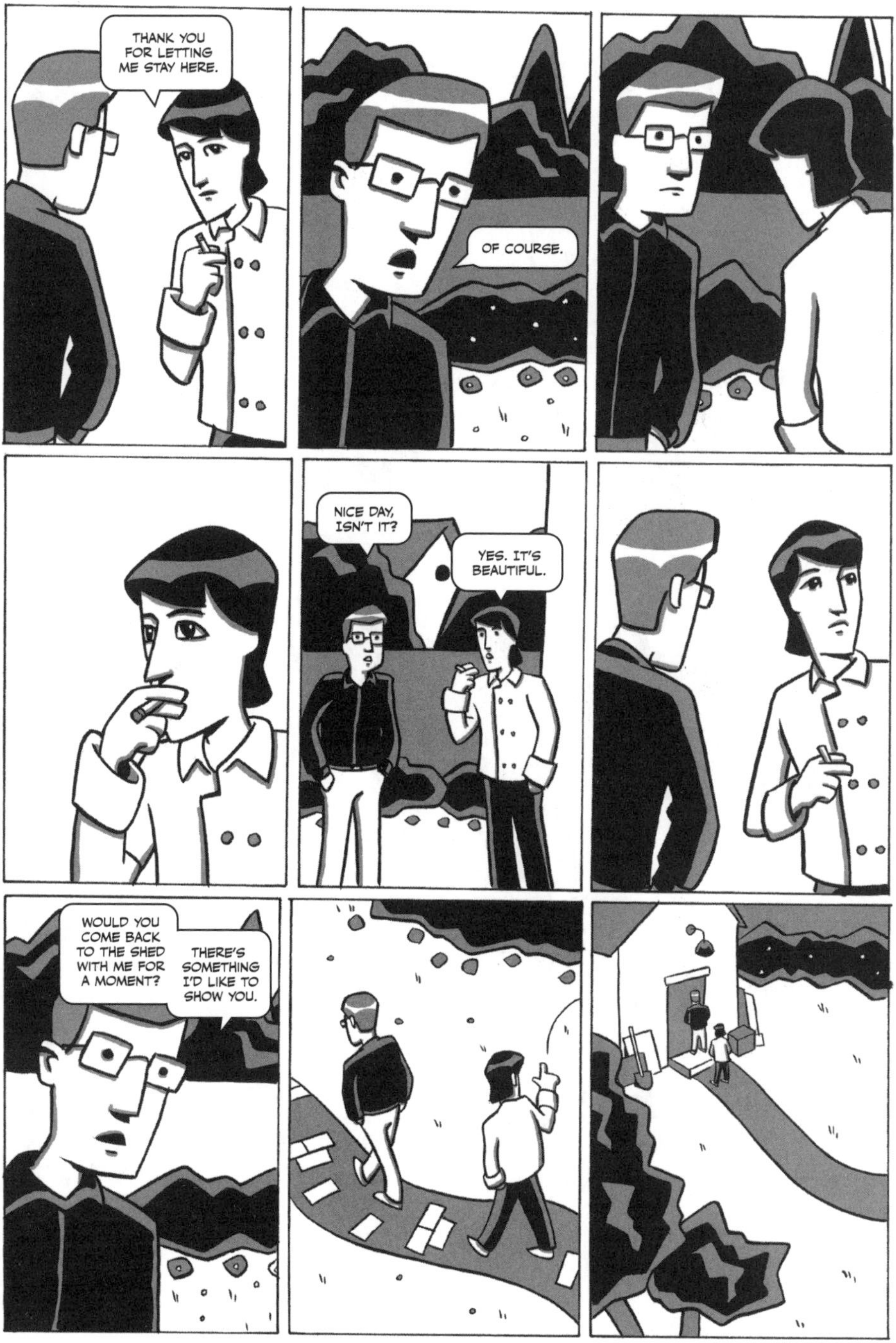
THANK YOU FOR LETTING ME STAY HERE.
OF COURSE.
NICE DAY, ISN'T IT?
YES. IT'S BEAUTIFUL.
WOULD YOU COME BACK TO THE SHED WITH ME FOR A MOMENT?
THERE'S SOMETHING I'D LIKE TO SHOW YOU.

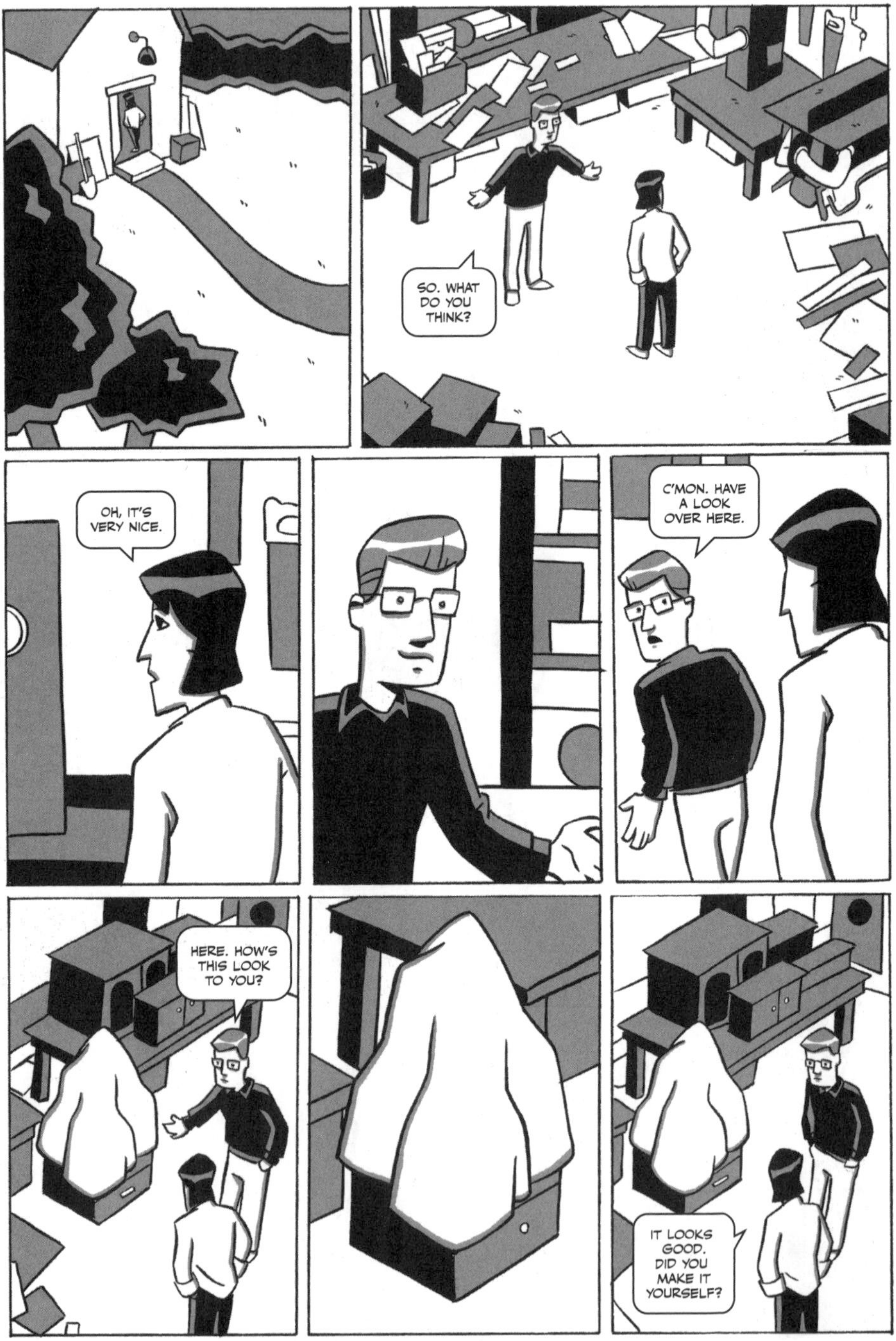
SO. WHAT DO YOU THINK?
OH, IT'S VERY NICE.
C'MON. HAVE A LOOK OVER HERE.
HERE. HOW'S THIS LOOK TO YOU?
IT LOOKS GOOD. DID YOU MAKE IT YOURSELF?

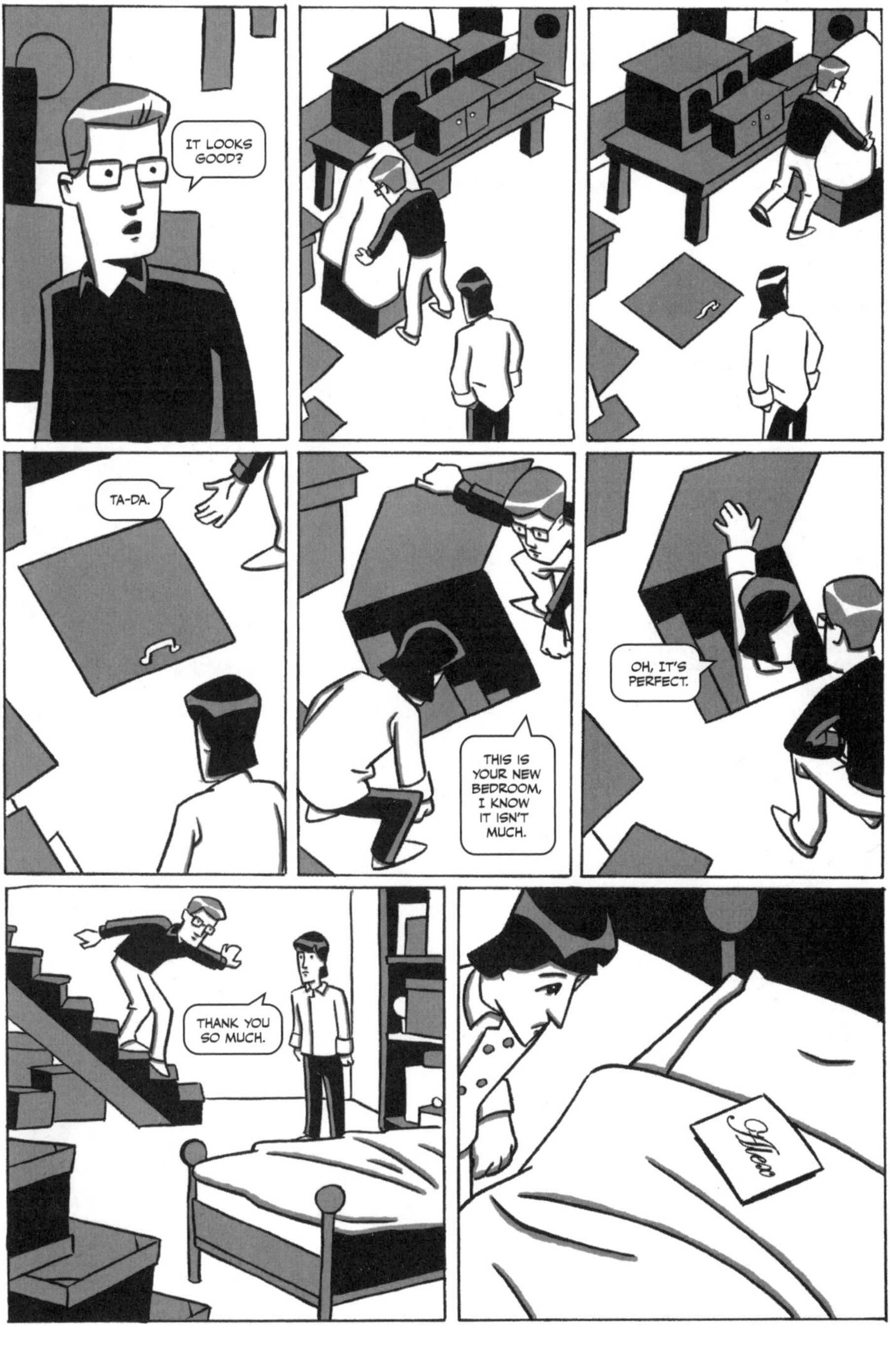
IT LOOKS GOOD?
TA-DA.
THIS IS YOUR NEW BEDROOM, I KNOW IT ISN'T MUCH.
OH, IT'S PERFECT.
THANK YOU SO MUCH.

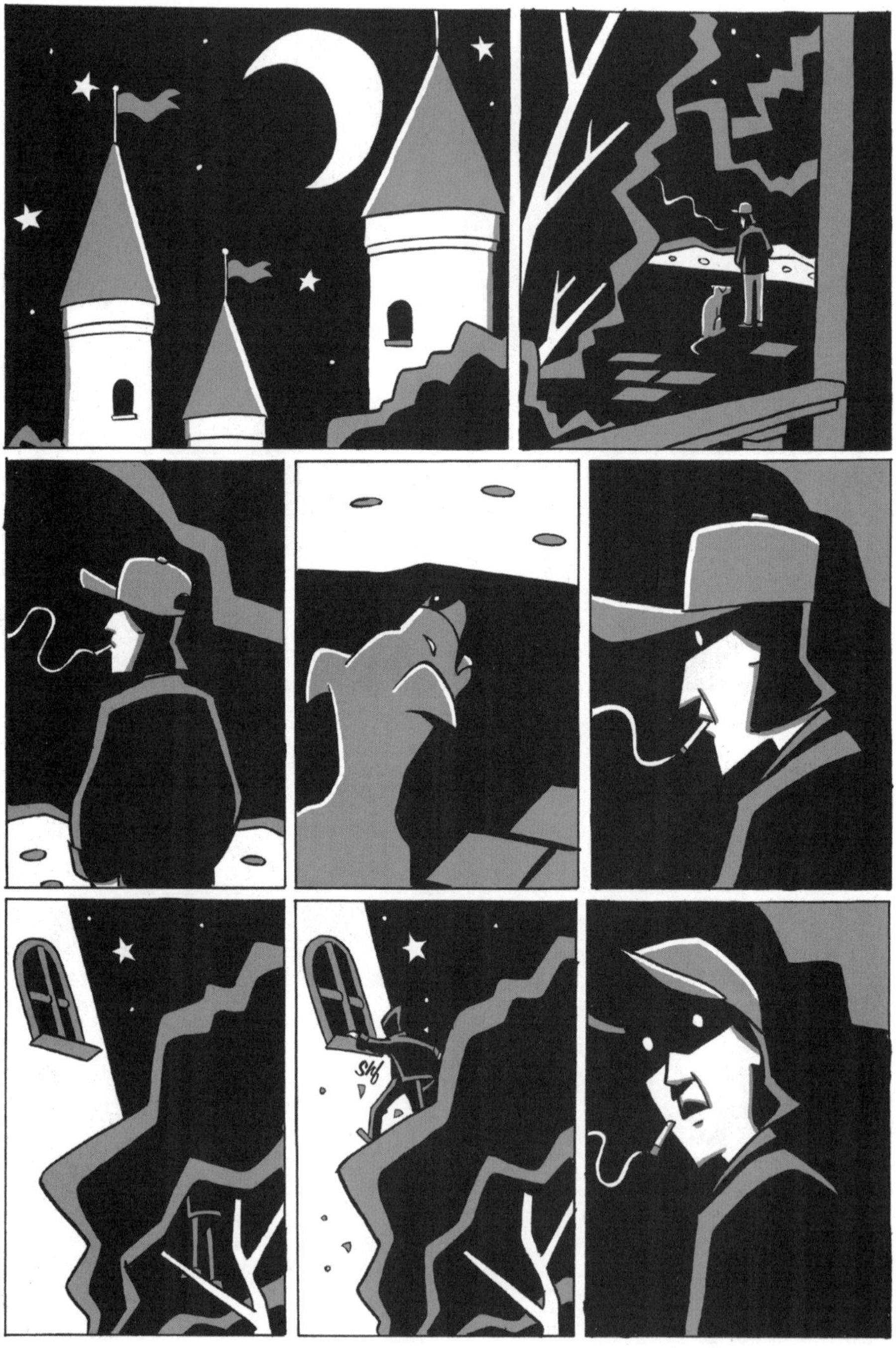
shf

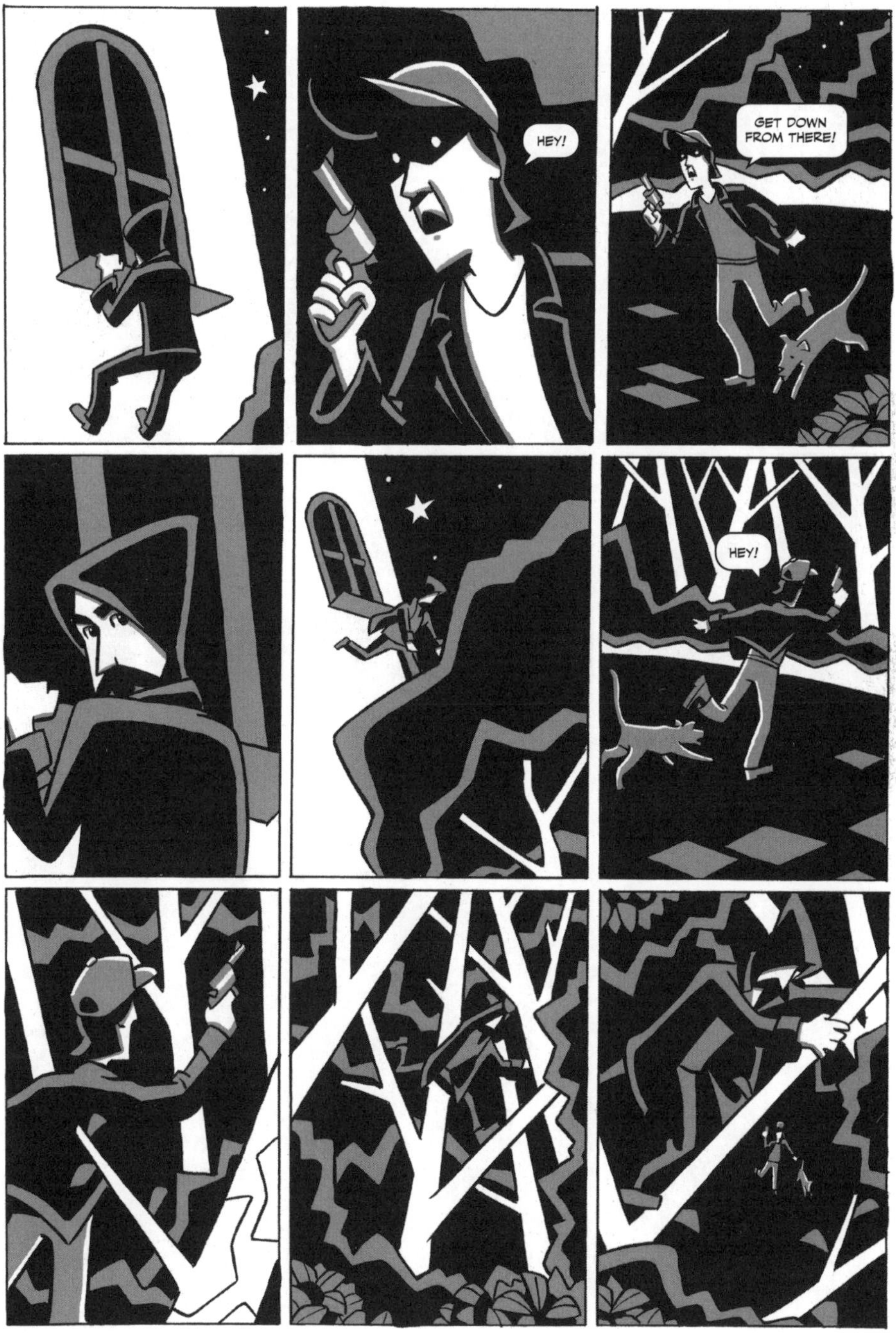
HEY!
GET DOWN FROM THERE!
HEY!

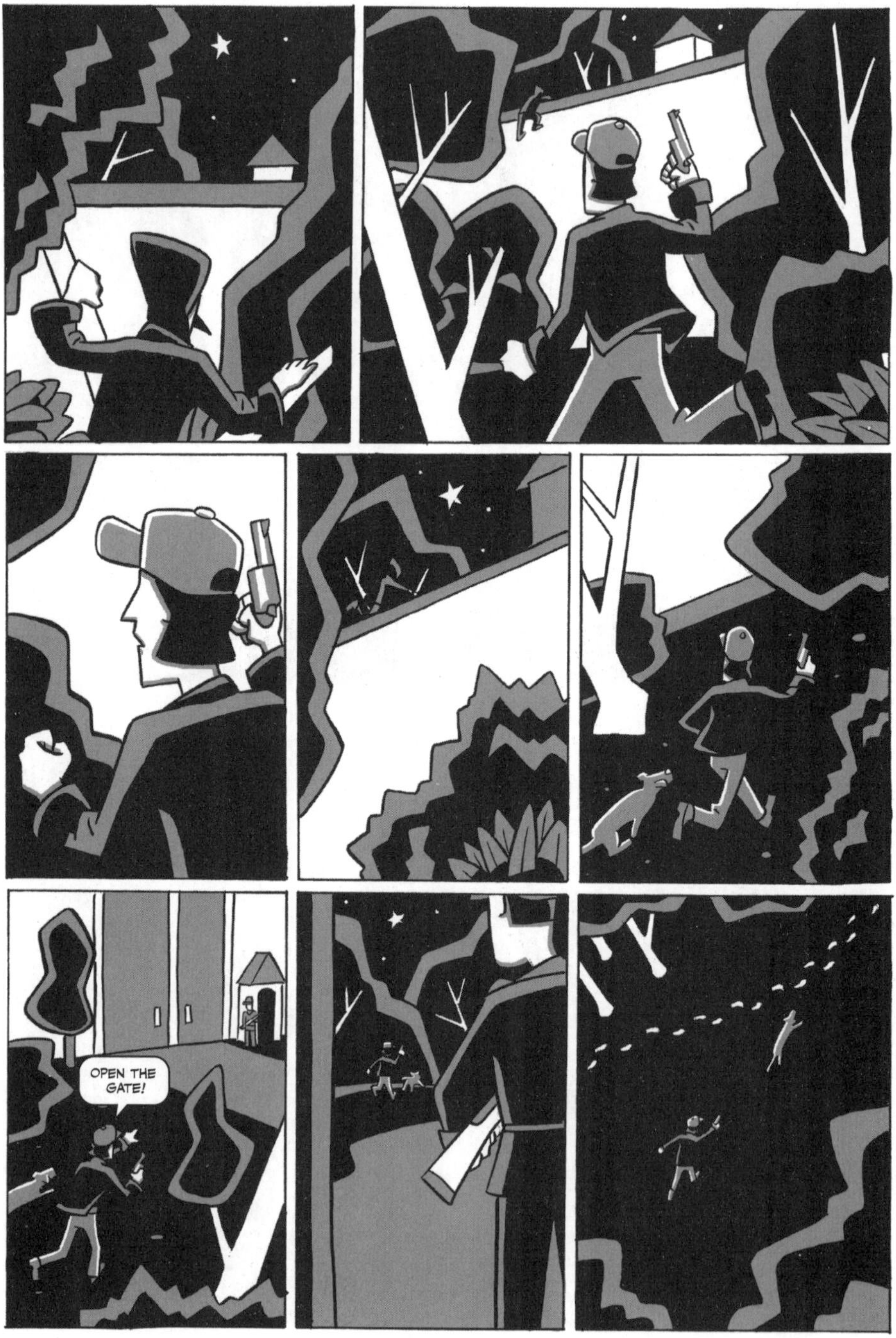
OPEN THE GATE!

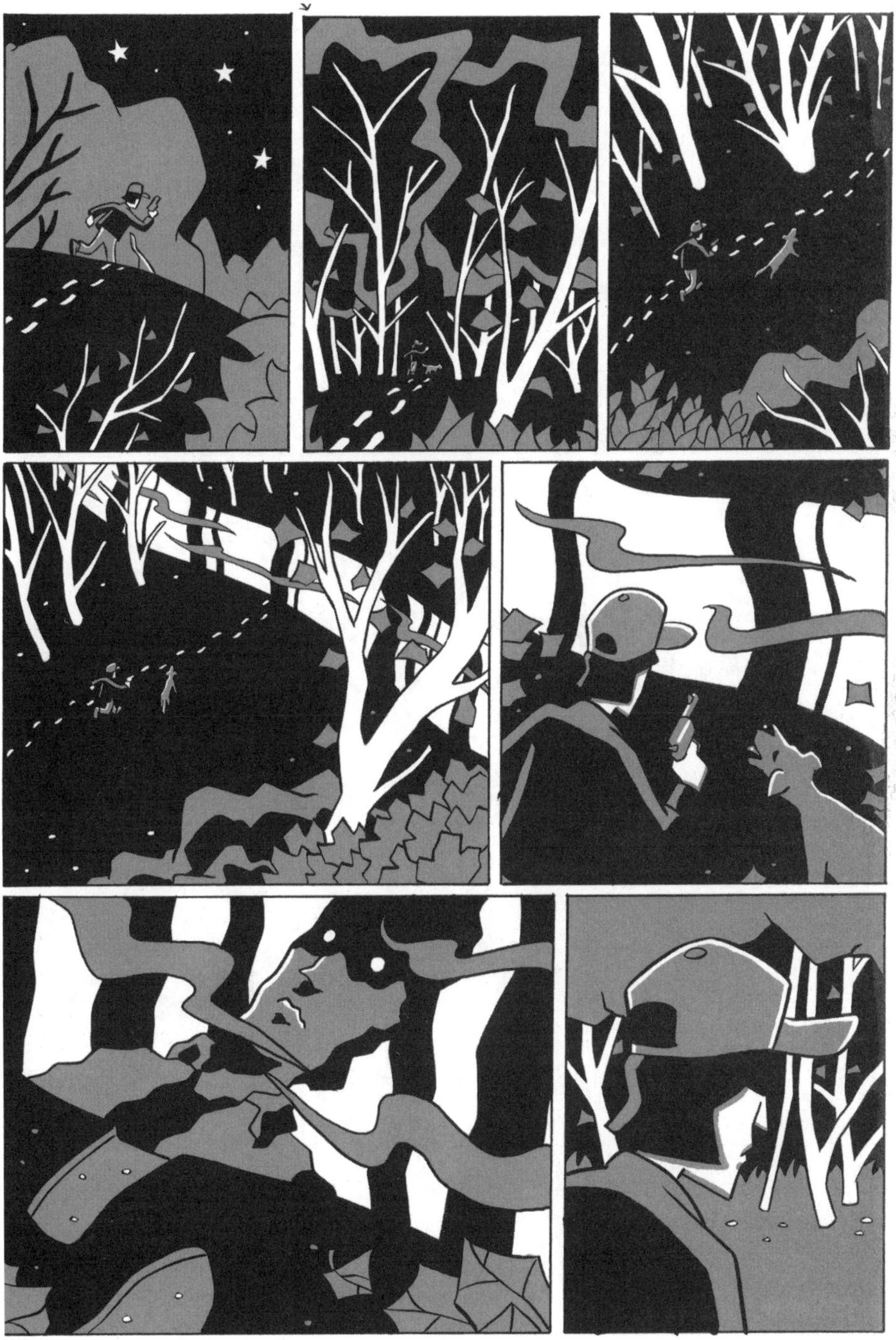

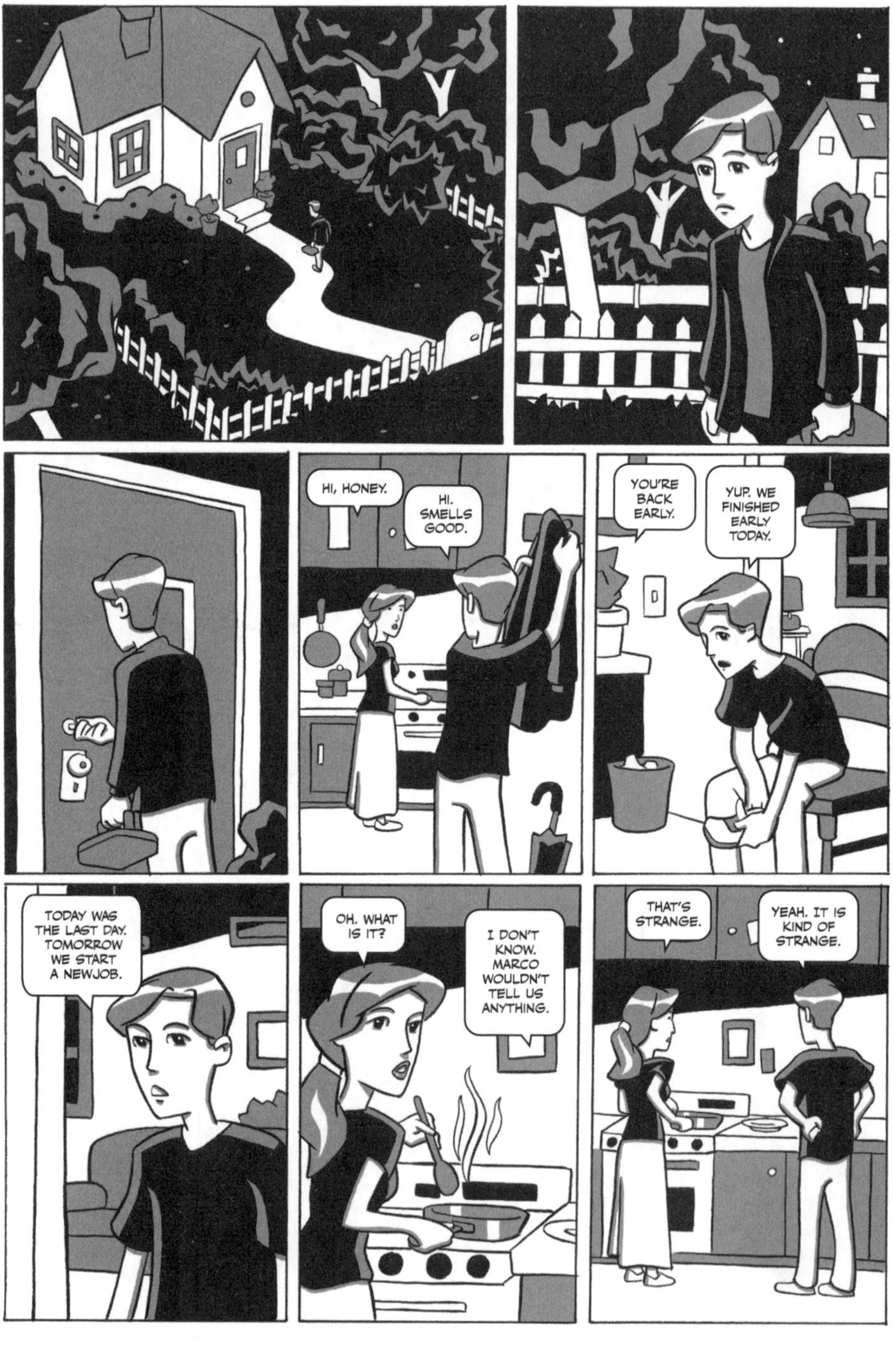
HI, HONEY.
HI. SMELLS GOOD.
YOU'RE BACK EARLY.
YUP. WE FINISHED EARLY TODAY.
TODAY WAS THE LAST DAY. TOMORROW WE START A NEWJOB.
OH. WHAT IS IT?
I DON'T KNOW. MARCO WOULDN'T TELL US ANYTHING.
THAT'S STRANGE.
YEAH. IT IS KIND OF STRANGE.

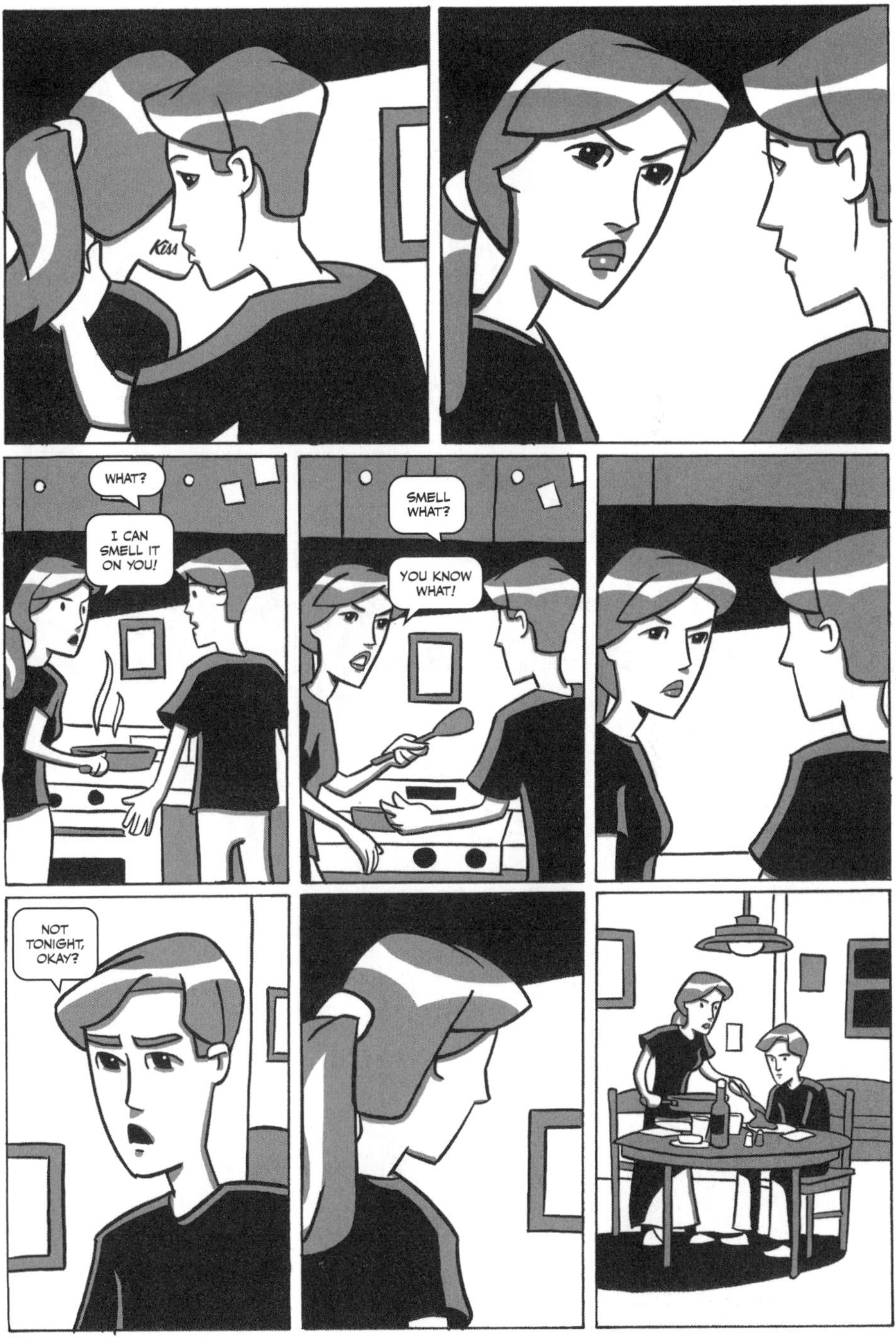
Kiss
WHAT?
I CAN SMELL IT ON YOU!
SMELL WHAT?
YOU KNOW WHAT!
NOT TONIGHT, OKAY?

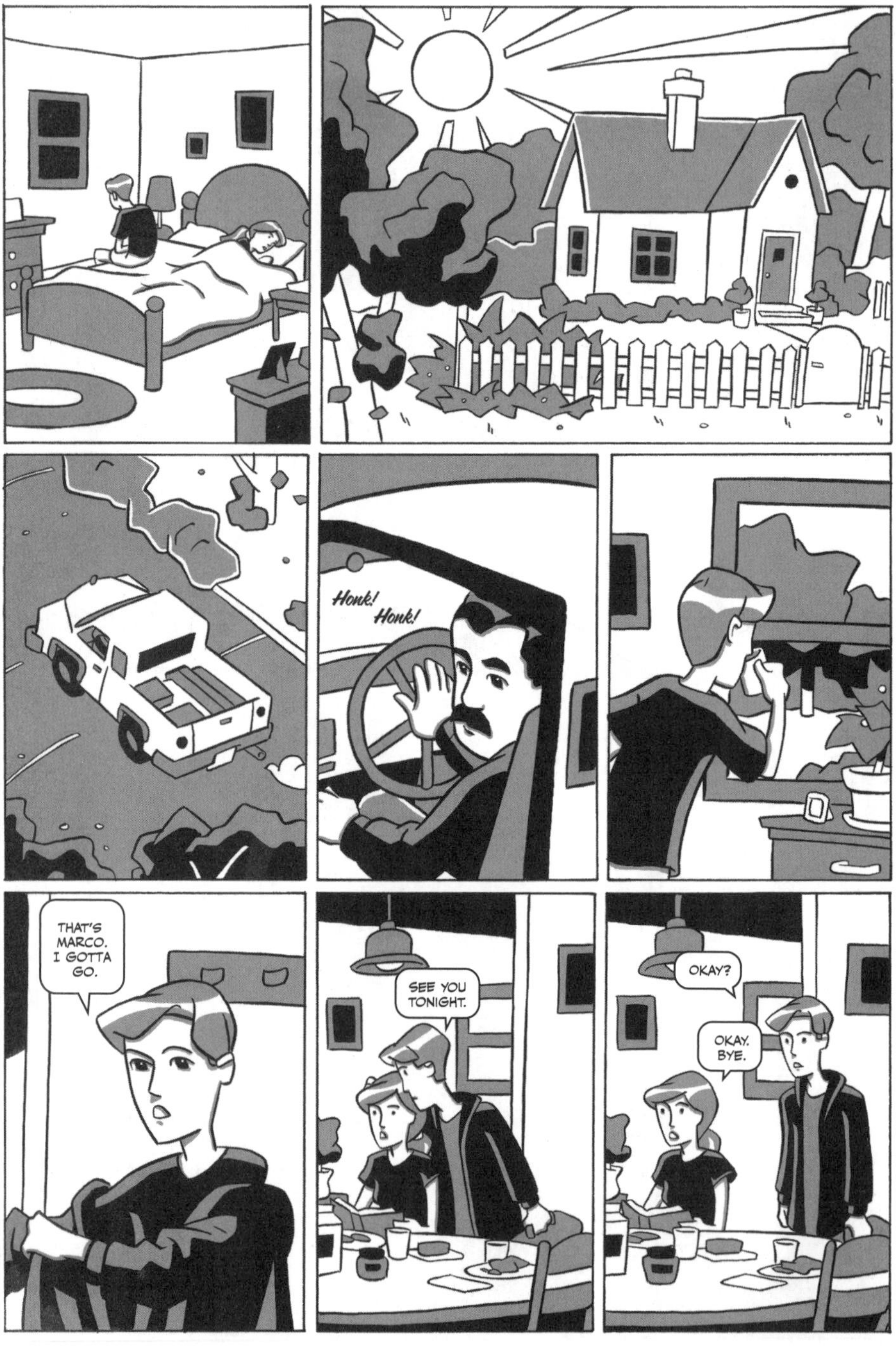
Honk!
Honk!
THAT'S MARCO. I GOTTA GO.
SEE YOU TONIGHT.
OKAY?
OKAY. BYE.

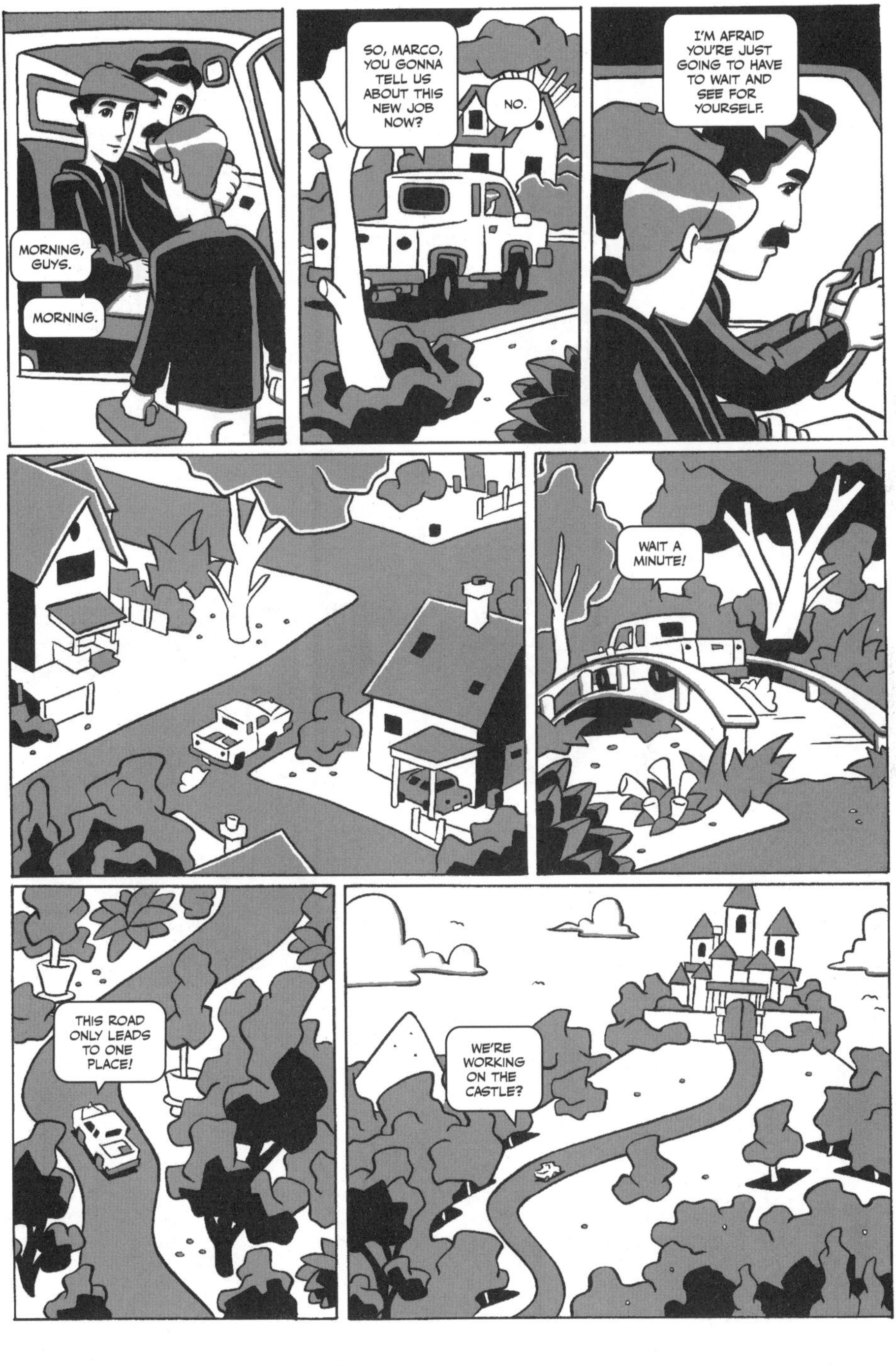
MORNING, GUYS.
MORNING.
SO, MARCO, YOU GONNA TELL US ABOUT THIS NEW JOB NOW?
NO.
I'M AFRAID YOU'RE JUST GOING TO HAVE TO WAIT AND SEE FOR YOURSELF.
WAIT A MINUTE!
THIS ROAD ONLY LEADS TO ONE PLACE!
WE'RE WORKING ON THE CASTLE?

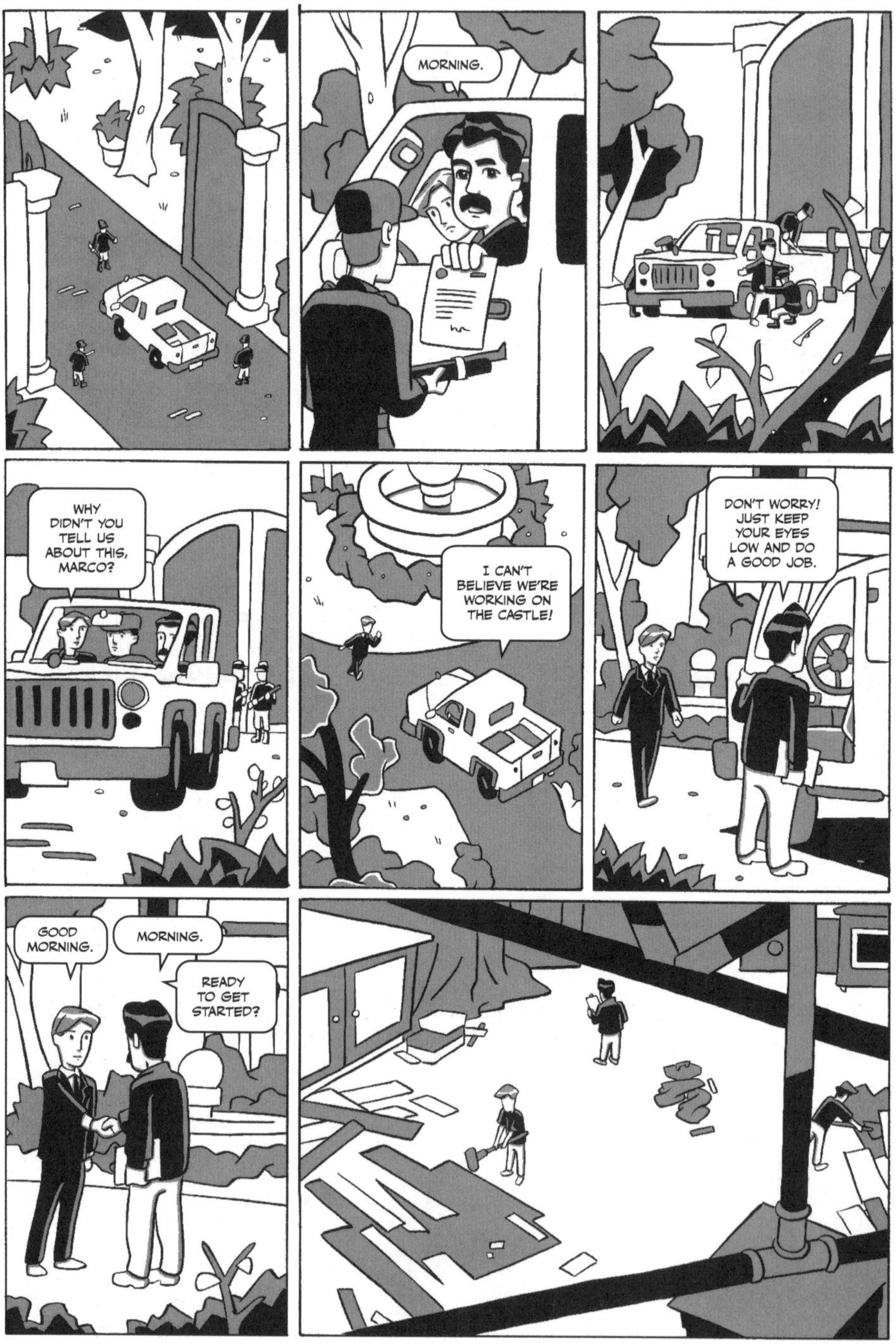
MORNING.
WHY DIDN'T YOU TELL US ABOUT THIS, MARCO?
I CAN'T BELIEVE WE'RE WORKING ON THE CASTLE!
DON'T WORRY! JUST KEEP YOUR EYES LOW AND DO A GOOD JOB.
GOOD MORNING.
MORNING.
READY TO GET STARTED?

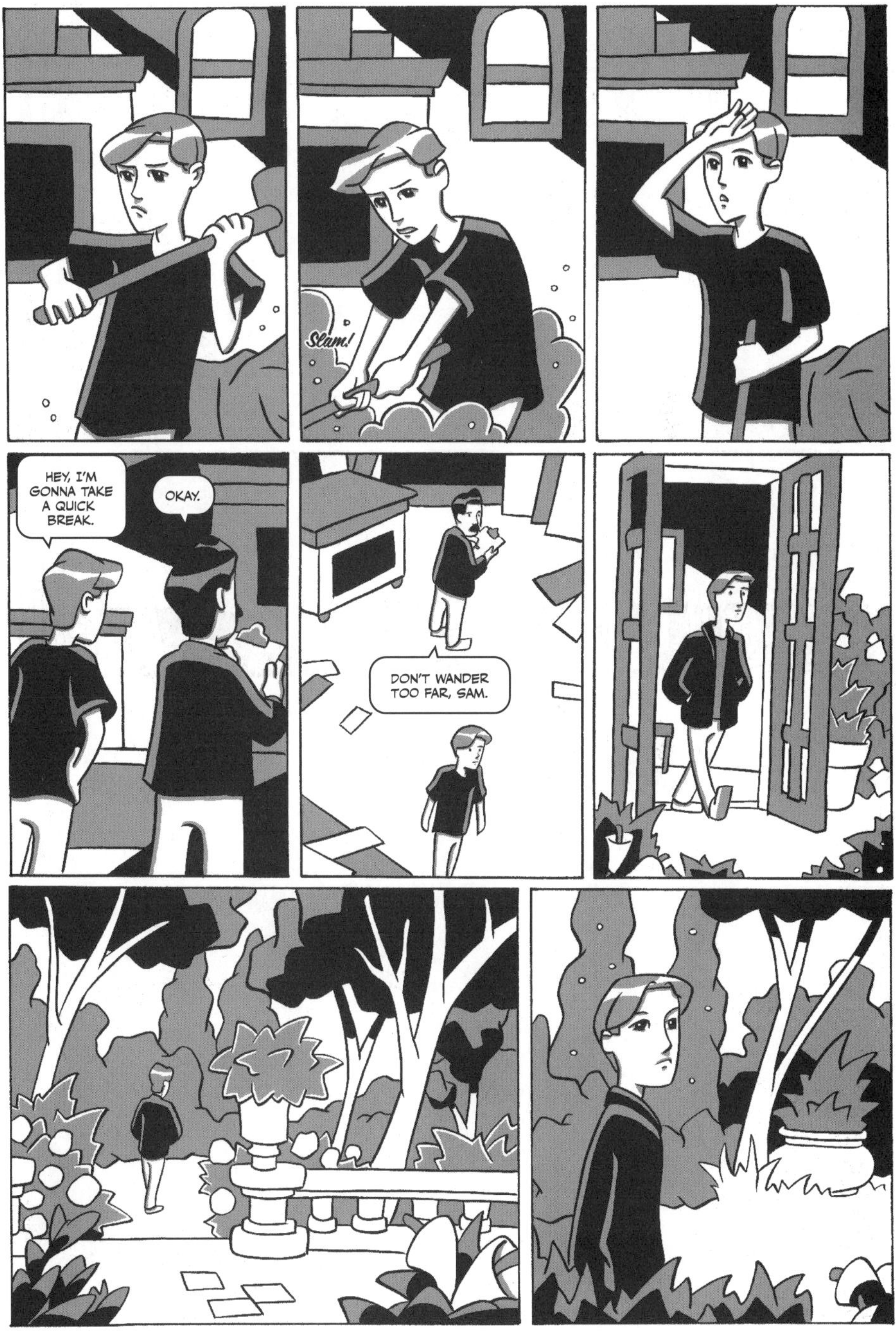

Slam!
HEY, I'M GONNA TAKE A QUICK BREAK.
OKAY.
DON'T WANDER TOO FAR, SAM.

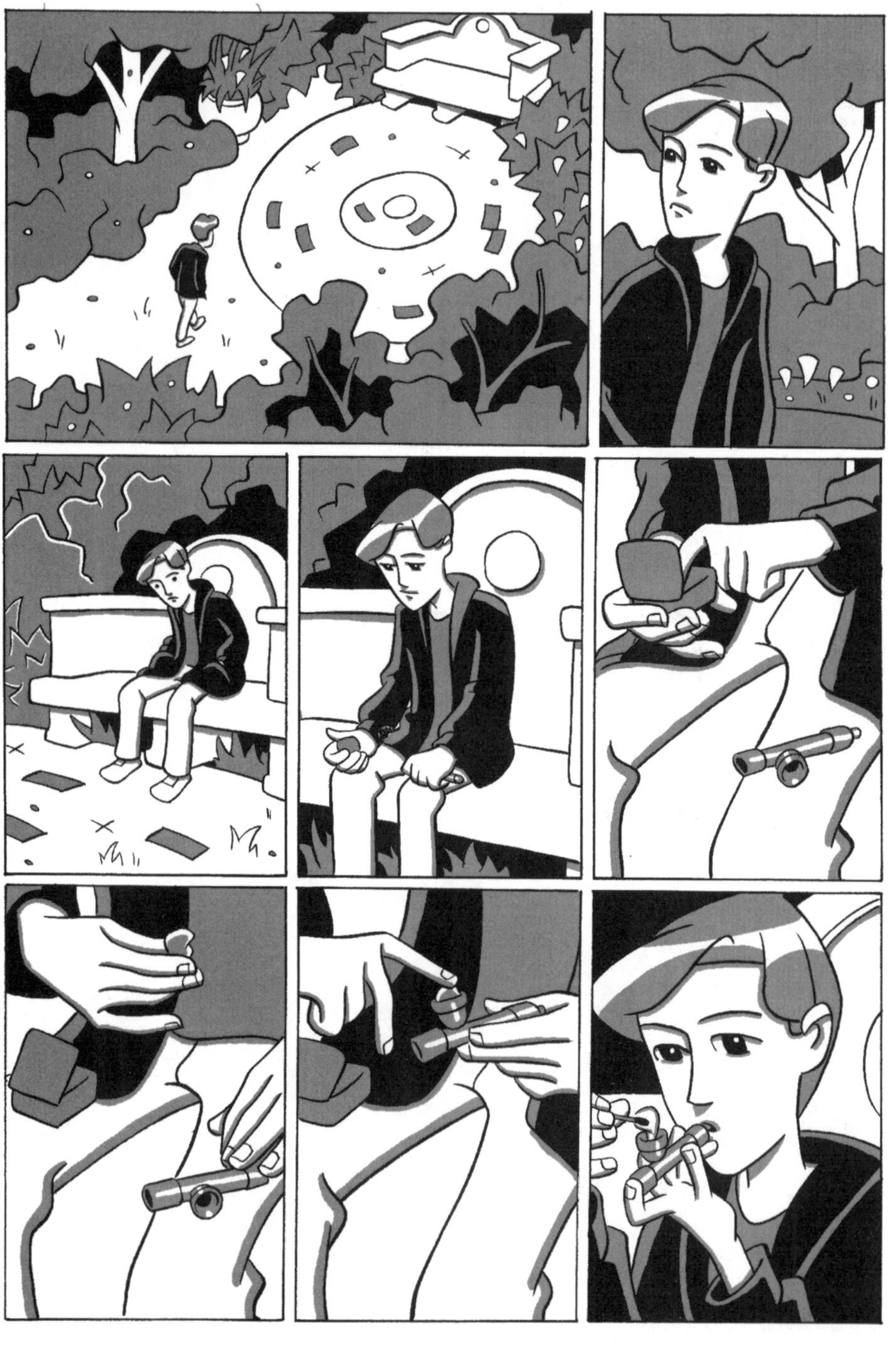

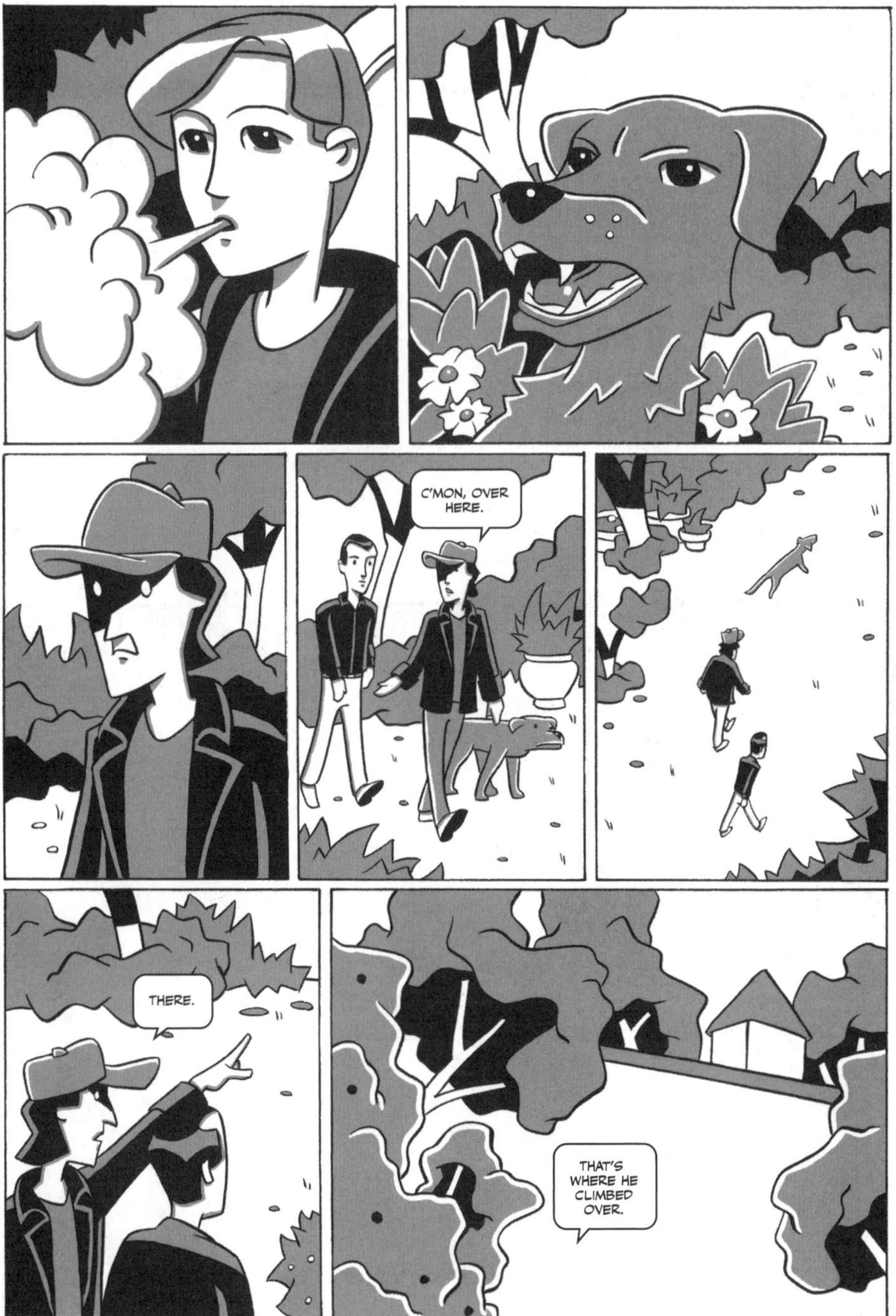
C'MON, OVER HERE.
THERE.
THAT'S WHERE HE CLIMBED OVER.

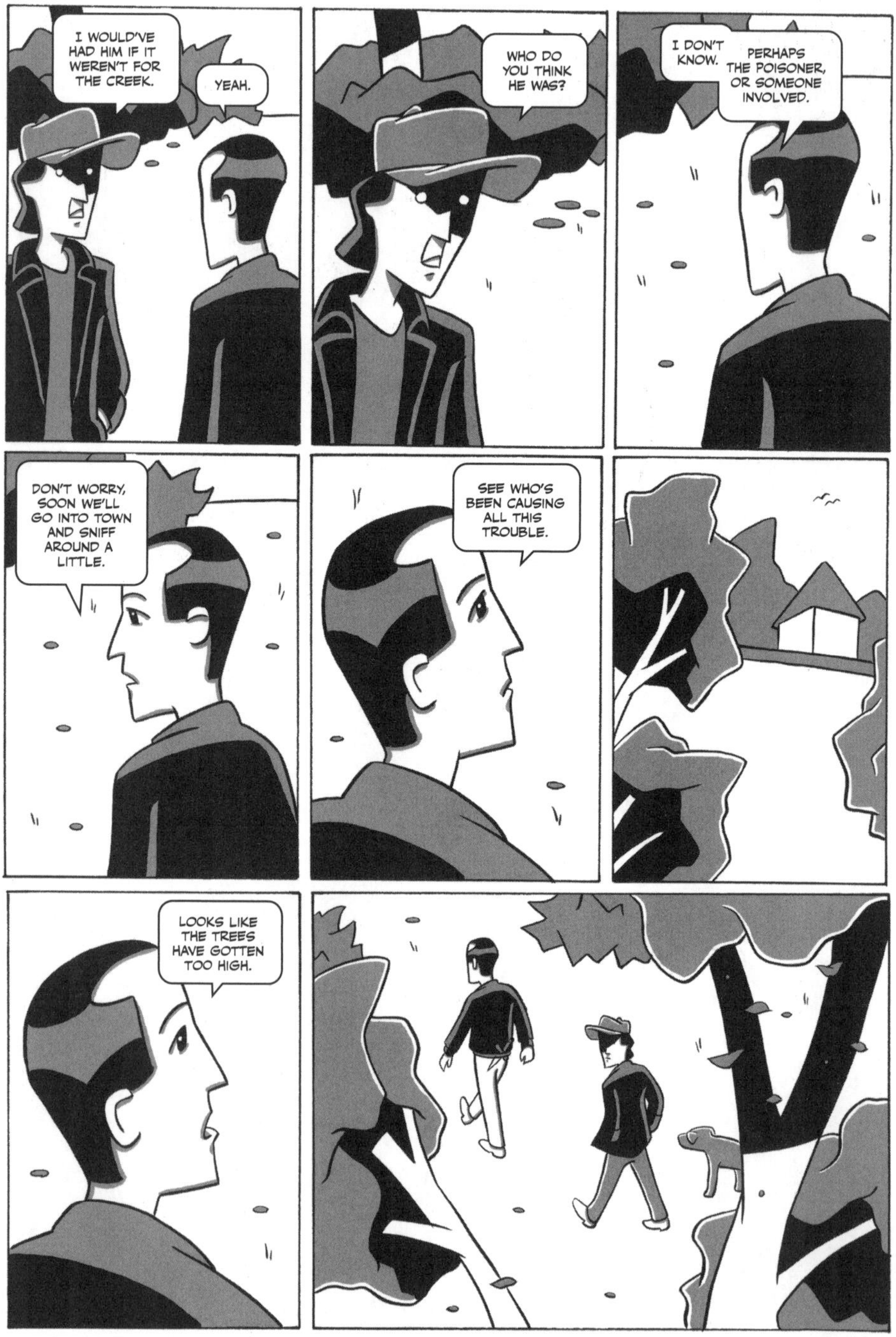
I WOULD'VE HAD HIM IF IT WEREN'T FOR THE CREEK.
YEAH.
WHO DO YOU THINK HE WAS?
I DON'T KNOW.
PERHAPS THE POISONER, OR SOMEONE INVOLVED.
DON'T WORRY, SOON WE'LL GO INTO TOWN AND SNIFF AROUND A LITTLE.
SEE WHO'S BEEN CAUSING ALL THIS TROUBLE.
LOOKS LIKE THE TREES HAVE GOTTEN TOO HIGH.

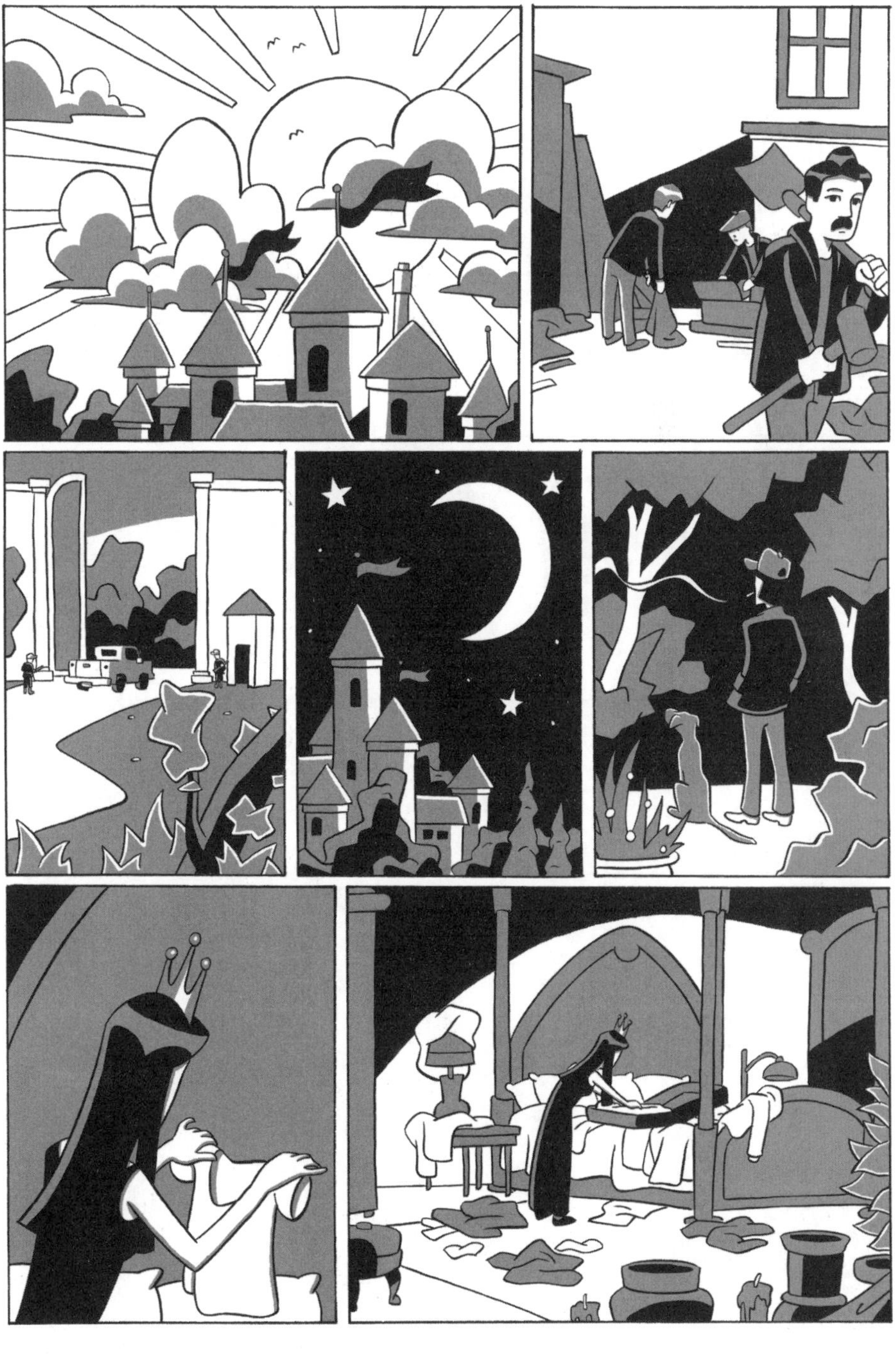

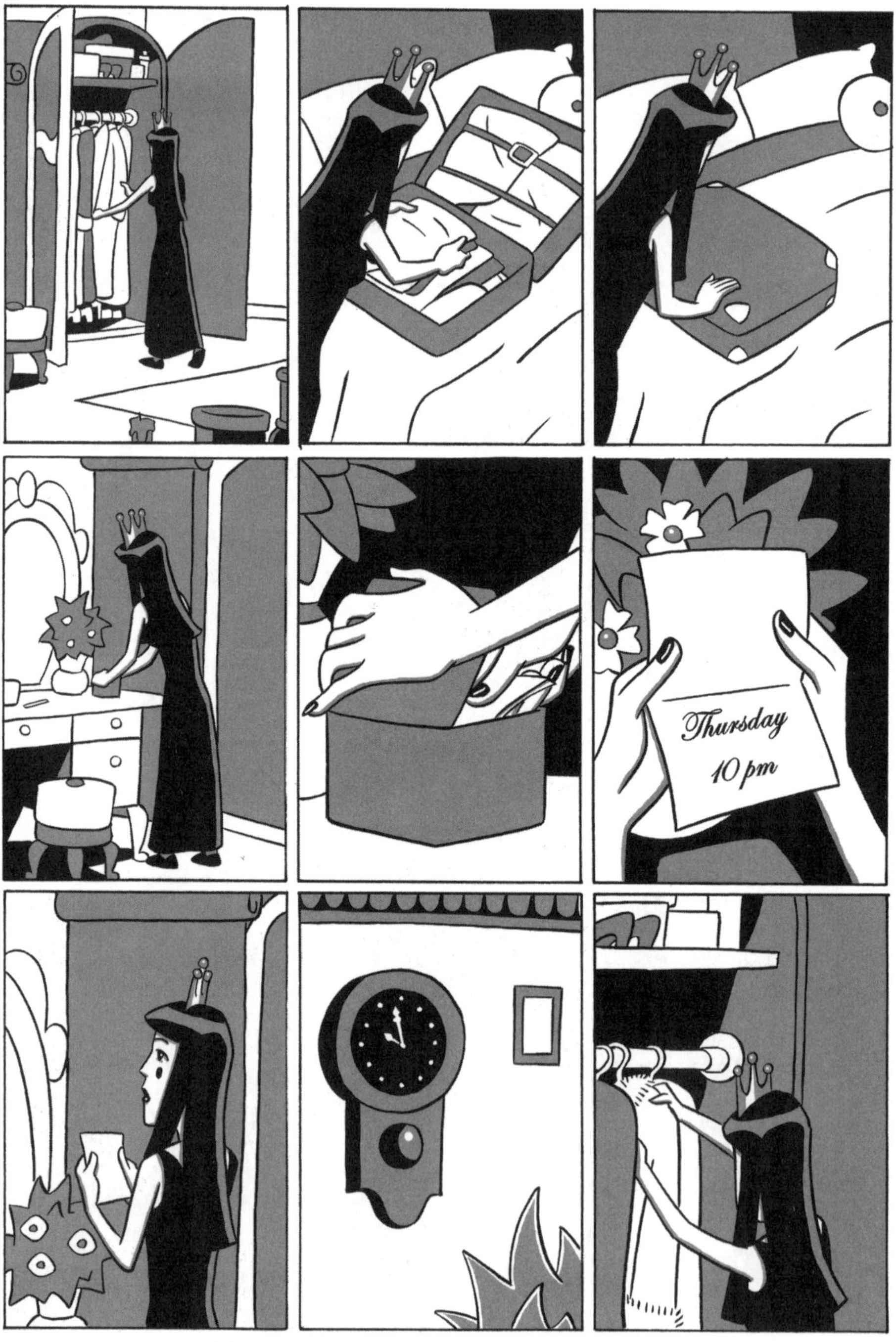
Thursday
10 pm

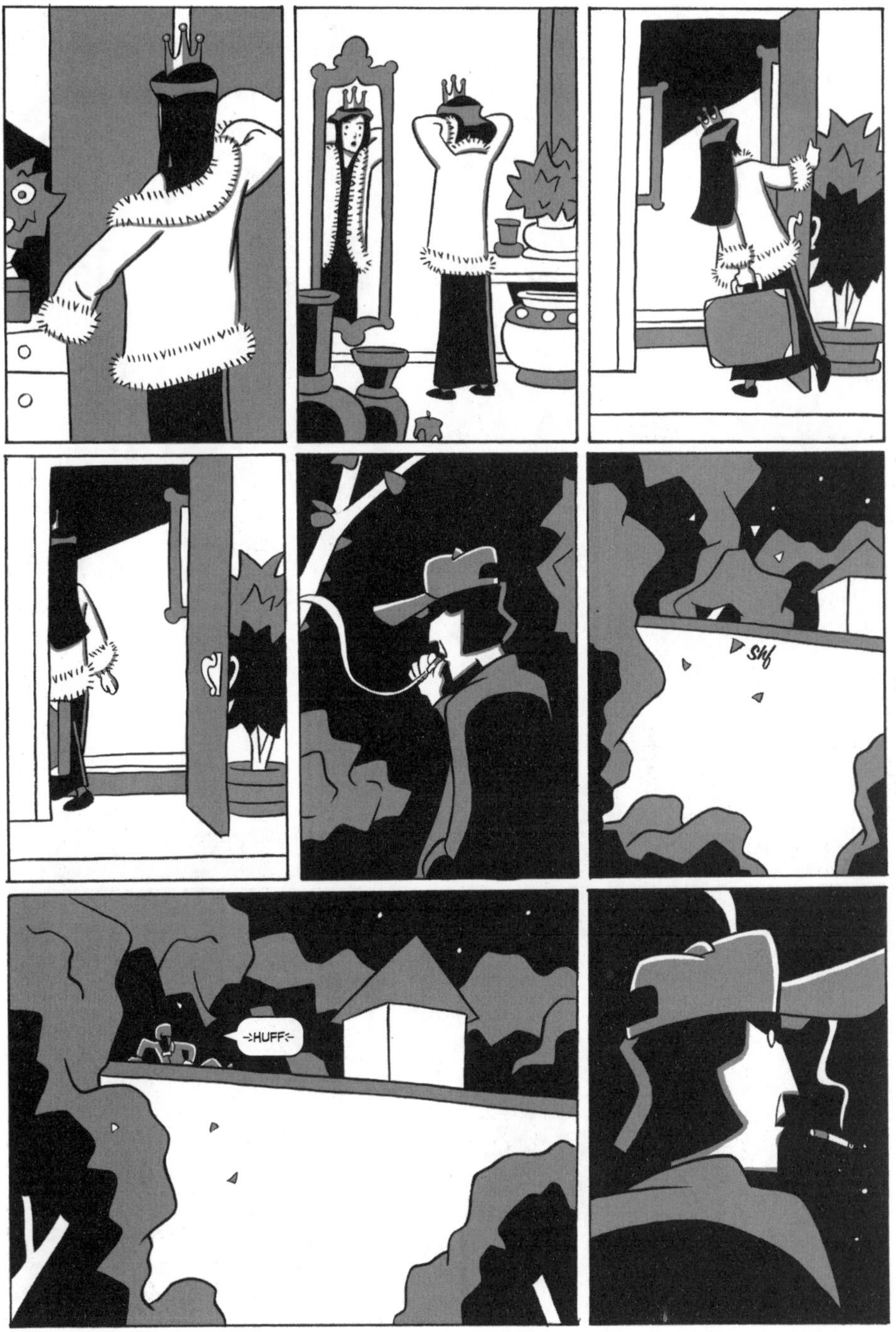
shf
HUFF

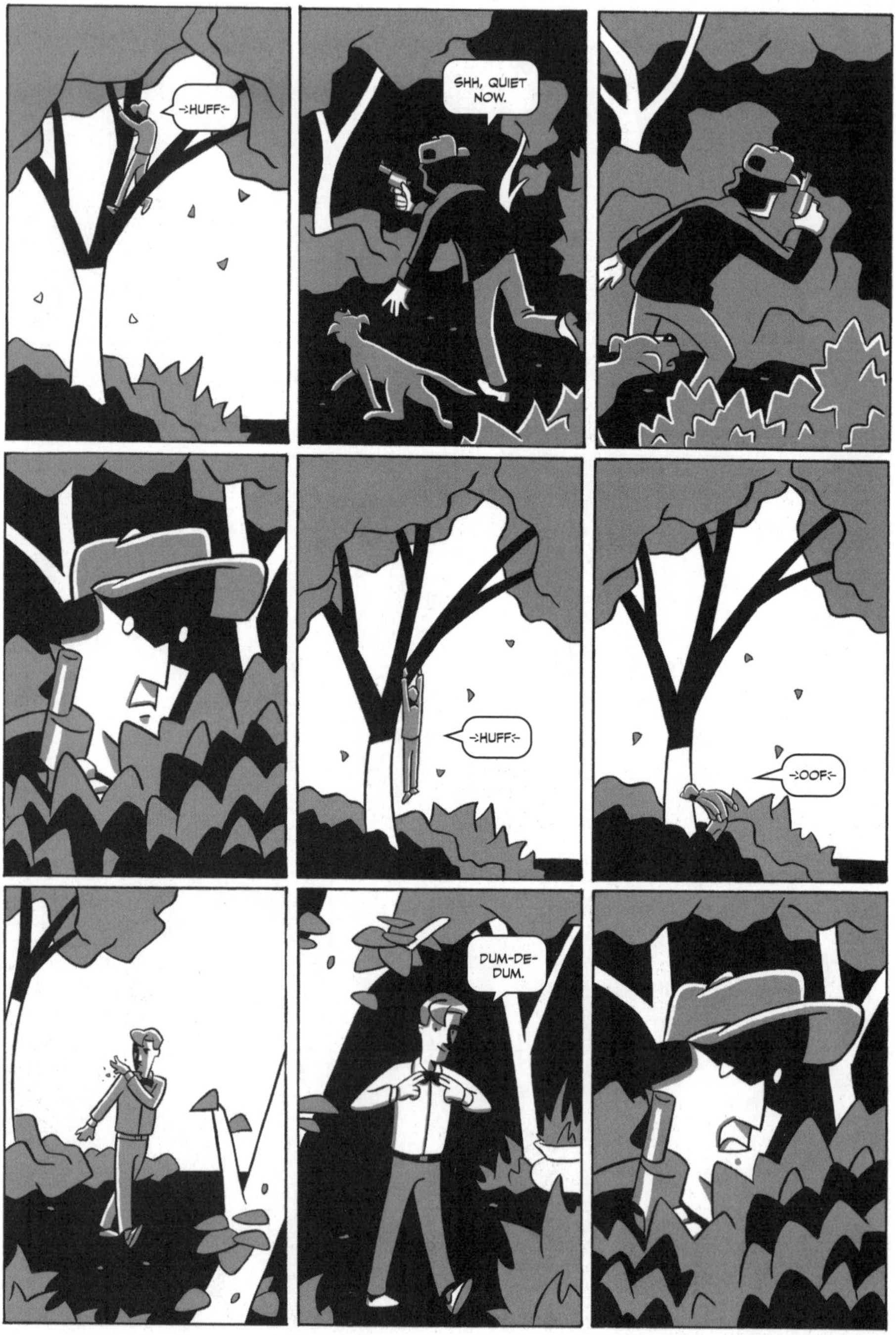
-HUFF-
SHH, QUIET NOW.
-HUFF-
-OOF-
DUM-DE-DUM.

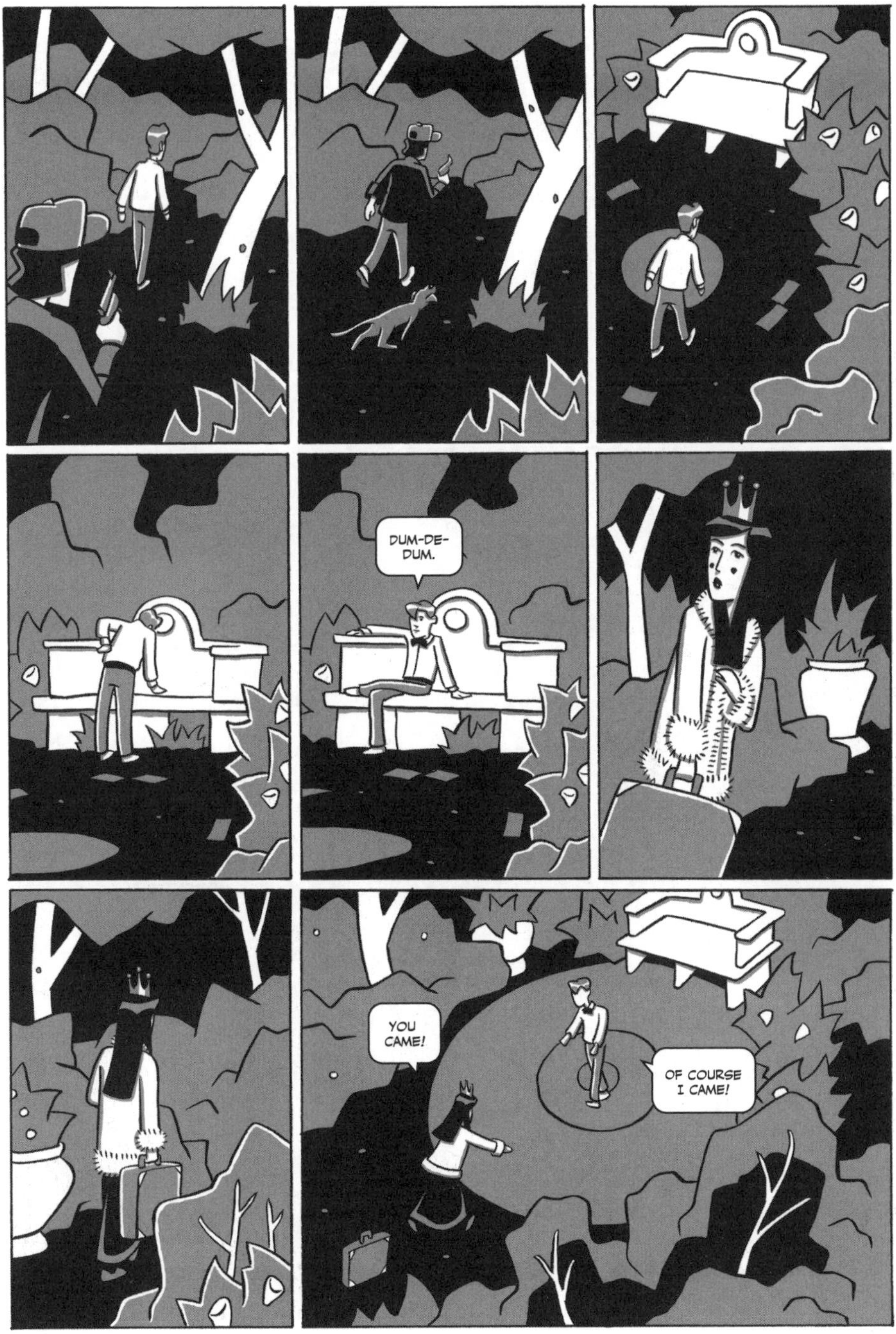
DUM-DE-DUM.
YOU CAME!
OF COURSE I CAME!

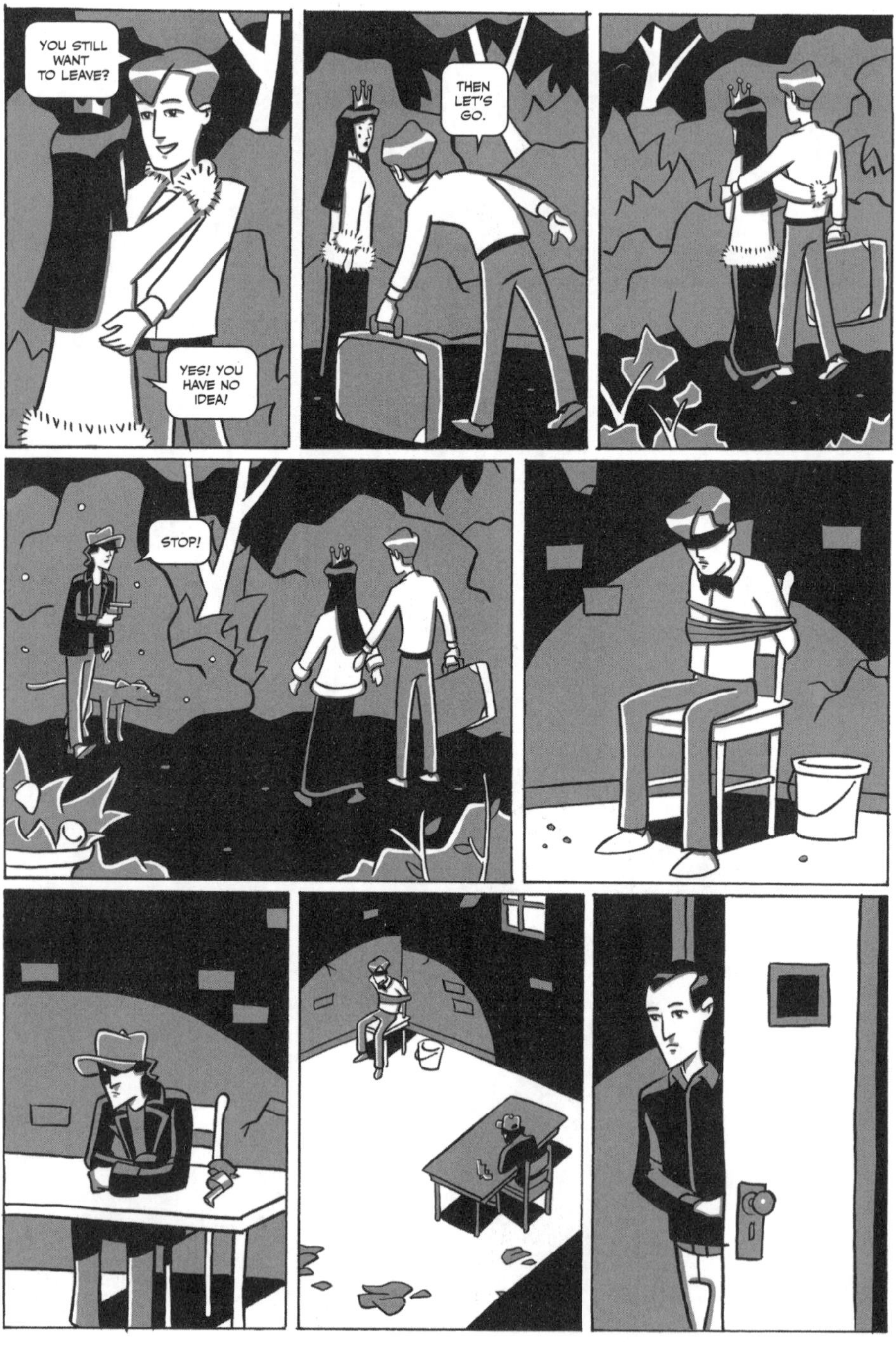
YOU STILL WANT TO LEAVE?
YES! YOU HAVE NO IDEA!
THEN LET'S GO.
STOP!

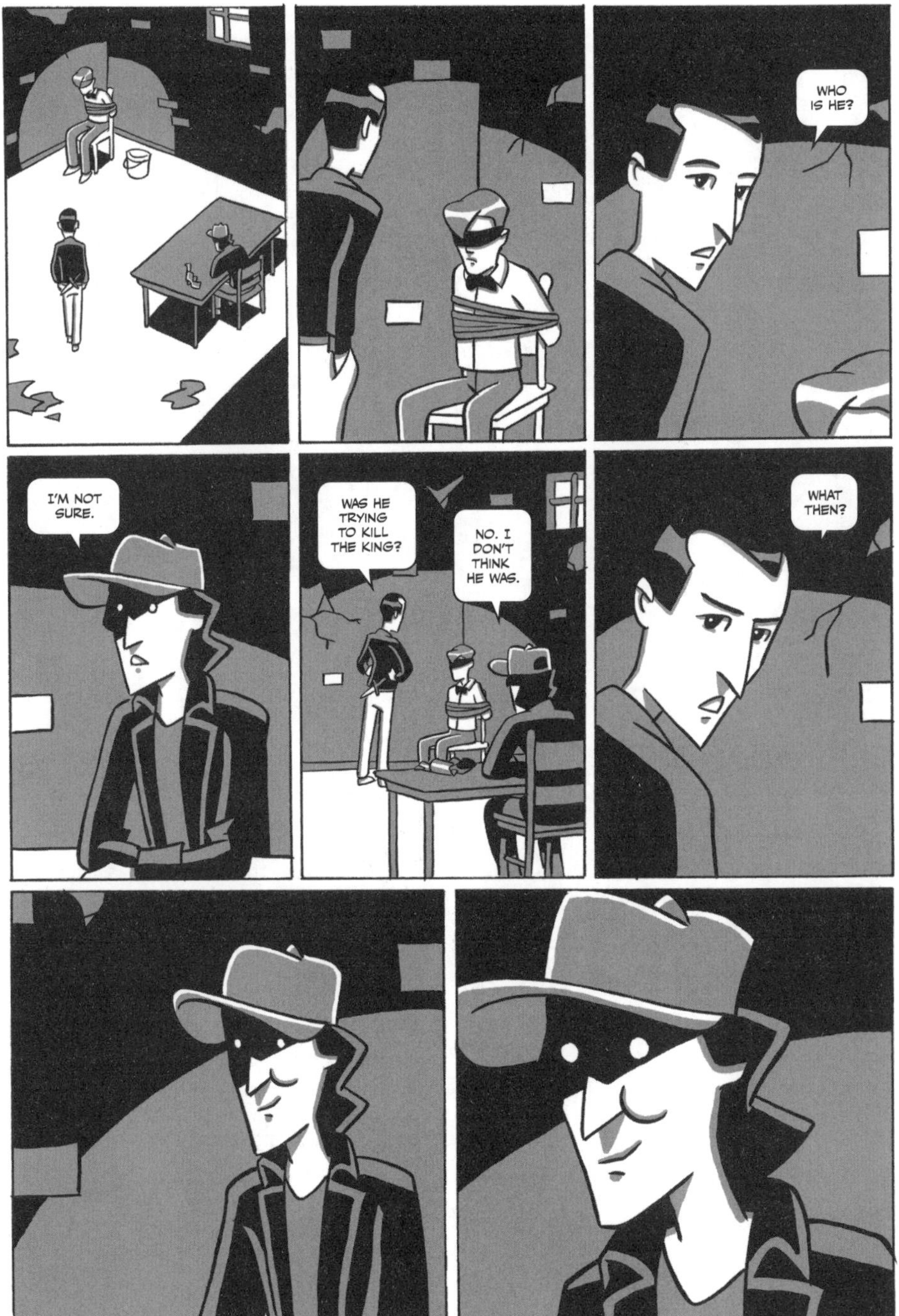
WHO IS HE?
I'M NOT SURE.
WAS HE TRYING TO KILL THE KING?
NO. I DON'T THINK HE WAS.
WHAT THEN?

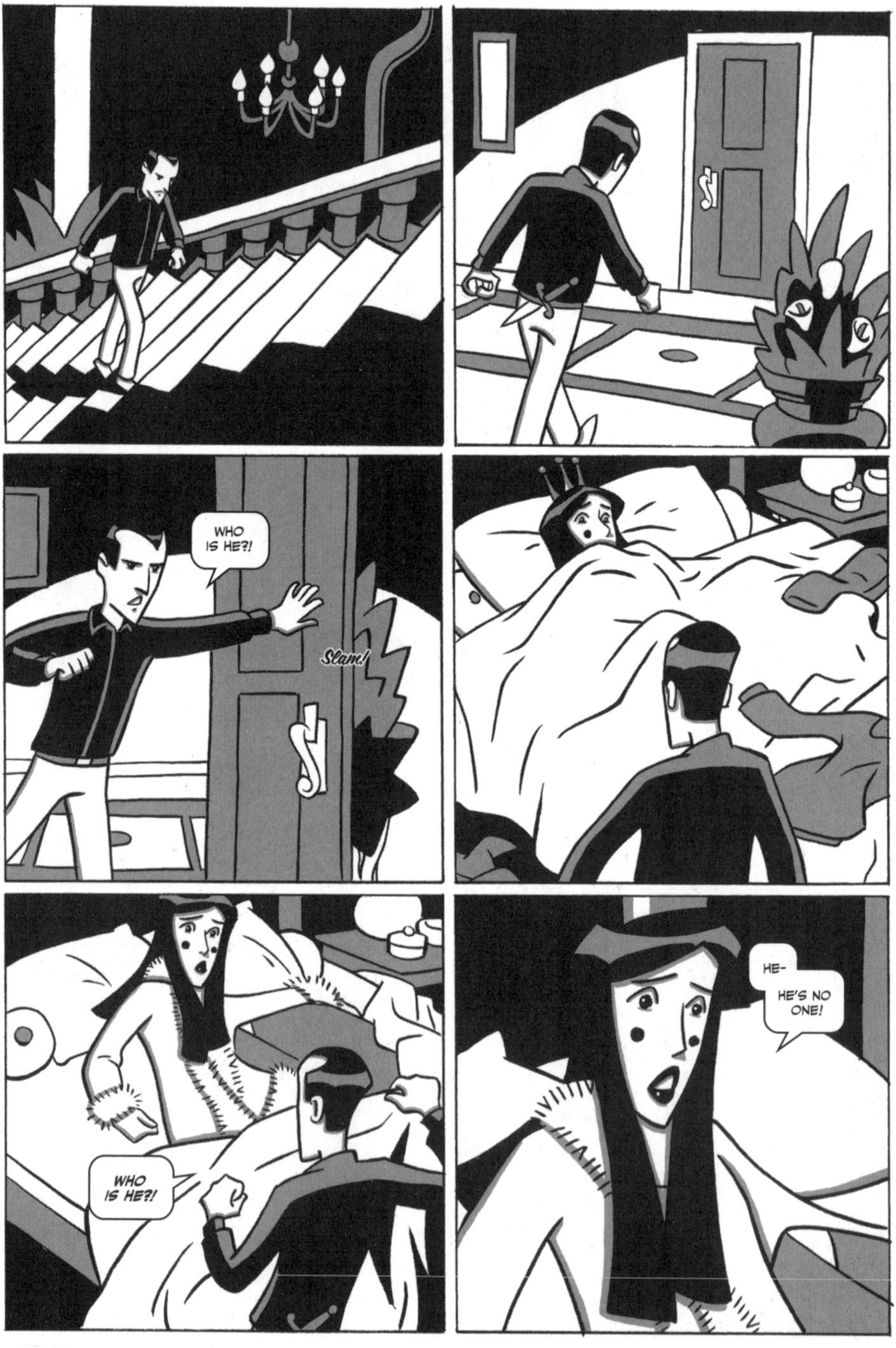

WHO IS HE?!
Slam!
WHO IS HE?!
HE-
HE'S NO ONE!

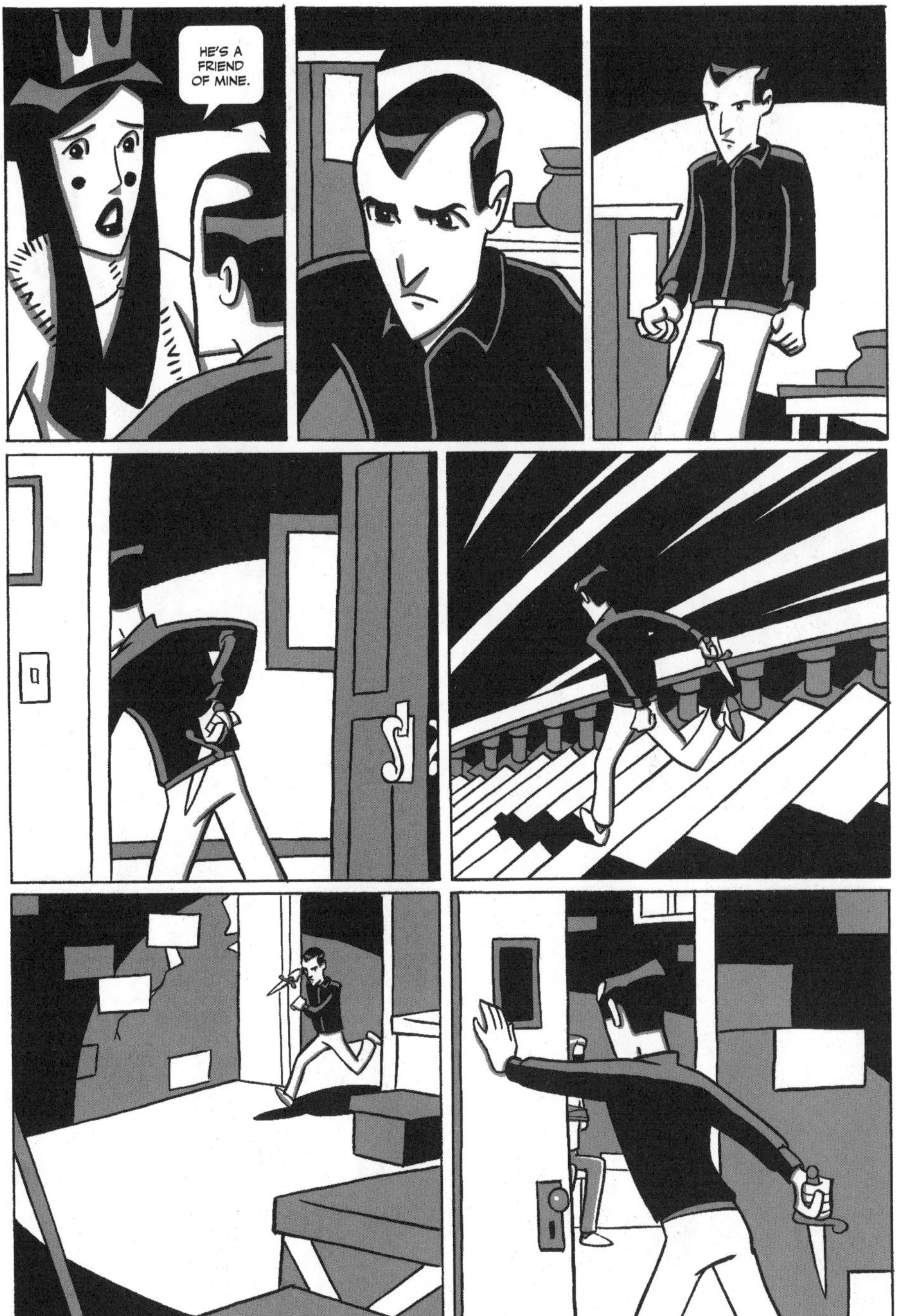
HE'S A FRIEND OF MINE.

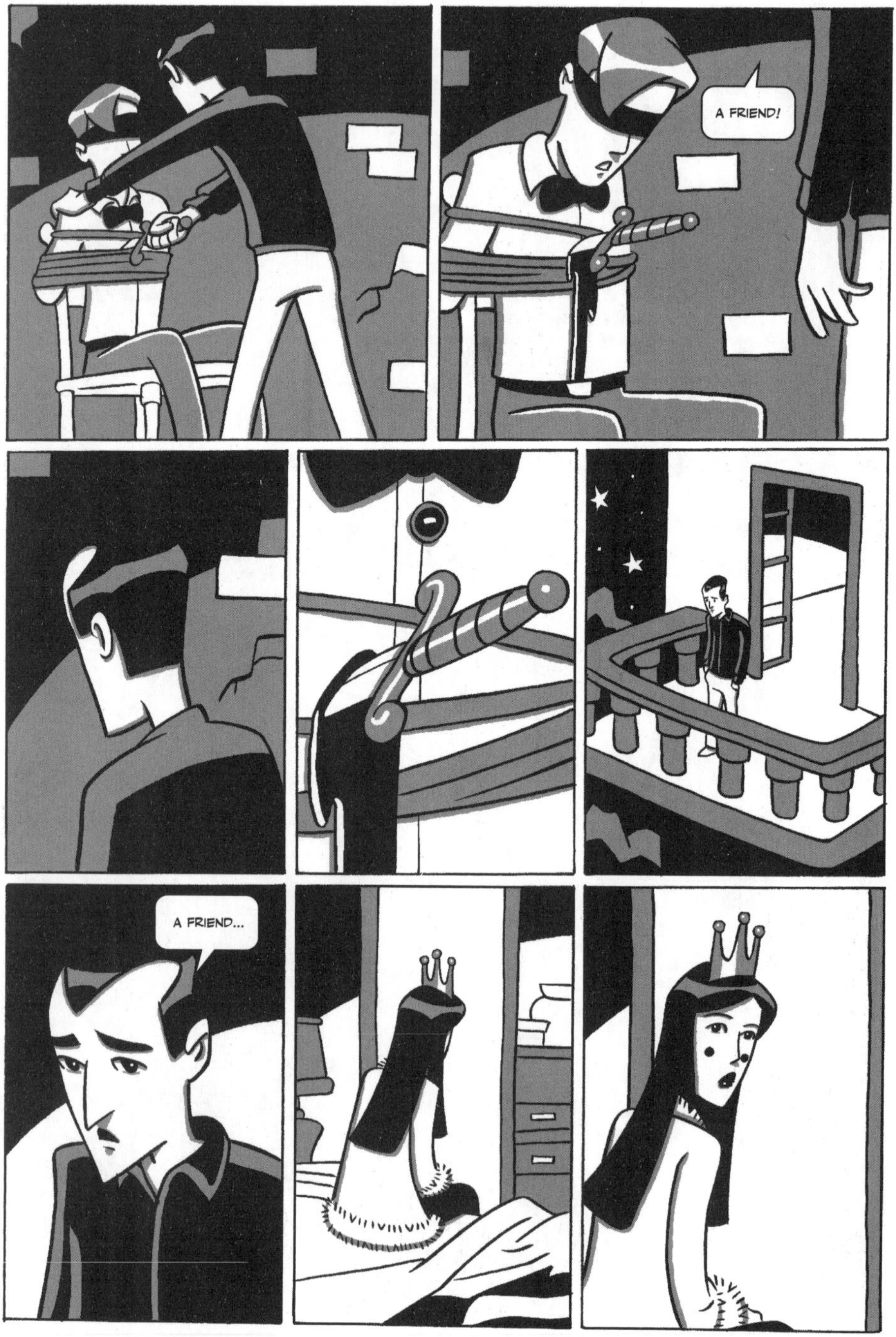
A FRIEND!
A FRIEND...

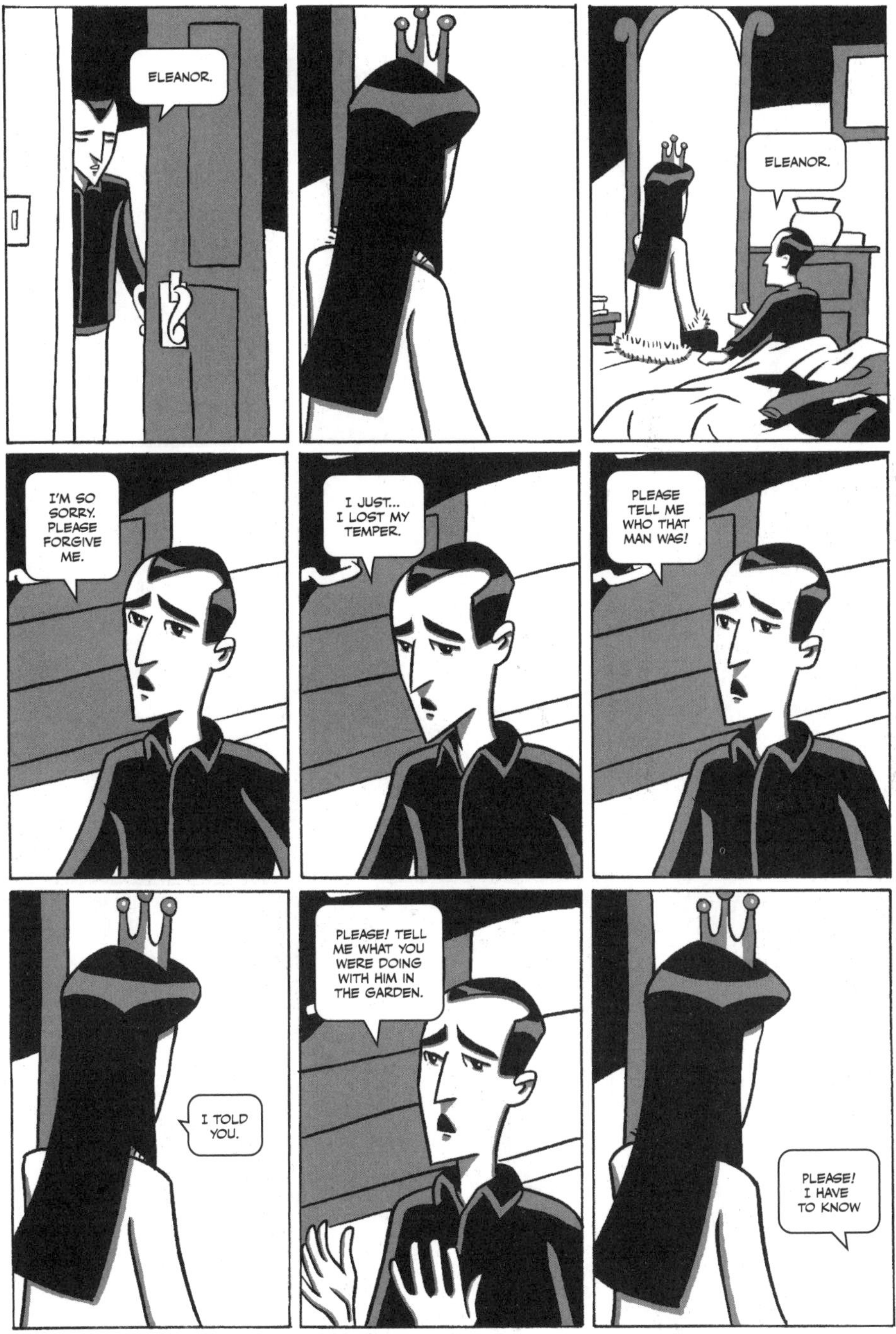
ELEANOR.
ELEANOR.
I'M SO SORRY. PLEASE FORGIVE ME.
I JUST... I LOST MY TEMPER.
PLEASE TELL ME WHO THAT MAN WAS!
I TOLD YOU.
PLEASE! TELL ME WHAT YOU WERE DOING WITH HIM IN THE GARDEN.
PLEASE! I HAVE TO KNOW

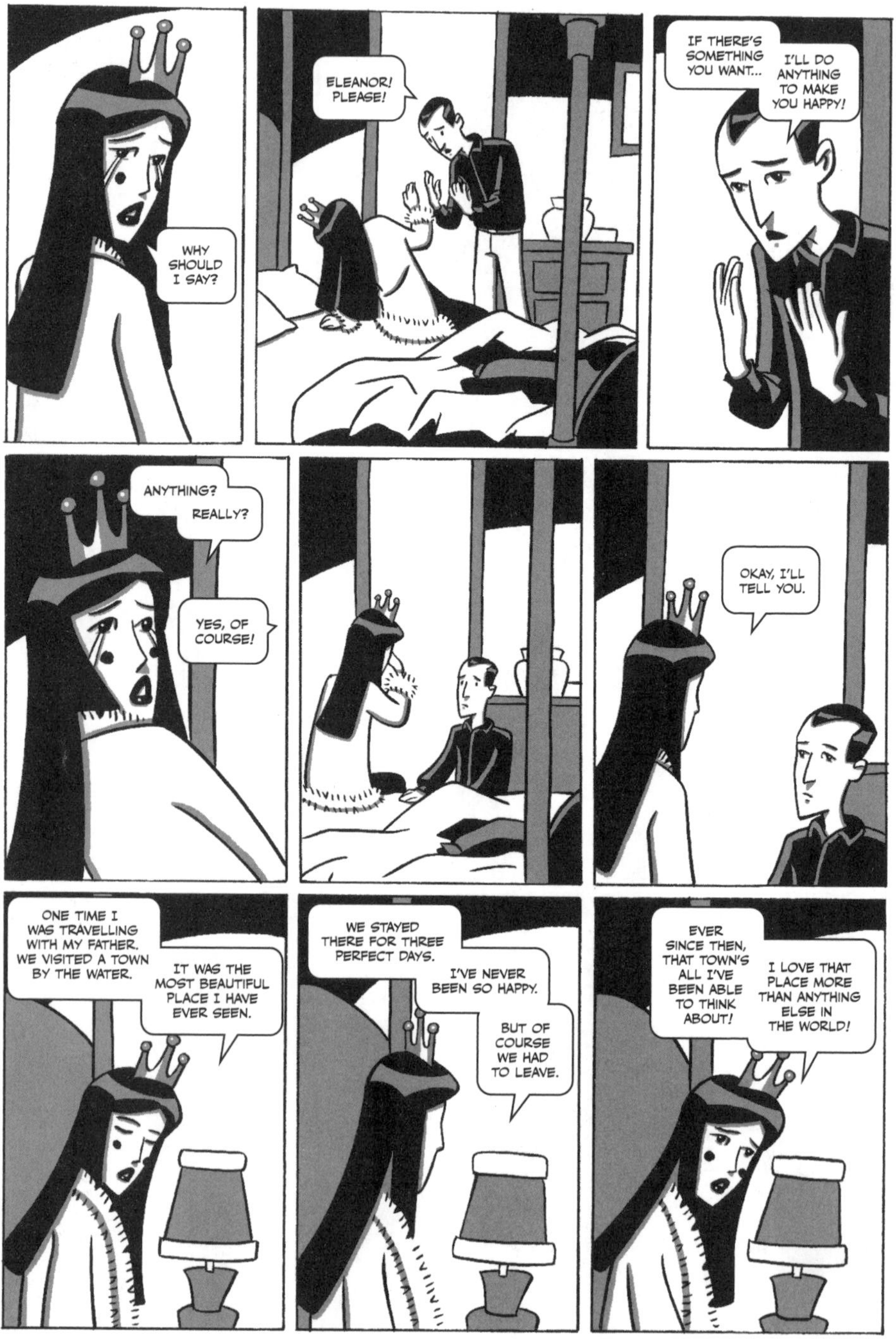
WHY SHOULD I SAY?
ELEANOR! PLEASE!
IF THERE'S SOMETHING YOU WANT...
I'LL DO ANYTHING TO MAKE YOU HAPPY!
ANYTHING?
REALLY?
YES, OF COURSE!
OKAY, I'LL TELL YOU.
ONE TIME I WAS TRAVELLING WITH MY FATHER. WE VISITED A TOWN BY THE WATER.
IT WAS THE MOST BEAUTIFUL PLACE I HAVE EVER SEEN.
WE STAYED THERE FOR THREE PERFECT DAYS.
I'VE NEVER BEEN SO HAPPY.
BUT OF COURSE WE HAD TO LEAVE.
EVER SINCE THEN, THAT TOWN'S ALL I'VE BEEN ABLE TO THINK ABOUT!
I LOVE THAT PLACE MORE THAN ANYTHING ELSE IN THE WORLD!

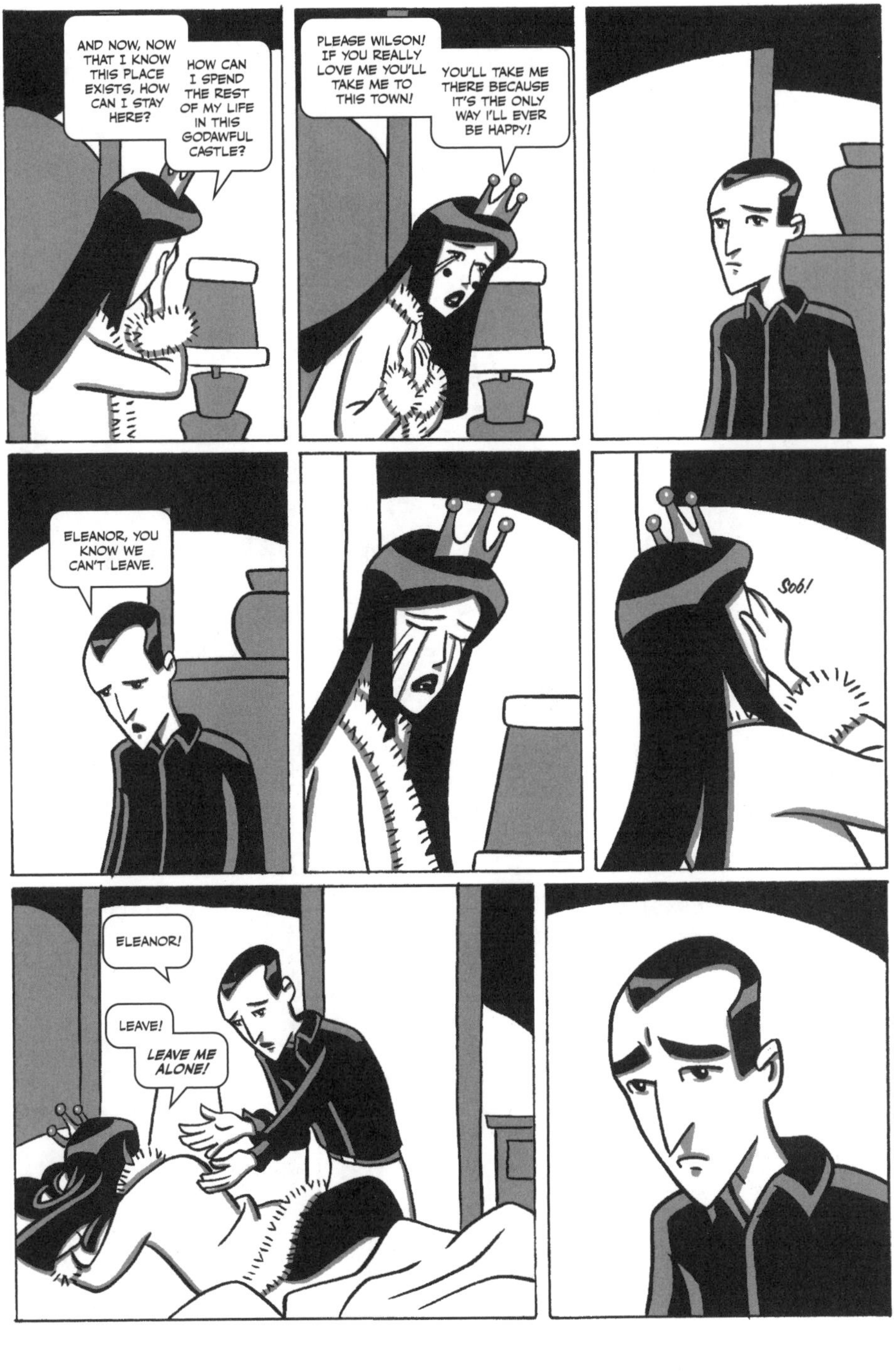
AND NOW, NOW THAT I KNOW THIS PLACE EXISTS, HOW CAN I STAY HERE?
HOW CAN I SPEND THE REST OF MY LIFE IN THIS GODAWFUL CASTLE?
PLEASE WILSON! IF YOU REALLY LOVE ME YOU'LL TAKE ME TO THIS TOWN!
YOU'LL TAKE ME THERE BECAUSE IT'S THE ONLY WAY I'LL EVER BE HAPPY!
ELEANOR, YOU KNOW WE CAN'T LEAVE.
Sob!
ELEANOR!
LEAVE!
LEAVE ME ALONE!

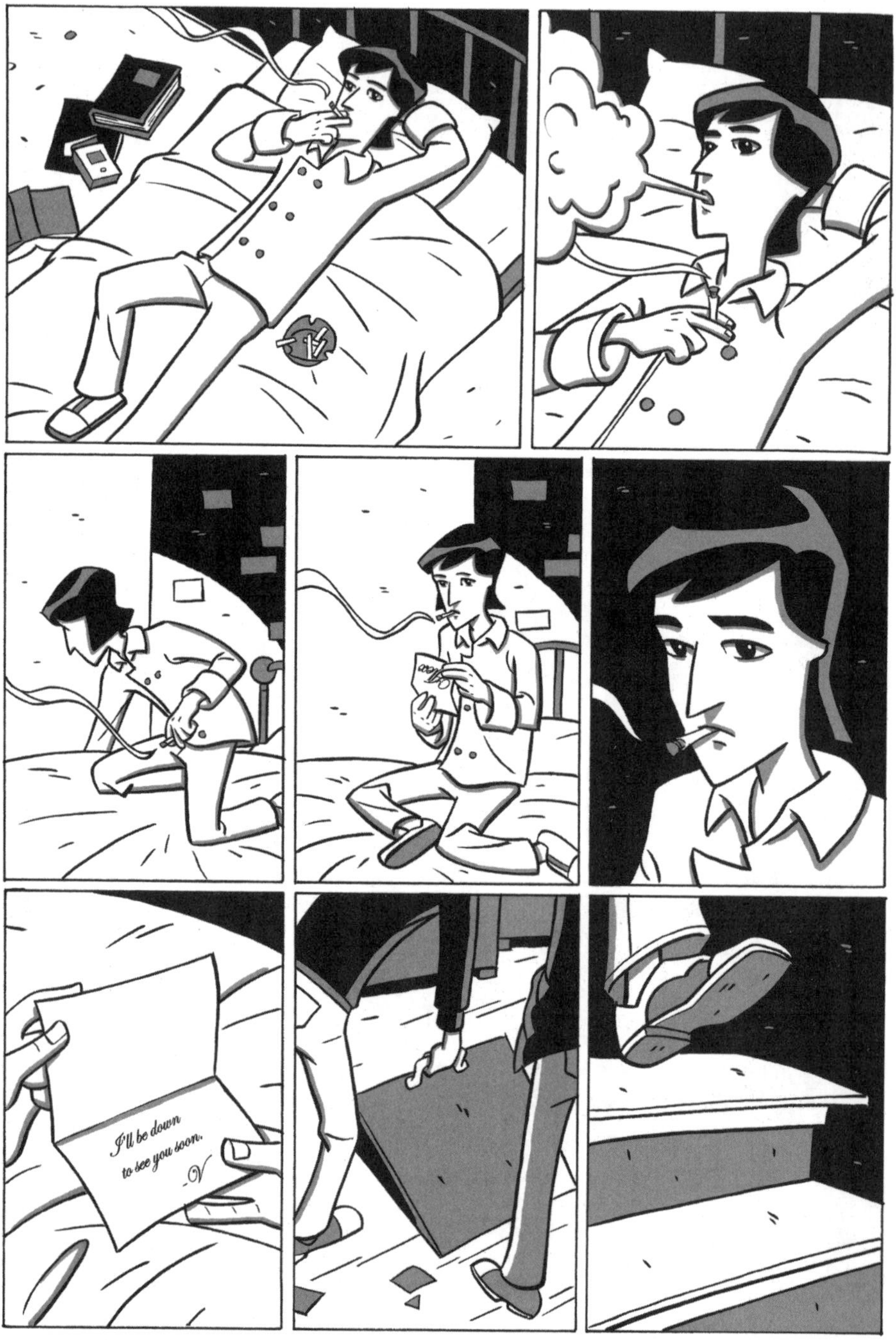
I'll be down
to see you soon.
-V

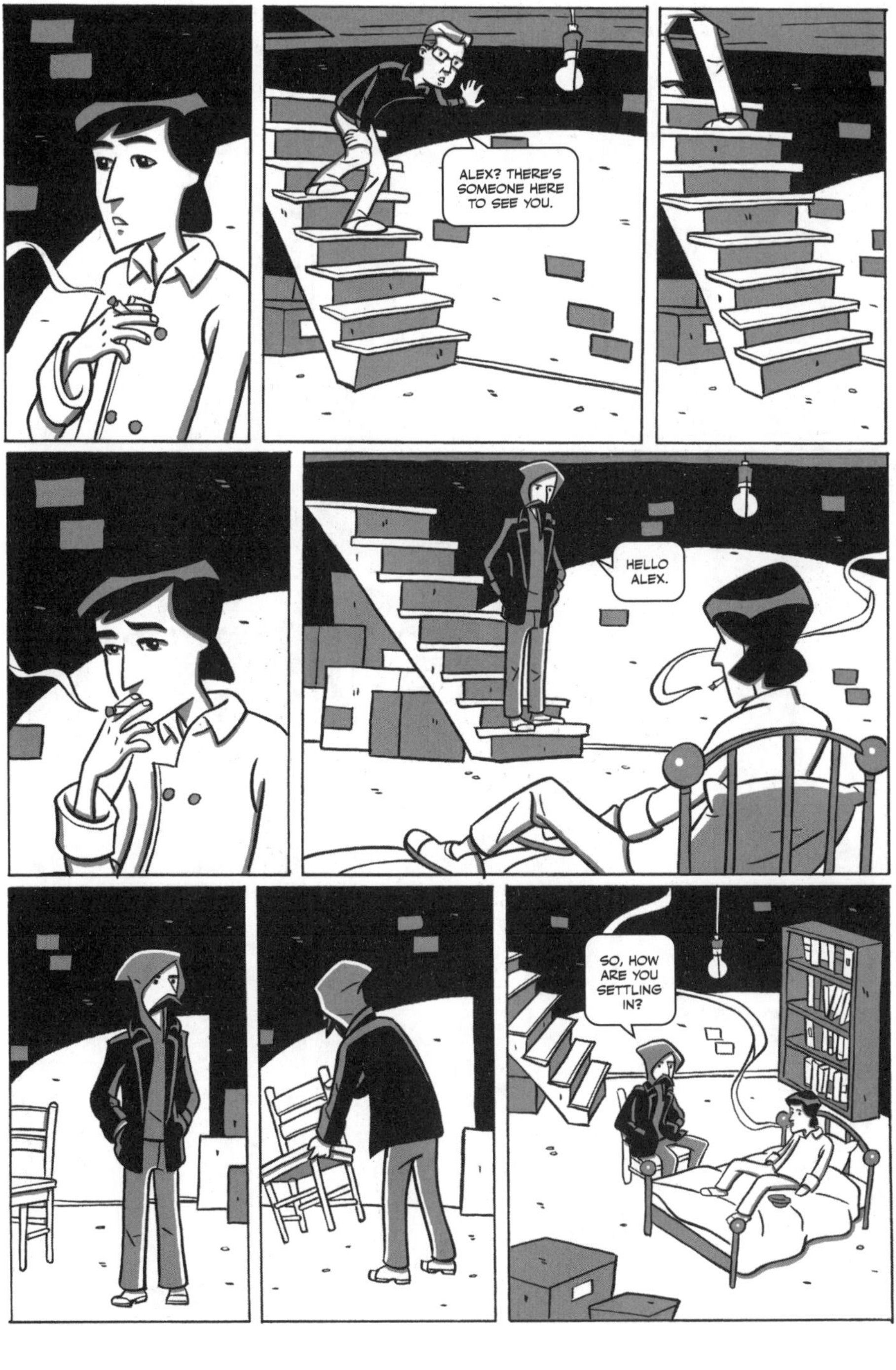
ALEX? THERE'S SOMEONE HERE TO SEE YOU.
HELLO ALEX.
SO, HOW ARE YOU SETTLING IN?

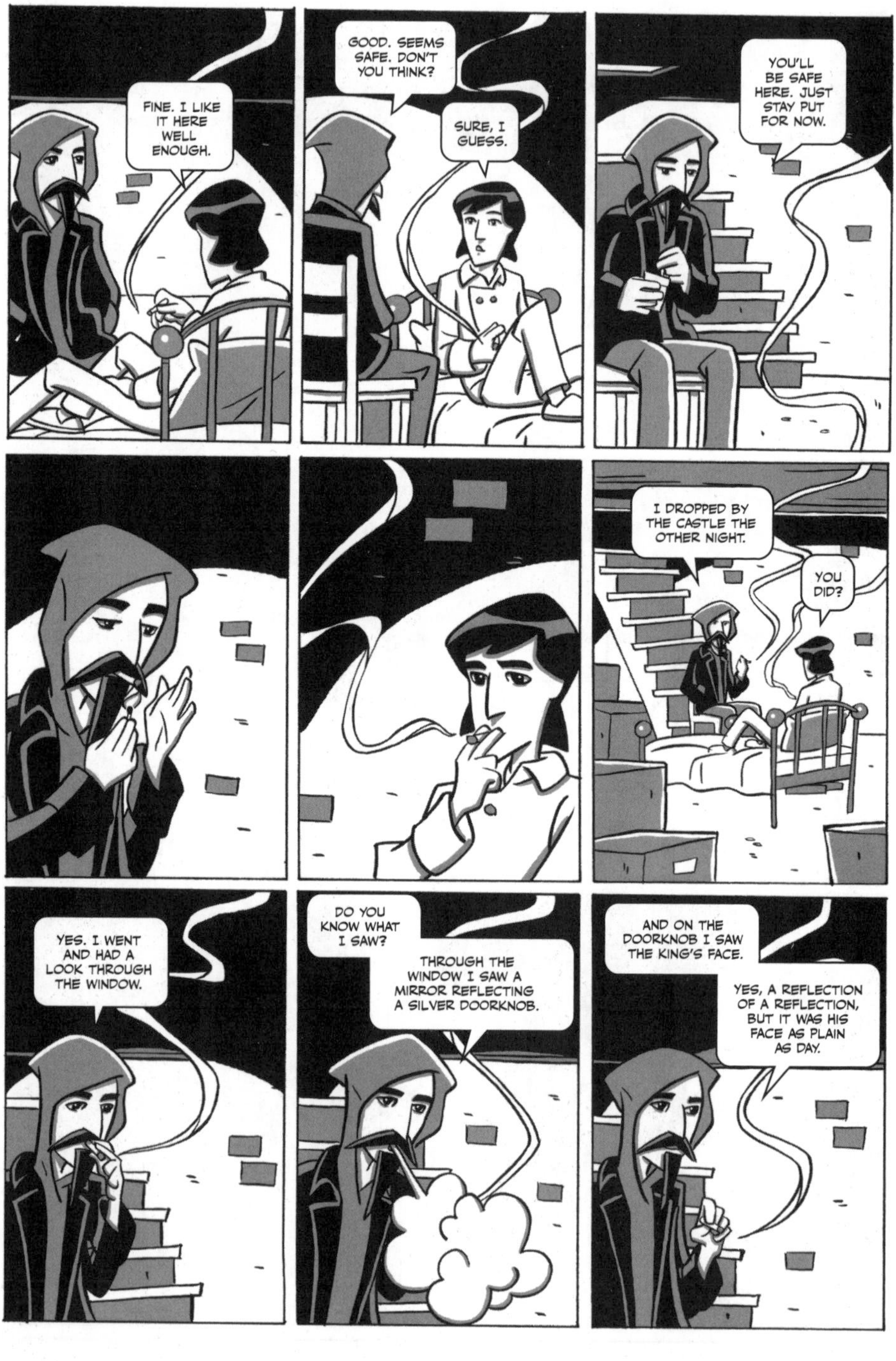
FINE. I LIKE IT HERE WELL ENOUGH.
GOOD. SEEMS SAFE. DON'T YOU THINK?
SURE, I GUESS.
YOU'LL BE SAFE HERE. JUST STAY PUT FOR NOW.
I DROPPED BY THE CASTLE THE OTHER NIGHT.
YOU DID?
YES. I WENT AND HAD A LOOK THROUGH THE WINDOW.
DO YOU KNOW WHAT I SAW?
THROUGH THE WINDOW I SAW A MIRROR REFLECTING A SILVER DOORKNOB.
AND ON THE DOORKNOB I SAW THE KING'S FACE.
YES, A REFLECTION OF A REFLECTION, BUT IT WAS HIS FACE AS PLAIN AS DAY.

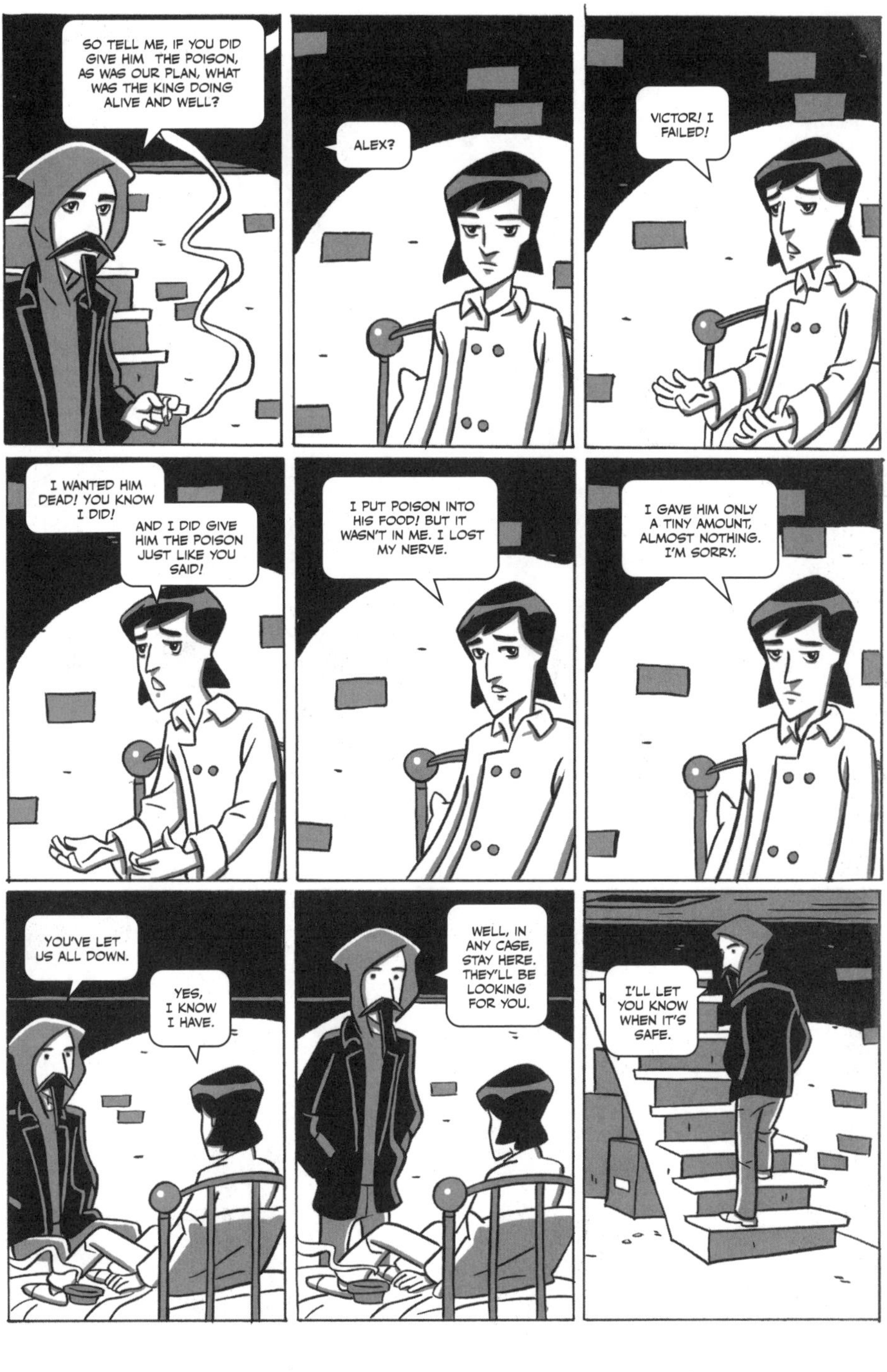
SO TELL ME, IF YOU DID GIVE HIM THE POISON, AS WAS OUR PLAN, WHAT WAS THE KING DOING ALIVE AND WELL?
ALEX?
VICTOR! I FAILED!
I WANTED HIM DEAD! YOU KNOW I DID!
AND I DID GIVE HIM THE POISON JUST LIKE YOU SAID!
I PUT POISON INTO HIS FOOD! BUT IT WASN'T IN ME. I LOST MY NERVE.
I GAVE HIM ONLY A TINY AMOUNT, ALMOST NOTHING. I'M SORRY.
YOU'VE LET US ALL DOWN.
YES, I KNOW I HAVE.
WELL, IN ANY CASE, STAY HERE. THEY'LL BE LOOKING FOR YOU.
I'LL LET YOU KNOW WHEN IT'S SAFE.

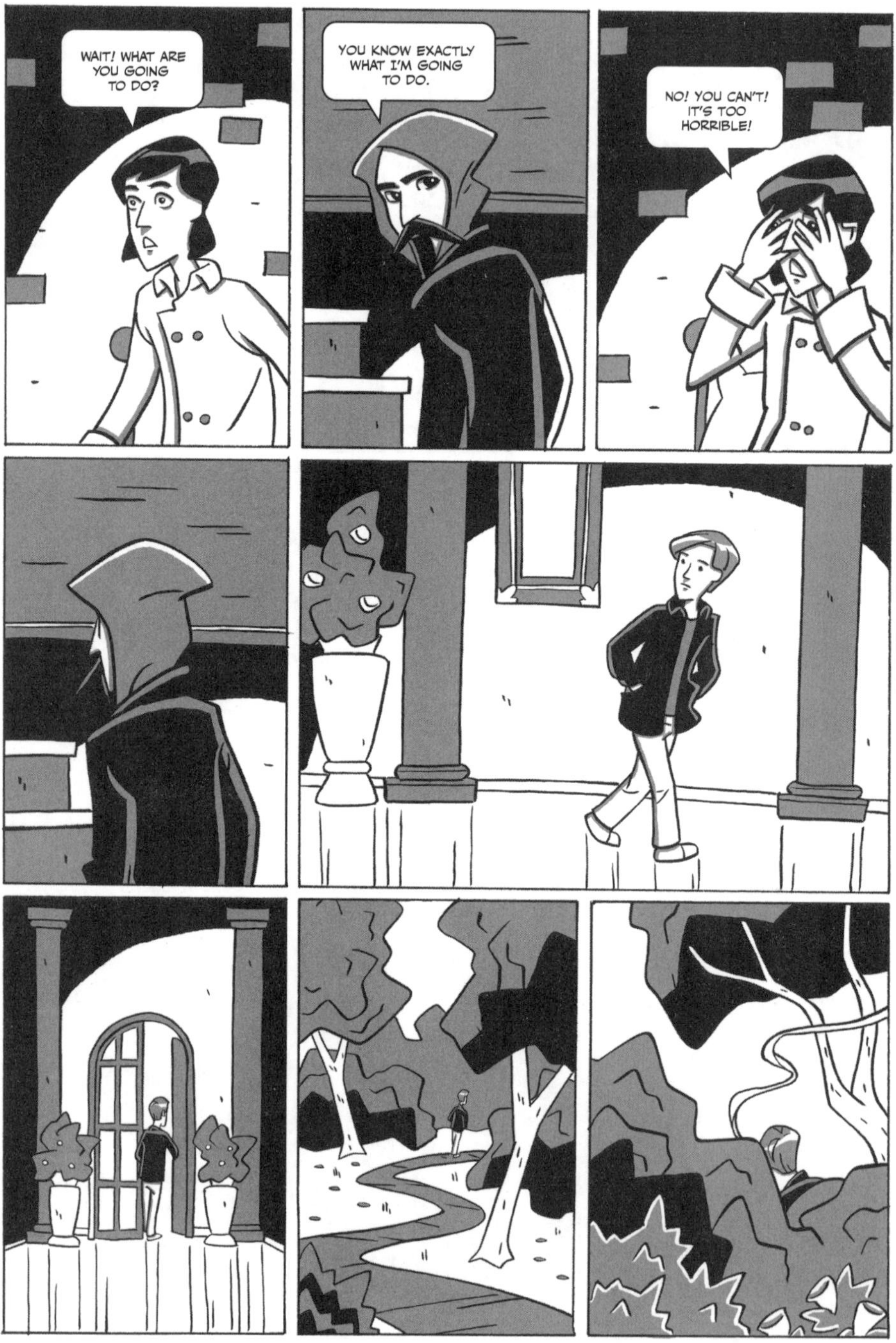
WAIT! WHAT ARE YOU GOING TO DO?
YOU KNOW EXACTLY WHAT I'M GOING TO DO.
NO! YOU CAN'T! IT'S TOO HORRIBLE!

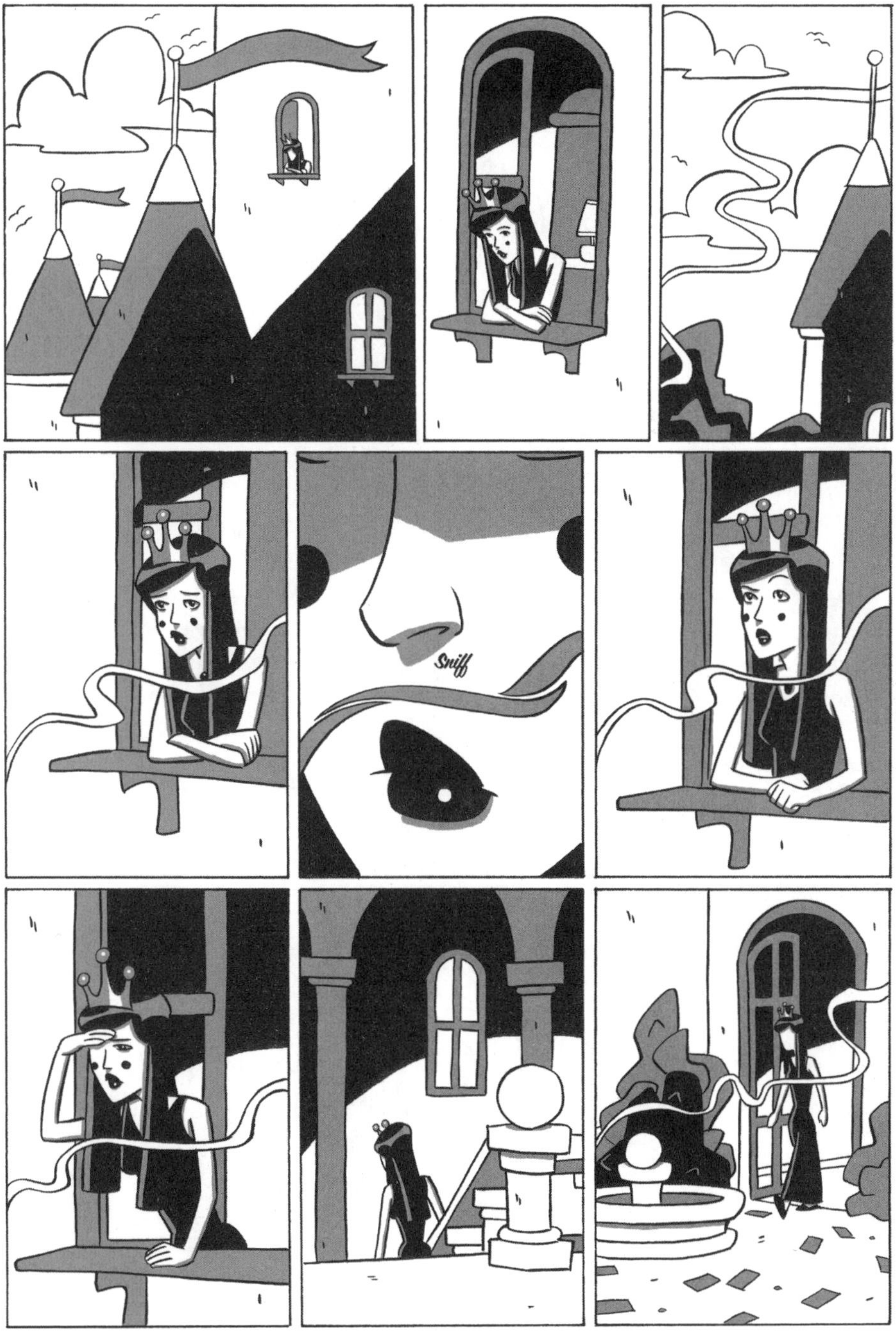
Sniff

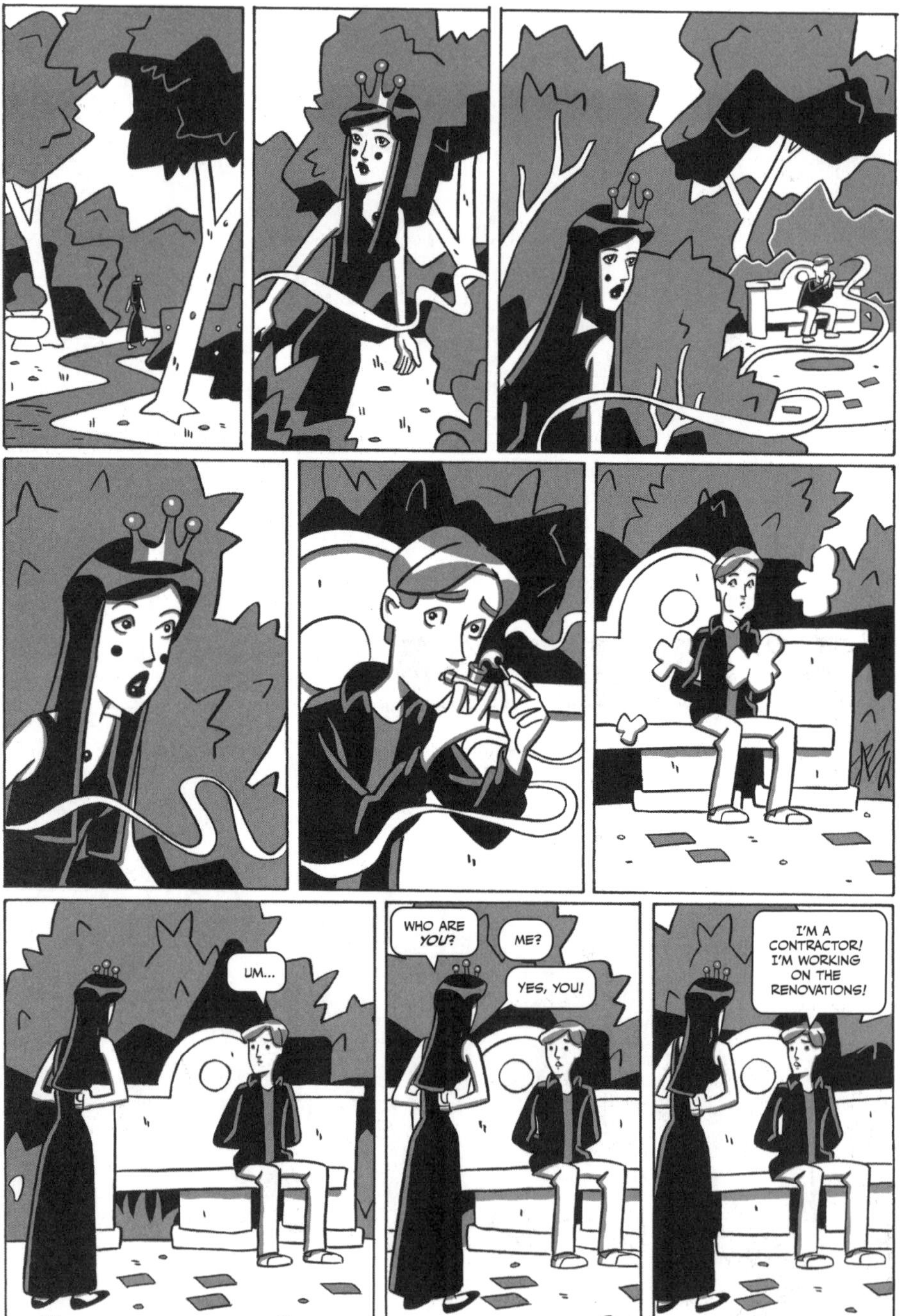
UM...
WHO ARE YOU?
ME?
YES, YOU!
I'M A CONTRACTOR! I'M WORKING ON THE RENOVATIONS!

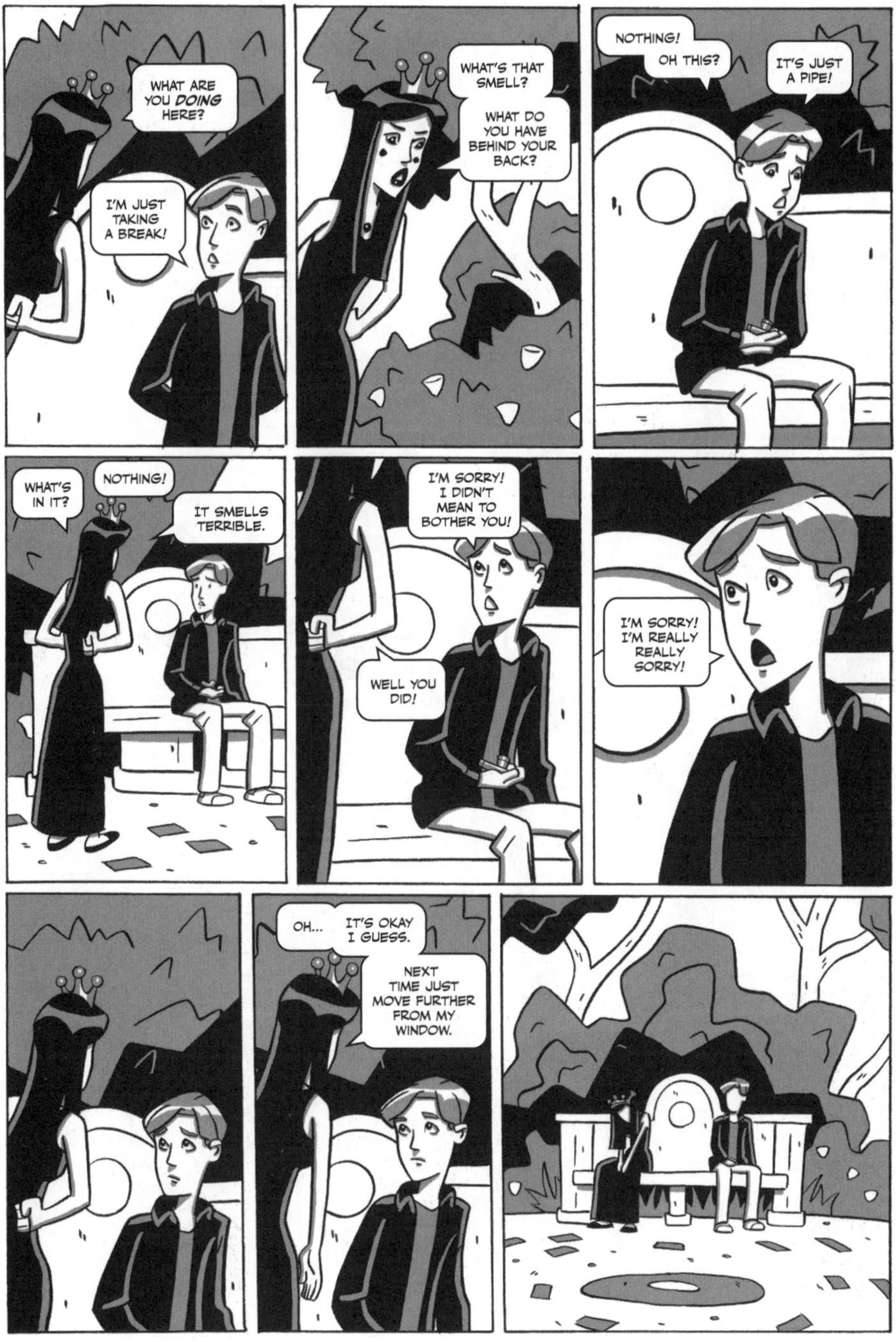
WHAT ARE YOU *DOING* HERE?
I'M JUST TAKING A BREAK!
WHAT'S THAT SMELL?
WHAT DO YOU HAVE BEHIND YOUR BACK?
NOTHING!
OH THIS?
IT'S JUST A PIPE!
WHAT'S IN IT?
NOTHING!
IT SMELLS TERRIBLE.
I'M SORRY! I DIDN'T MEAN TO BOTHER YOU!
WELL YOU DID!
I'M SORRY! I'M REALLY REALLY SORRY!
OH...
IT'S OKAY I GUESS.
NEXT TIME JUST MOVE FURTHER FROM MY WINDOW.

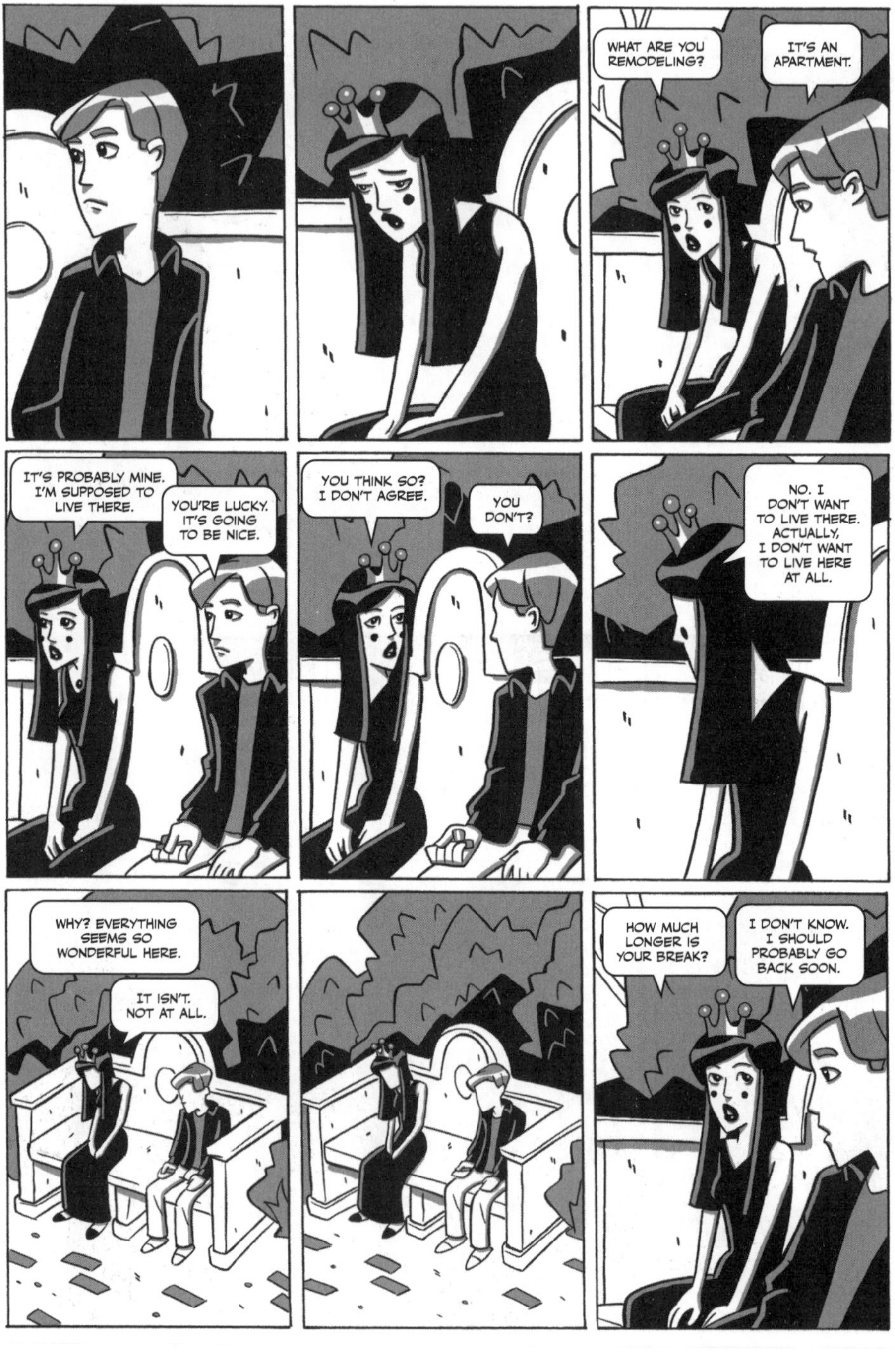
WHAT ARE YOU REMODELING?
IT'S AN APARTMENT.
IT'S PROBABLY MINE. I'M SUPPOSED TO LIVE THERE.
YOU'RE LUCKY. IT'S GOING TO BE NICE.
YOU THINK SO? I DON'T AGREE.
YOU DON'T?
NO. I DON'T WANT TO LIVE THERE. ACTUALLY, I DON'T WANT TO LIVE HERE AT ALL.
WHY? EVERYTHING SEEMS SO WONDERFUL HERE.
IT ISN'T. NOT AT ALL.
HOW MUCH LONGER IS YOUR BREAK?
I DON'T KNOW. I SHOULD PROBABLY GO BACK SOON.

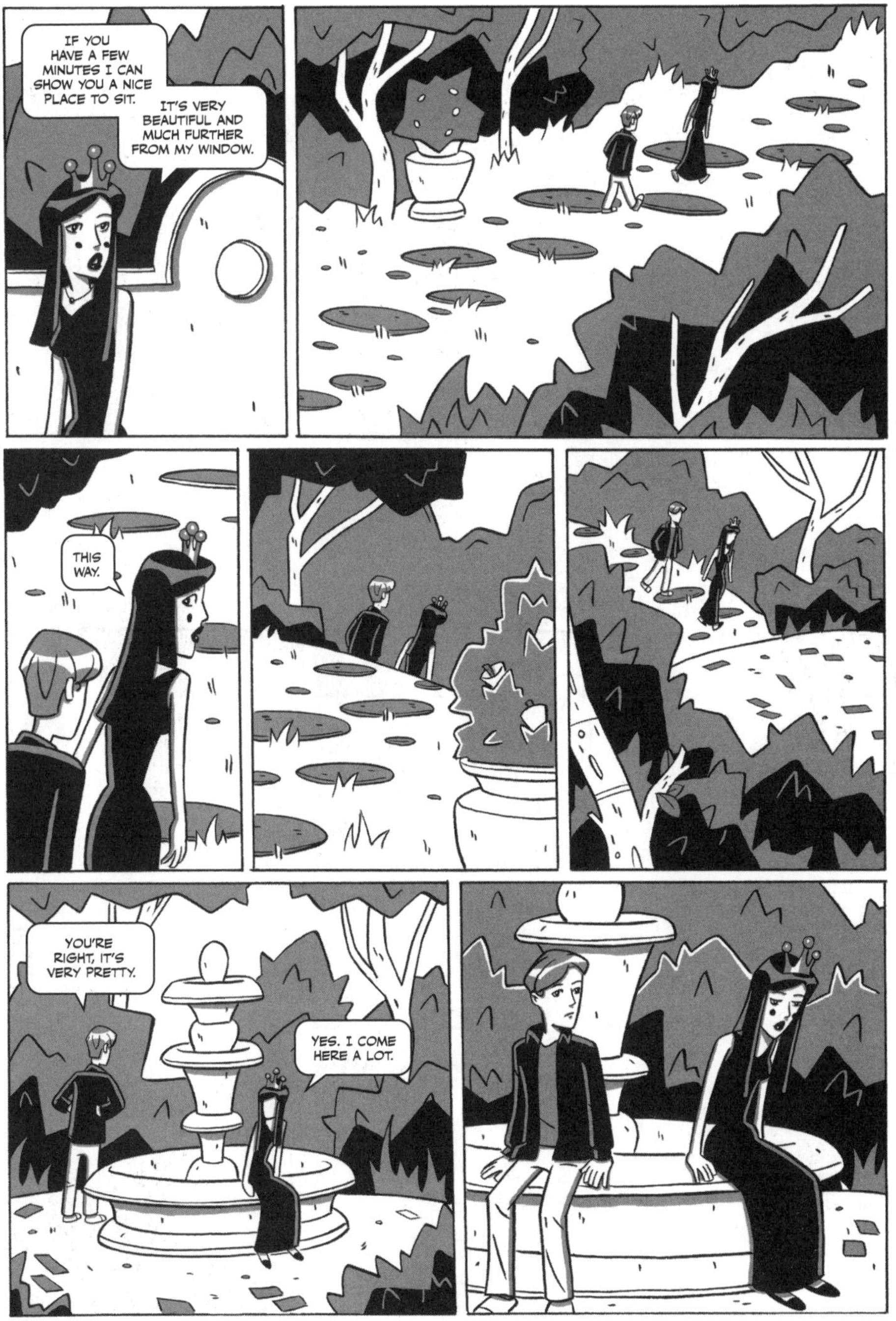
IF YOU HAVE A FEW MINUTES I CAN SHOW YOU A NICE PLACE TO SIT.
IT'S VERY BEAUTIFUL AND MUCH FURTHER FROM MY WINDOW.
THIS WAY.
YOU'RE RIGHT, IT'S VERY PRETTY.
YES. I COME HERE A LOT.

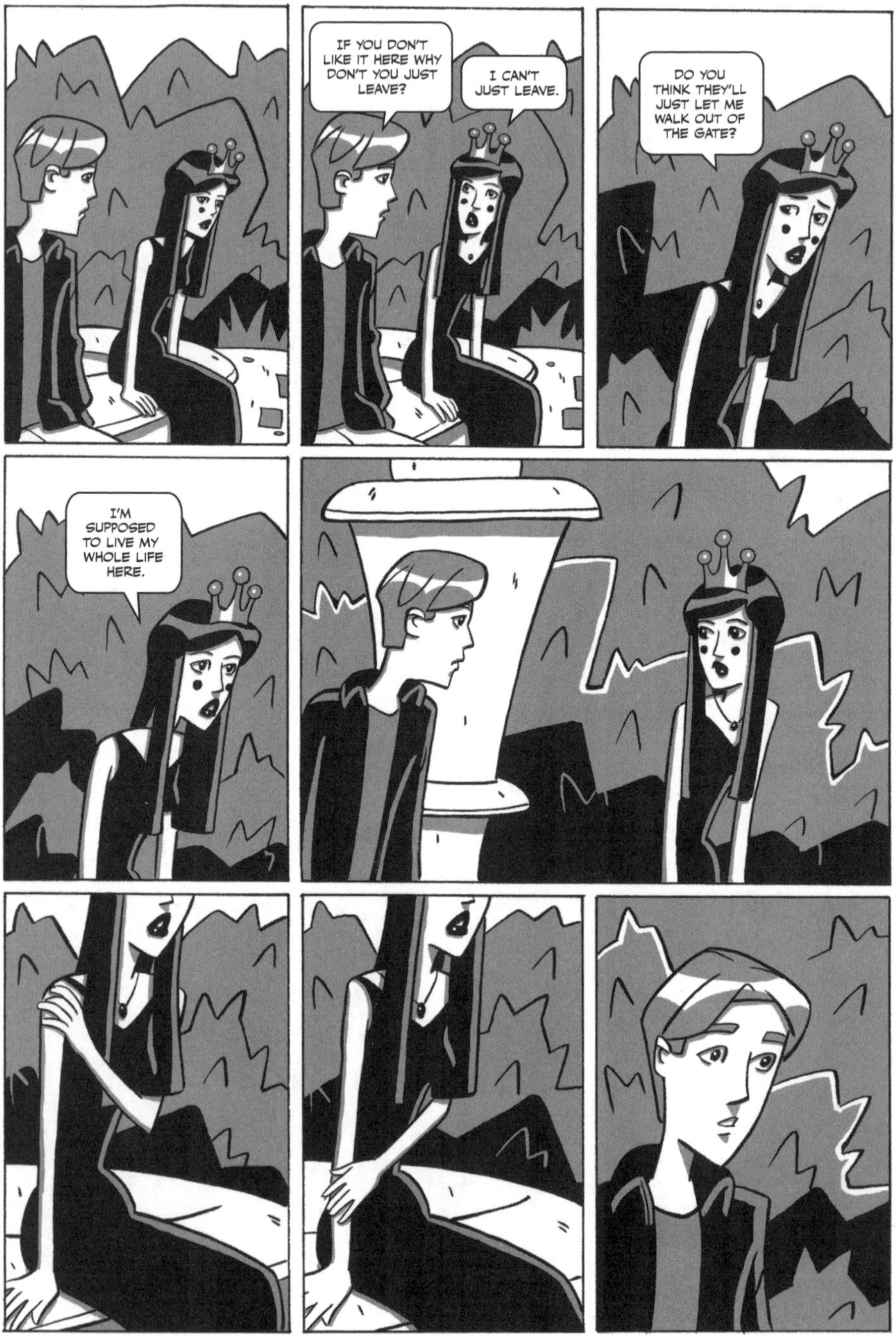
IF YOU DON'T LIKE IT HERE WHY DON'T YOU JUST LEAVE?
I CAN'T JUST LEAVE.
DO YOU THINK THEY'LL JUST LET ME WALK OUT OF THE GATE?
I'M SUPPOSED TO LIVE MY WHOLE LIFE HERE.

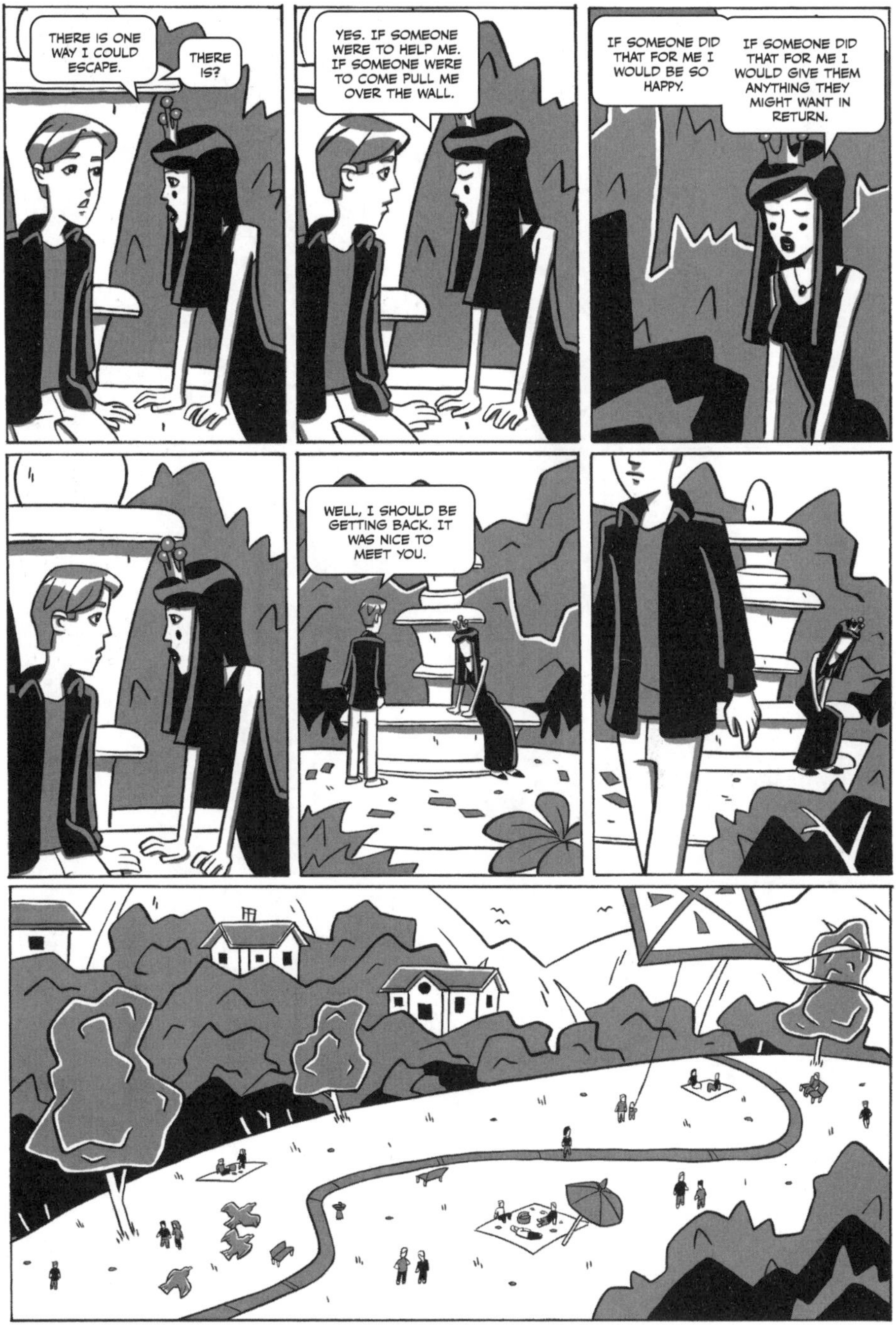
THERE IS ONE WAY I COULD ESCAPE.
THERE IS?
YES. IF SOMEONE WERE TO HELP ME. IF SOMEONE WERE TO COME PULL ME OVER THE WALL.
IF SOMEONE DID THAT FOR ME I WOULD BE SO HAPPY.
IF SOMEONE DID THAT FOR ME I WOULD GIVE THEM ANYTHING THEY MIGHT WANT IN RETURN.
WELL, I SHOULD BE GETTING BACK. IT WAS NICE TO MEET YOU.

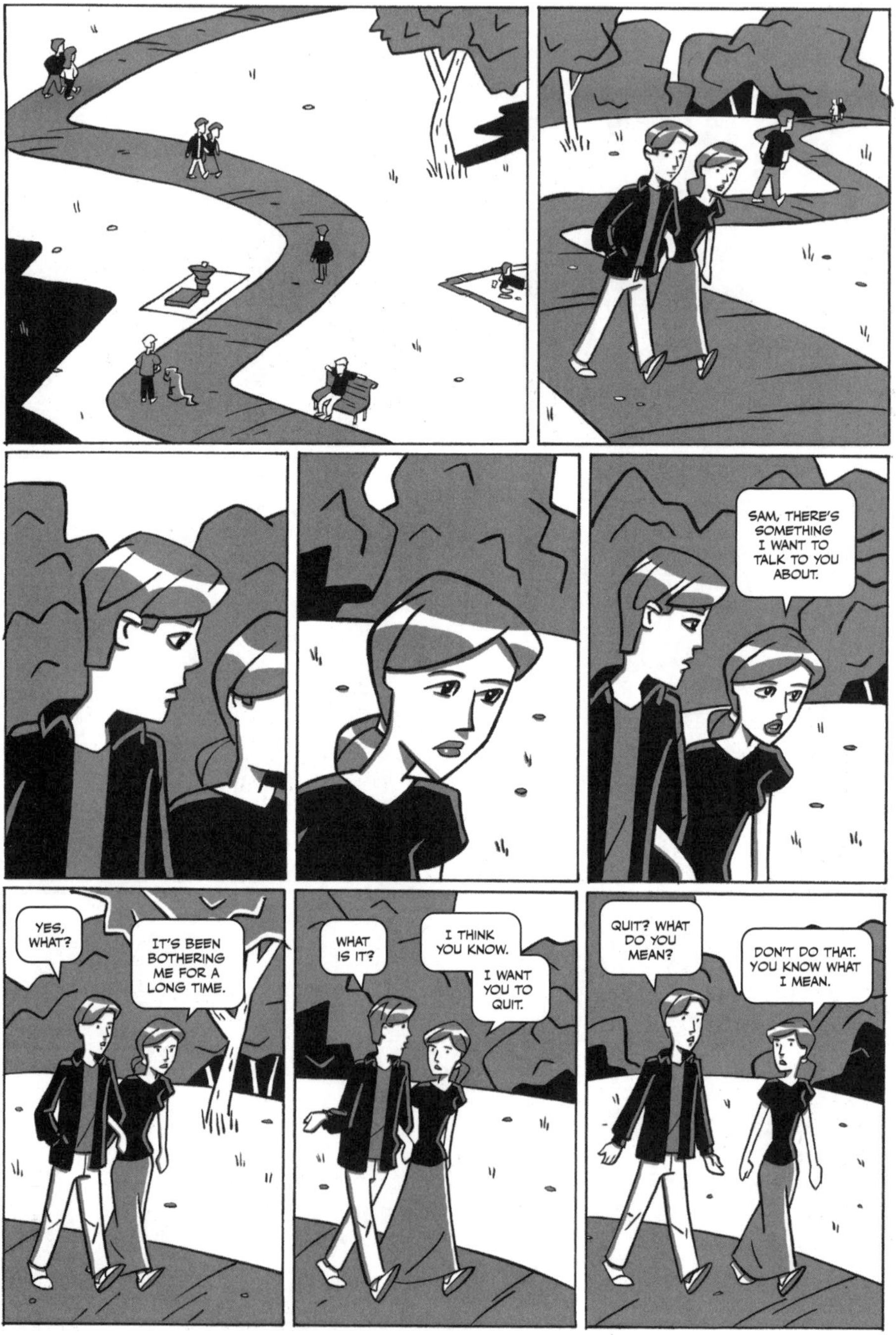
SAM, THERE'S SOMETHING I WANT TO TALK TO YOU ABOUT.
YES, WHAT?
IT'S BEEN BOTHERING ME FOR A LONG TIME.
WHAT IS IT?
I THINK YOU KNOW.
I WANT YOU TO QUIT.
QUIT? WHAT DO YOU MEAN?
DON'T DO THAT. YOU KNOW WHAT I MEAN.

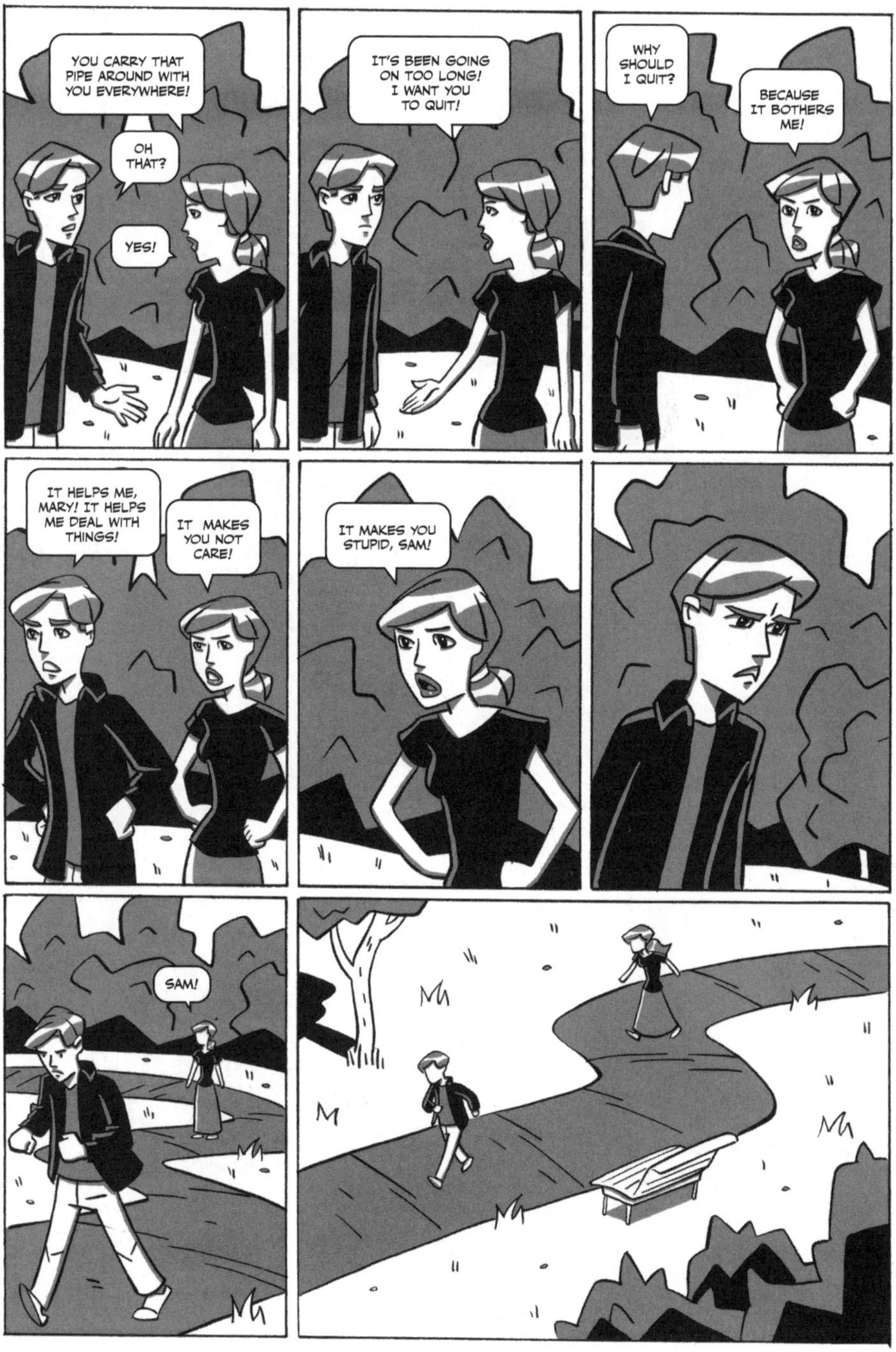
YOU CARRY THAT PIPE AROUND WITH YOU EVERYWHERE!
OH THAT?
YES!
IT'S BEEN GOING ON TOO LONG! I WANT YOU TO QUIT!
WHY SHOULD I QUIT?
BECAUSE IT BOTHERS ME!
IT HELPS ME, MARY! IT HELPS ME DEAL WITH THINGS!
IT MAKES YOU NOT CARE!
IT MAKES YOU STUPID, SAM!
SAM!

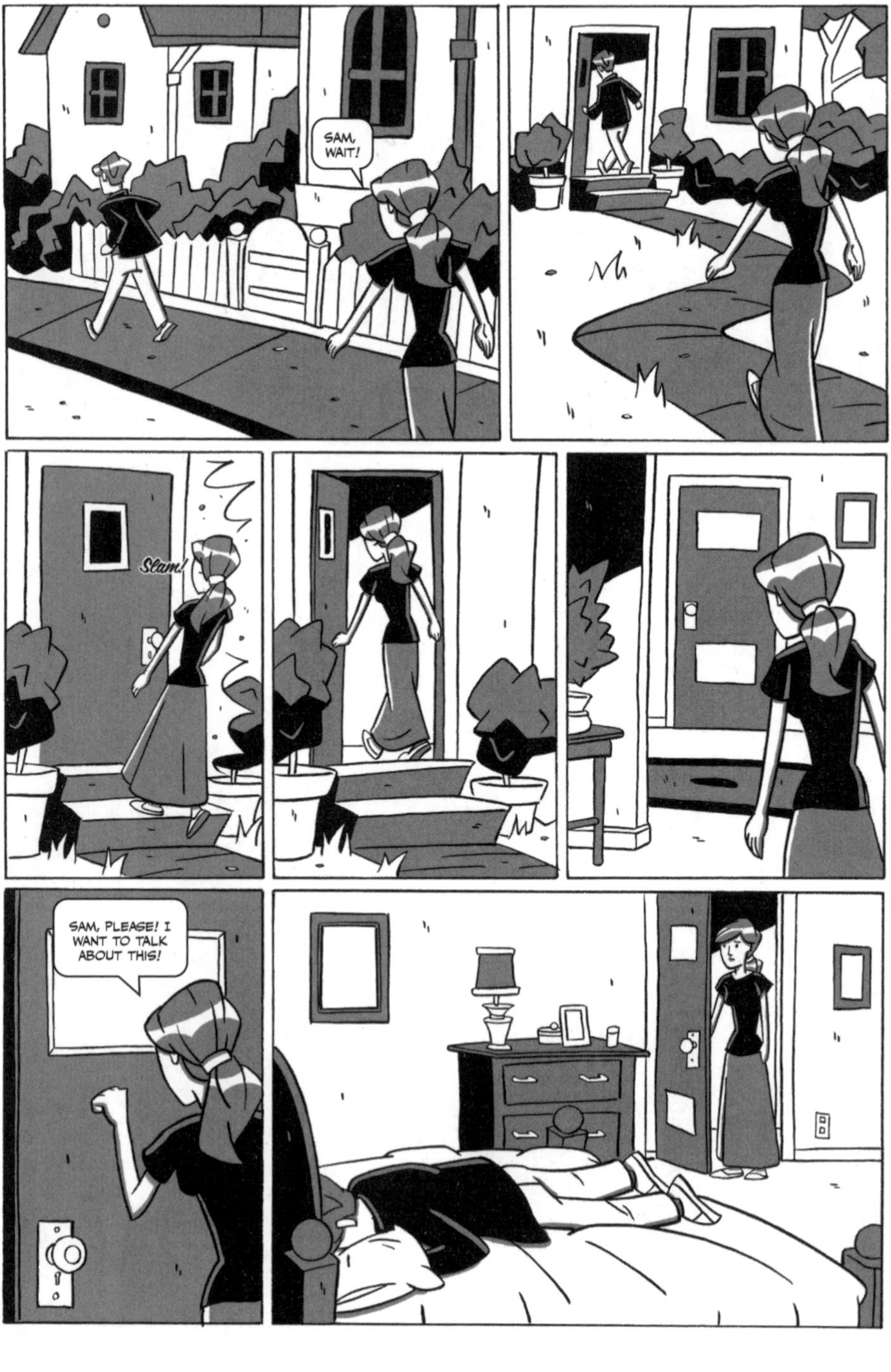
SAM, WAIT!
Slam!
SAM, PLEASE! I WANT TO TALK ABOUT THIS!

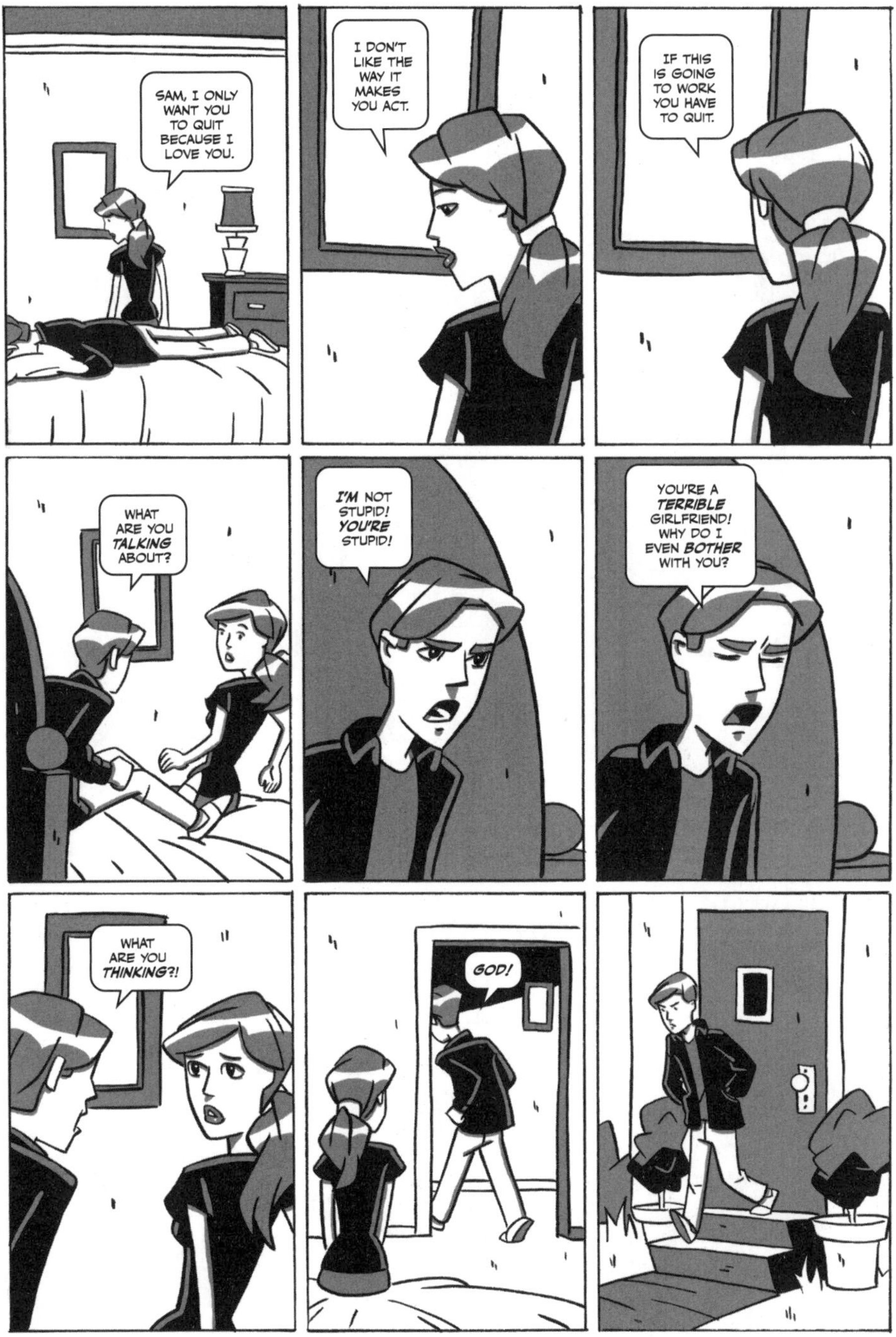
SAM, I ONLY WANT YOU TO QUIT BECAUSE I LOVE YOU.
I DON'T LIKE THE WAY IT MAKES YOU ACT.
IF THIS IS GOING TO WORK YOU HAVE TO QUIT.
WHAT ARE YOU *TALKING* ABOUT?
*I'M* NOT STUPID! *YOU'RE* STUPID!
YOU'RE A *TERRIBLE* GIRLFRIEND! WHY DO I EVEN *BOTHER* WITH YOU?
WHAT ARE YOU *THINKING*?!
*GOD!*

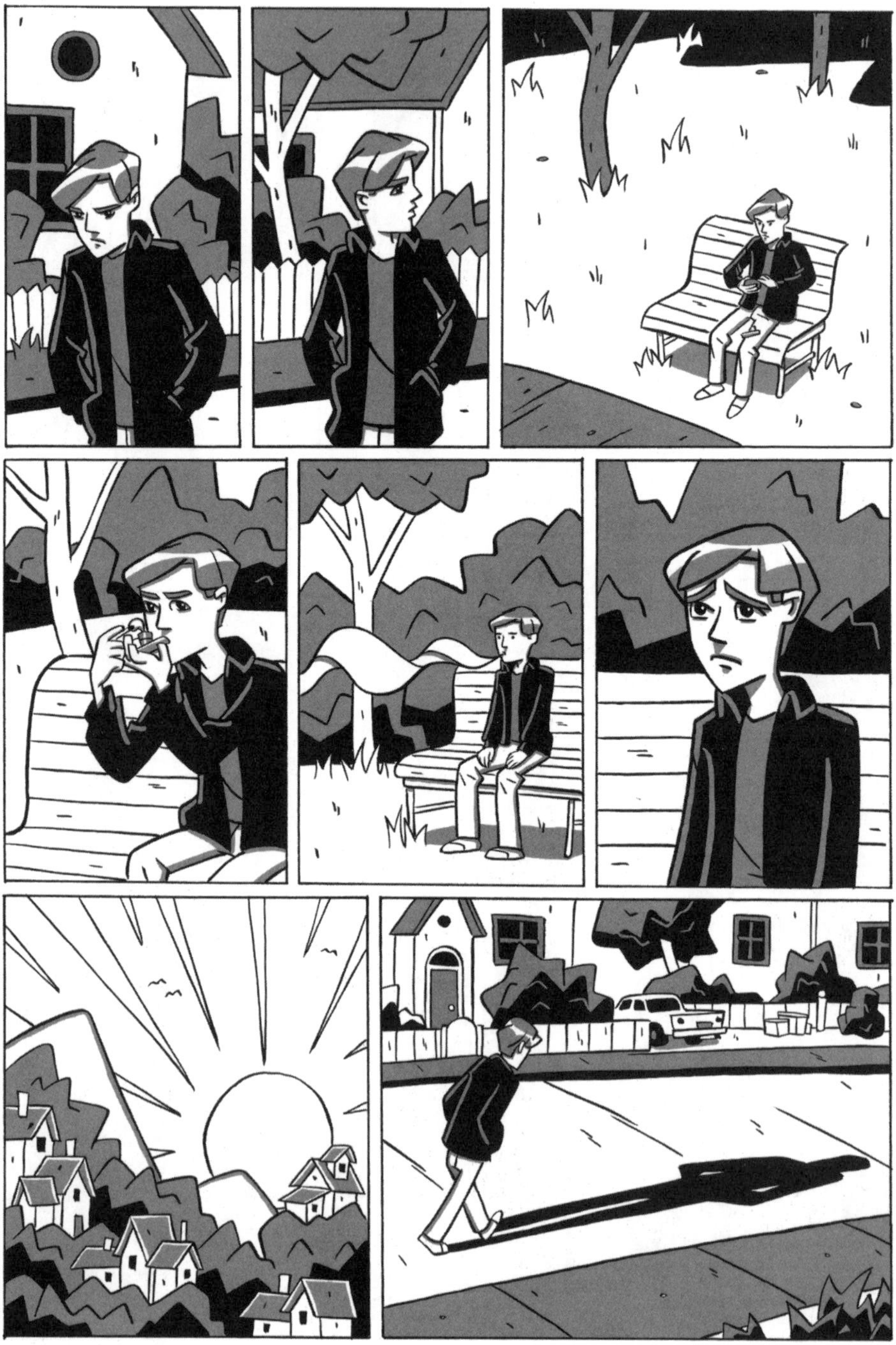

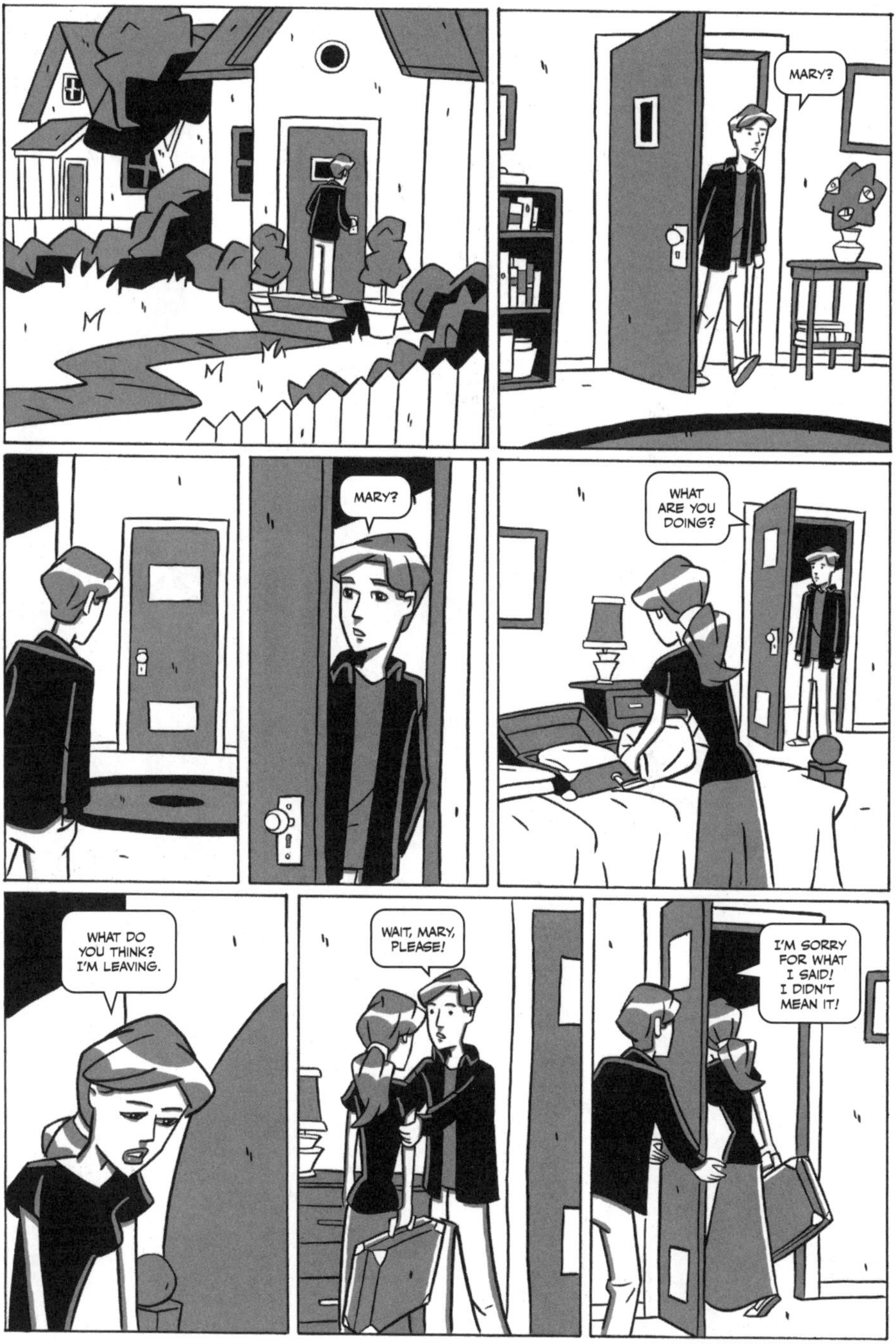
MARY?
MARY?
WHAT ARE YOU DOING?
WHAT DO YOU THINK? I'M LEAVING.
WAIT, MARY, PLEASE!
I'M SORRY FOR WHAT I SAID! I DIDN'T MEAN IT!

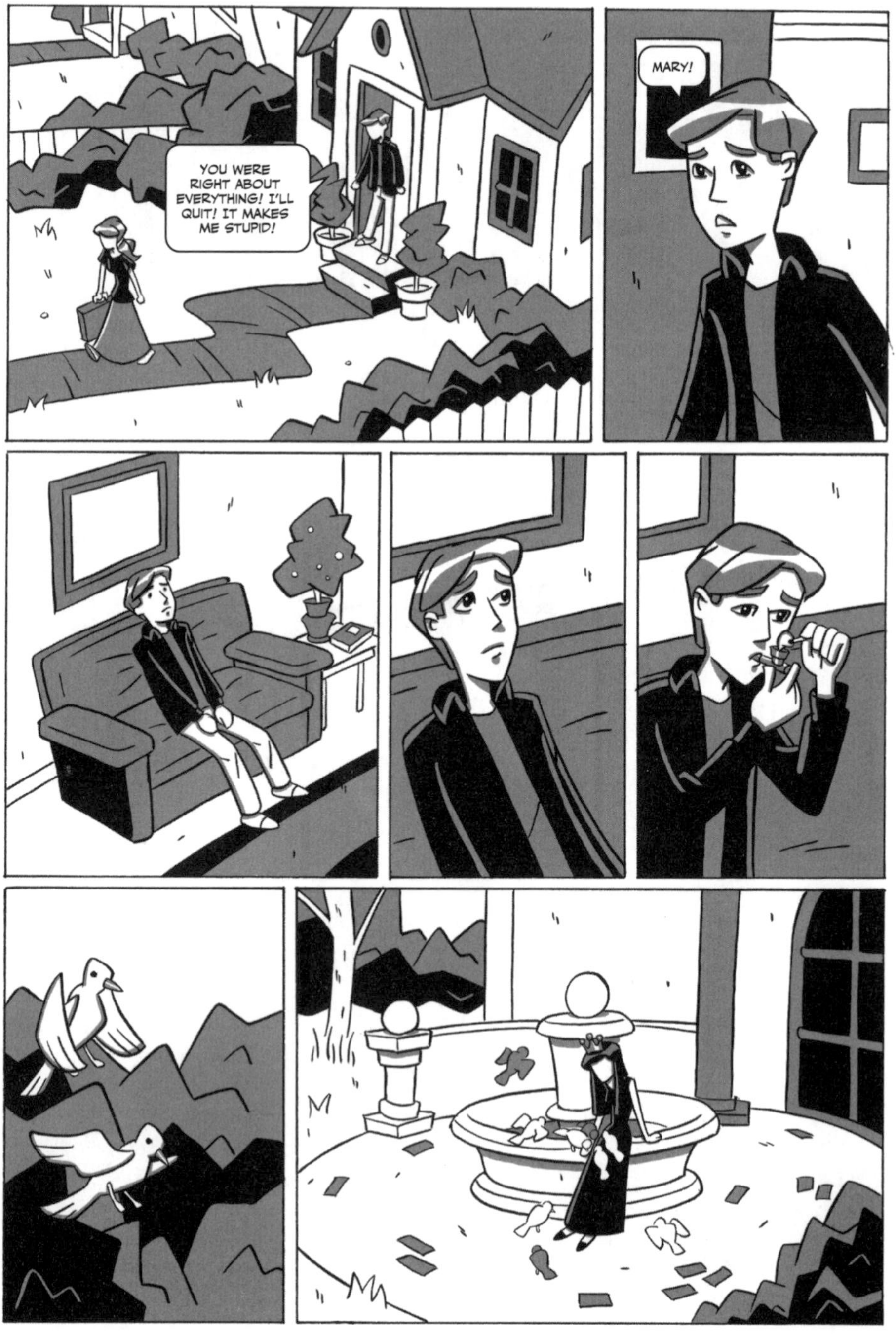
YOU WERE RIGHT ABOUT EVERYTHING! I'LL QUIT! IT MAKES ME STUPID!
MARY!

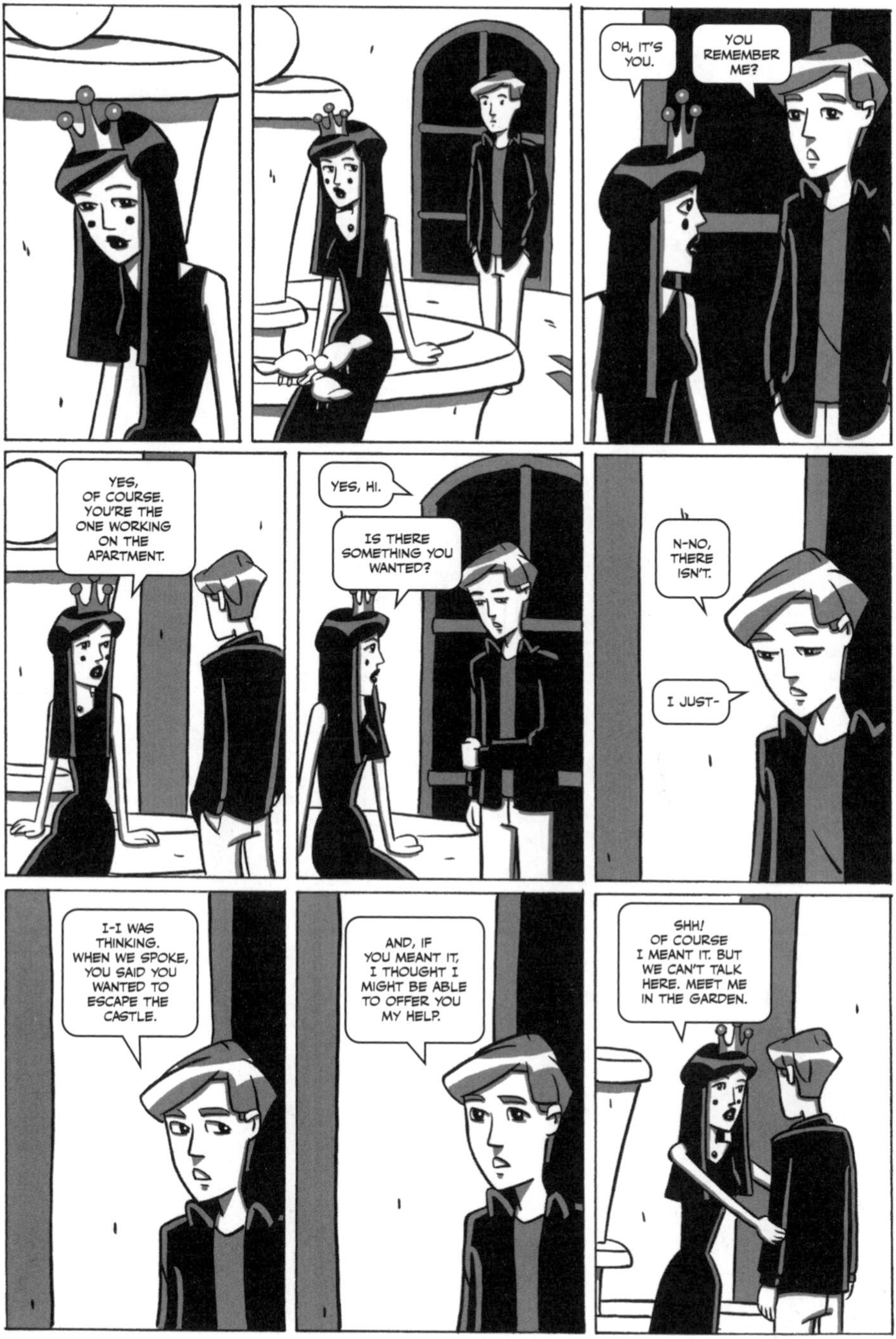
OH, IT'S YOU.
YOU REMEMBER ME?
YES, OF COURSE. YOU'RE THE ONE WORKING ON THE APARTMENT.
YES, HI.
IS THERE SOMETHING YOU WANTED?
N-NO, THERE ISN'T.
I JUST-
I-I WAS THINKING. WHEN WE SPOKE, YOU SAID YOU WANTED TO ESCAPE THE CASTLE.
AND, IF YOU MEANT IT, I THOUGHT I MIGHT BE ABLE TO OFFER YOU MY HELP.
SHH! OF COURSE I MEANT IT. BUT WE CAN'T TALK HERE. MEET ME IN THE GARDEN.

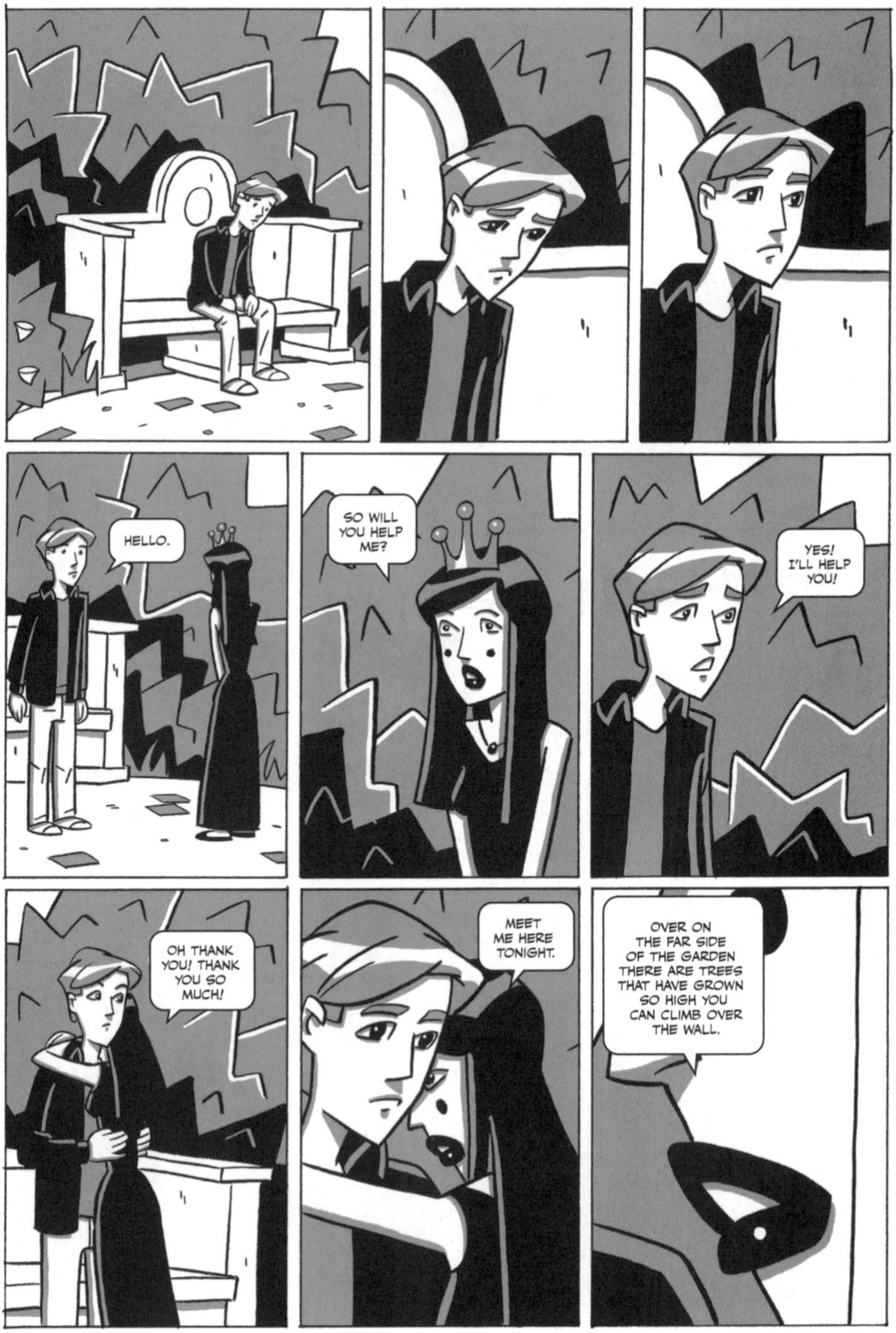
HELLO.
SO WILL YOU HELP ME?
YES! I'LL HELP YOU!
OH THANK YOU! THANK YOU SO MUCH!
MEET ME HERE TONIGHT.
OVER ON THE FAR SIDE OF THE GARDEN THERE ARE TREES THAT HAVE GROWN SO HIGH YOU CAN CLIMB OVER THE WALL.

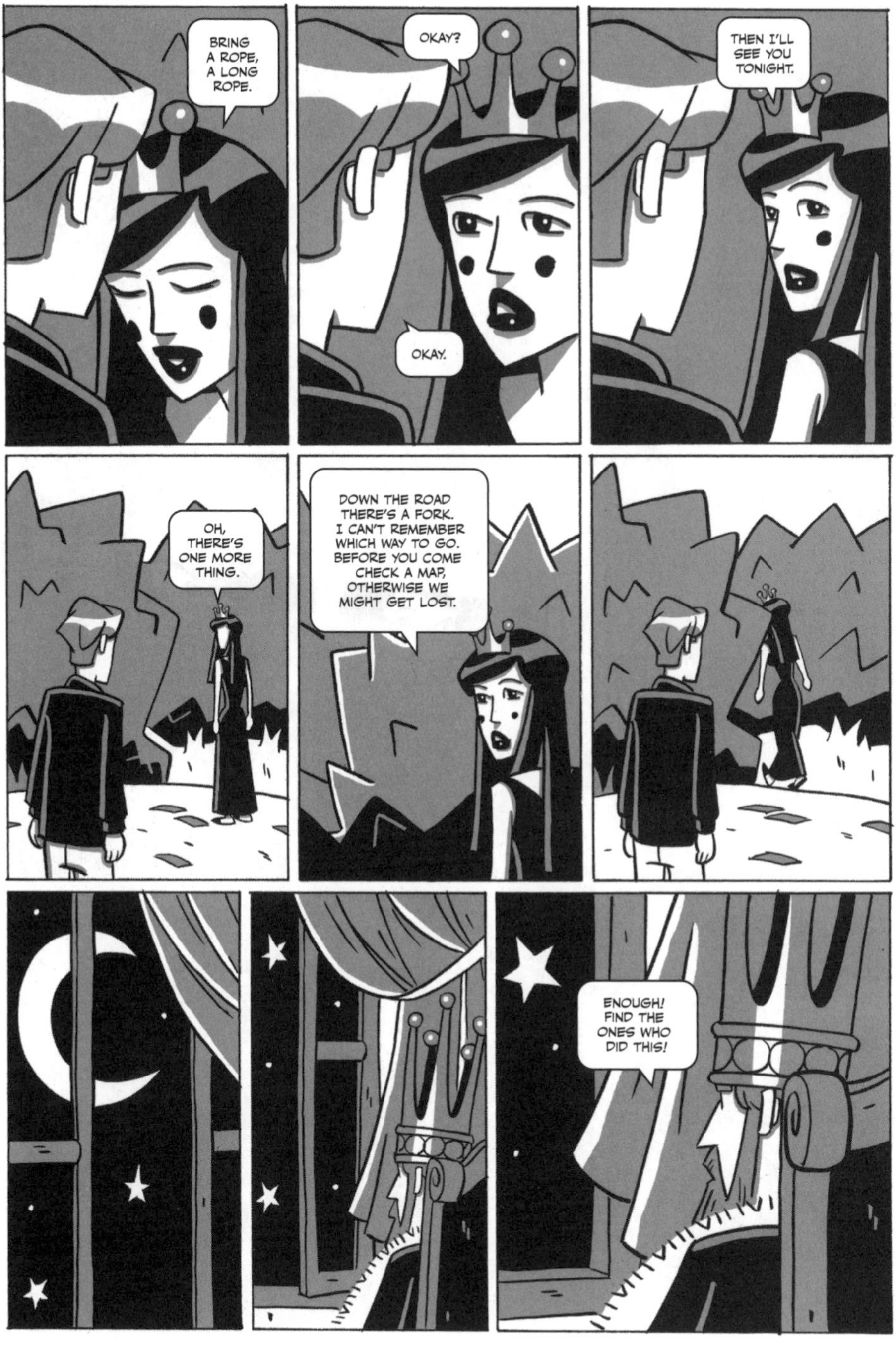
BRING A ROPE, A LONG ROPE.
OKAY?
OKAY.
THEN I'LL SEE YOU TONIGHT.
OH, THERE'S ONE MORE THING.
DOWN THE ROAD THERE'S A FORK. I CAN'T REMEMBER WHICH WAY TO GO. BEFORE YOU COME CHECK A MAP, OTHERWISE WE MIGHT GET LOST.
ENOUGH! FIND THE ONES WHO DID THIS!

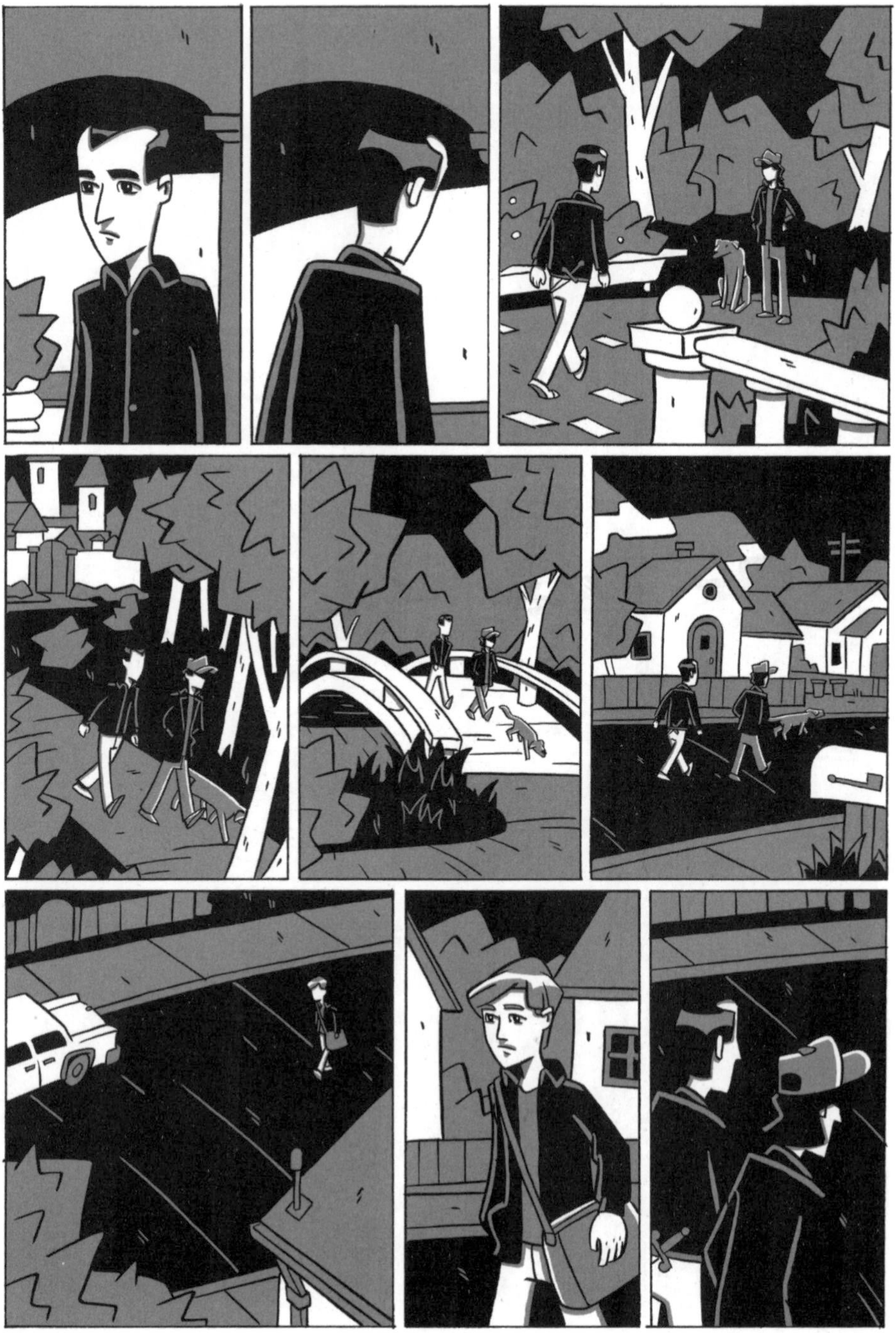

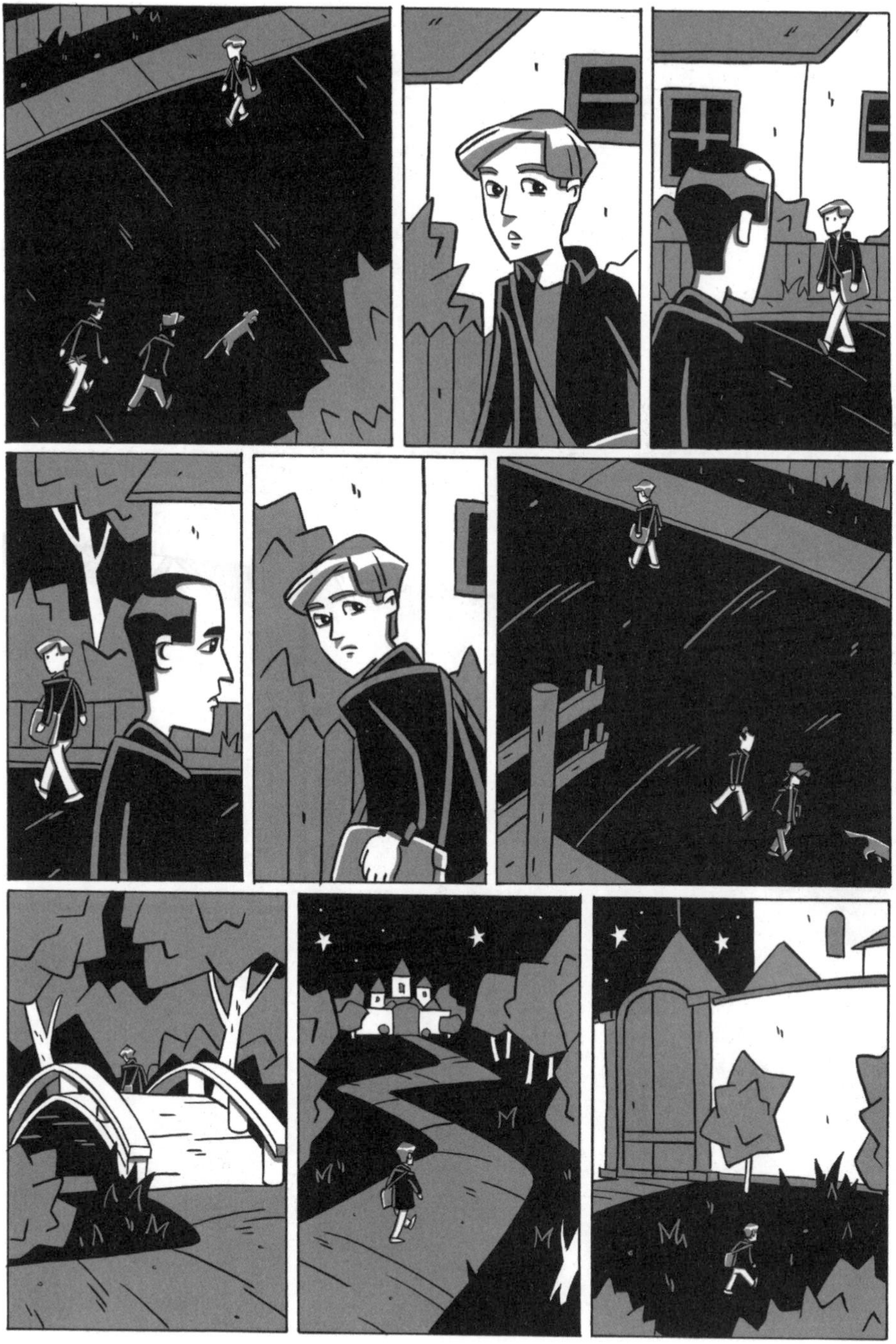

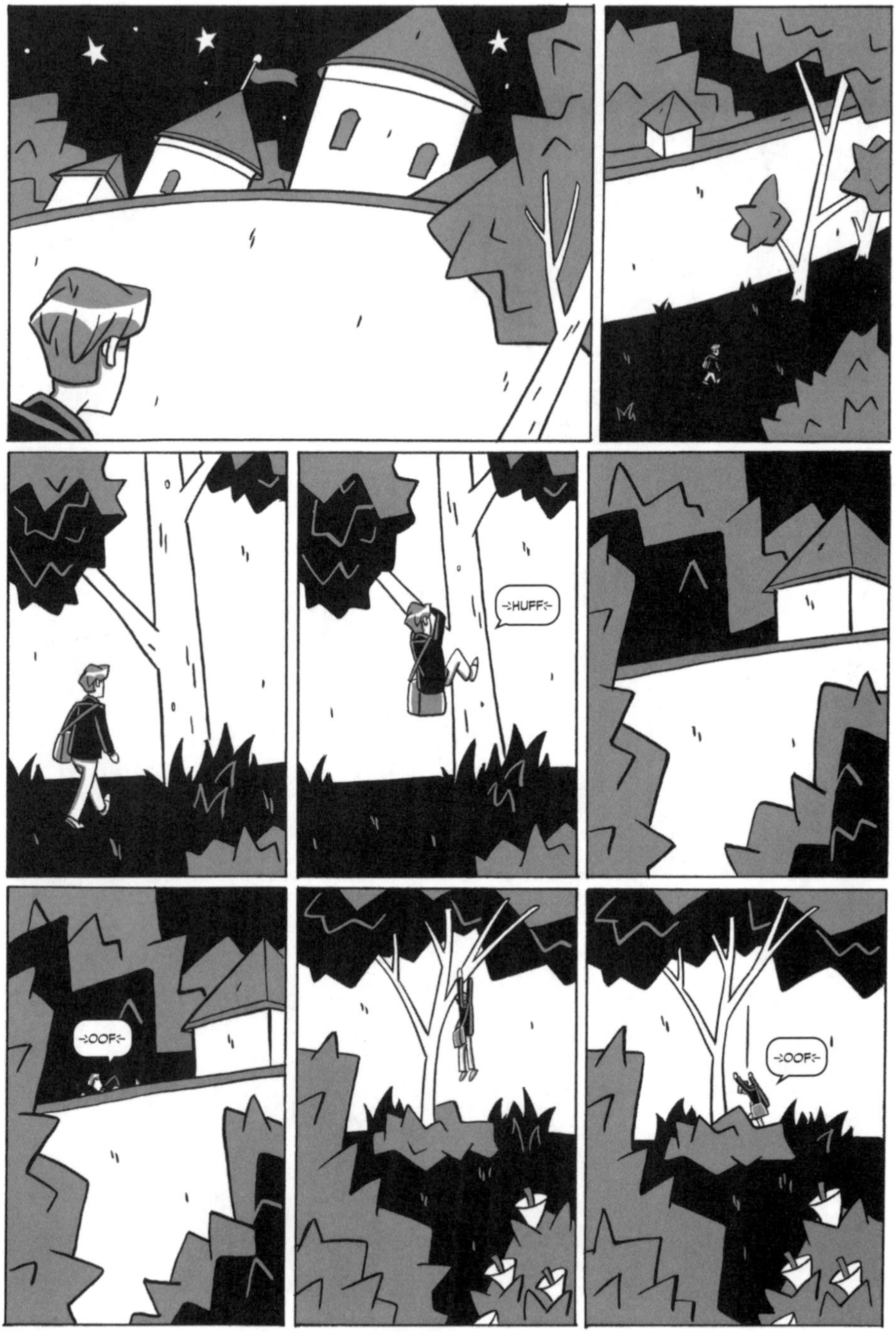
HUFF
OOF
OOF

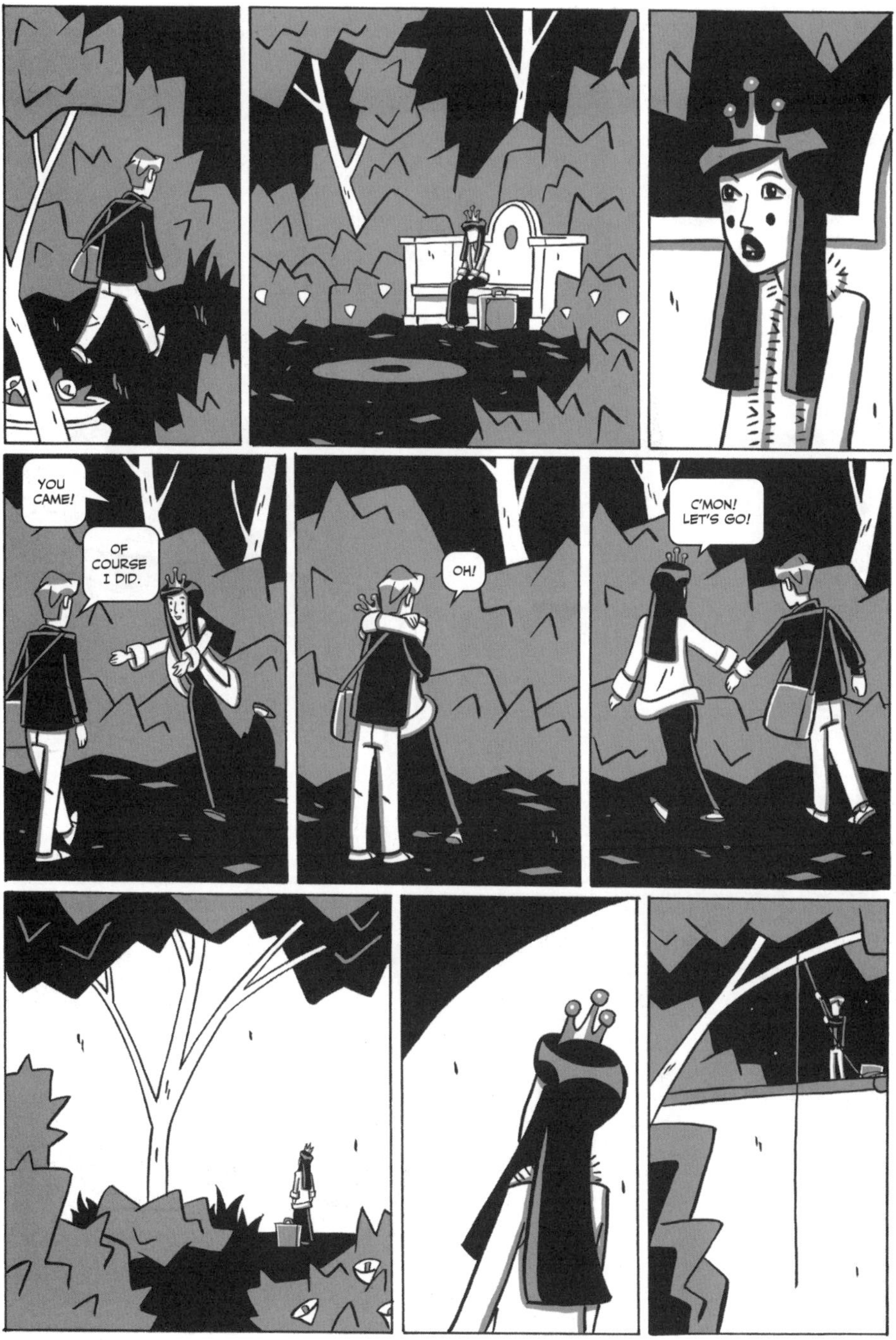
YOU CAME!
OF COURSE I DID.
OH!
C'MON! LET'S GO!

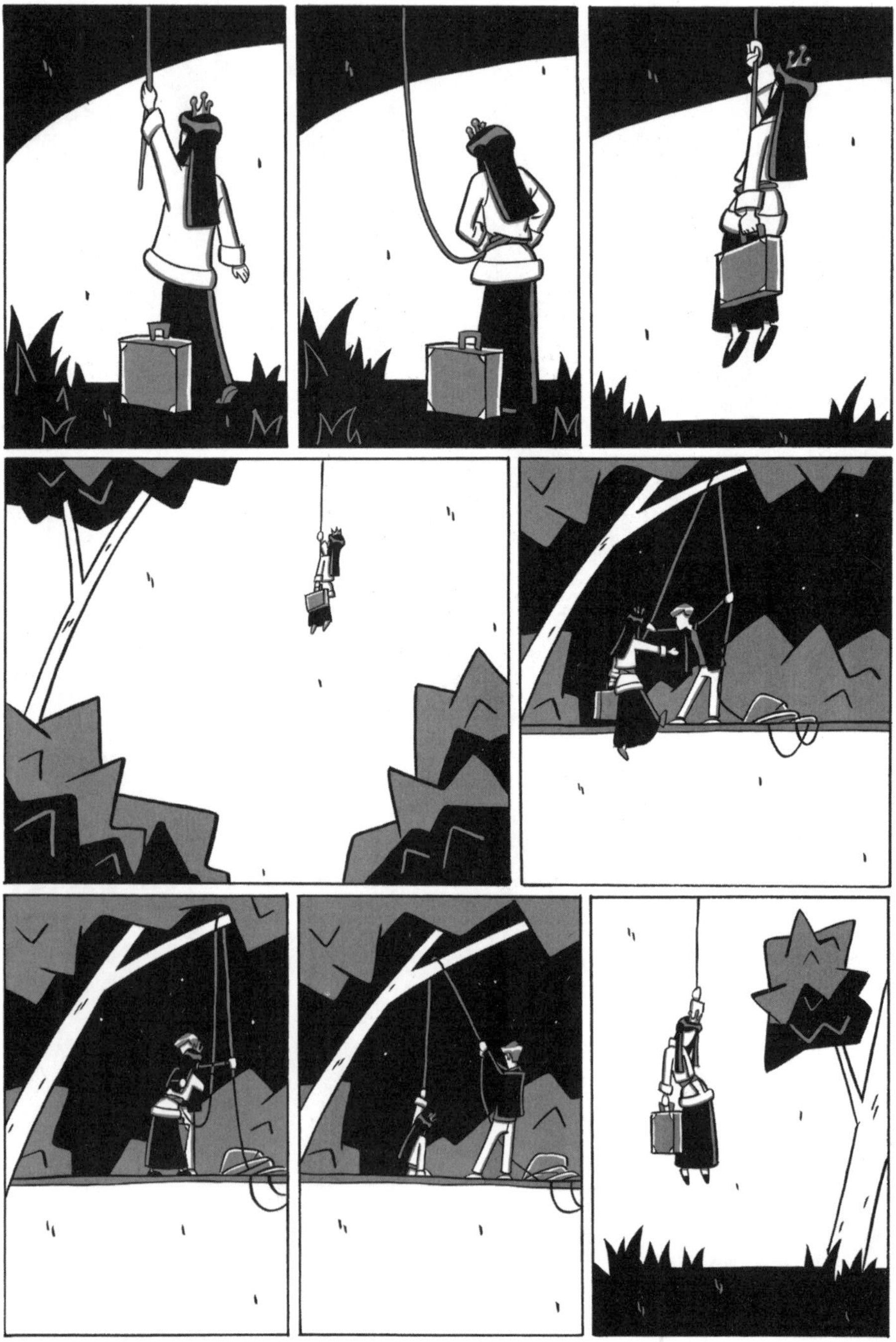

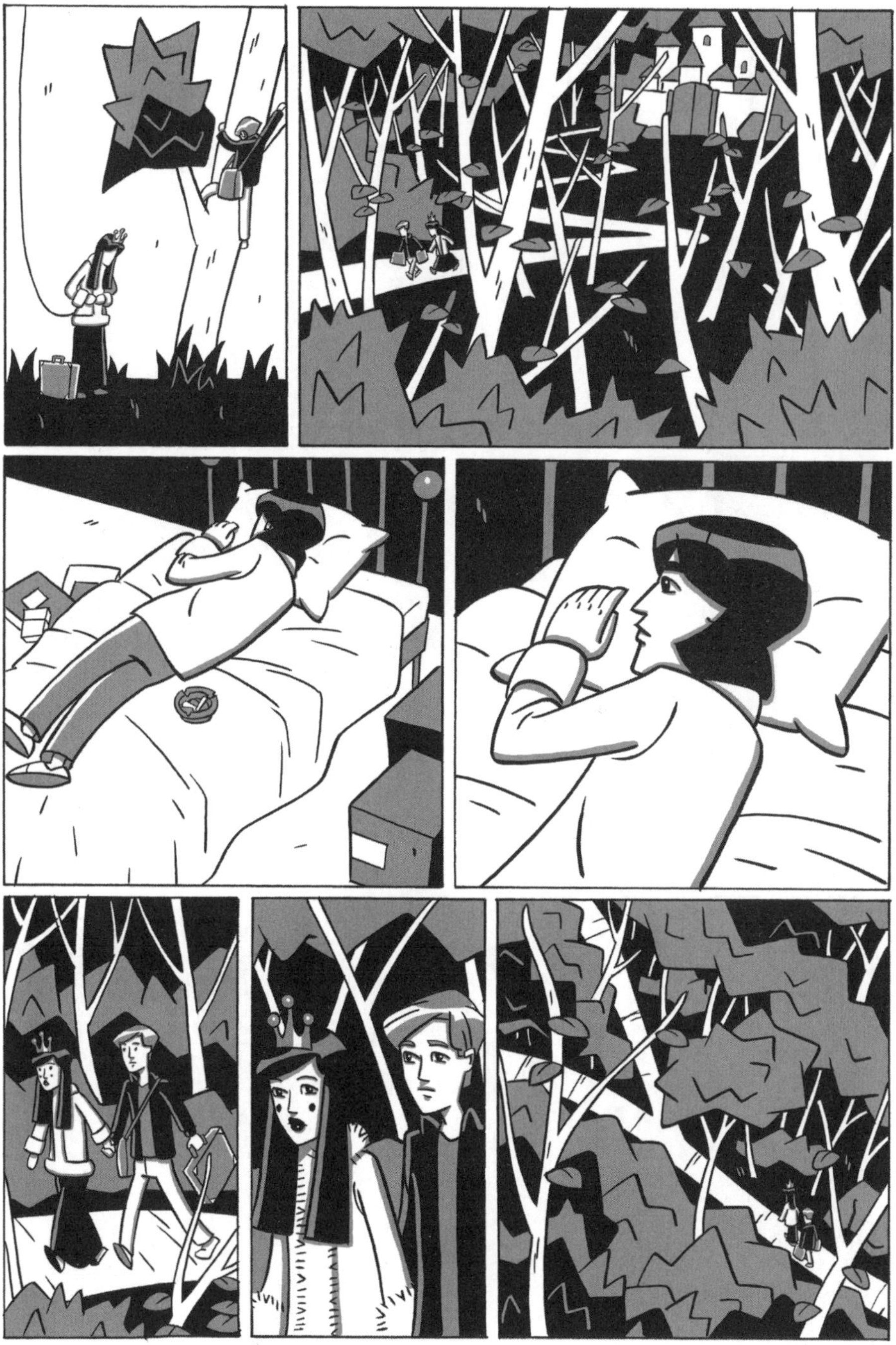

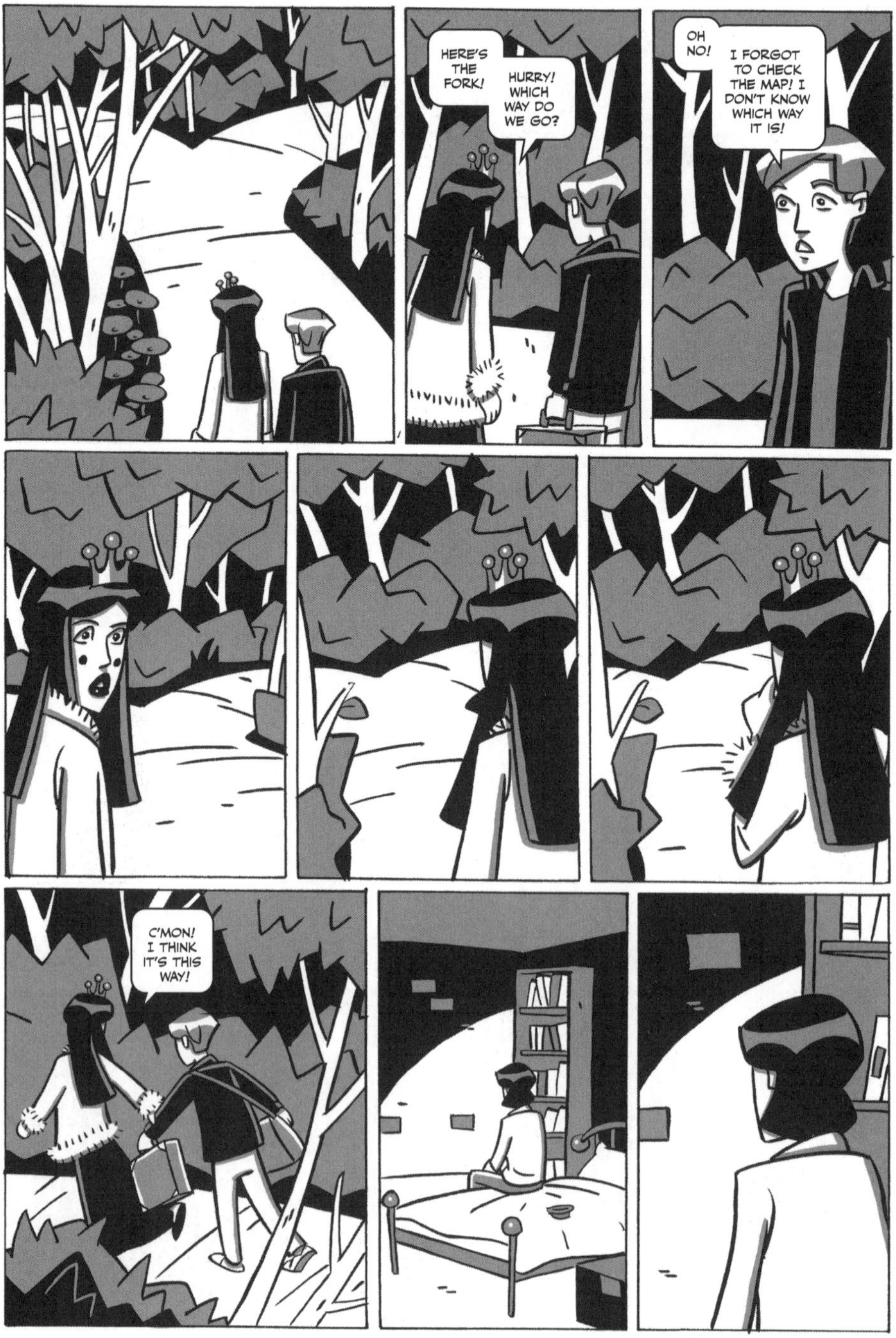
HERE'S THE FORK!
HURRY! WHICH WAY DO WE GO?
OH NO!
I FORGOT TO CHECK THE MAP! I DON'T KNOW WHICH WAY IT IS!
C'MON! I THINK IT'S THIS WAY!

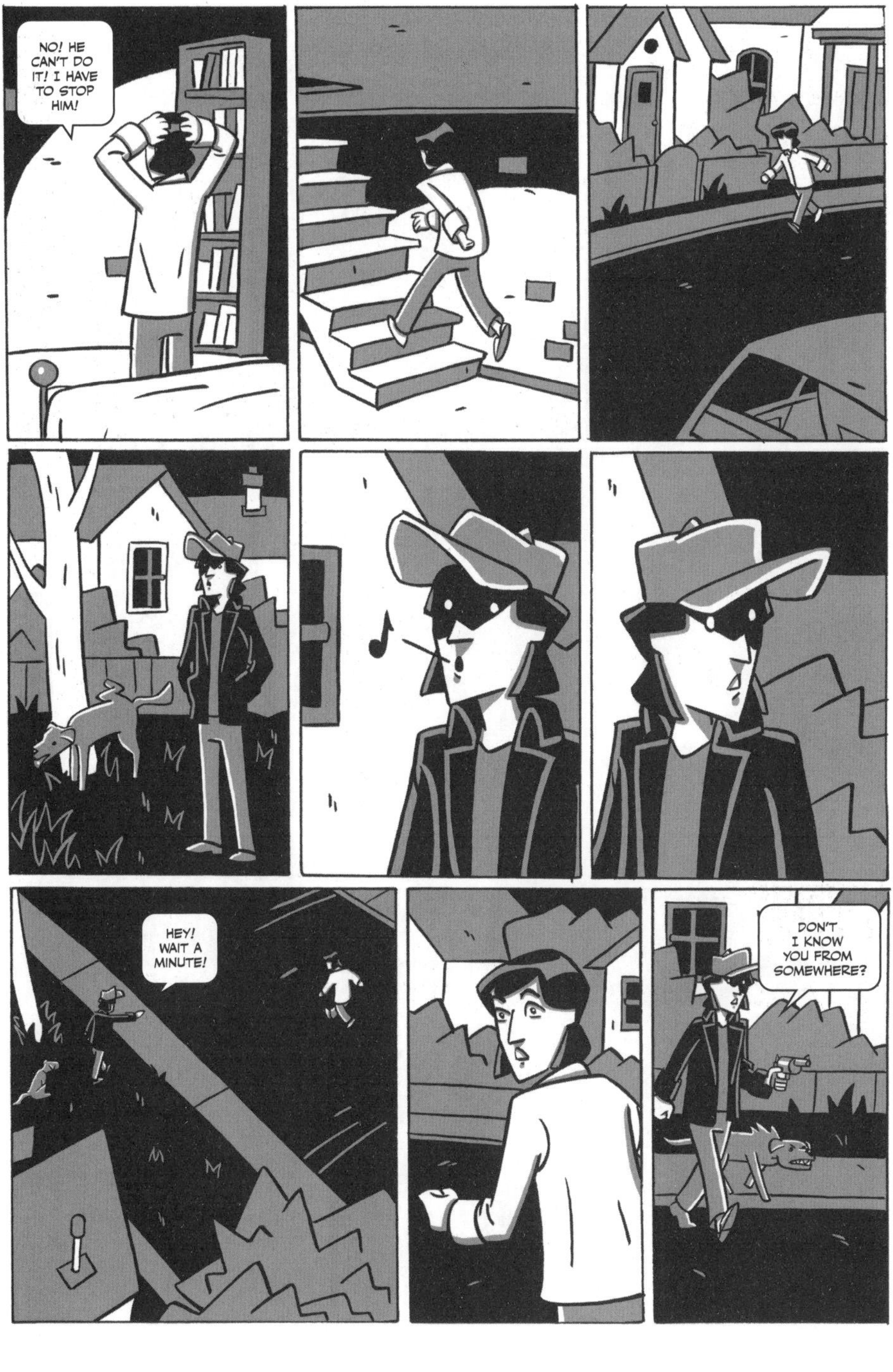
NO! HE CAN'T DO IT! I HAVE TO STOP HIM!
HEY! WAIT A MINUTE!
DON'T I KNOW YOU FROM SOMEWHERE?

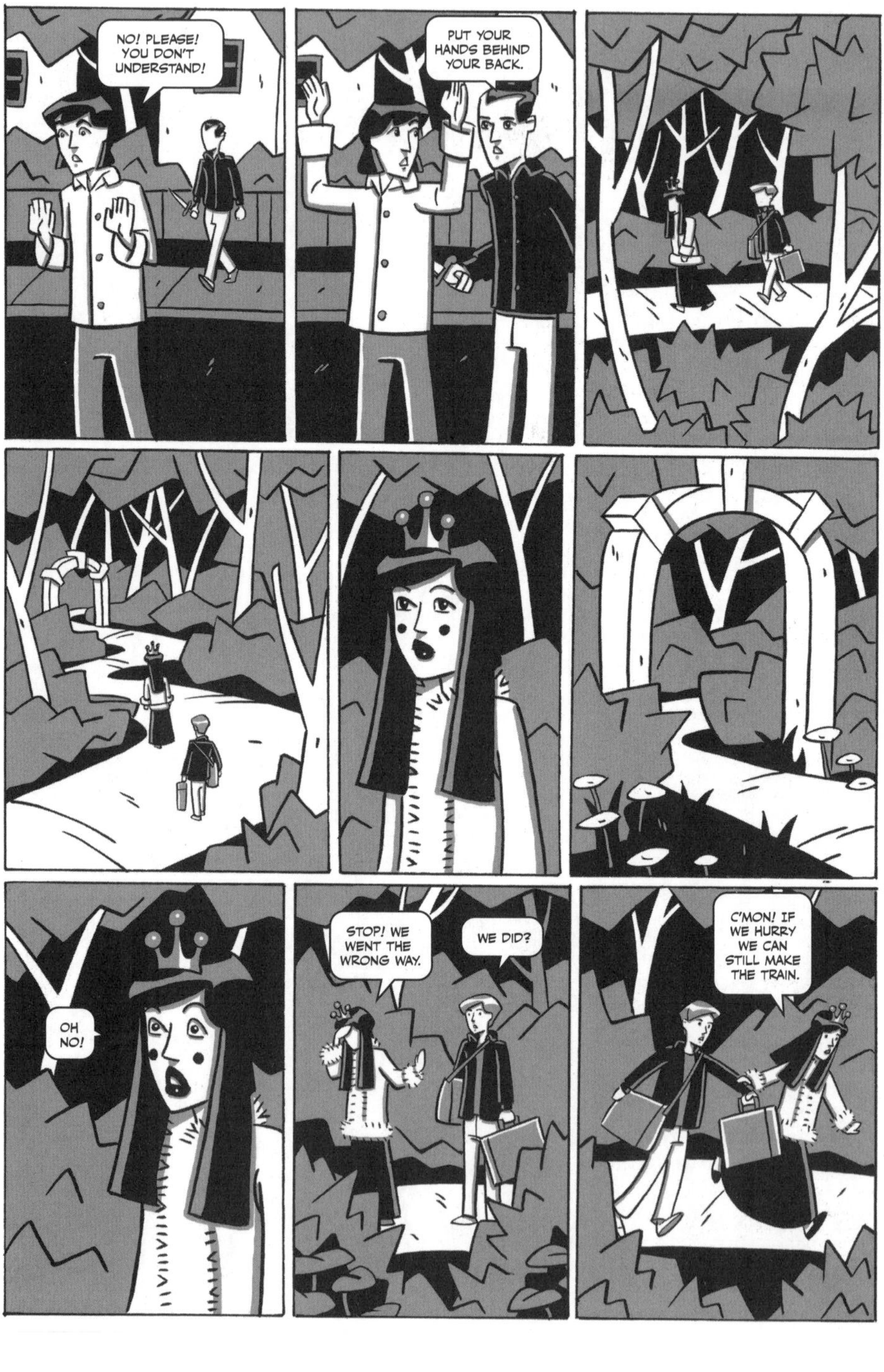
NO! PLEASE! YOU DON'T UNDERSTAND!
PUT YOUR HANDS BEHIND YOUR BACK.
OH NO!
STOP! WE WENT THE WRONG WAY.
WE DID?
C'MON! IF WE HURRY WE CAN STILL MAKE THE TRAIN.

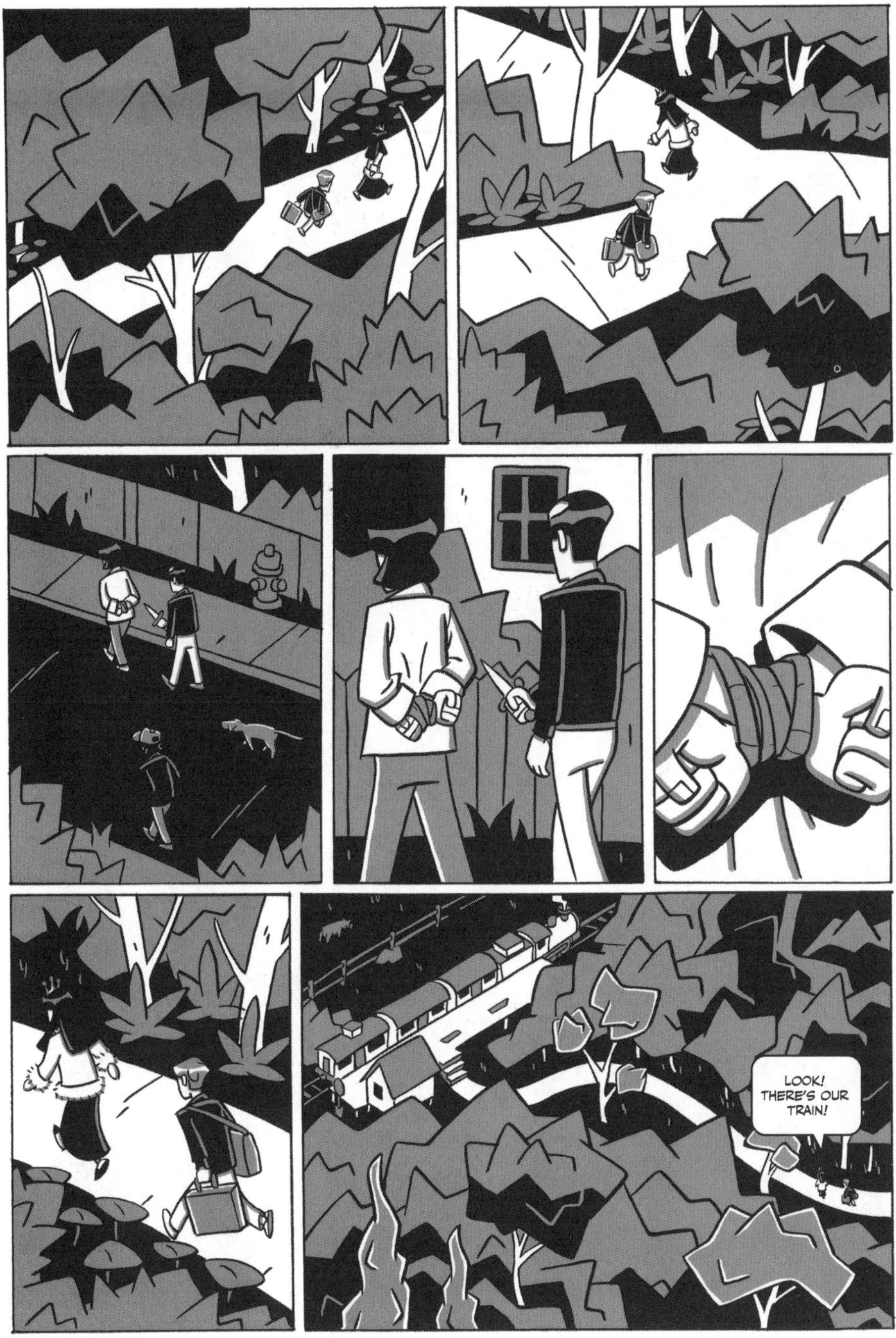
LOOK! THERE'S OUR TRAIN!

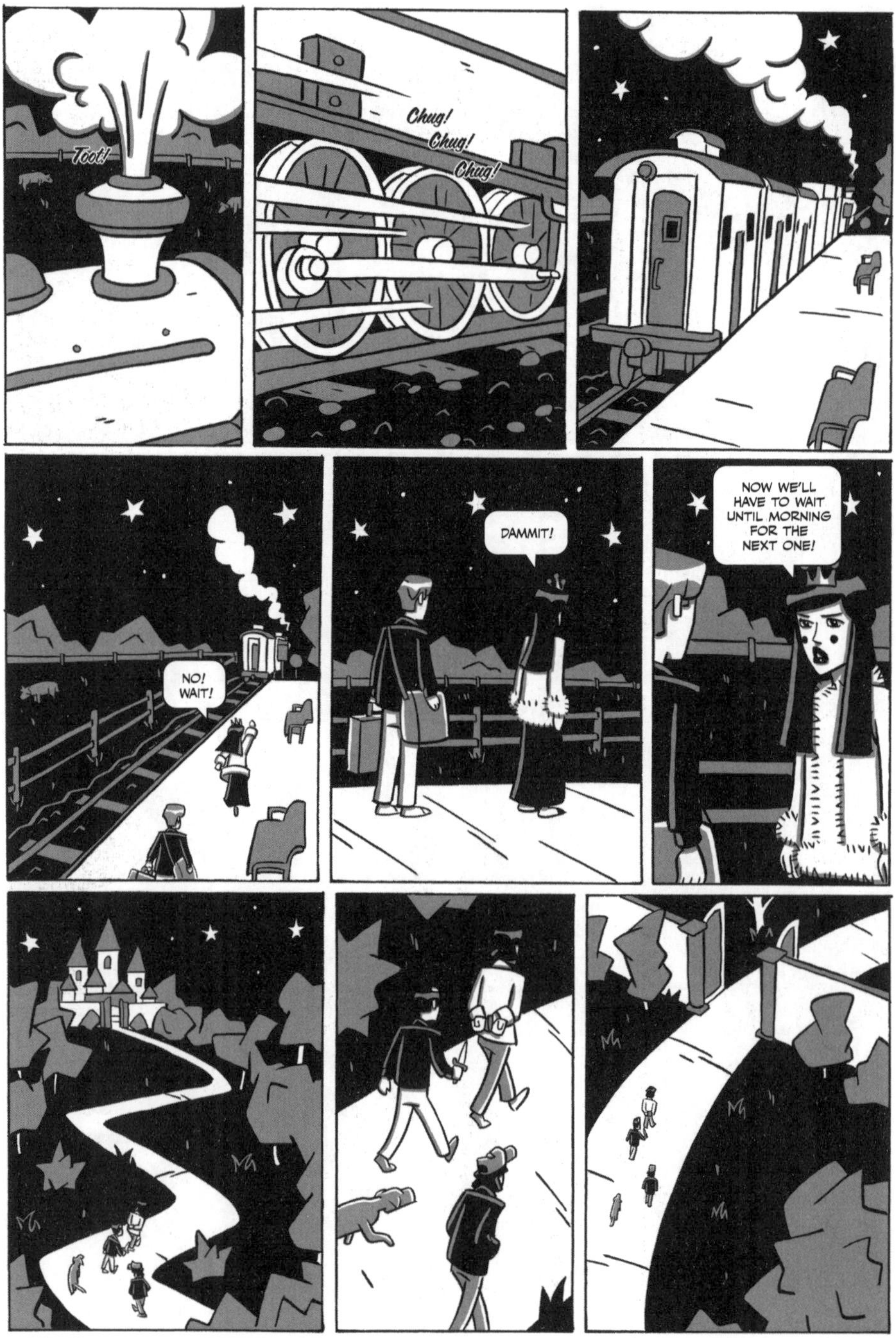
Toot!
Chug!
Chug!
Chug!
NO! WAIT!
DAMMIT!
NOW WE'LL HAVE TO WAIT UNTIL MORNING FOR THE NEXT ONE!

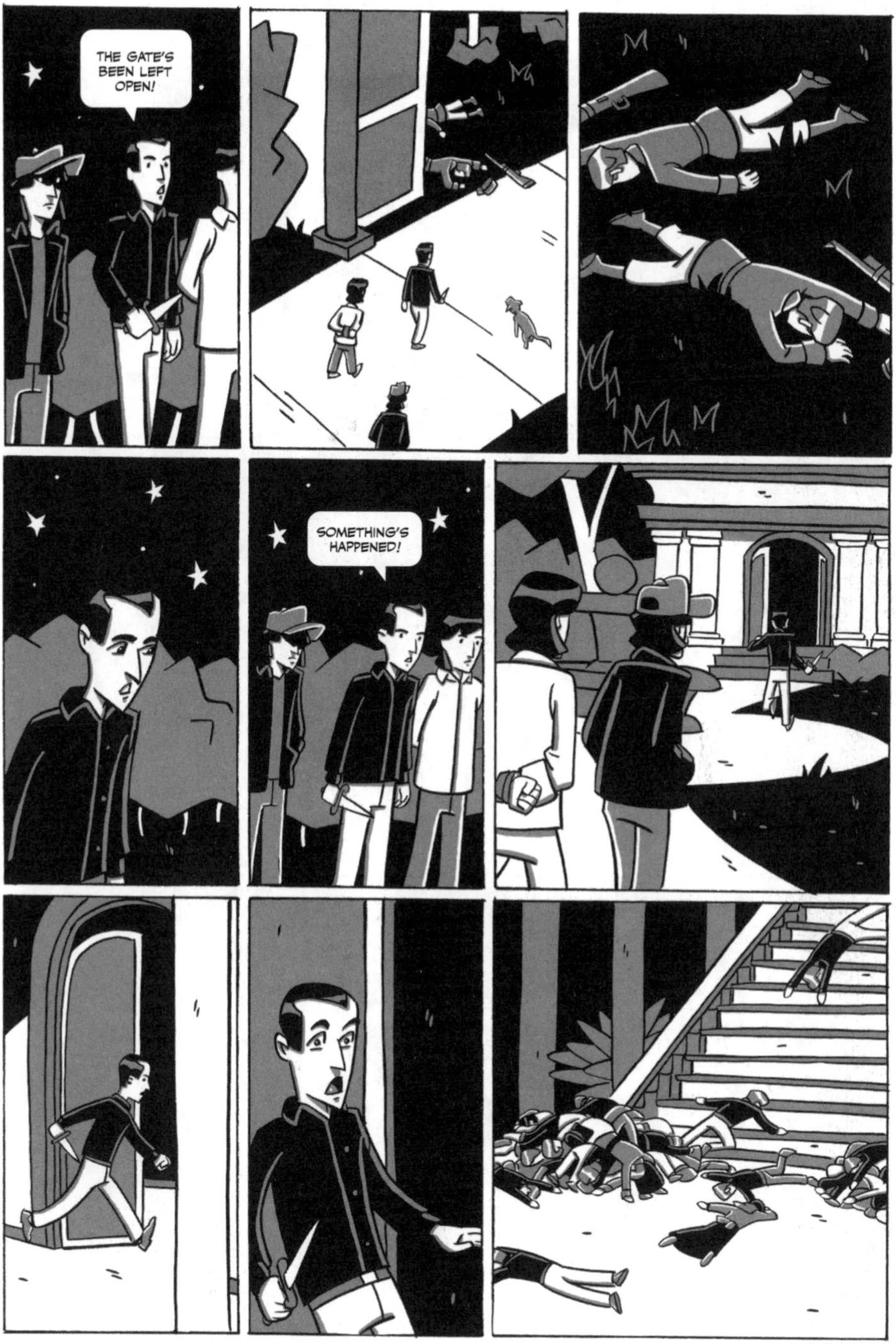
THE GATE'S BEEN LEFT OPEN!
SOMETHING'S HAPPENED!

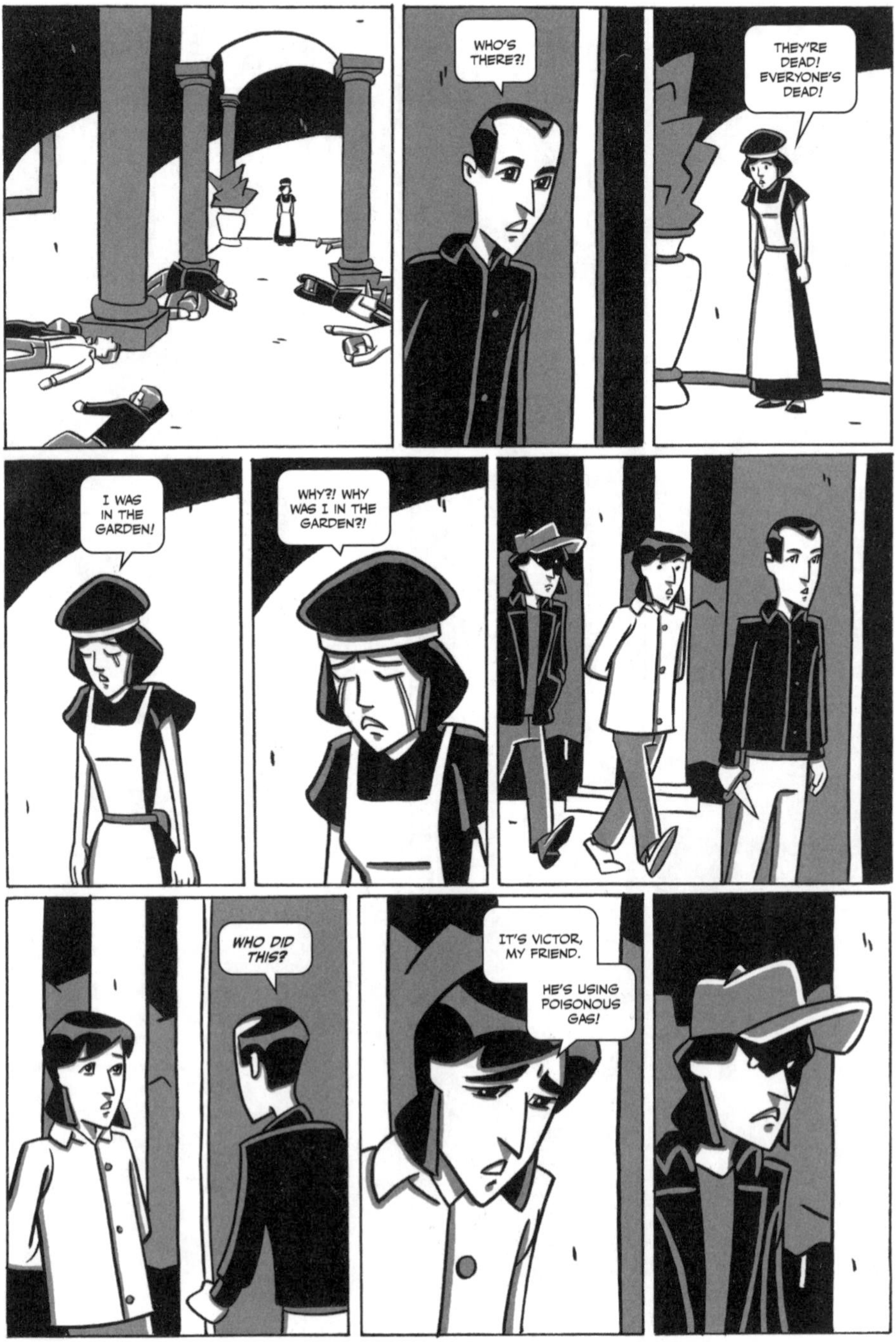
WHO'S THERE?!
THEY'RE DEAD! EVERYONE'S DEAD!
I WAS IN THE GARDEN!
WHY?! WHY WAS I IN THE GARDEN?!
WHO DID THIS?
IT'S VICTOR, MY FRIEND.
HE'S USING POISONOUS GAS!

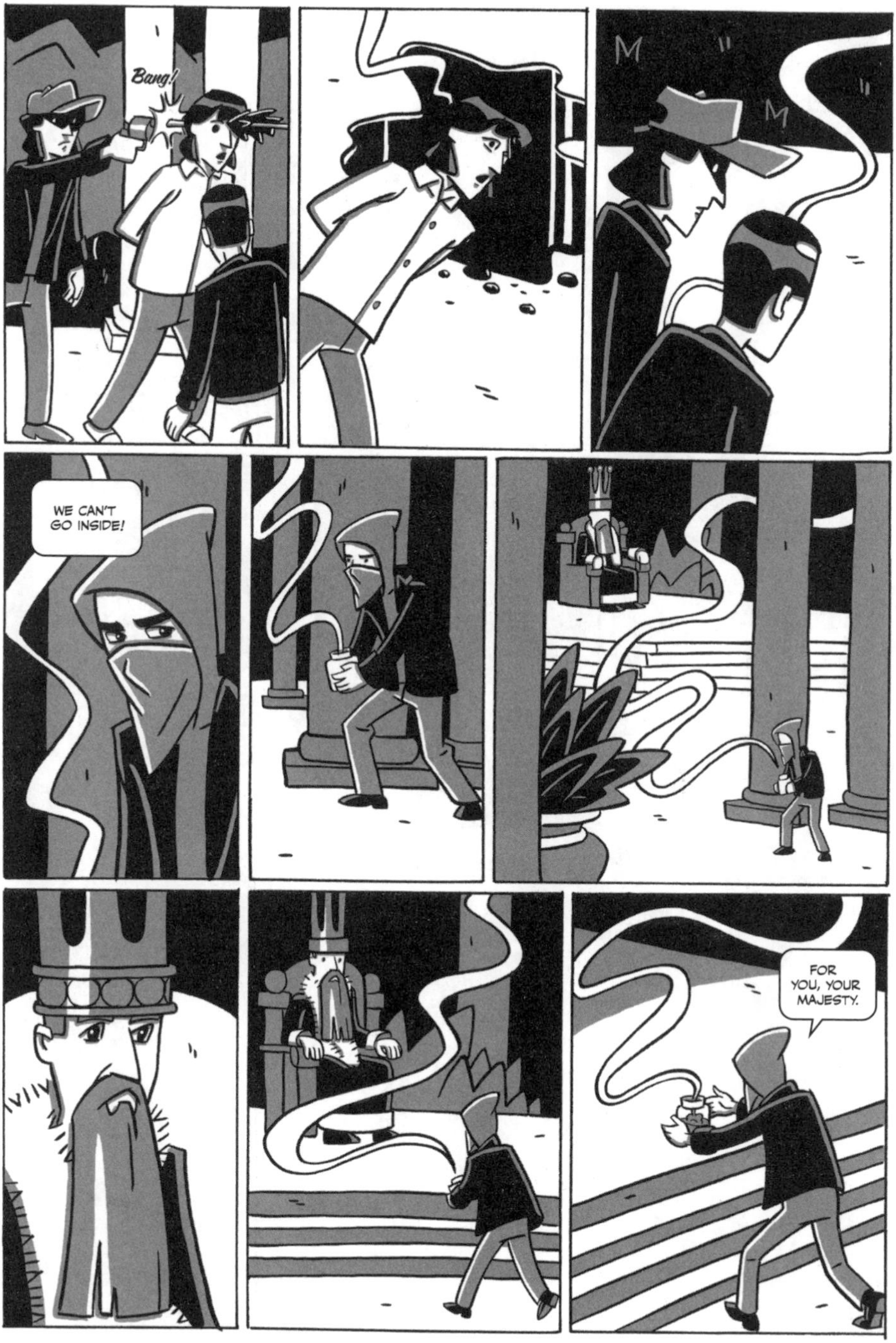
Bang!
M
M
WE CAN'T GO INSIDE!
FOR YOU, YOUR MAJESTY.

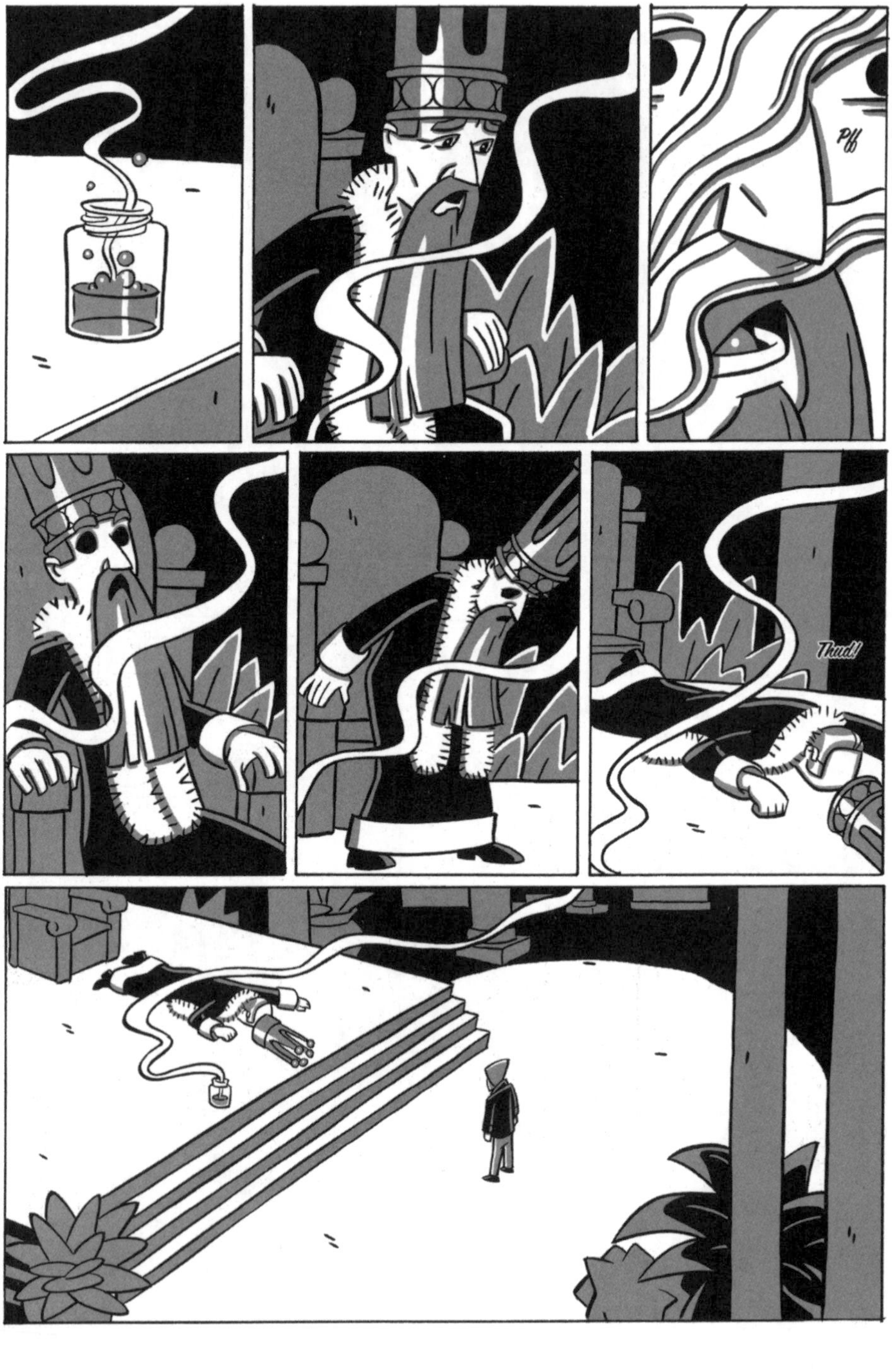
Pff
Thud!

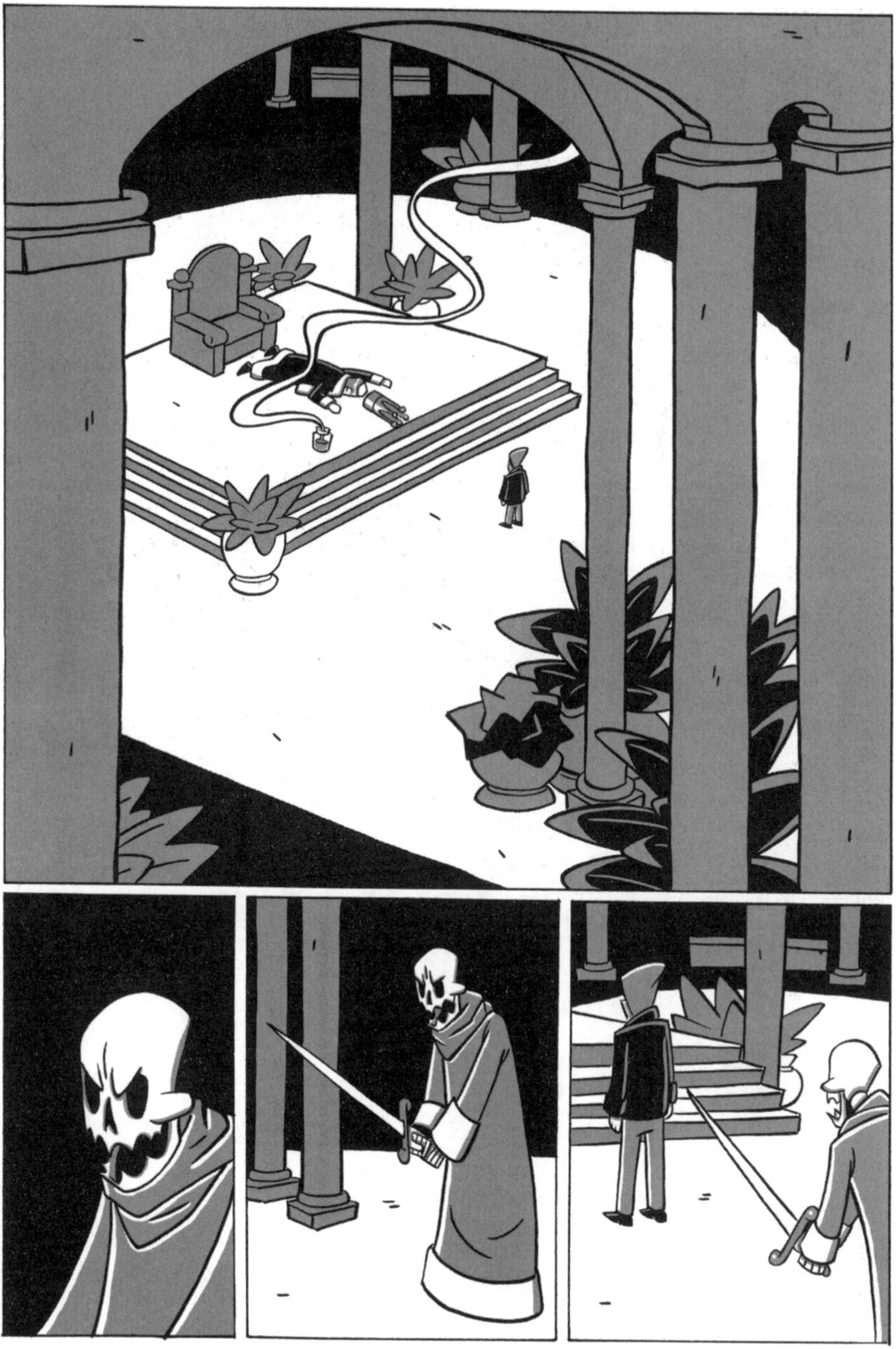

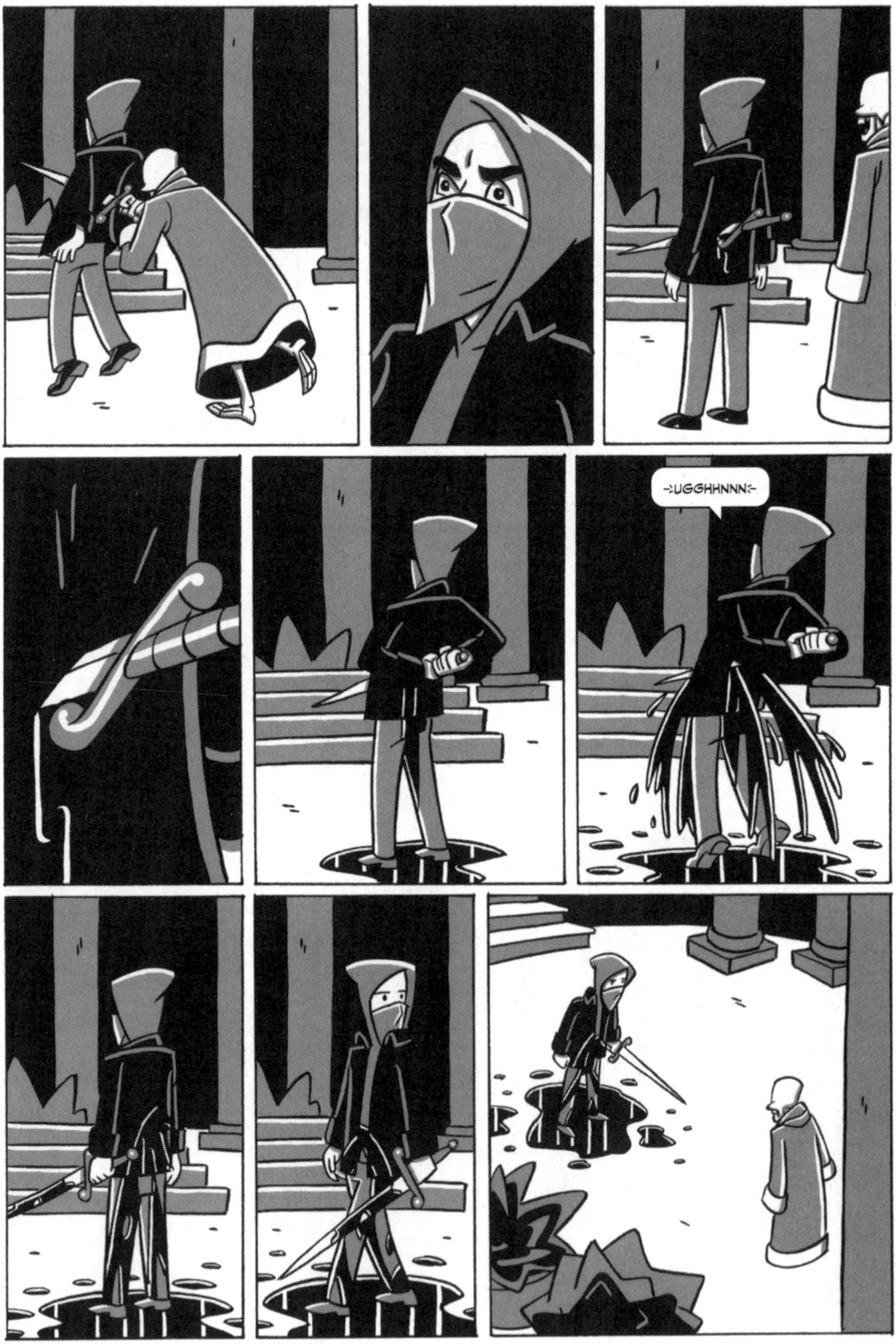
-UGGHHNNN-

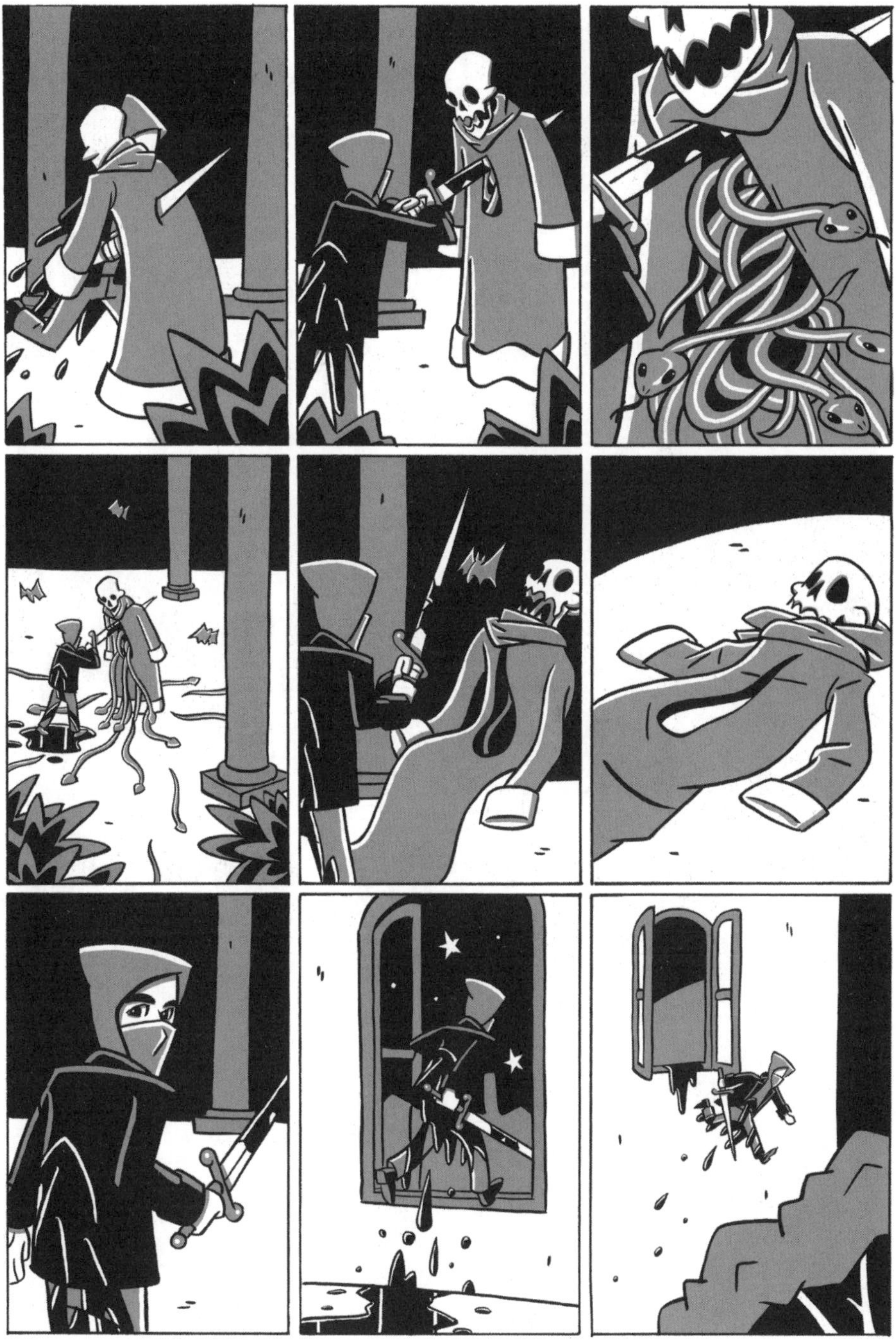

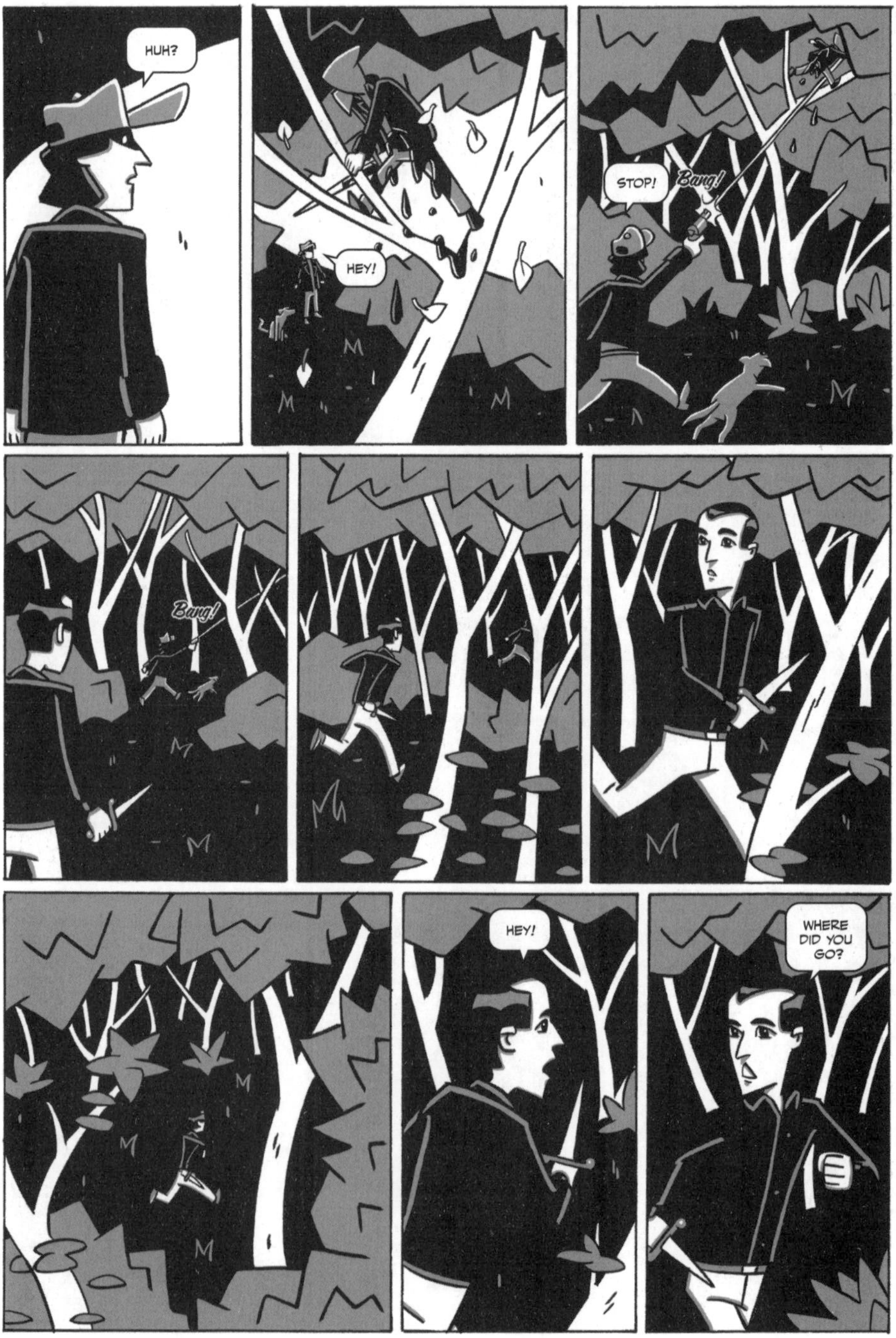
HUH?
HEY!
STOP!
Bang!
Bang!
HEY!
WHERE DID YOU GO?

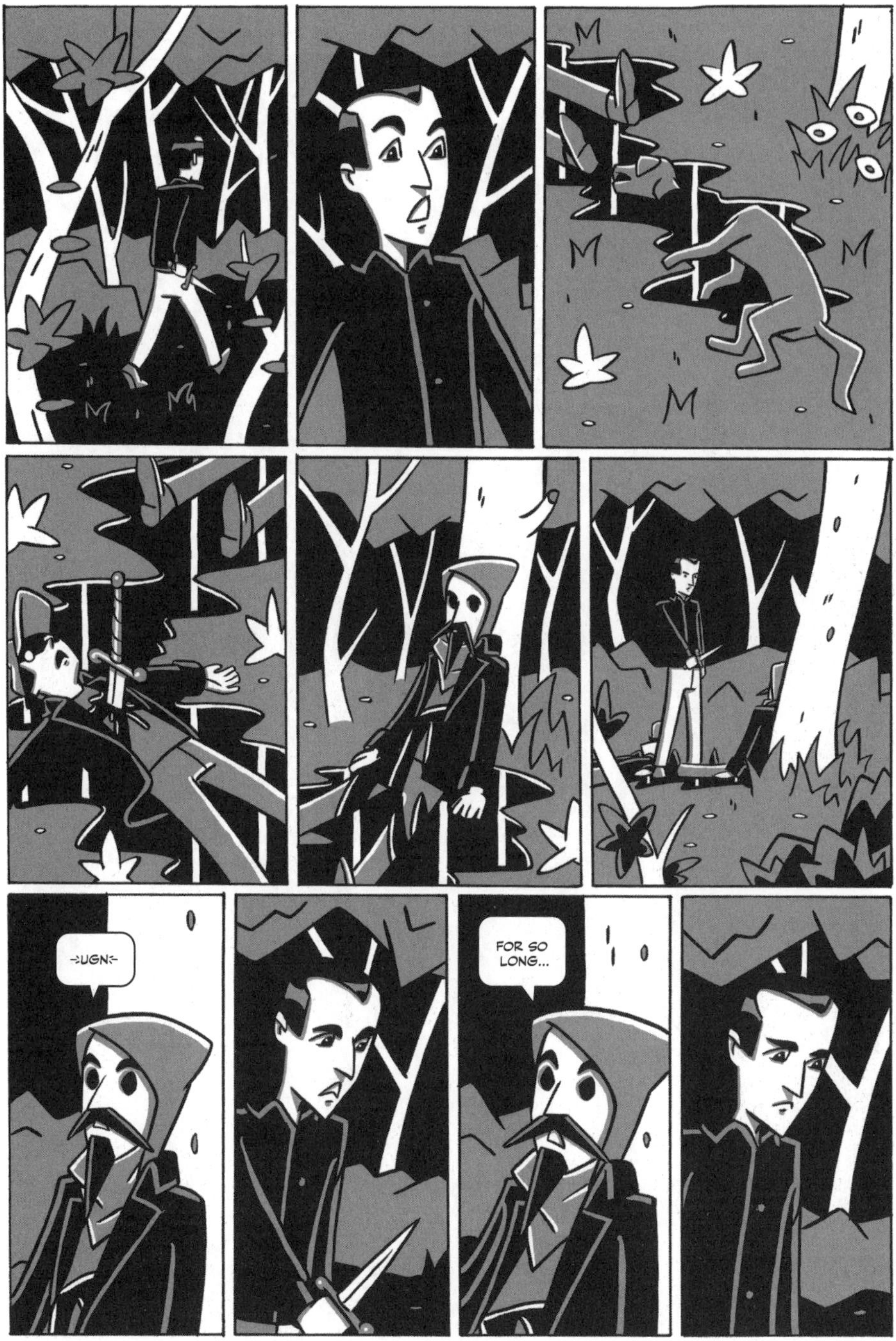
-UGN-
FOR SO LONG...

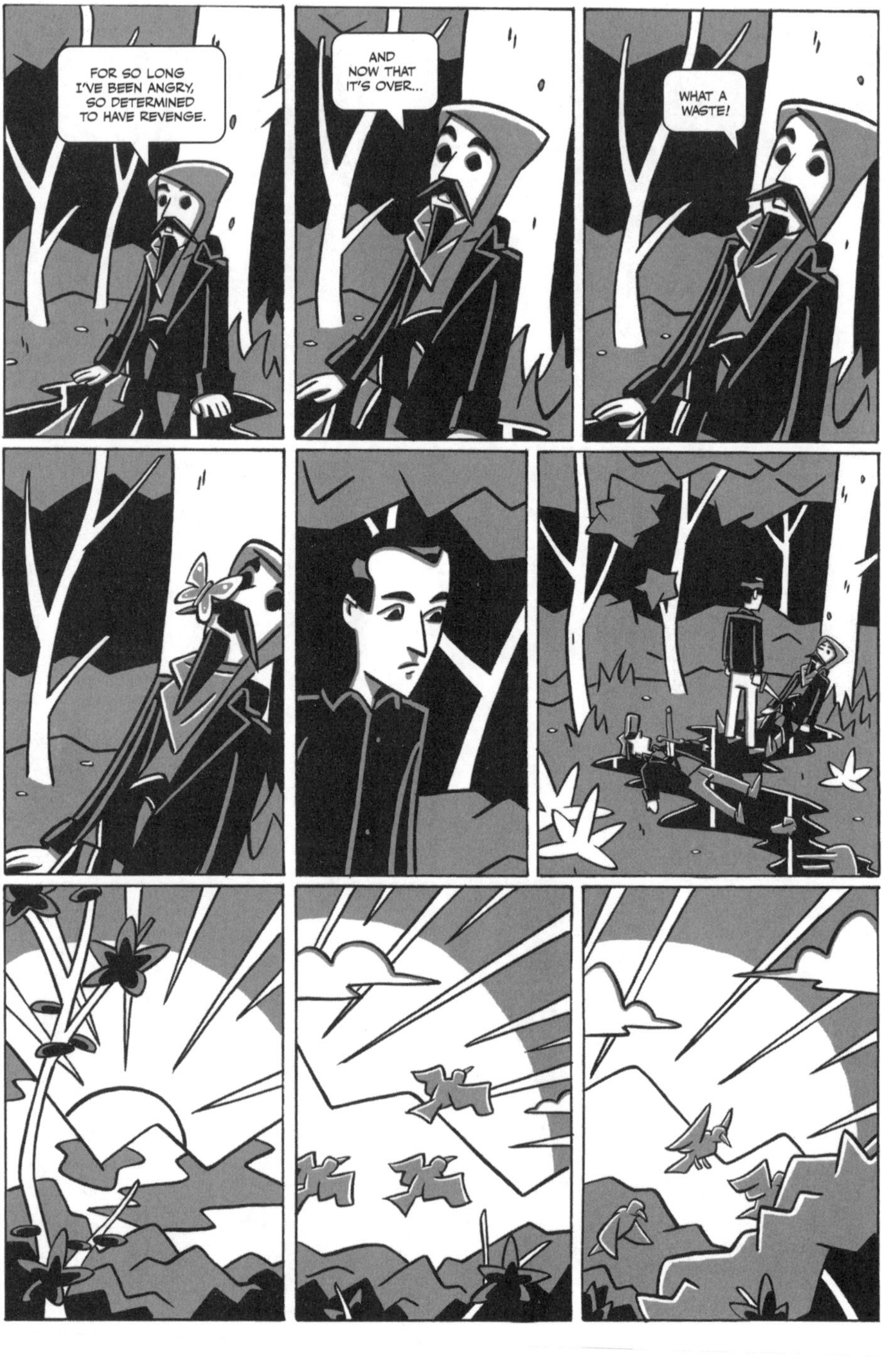
FOR SO LONG I'VE BEEN ANGRY, SO DETERMINED TO HAVE REVENGE.
AND NOW THAT IT'S OVER...
WHAT A WASTE!

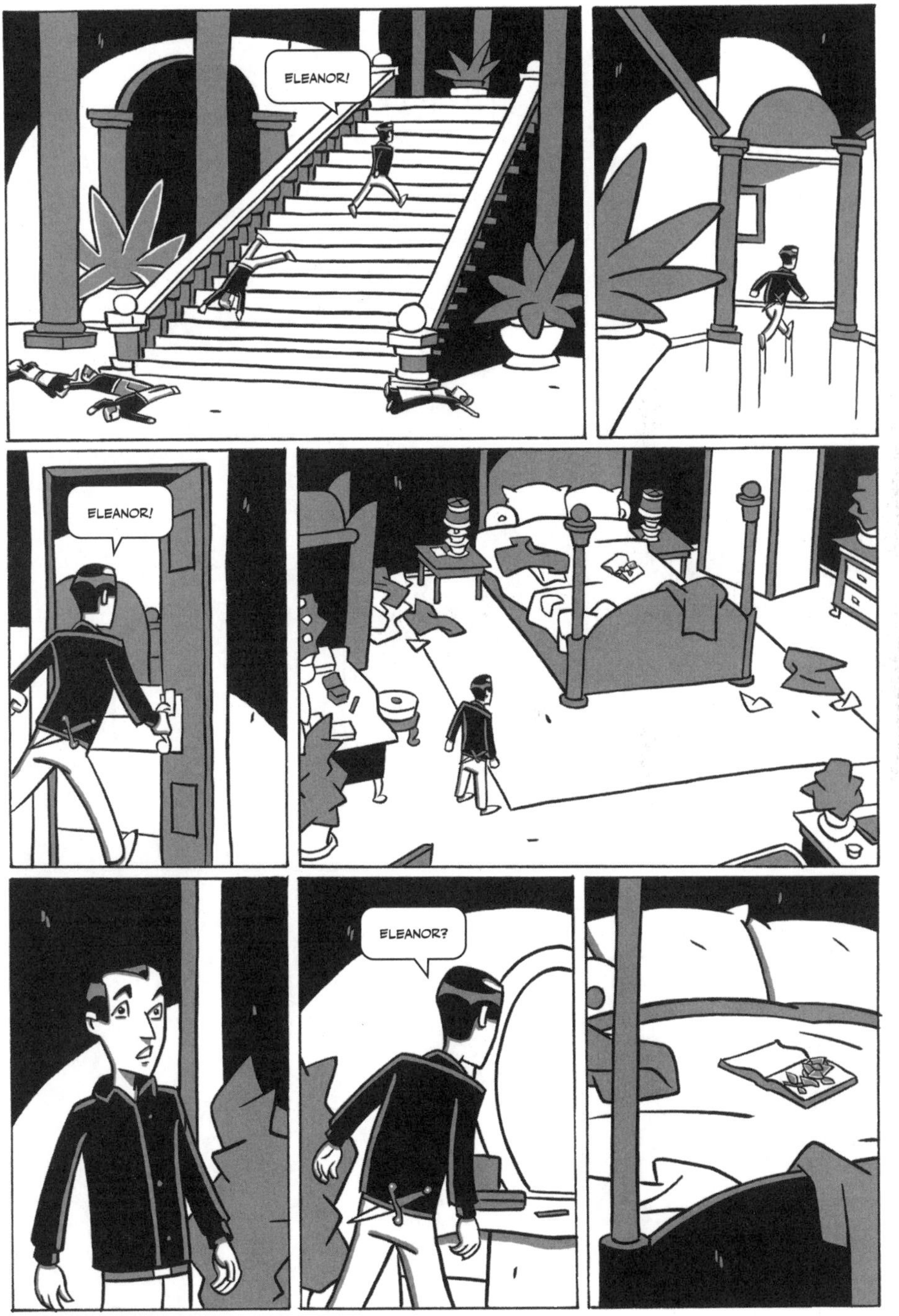
ELEANOR!
ELEANOR!
ELEANOR?

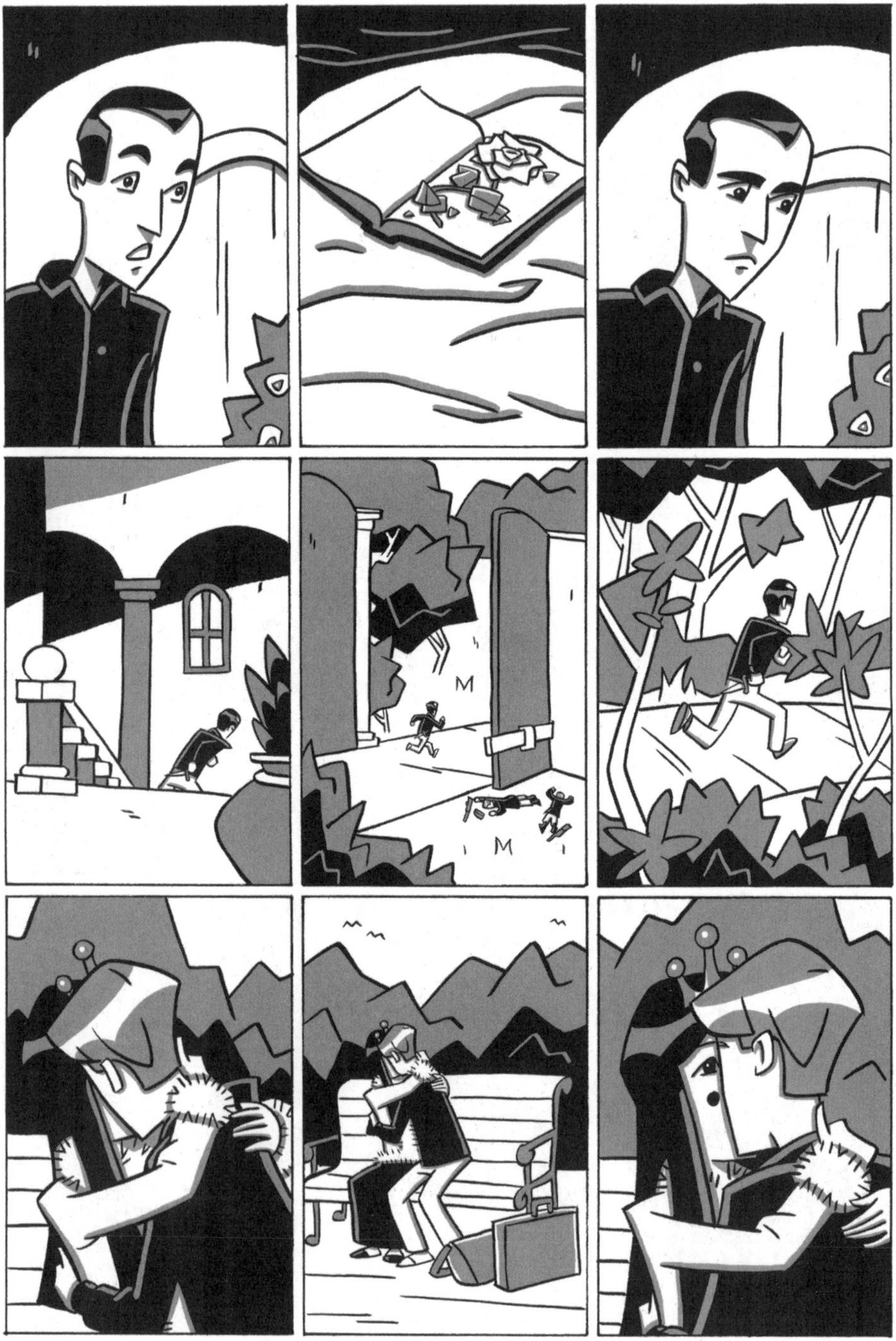

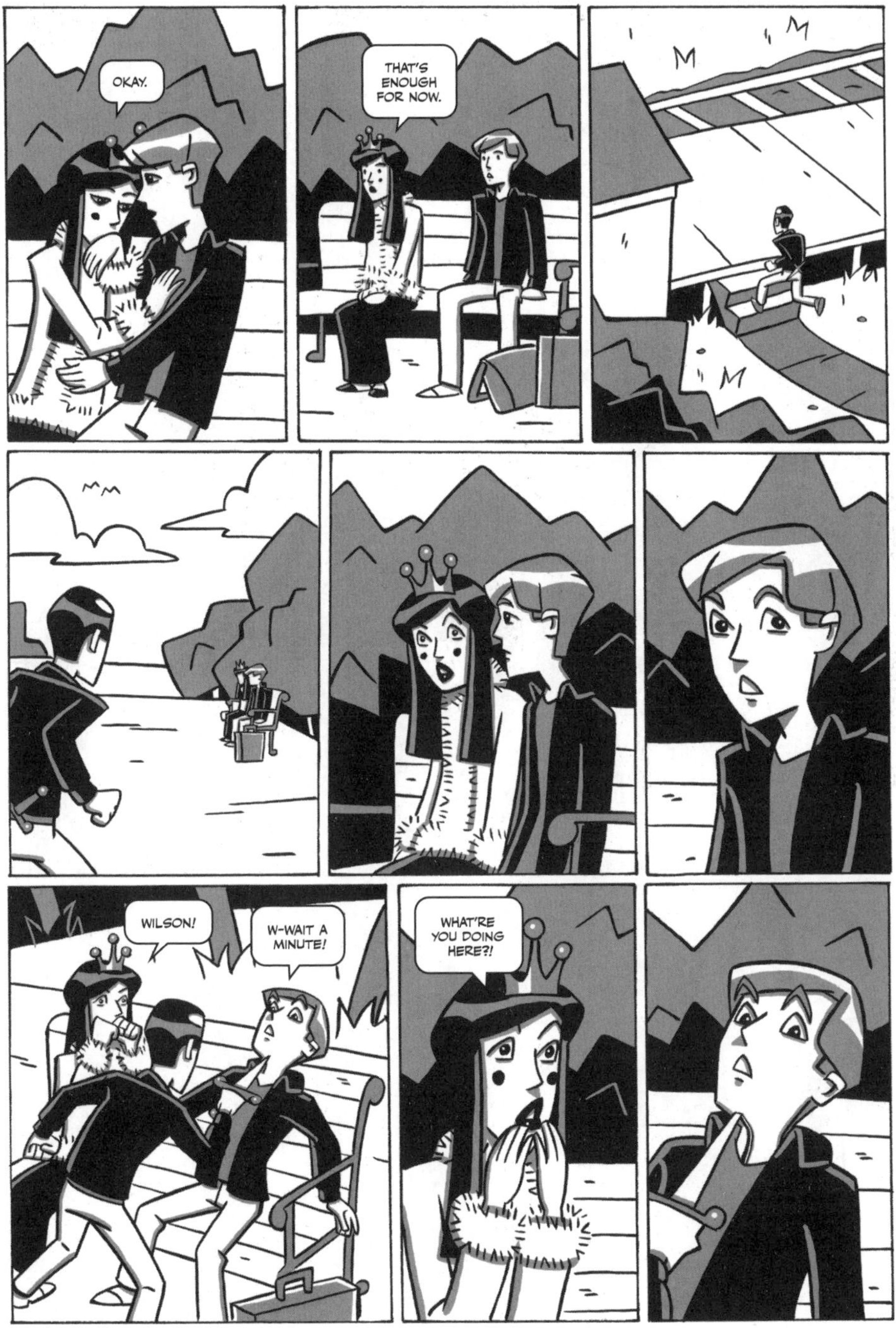
OKAY.
THAT'S ENOUGH FOR NOW.
WILSON!
W-WAIT A MINUTE!
WHAT'RE YOU DOING HERE?!

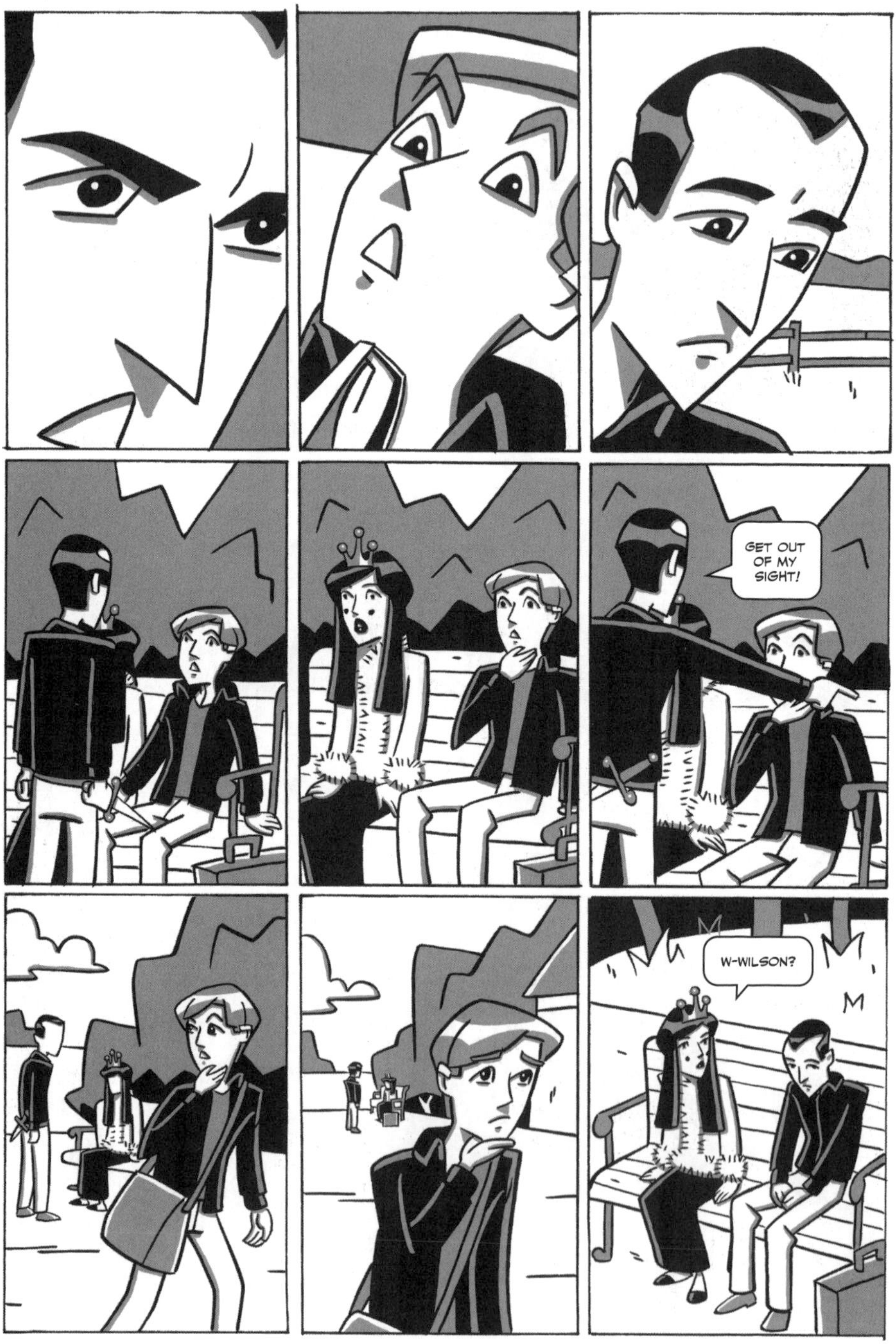
GET OUT OF MY SIGHT!
W-WILSON?

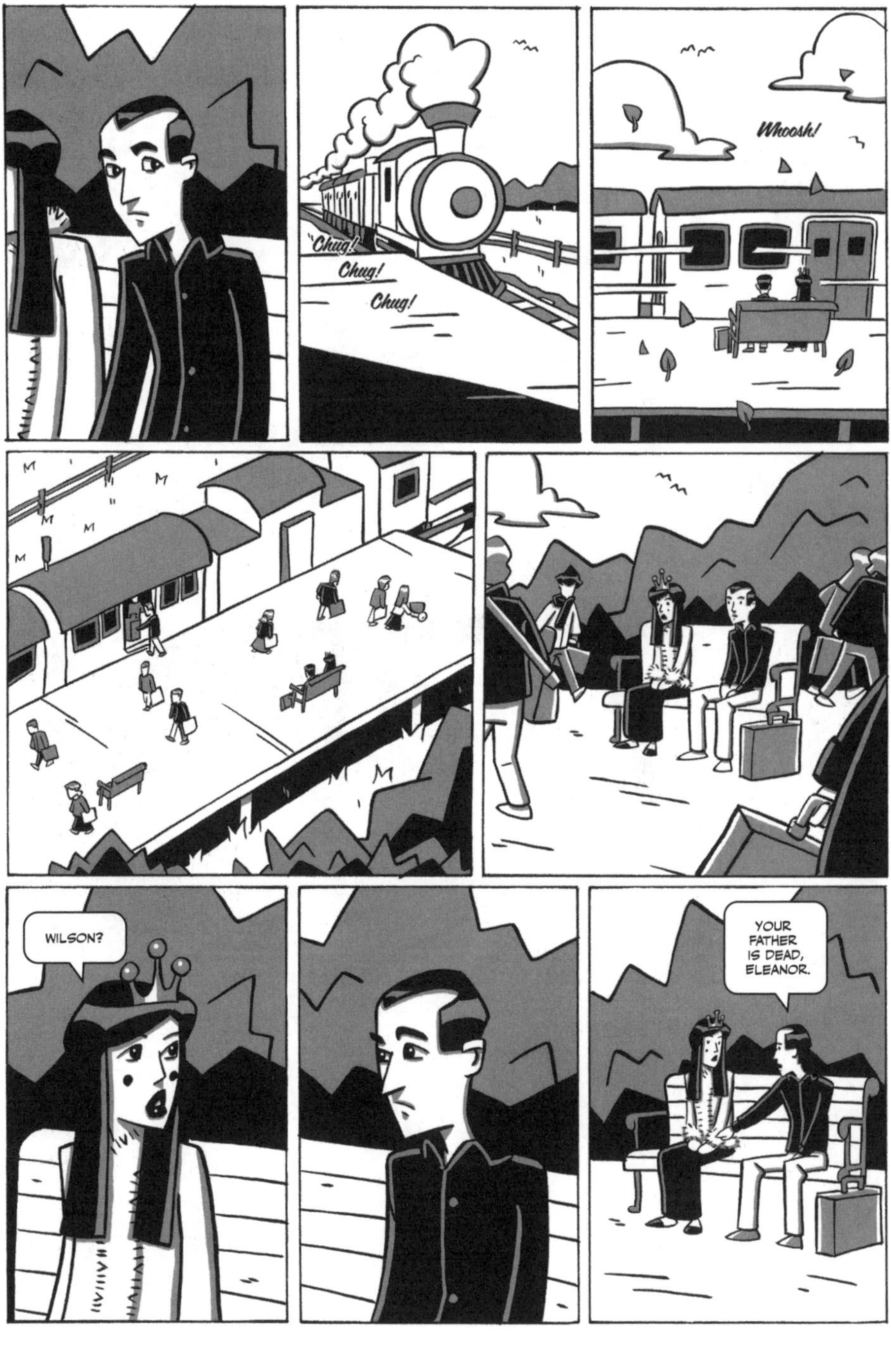
Chug!
Chug!
Chug!
Whoosh!
WILSON?
YOUR FATHER IS DEAD, ELEANOR.

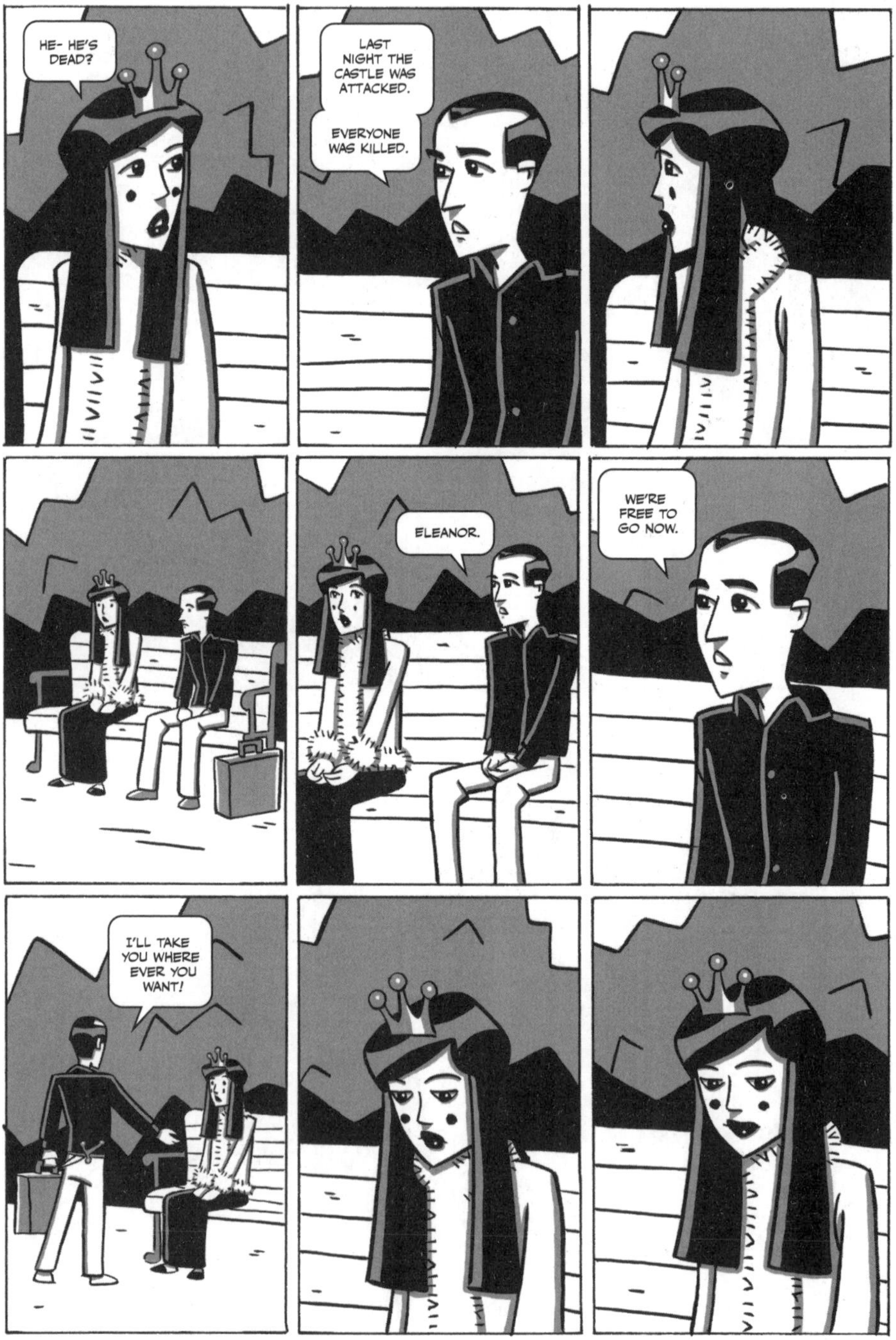
HE- HE'S DEAD?
LAST NIGHT THE CASTLE WAS ATTACKED.
EVERYONE WAS KILLED.
ELEANOR.
WE'RE FREE TO GO NOW.
I'LL TAKE YOU WHERE EVER YOU WANT!

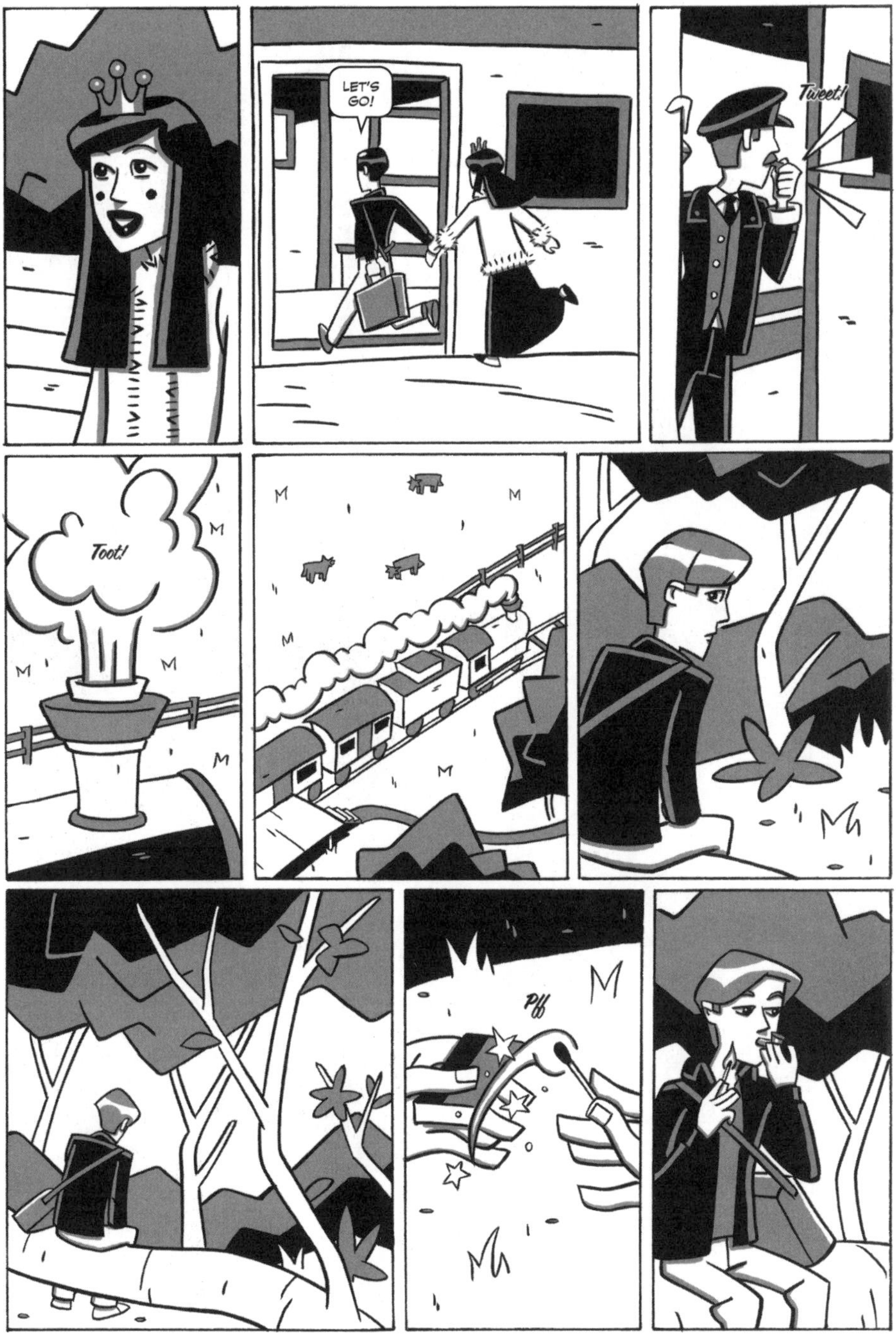

LET'S GO!
Tweet!
Toot!
Pff

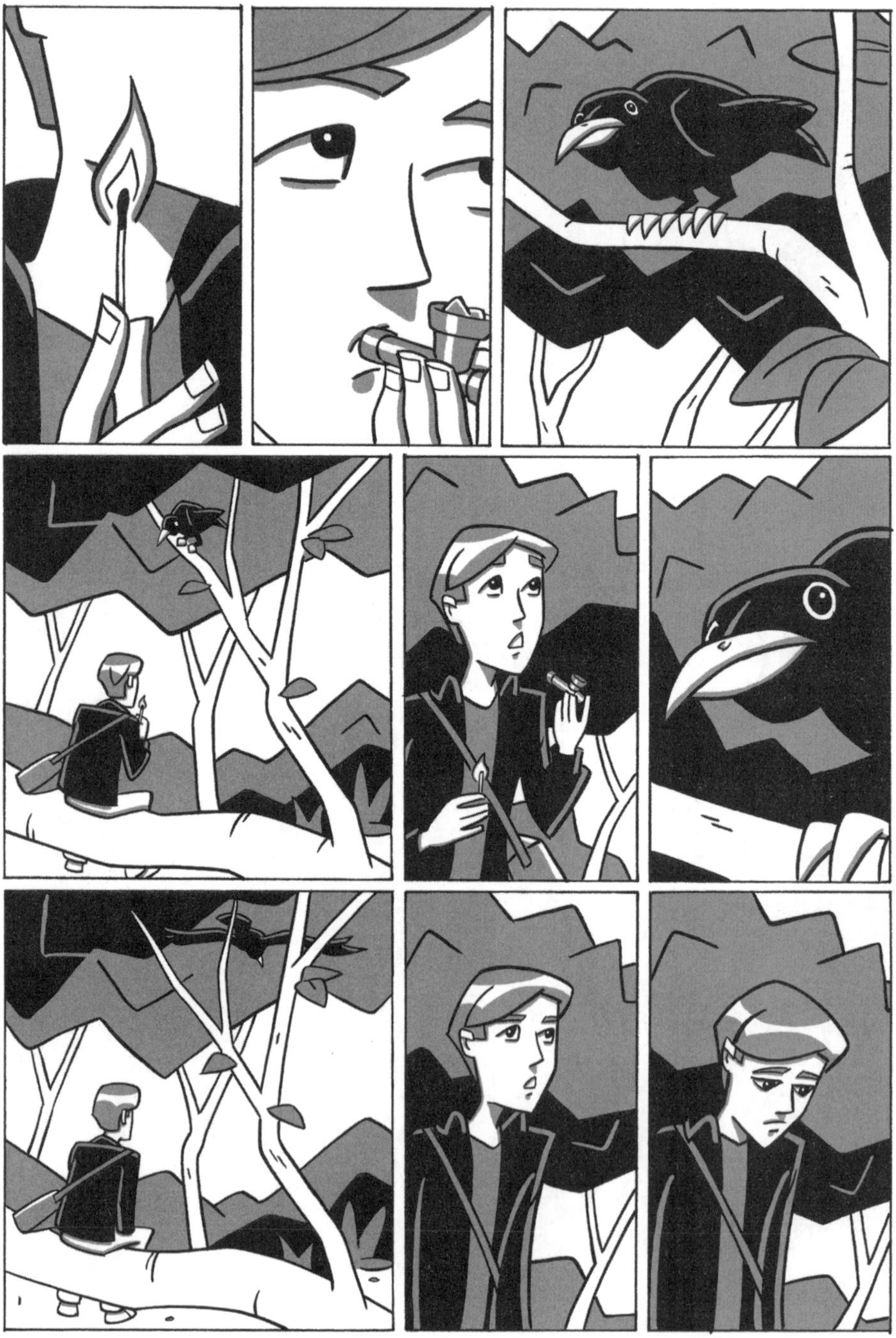

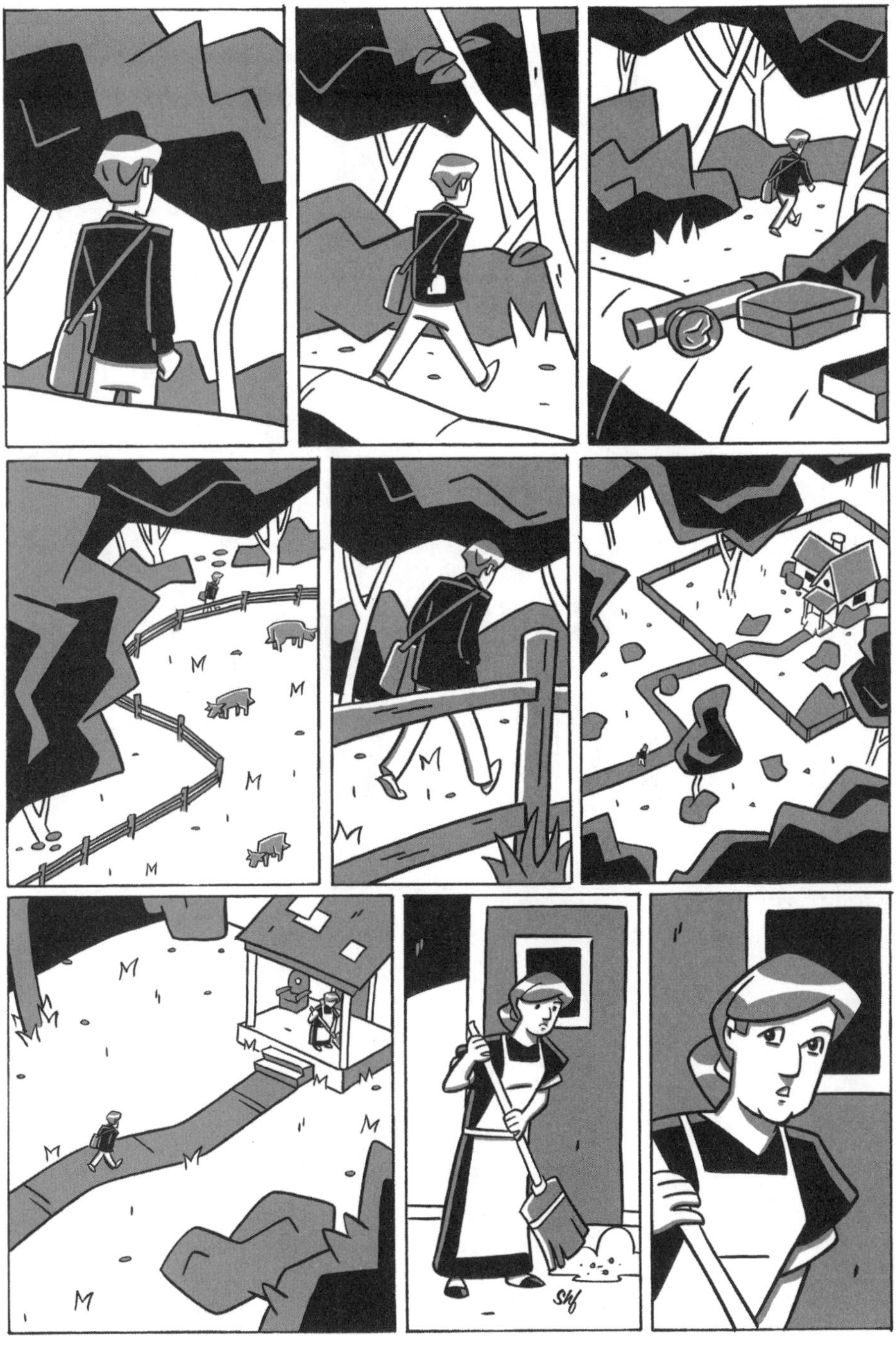

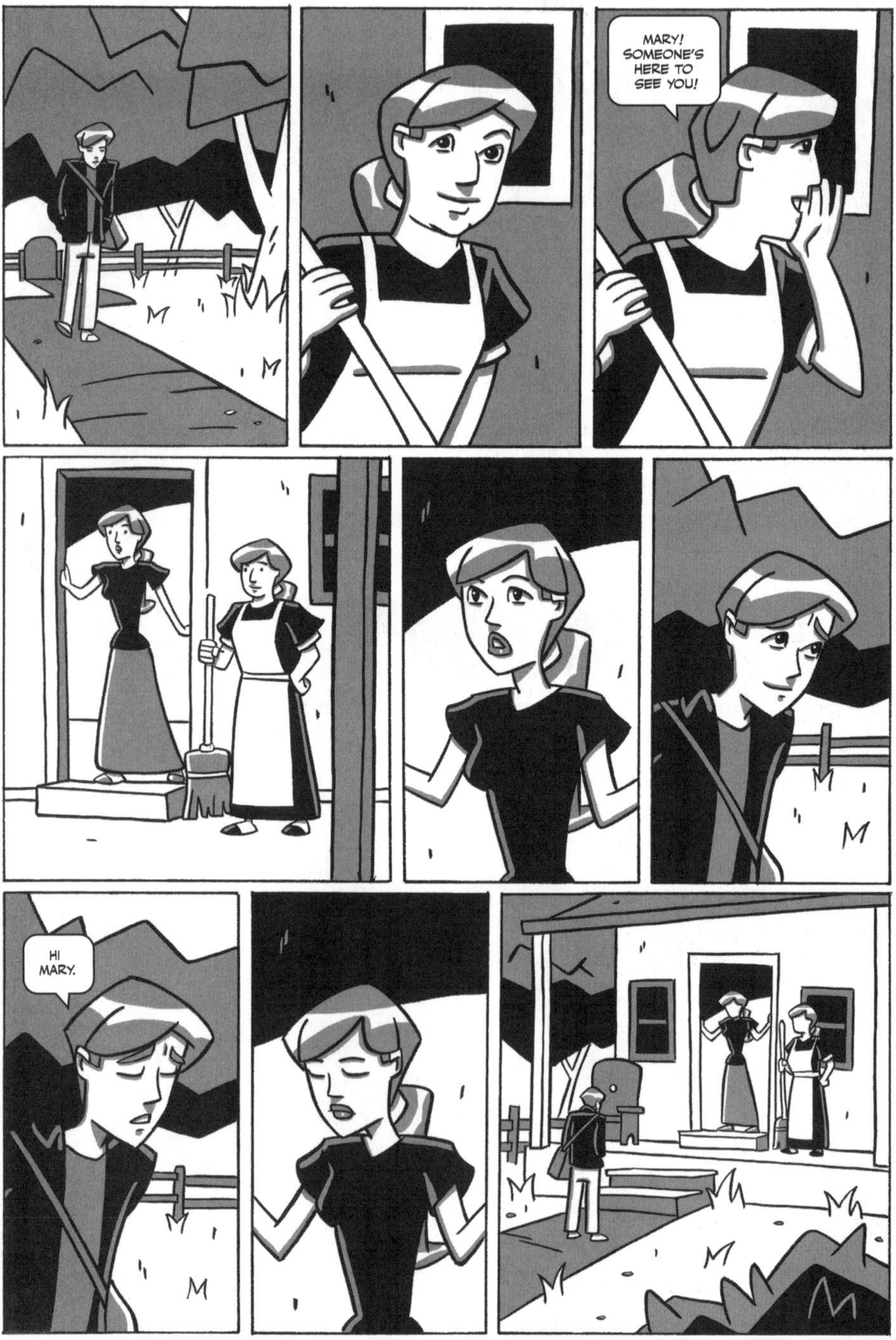
MARY! SOMEONE'S HERE TO SEE YOU!
HI MARY.

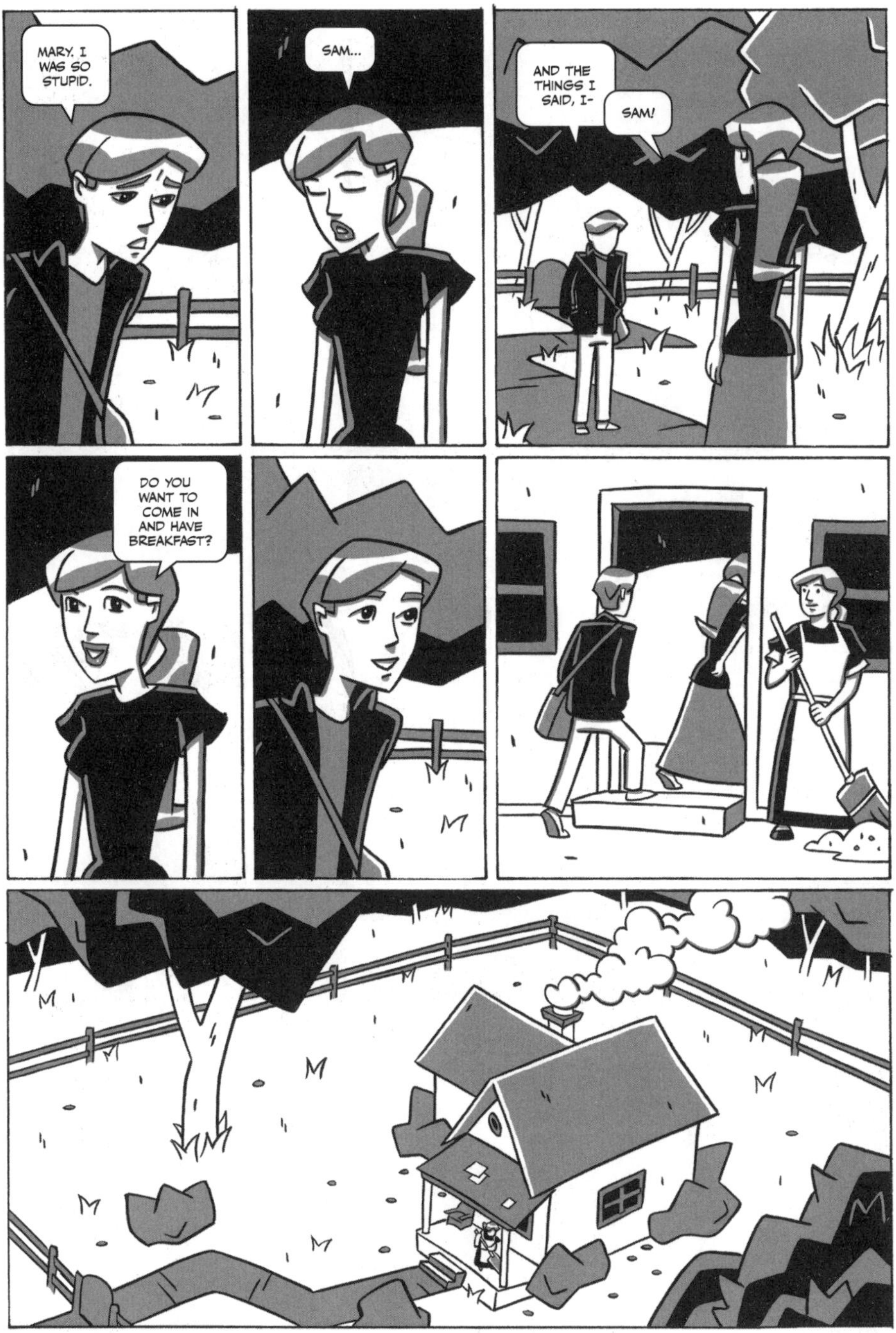
MARY. I WAS SO STUPID.
SAM...
AND THE THINGS I SAID, I-
SAM!
DO YOU WANT TO COME IN AND HAVE BREAKFAST?

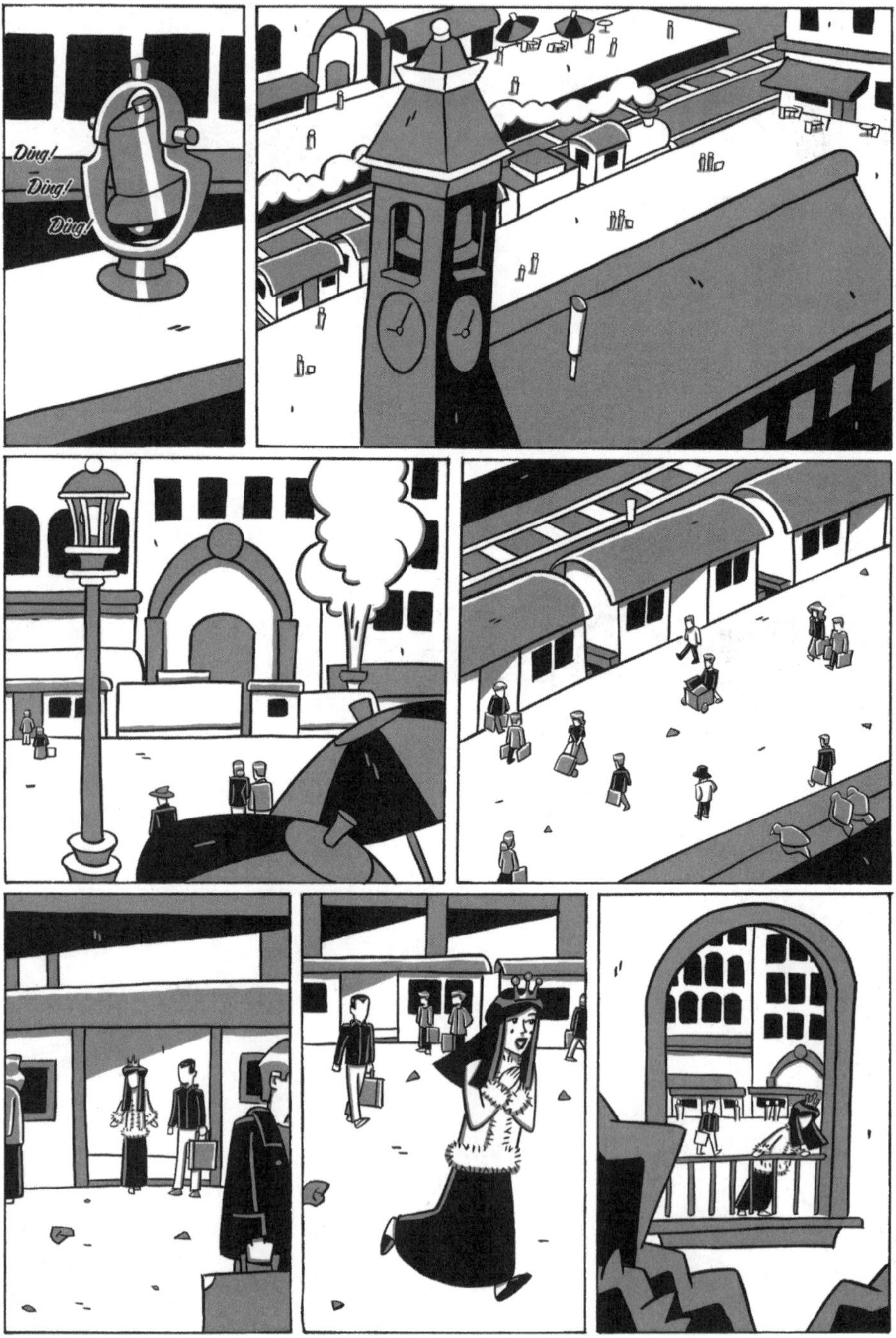
Ding!
Ding!
Ding!

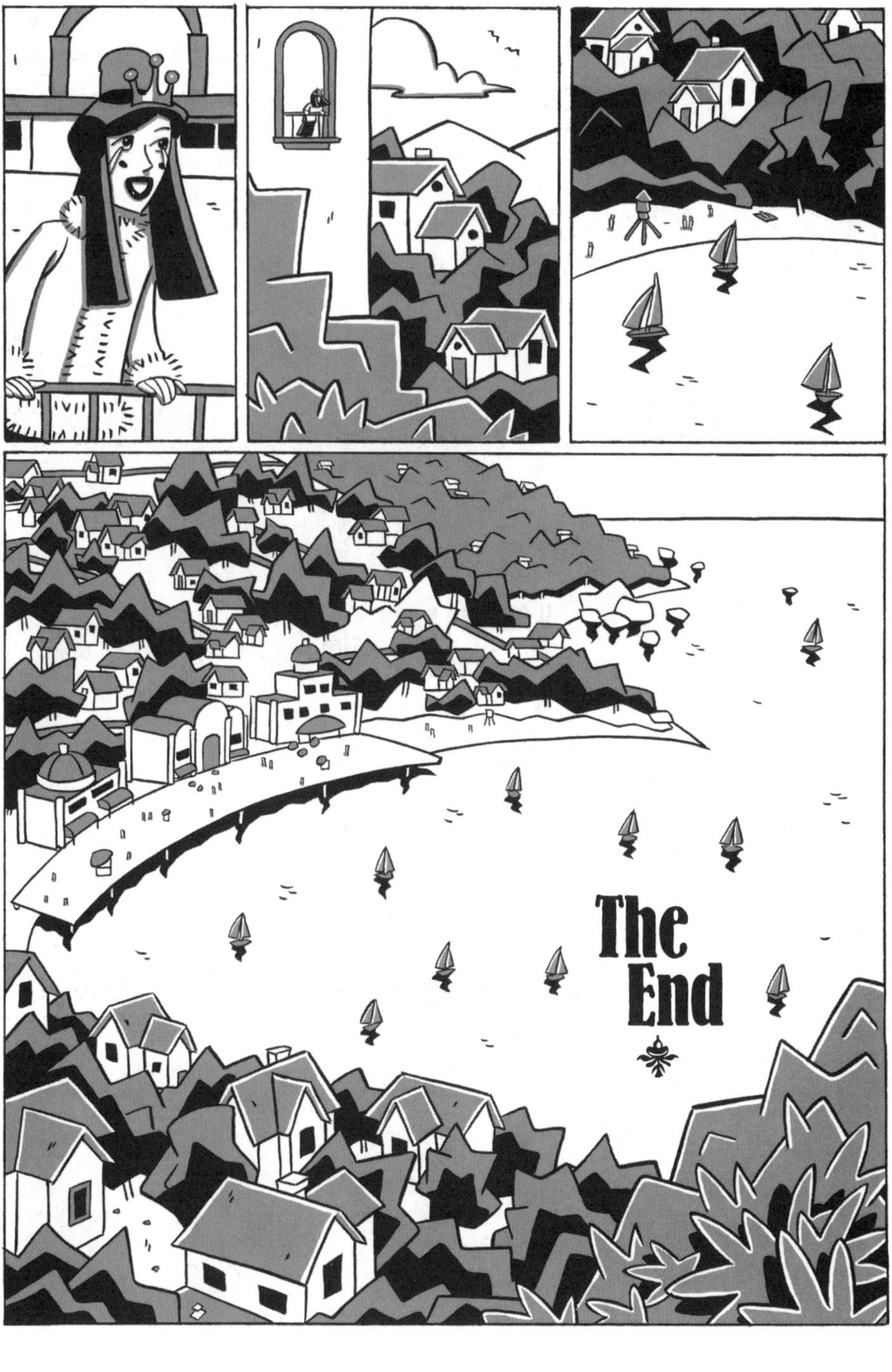
The End

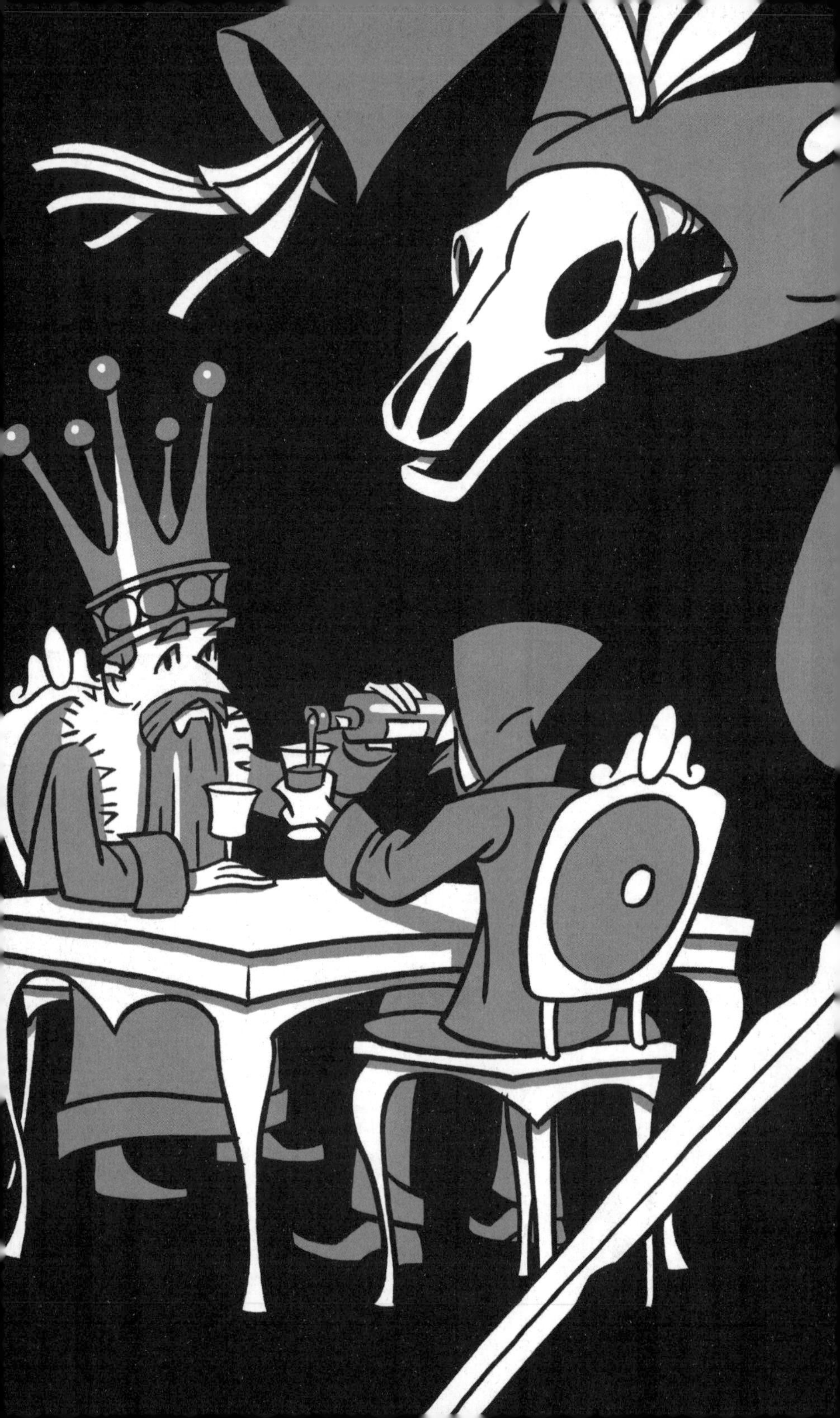

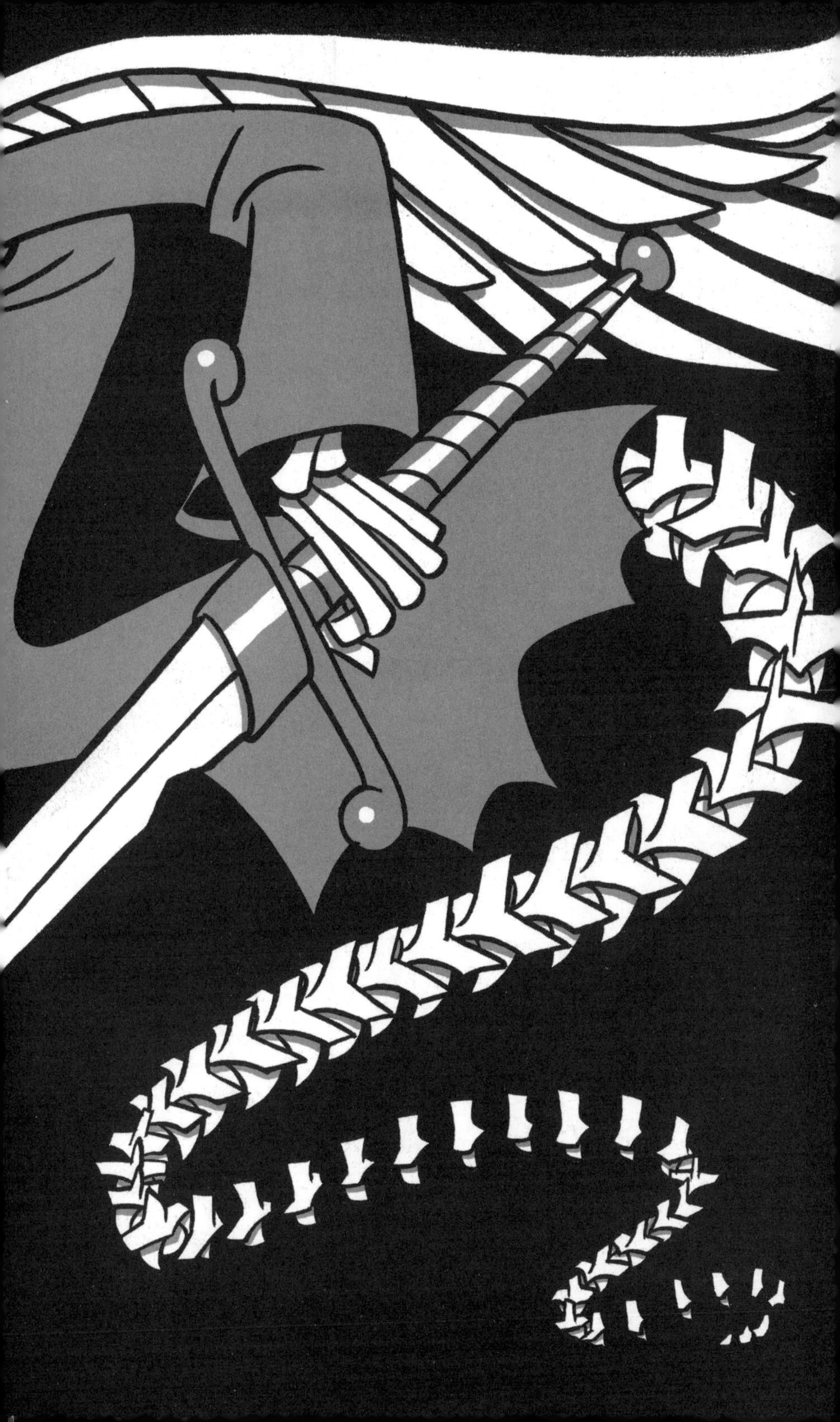

Love Like Fishes

tin bird press

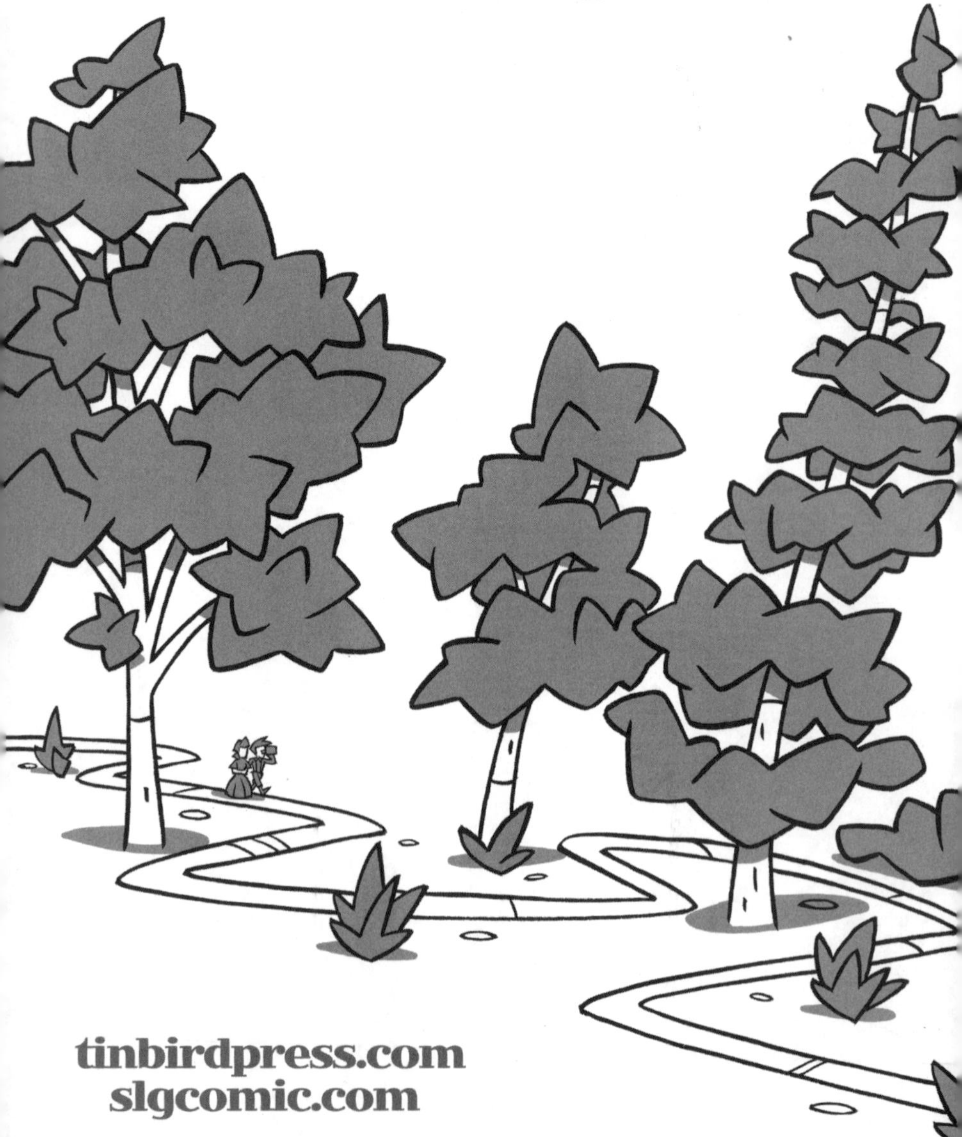

tinbirdpress.com
slgcomic.com

Praise for *The White Devil* and Domenic Stansberry

'Edgar-winner Stansberry takes the reader on a wild ride in this exceptional noir . . . Compelling reading'
*Publishers Weekly* starred review

'Freaking incredible'                                                   *Crimespree*

'Stansberry nails the sultry, decadent, and erotically charged tone with one perfectly placed hammer stroke after another'   *Booklist*

'More than a murder mystery: a story of Italy, obsessions, candid cultural observations, and a sense of place and confused purpose that keeps readers guessing, entertained, and thoroughly immersed'                                      *Midwest Book Review*

'Perhaps the most surprising feature of this *tour de force* is its pervasive links to both Jacobean tragedy and contemporary Mediterranean noir. Who knew?'                                 *Kirkus*

'A sensitive writer and observer'                      *New York Times*

'Stansberry is an extraordinarily evocative writer'
George Pelecanos, writer/producer for *The Wire*

'One of the genre's best writers right now'
Sarah Weinman, author of *The Real Lolita*

'Stansberry is a hard-hitting, uncompromising writer'
Bookreporter.com

**Domenic Stansberry** is the Edgar Award-winning author of ten novels and a collection of stories. His North Beach Mystery series has won wide praise for its portrayal of the ethnic and political subcultures of San Francisco. Books from that series include *The Ancient Rain*, named one of the best crime novels of the last decade by *Booklist*. An earlier novel, *The Confession*, received the Edgar Allan Poe Award for its controversial portrait of a Marin County psychologist accused of murdering his mistress. *The White Devil* was the winner of the 2016 Hammett Prize for best crime fiction. Stansberry grew up in the San Francisco area and currently lives with his wife, the poet Gillian Conoley, and their daughter Gillis in a small town north of that city.

*Also by Domenic Stansberry*

THE NORTH BEACH MYSTERIES

Chasing the Dragon

The Big Boom

The Ancient Rain

Naked Moon

The Spoiler

The Last Days of Il Duce

Manifesto for the Dead

The Confession

Exit Paradise

# THE
# WHITE DEVIL
## DOMENIC STANSBERRY

WEIDENFELD & NICOLSON

First published in the USA in 2016 by Molotov Editions.
First published in Great Britain as an ebook in 2018
by Weidenfeld & Nicolson.
This paperback edition first published in 2018
by Weidenfeld & Nicolson
an imprint of The Orion Publishing Group Ltd
Carmelite House, 50 Victoria Embankment
London EC4Y 0DZ

An Hachette UK Company

1 3 5 7 9 10 8 6 4 2



All the characters in this book are fictitious, and any resemblance to actual persons, living or dead, is purely coincidental.

A CIP catalogue record for this book is available from the British Library.

ISBN (Mass Market Paperback) 978 1 4746 1010 0
ISBN (eBook) 978 1 4746 1011 7

Printed in Great Britain by Clays Ltd, Elcograf S.p.A.

MIX
Paper from responsible sources
FSC® C104740

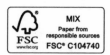

www.orionbooks.co.uk

*"She hath no faults, who hath the art to hide them."*
John Webster

# PART ONE

# 1.

THERE'S BEEN ANOTHER MURDER, this one in Los Angeles, in the sand under the Palisades. Both of my husbands are dead. I am young to have been married twice, let alone widowed.

Others are dead, too—a woman I admired; a boy.

I have taken refuge in a distant city, in a second-story flat off the Avenida. It's an older neighborhood, where the once stolid houses now smell of decay. The front gate is iron, the windows barred. At the end of the Avenida the shanties start up, sprawling over the canyons and railroad gullies onto the pampas. Before this, I lived a different kind of life. There were stories.

I do my best to stay out of sight . . . to remain anonymous . . . but I get weary sometimes . . . reckless . . .

I wander onto the balcony in my nightgown, foolish, a little bit drunk. A car door slams.

I hear a man out in the street. He speaks in Spanish, "*puta*"—hissing in my direction, I think, but no, a woman staggers alongside him, a girlfriend or wife, a mistress, someone used to his insults. They muck along the dark avenue, insulting each other, then embrace in a dark cranny.

I envy them, even though it's embraces like that which have gotten me in so much trouble.

I tell myself I am safe in this sprawling city, that I have escaped—but only a few days ago a woman recognized me, I fear, a cashier who studies the gossip sites. This has happened before. I let my guard down in the way I walk or dress. I remove my glasses while examining a necklace in a window or a menu at a café— and some clerk, some passerby, a couple two tables over, their eyes spark with recognition.

There is no such thing as a secret life.

Not for me.

Blink and I am captured. Whereabouts known.

With the cameras not far behind.

And others.

Who wish me greater harm.

## 2.

THIS ALL STARTED IN ROME, not long ago. It wasn't quite the Rome of my imagination, full of motor scooters and ruins, an endless film set where I might wander in a sleeveless dress, immune to heat and noise. I was naive that way. The streets were dirty and hot. Flies swarmed the Colosseum. The spring was so short that year, nonexistent. Everything stank of itself. The Italians in their bright synthetics. The Pakistani vendors. The streets, too, the old stones, the restaurants, the English women with their toy dogs drenched in cologne.

It wasn't what I'd expected, but I grew to like it: my own stink mixed with all the others, the dampness beneath my clothes when I went walking or sat with my legs crossed on the metro.

I lived with Frank Paris, my first husband, in a small flat by the Tiber. He was running out of money, but it wasn't something we talked about. I had my own secrets. Maybe it's the same with everyone, I don't know: a place inside, an emptiness, where matters get lost. At night Frank would lie there and study my features. The curtain billowed and the shadows moved. He didn't press me, not at first. I lay with my eyes closed, feigning sleep—

but I felt him watching. He'd kiss my cheek, run a finger down my leg.

Frank was quite a bit older than me. He was a thin man with sandy gray hair and a nose something like a boxer's—a bit crooked, pushed to one side. Despite that injury, or maybe because of it, his face had a wry character. I liked that about him. I liked touching his wide, battered nose and straddling him in the dark*
. . . I put my hand on his gray chest . . . He disappeared underneath me . . . Then he rolled me over and I disappeared, too . . . Eyes closed, falling into the darkness, we might have been anyone . . . his tongue, my tongue, his hands on my breasts, my legs in the air . . . Our sweat soaked through the sheets, the mattress damp like a riverbed . . . How I met Frank—he'd helped me out of a situation in Dallas involving my brother and an ex-boyfriend that had ended in a pretty ugly way.

I tried not to think about that, and Frank never mentioned it.

When we were done in bed, we'd go outside.

I walked beside him with nothing in my head—no past, no future—feeling just barely outside myself in the Italian night. I liked being empty like that. I liked the sultriness of the night, the dampness and the heat. We ended up under the umbrellas by the Tiber. Frank drank. Sitting there—in that black night, watching the people, listening to them laugh and flirt—I ached with vagrant desire. A longing to become someone else, to disappear. Afterward, we strolled along the glistening river.

All of that now seems like it happened to someone else.

Frank stopped on the bridge. He got morose all of a sudden, and whatever youth remained fell out of his face.

"There's something I need to tell you . . ."

"Hush," I said.

He let it go. He kissed me instead. That was how it was between us. He put his arm around my waist and dropped his hand onto my hip. He liked to feel me move against him as we walked. Meanwhile I could feel the young Italian men, loitering there along the river wall, watching as we passed.


AFTER MY BROTHER, JOHNNY, CAME to Rome, things changed. It would be easy to blame Johnny: his smile, his brown eyes and tousled hair. Strictly speaking, Johnny wasn't my brother but my half brother. We were very close: almost inseparable.

My brother had always been a bit of a delinquent, but he knew how to take care of himself. He had his own apartment across the Tiber, and work that took him back and forth from Naples. He spoke Italian well and had a way of getting around, slumming it, working both sides. He moved in circles you might not expect.

I went with him sometimes to the clubs. On one of those nights Johnny introduced me to Paolo Orsini, an Italian senator who'd spent time in New York. Because Orsini was a bit of a celebrity—nice-looking and married to a famous woman—Johnny thought we should meet.

"*Mia sorella bella*," my brother said. "The actress and poet. Vittoria."

This was typical Johnny. I'd done some acting, it was true—more modeling, if I am honest—but I wasn't a poet. That was just Johnny talking. The name, one I'd taken since coming to Rome, wasn't mine, either.

My real name was Vicki.

Vicki Wilson.

"We've met," said Paolo.

"Oh?"

The man's eyes went shy. He had black, unruly hair. The way he looked at me, dark eyed and glassy, as if he didn't quite know what to do with himself—I hadn't expected that.

"Not actually . . . but I saw you, at the Cinema Aventine," he explained. "So I've admired you from a distance . . ."

He was speaking of my brief appearance in a film by the Italian director Marino. It was a small role, won partly by chance: because of a night like this, some time back, stumbling into a casting director, a small, ruddy man I hadn't taken seriously at first. I looked the part, the man said. Or maybe it had something to do with the fact my husband was a writer, or had been once. Though I was American and my Italian could be clumsy, the audience had found the moment arresting. I had been written about in the expatriate newspapers and featured in *Roma*, one of the Italian gossip sites.

*Stellita*, they called me.

"Little star." Or "little knife." I was never quite sure of the translation.

In the scene my hair was pulled back from my face, and the camera lingered on the knowing expression in my character's eyes, the flirtatious engagement I held with the camera.

Like I said, it hadn't amounted to much. There'd been some modeling afterward, for an Italian department store, but that was all done.

WE WERE AT THE PURPLE Café, an American bar in the Testaccio district not far from the Circus Maximus. The Purple was an older place no longer in the guidebooks. Its heyday had passed, but the place could still come alive. Going there, you felt as if you had slipped back into another decade. I often felt like that. At the moment, a jazz group from Barcelona was playing.

My brother had gotten to know Orsini through one of his clients in Naples. Johnny did procurement work for a cruise line catering to wealthy travelers. He had his own reasons for introducing us, but I didn't mind. Orsini was somewhere in his forties, not young exactly, but a good deal younger than Frank, and I was flattered by his attention. The jazz played in the background, an old tune I couldn't quite recognize, mixed with something else, a fusion of sorts, the melody playing as if on the verge of falling apart. I could smell the crowd, the perspiration and the alcohol. Their smartphones glowed in the dark. It was a warm night, and people were looking at us, recognizing Orsini and muttering his name, his name and his wife's, about whom there were always stories.

Orsini touched my shoulder. I wore a strapless dress and turned at his touch.

"My husband . . ."

"What about him?"

"He should be here soon," I said. "He's a little late."

Orsini gave me a look. The shyness was gone. He had brown eyes, almost black. Every woman sees eyes like these on occasion—or imagines them in the shadows, like the eyes of those Italian boys down by the river. Most often, you don't look back.

This time was different.

It was one of those moments when you feel like you are meeting a familiar, someone you knew in another life, for better or worse, and are destined to know in this one, as well.

I saw myself from that place outside myself: standing there in my strapless dress, dark eyed and foolish, a little bit gangly.

"We should find a table?"

All this while my brother stood close by watching. He smiled at me in the way only Johnny could.

BECAUSE OF THE WAY JOHNNY and I are with each other, people make insidious comments. Nasty things I will leave to your imagination. It's always been that way, ever since we were kids. We touch, we hold hands, we go places together. You'd think the Italians, with their love of family, would understand this kind of thing, but their minds, too, roam the gutter.

There are reasons Johnny and I are so close.

We grew up in Houston, in one of those aging suburbs meant by the original developers to look like Palm Springs, except the houses were smaller, without central air, and the effect—of all those sharp angles hovering over the shrubbery—was of a place that didn't quite exist. We didn't fit in. We weren't Texans, not really. Our accents were wrong. Our mother was from a little town outside Chicago—a good family, she insisted—but Johnny's father had ditched out before he was born. Afterward, my mother married an oil engineer. That man was my father. I don't remember much about him—just a vague shape, a face hovering over me—but there were other men after. Some of those men were good to us, some weren't.

Like I said, there are reasons Johnny and I are so close.

My mother did what she could. She found money for private schools. When Johnny was older he had to go away for a while, but he caught up with me later, in Dallas, when I was in college.

That was where the incident occurred . . . that ugly business I didn't much want to think about . . .

It involved a young man, the close-cropped type you see at places like SMU . . . thick shoulders, gray eyes . . . polite on the surface, like all those Texas boys . . . *yes, ma'am, no, sir* . . . but brazen underneath . . . I was used to that, but this one, there was something off . . . Not in the usual way but somehow else . . . not entirely stable . . . Johnny brought him over after a long night in a bar, high as a kite . . . That's how I met him . . . His family had money. He liked to buy me things . . . jewelry . . . clothes . . . but eventually, well . . . He was obsessive and had a hard time letting go . . . He followed me to the grocery, to class . . . He paced around outside my apartment building . . . Johnny tried talking to him, telling him it was over, to let me be. They got pretty loud . . . pushing and shoving . . . The guy disappeared for a while . . . Then late one night he came back . . . he got into the building . . .

The maintenance woman found him the next morning, around dawn, heaped on the concrete, in the service alley six floors beneath my balcony.

There was a good deal of confusion about what had happened. Johnny and I weren't home when the police came by, not the first time. The girls next door, sorority sisters, said they'd heard noise in our apartment the night before, the sound of a scuffle, someone running down the hall. The forensics—the nature of the injuries, the shattering of the skull, the broken neck—together with the state of congealment—confirmed the impression that he'd fallen to his death from some sixty feet above, the distance from my balcony to the pavement, and that this had happened about two in morning. The lab tests showed alcohol in his blood, also Risperdal and amphetamines. The police found latents on my railing but of course there would be. He'd visited more than once. His parents were wealthy, like I said, and insisted on a full investigation.

Despite the sorority girls, the detectives could not put Johnny and I at the scene, not definitively. Meanwhile, the dead boy had a history. A key to my apartment he'd never returned. Manic episodes, suicidal behavior. He'd overjuked on his meds before, after a broken engagement, and driven his car into a pylon on the Galveston causeway. There was nothing to say he hadn't come unhinged again. Suicide: entering the apartment while I was gone and pitching himself from the balcony. Ultimately there was not enough evidence to prove either way. Even so, the investigation might have remained open if Frank Paris hadn't stepped forward, insisting that on the night in question my brother and I had been with him at his apartment. Frank had a position at the university then—a one-year post. The parents called him a liar. They were grief stricken and wanted to blame their son's death on someone. On Johnny and me, I guess, for luring him into our lives.

"This man," my mother said. "This Frank Paris. Just because he testified, it doesn't mean you owe him anything."

"He has an apartment in Rome."

"Rome?"

Her black eyes fluttered. She had a nice figure, my mother, more voluptuous than mine. She filled her dresses in way I'd always envied, ever since I was a child, but would never match.

"You've always been this way," she said. "Off in some world of your own. But you get yourself in these situations with men. And your brother, he . . ." She hesitated. "Your poor brother, he does his best to get you out."

I said nothing.

"This Frank Paris . . . a man his age . . . It might be good now," she said. "But in a few years . . ."

I understood where she was headed. Most men don't die all of a sudden but slowly, like old trees rotting from the inside—but I didn't care. After what had happened, I couldn't live in Dallas anymore, or even Houston. Texas society is a small town.

"I'm a pariah now."

"Don't worry. I'll fly out to see you."

"In Italy?"

"I'll visit you in Rome."

"His apartment is small."

"We can walk the Spanish Steps."

"Not right away."

"Pardon?"

I could hear in her voice the flat, sad sound of the midwestern town where she'd grown up.

"As soon as we get settled."

"I'm not planning to move in with you."

"I didn't mean it that way. I want you to come. I miss you already."

Maybe everyone feels this way after the fact, I don't know. Truth was I didn't miss her, at least not as much as I should have. Rather I felt her disappear into that empty space inside me, in the dark hollows, in one of her tight-fitting dresses that flattered her figure. Then one day my brother stopped by Frank's place in Rome, on the Campo de' Fiori, to tell me she'd died in a car accident along the Biloxi coast. She had been riding in a convertible with the top down, in the passenger seat, her latest husband behind the wheel.

"It's just us now," Johnny said.

"Poor Mama."

I didn't cry, not then. Johnny let loose and I petted him. He put his head against my chest. I stroked his hair. He could be very sweet, and I comforted him the best I could.

I SHOULD HAVE STEPPED AWAY then—from Paolo and my brother, that night at the Purple Café—but people at the tables nearby were cutting glances in our direction and bending their heads toward one another, whispering. Paolo Orsini attracted attention. He was a good-looking man whose face was often in the news, and in the scandal sheets, too. Much of the attraction had to do with the fact he was married to Isabella.

Maybe that attracted me, too.

Isabella was an actress, famous for her dark-eyed pout, her round cheeks, her role as the ingenue once upon a time, stumbling about the ruins in a tattered dress. She was older now, but her allure hadn't faded. She might no longer appear in American films, and Italian directors, too, might have abandoned her for younger stars, but the Italians themselves clung to her. At the same time, the tabloids relished Paolo's inconstancies.

The marriage was on the skids.

Paolo was a gigolo and a brute.

He had taken control of Isabella's estate, owned an interest in an online casino, and played silent partner in a construction firm controlled by the Mafia.

The truth of such stories was hard to know. The details of his life with Isabella were often contradictory.

"Over here—a table," said Johnny.

We started moving, the three of us, toward a table my brother had found in another corner of the room, and as we moved I felt myself stepping into some old-fashioned world—full of glamour and gossip, striped beach chairs and cocoa lotion and mint drinks in tall glasses. Gangsters in swimming trunks and sunglasses.

Johnny winked at me.

My brother had curly hair and soft eyes. Because of those eyes, he could communicate inexpressible things with a nod of his head. Though my brother had his flaws, he watched out for me. We had that bond. I looked where he was looking and saw Frank Paris making his way across the room. Frank hadn't spotted us yet. The way he walked, his posture, you could tell Frank was American. He wore a white shirt open at the collar, and jeans. He was a vigorous man but these last months that vigor had started to fade. He'd been drinking more, slipping into old habits, gambling.

His face still held that wry smile.

I made room for him at the table.

"What kept you?"

"Correspondence."

"Business?" my brother asked. His eyes met mine. Johnny knew about Frank's money problems.

"An old friend," Frank said. "E-mail. That's all."

"I hear you are a famous writer," Paolo said. "Your brother-in-law has told me all about you."

When he was younger, Frank had written a novel about a young man who ruined himself gambling on horses. It was a book of an autobiographical nature, neglected in America but adored by the French, who'd made it into a movie that had a lingering reputation. The interest in horses was something Paolo and

Frank shared. Paolo kept a small stable outside his villa in Florence and owned a stallion who had run in the Palio di Siena a few years earlier.

"The stallion is a handsome animal," Paolo said. "You should see him."

"I'd like to ride him."

Paolo hesitated. "He can be hard to handle."

"I wouldn't worry about Frank. He grew up around horses," said Johnny. He often flattered Frank a little too much, overdoing it. "And anyway, he's quite the famous writer.".

"Just the one book," said Frank.

"And influential with the Roman clergy."

"Hardly," said Frank.

"What do you mean?" asked Paolo.

"Cardinal Whiting is his uncle."

"Well, then, perhaps he will make me pope," said Paolo.

We laughed then, and Frank Paris laughed too—though uncomfortably, since his uncle was an embarrassment to him, a public moralizer, influential in certain circles but with a worldview inimical to his own.

People watched us. They recognized Paolo, and I wondered if anyone recognized me as well, from my small role or my pictures in the magazines, in fashion advertisements. These latter had shown me in the guise of a poet—somewhat ridiculous, wearing long-sleeved, billowing blouses—and the ads included snippets from my imaginary journal. The campaign had been well displayed, and I thought for a second I heard my name whispered. I wondered if Paolo and I would be an item in the gossips tomorrow, if someone here would snap our picture.

"I'll be having a get-together in a few weeks," said Paolo.

His eyes stayed fixed on my husband, but he was addressing me, I thought. He wanted to see me again.

The music grew more chaotic. I felt it inside me. The violet light spilled over the small stage and onto the audience. I felt that, too. A couple started making out at a table nearby, showing off. Orsini was watching me and I felt something brush against my knee. I started to look up surreptitiously—to catch the look in Orsini's eyes—but just as I did so my husband reached down into my lap, curling his hand about my fingers.

# 3.

I HAVE A TABLET HERE on the Avenida. When I type in my name, the past, imagined or otherwise, rushes back. Pictures of myself on blogs, in news feeds, many taken without my knowledge, from unfamiliar angles, with scarce resemblance. Though some of these women are me, others are falsely labeled.

*Isabella* . . .

Lying with one cheek pressed to the floor, lips parted, eyes open, glazed like the surface of some forgotten lake. Hair mussed. A dark tendril splitting her forehead, curling across her bruised face.

In the stories of her death, my name is mentioned, and Johnny's, too. We're not innocent of everything . . . I don't pretend that . . . we were typical tourists . . . glamour struck. . . enamored of the surface of things . . . but there were others more brutal.

There had been another man there that night at the Purple Café. Maybe I had noticed him then—sitting in one of those stiffed-back chairs, drinking at one of the tables that lined the rear wall. The Purple was not a large place. Over the course of an evening, the clientele had a chance to look one another over pretty well. It was part of the design of the place, part of the attraction. He was a wide-shouldered man—sharply dressed, with a loose-lipped smile and a black, penetrating glance. He had a receding hairline and wore his hair slicked back. Though I didn't pay so much attention to him at the time, he saw me. If I'm to believe this little device.

These pictures, these scrawls of light in the dark . . .

The man's name . . .

Ernesto Lodovico.

A bodyguard in Orsini's service.

Ordinarily assigned to Isabella.

He watched over Paolo Orsini that night, on surveillance, filling in because the staff was shorthanded. Beneath the surface, there was a conflict of loyalties—and a growing enmity. I didn't know any of this then, just as I didn't catch the contempt in the man's eyes. I listened to my brother as he took me aside and leaned me delicately against the tavern wall. We had an intimacy between us, as brother and sister, in the way we chatted and touched.

"Orsini's quite smitten with you."

"I'm flattered. But I'm a married woman."

"He's married, too."

"So it can't come to anything."

"Of course not," my brother said.

"I wouldn't want it to."

"Of course you wouldn't."

"No. I wouldn't."

"But you will come to his party? There will be beautiful people there." Johnny laughed. His eyes shone. "And Isabella. Whom I'm sure you want to meet."

# 4.

THE APARTMENT WHERE I LIVED with Frank was at the edge of the Campo de' Fiori. The building was an old palazzo gone to seed, constructed on the site of the ancient Theater of Pompey—where Caesar was assassinated. Somewhere beneath the oldest part of the building, there had been caves that once housed a statue of Venus. The caves were history now, backfilled with mud and crumbling marble. Our apartment felt cramped even by Italian standards, and the plumbing was bad.

It was the evening of Orsini's party. We were supposed to go—I'd promised Johnny—but Frank looked pretty battered. He'd been drinking the night before, alone, and I'd found him asleep on the bed when I'd come home.

"Last night," he said now. "What time did you get in?"

I didn't answer. We'd been through this already.

"This shirt," I said. "This one, the color is good on you."

It was rust colored, nice material, with an Italian collar. He buttoned it partway and regarded himself in the glass: an old-fashioned panel mirror he'd bought for me, and to give the room some extra dimension.

"The shirt hangs well."

"I stink," he said. "I smell like a goat."

"All the men in Italy smell like goats."

There was some truth to this. It was only Americans who showered four times a day.

"You should go without me."

"Don't be silly . . . just wear cologne."

"You are bored of me." His hands were shaking.

I poured him a drink.

"Your brother . . . he says I should play hard to get."

"You talk to my brother about us?"

"Who else should I speak to?"

"Me, I suppose."

I didn't have any makeup on, so my eyes were unadorned, my lips pale. I have wide eyes and high cheekbones, and my body is thin and angular. Without makeup I can look very much younger than I am, childlike and boyish. My looks at such times affected him deeply, I knew; he'd told me so himself. And I'd seen pictures of his first wife and daughter, both estranged. I resembled the girl when she was young.

"I'm completely dedicated to you," I said.

"Not completely."

"Yes, completely."

"You're only flattering me."

"No," I insisted.

I lowered my head and felt the empty space inside me. I looked deep down into it but couldn't see anything. I had a million desires, but I couldn't name them, they all vanished—all except the ugliest, the kind you can't admit—and suddenly the only thing I wanted was to get away. Frank studied me in the mirror. I smiled, a warm smile. I could see myself in the glass: my brown eyes, the sudden shyness, the crook of my lips.

"I'm completely dedicated to you," I said again.

"You own me."

"Don't be absurd."

"I'm possessed by you."

"I think it's quite the opposite."

"Once a person possesses something, it's easy to lose interest. Maybe that's how it is with us."

My blouse was half-undone. I stood facing the mirror, hand on hip, and Frank studied me from behind. The blouse was an older one. A new one, from Biagotti, lay on the bed.

"Your brother says—"

"Oh, Johnny says a lot of things, you know that. It's just because he wants someone to go to the races with him."

They'd been doing that lately, playing the odds on the horses. Johnny liked to gamble, too. He and Frank had that in common.

"Does it bother you?"

"No, it's just—yesterday our credit was denied. Down at Biagiotti. I didn't want to say anything."

He glanced at the open carton on the bed, the new blouse inside its tissue.

"You got something."

"A new blouse. But there was a skirt, too. And some other things I put back."

"I'm sorry . . . our finances . . . "

"I don't care about the clothes," I insisted.

This wasn't exactly true. I loved the touch of new clothes . . . different outfits . . . Frank knew this . . . He enjoyed it, too, watching me in front of the mirror, posing. It was something we did.

"Your brother's a fool for the horses."

"Did you lose money?"

"I might lose sometimes, but in the long run . . ." He paused. "Johnny says there are some beautiful trails in Tuscany—out by Orsini's stables. I wouldn't mind getting on a horse again. They've got that stallion, the one that ran at Siena."

Johnny had been working for Orsini lately, traveling back and forth from Reggio, down in the toe of the country, in the lower part of the boot. In between these excursions, he'd been hanging out a lot with Frank. I knew Johnny, and I wondered what he was up to.

I thought of that boy back in Dallas, the one who had tumbled over my balcony railing.

I thought of the inquest, and the police, and how the incident hadn't happened exactly as we'd described.

I thought of the boy's body crumpled on the sidewalk.

Maybe Frank was thinking of all that, too. Or maybe he was just thinking of his ex-wife. Of the daughter who wanted nothing to do with him.

"You love your brother."

"Of course."

"I'm fond of him, too. He's been a friend to me. More than that—like a son."

I picked up the blouse that had finished off our credit at Biagiotti. Like most beautiful things, it was simple, really, the way it was cut, how it hung.

"I should take it back."

"No."

"But—"

"Put it on," Frank said.

When he kissed me, I closed my eyes. It was a tender kiss, but Frank watched me the whole while. Most men, when they look at you like that, while you kiss, it's not you they see but the thing in their imaginations. I pulled him close.

"Last night . . ." he said.

"I went for a walk."

"You were out for a while."

"The blouse," I said, pulling away. "Let me put it on. And you can tell me how I look."

# 5.

FTER ISABELLA'S DEATH, THE INVESTIGATION kept coming back to that evening at Palazzo Orsini. Though evidence was thin, the investigators sought to establish motive, a connection. It was a sensational case, and people wanted to know about the events leading up to Isabella's death, to that moment when she was found lying bruised on the tile in her blue silk.

There was a lot of speculation.

I have read accounts of my own behavior that evening. It's true I followed Isabella into the garden, as people say. And I was flirtatious, maybe, with her husband, and foolish, and perhaps my blouse slipped off my shoulder, and the champagne went too much to my head.

It's also true Frank and I exchanged words on the pavement before entering, when he asked once again where I'd been the evening before.

"I was with my brother," I said. "I told you."

"No, you didn't."

"Yes, I did."

Whether that comforted him and whether he believed me, I don't know. He was jealous of Johnny sometimes—of the closeness between us—but afterward he would feel silly. Once we got inside the party, the issue vanished. Johnny and Frank talked like the best of friends and left me to mingle on my own.

THOUGH THE PLACE BRIMMED WITH celebrity, I didn't recognize the names, not then. I didn't know the man leaning against the fireplace was Jimmy Luciano, grandson of the American gangster. Or that the man talking to him was Alberto Fadini, a cabinet minister whose father had served under Mussolini. A number of Italian actors milled about the room, and also some directors with young women, aspiring actresses on the arms of older men. The director von Stromberg had a French girl with him, and Francesco Olivetti, the typewriter heir, boasted a runway model from Milan. There was Johnny Marco, the star of the new Coppola movie, and a British director by the name of James Mawk whom the Italian Film Commission hoped might use Studio Cinecittà as the central shooting location for his new project. Mawk was working on a series about ancient Rome for an American network, and he had a coterie of aspiring cast members around him. I didn't pay too much attention to any of these, though. Because at the edge of his coterie stood Isabella, dark haired, alone, holding a glass of champagne. She had a smoldering beauty. She stood alone, though there was a sense in which she was never alone, not the way people watched her. She held herself straight, shoulders back—in that way beautiful women do. She bowed her head to sip from the glass, and her lips left a stain on the rim.

When she looked up, her eyes seemed very bright. Our glances met then—mine and Isabella's.

I might have approached her, but a man stood just behind her, and the man gave me pause. This was the bodyguard, Lodovico, from that night at the Purple Café. He was a sharp-faced man with receding black hair. He wore it slicked back. He was well dressed and might have been good-looking except for the ugliness about his mouth and the familiar way he looked me over, full of derision. He tilted his head toward Isabella as if giving her confidential information. Isabella burst into laughter.

"That man," I told my brother.

"Which?"

"The one with Isabella."

"Yes?"

"He was mocking me."

"Poor sister."

"And now you mock me, too."

"No," my brother said. "That's not how I meant it."

He explained then something of how it was with Lodovico. He was rash and ill-tempered. He had a violent history and other traits—a menacing demeanor, a connection to the underworld—things Orsini maybe had found useful at one time, but now made his presence more problematic. Worse, lately he'd begun to ingratiate himself with Isabella at Orsini's expense.

"He's dangerous."

"He makes me nervous"

"I'll tell Paulo."

"No."

"You're not the only one," he said. "The way he eyes the guests . . . Also, he has a fetish . . . stilettos . . . knives . . ."

My brother went over to Orsini, and later I saw Paolo take the bodyguard aside. The two men didn't care for each other. If circumstances had been different, things might have grown ugly. In the end Lodovico left the party, and I was glad to see him go. Maybe I let my pleasure show in my face as he walked by me, I don't know. I might have been more cautious if I had known I would run into Lodovico again before the night was over.

Isabella walked the other way, through the portico doors into the garden beyond.

I REMEMBER WATCHING HER ON television, in Houston, in the back room that smelled of the air conditioner, while outside the landscape sweltered and baked. My mother and I watched a lot of movies. It was our way of escape, of being together. Isabella struck a chord with me even then. Sometimes I'd think of her when I was outside, sitting in the grass, the chiggers biting. I'd think of Isabella in that bedraggled dress with her torn stockings, standing in the dust—as she had looked once upon a time—playing the lost ingenue in a sentimental movie that showed over and over on afternoon cable. The movie had been made several years before I was born, almost thirty years ago, when Isabella was barely twenty.

Part of me back then had wanted to be her, I guess. Or what I had imagined her to be. Maybe that was still true.

I went through the portico and found her in the garden, smoking a cigarette. She wore a blouse in an old Venetian style with the bodice cut square. Her figure was fuller than mine, more voluptuous. Her eyes were darker, warmer. She looked at me appraisingly, as if she had seen the likes of me before and there was no reason to ask me what I wanted, or why I was approaching her, because she already knew. She had seen me before in a hundred guises.

"Do you have a cigarette?" I asked.

"You don't look like a smoker."

"I shouldn't. But I enjoy it so."

I smoked on occasion, but I didn't have any real passion for it. I wasn't an addict, not yet, but I enjoyed how the smoke spiraled upward, off the edge of my fingers, through the branches overhead. We smoked under an arbor hedged with wild roses.

"This rose," I said. "It's beautiful."

"It's red."

"The petals—the touch is very soft to the fingers. And the color—"

"I see the color."

"It's just so beautiful."

"Impatient?"

"I don't know what you mean."

"I think you do. Regardless, it will wilt and die."

"It's still on the branch."

"The oil from your fingers will kill the petals."

Isabella drew hard on her cigarette. The gesture accentuated the sharpness of her jaw and narrowed the lines about her mouth. I could see up close the fine spidering around her eyes. I saw her age. It didn't matter. When she let the smoke out, the way she turned her head in profile—she was devastating in her beauty.

"Well, I suppose everything shares the same fate," I said. "Except Rome, of course. Rome is eternal."

"No," she said. "Rome is dead. In all the important ways."

Behind us, the stones creaked. It was my brother. Isabella reached down and crushed her cigarette into a flowerpot. I did the same, imitating her, and felt a sudden craving for another.

"Yes, Rome is quite dead," said Johnny.

The sentiment was fashionable in certain circles, and Johnny was aware of that. More than once, we'd heard artists and writers complain about the very things that brought so many people to the city. All the ancient art, the massive efforts at restoration, the eternal focus on what had been done in the past—it was too much, they claimed. It stifled them. It made it impossible to do anything new.

"But I don't mind the dead," Johnny said.

"No?"

"They were hard workers," he said, gesturing at our surroundings. "And they left such beautiful things behind."

My brother looked Isabella up and down. He was a flirt, my brother. Everyone in Rome flirted. Isabella regarded him with a mix of suspicion and pleasure, the way people often regarded Johnny. My brother had that softness in the eyes, that smile.

"What do you do for my husband, exactly?"

"I keep people happy."

"You're just a boy."

"I'm thirty years old."

"A man, then."

"I'm helping with Stazione di Uzio."

Uzio Station was a public-works project—part of the Milan-Bologna railway—for which Orsini controlled the contracts. I didn't know it then, but Johnny had taken the place of Paolo's brother-in-law as an unofficial go-between, working with contractors—people with their own interests, of course—whom he had gotten to know through his work in Naples. The brother-in-law had proved himself unreliable, and greedy. Meanwhile Johnny was good at that kind of thing, moving in back channels.

"And this is my sister," my brother said. "Isn't she beautiful?"

Isabella reached out to touch my cheek. An affectionate gesture, almost, that reduced me to a child. I saw her beauty—the mole on her cheek, the sintered lips, the almond eyes.

"This is the little poet?"

She was mocking me—though not without sympathy, I thought. She had done plenty of silly ad work over the years.

"I have other aspirations."

Maybe that was the wrong thing to say. All I'd really wanted when I left Texas was to get out. And maybe a chance to be someone else. Who that might be . . .

I cast my eyes toward Isabella.

"The British director, Mawk—he's casting," said Isabella.

"I know," I said shyly. It came to me then—or maybe it had been on my mind all along—that Isabella might have some influence with him: that she saw something of herself in me, and that was the reason I had come here, why my brother had brought me to Orsini's attention.

"But you can forget about Mawk."

"Pardon?"

"You're closer to the age he likes, but he'll never cast you."

She paused.

"You have the wrong accent." The beat felt deliberate, like she'd contemplated the effect. "It's an American series. And Americans like their Romans to sound like Brits."

I felt the hot flush on my cheeks. I was embarrassed. I realized this was what she had intended. It was why Isabella had talked to me—so that she might dismiss me in just this way.

"Excuse me," she said.

She went to Paolo, and I watched them mingle as a couple. I watched his hand brush over her, running down her body. *A mindless gesture*, I told myself. Even as he touched her, he glanced my way.

Isabella and Paolo looked quite graceful together, quite beautiful. I felt a stir of envy. I felt desperate, as if I'd just discovered, just that moment, what I'd always wanted, and in that same moment it had all slipped away. Paolo and Isabella were talking to the director now. I saw Isabella's charm. Her hands were on her hips. Her head flashed back as she laughed. Her eyes were full of light.

# 6.

MURDER POSSESSES A RITUAL DIMENSION. Certain things are predictable, but not always. Human nature is infinite, complex, and there are random elements. This is what a homicide detective told me later, an American woman from Los Angeles—part Chinese, part Anglo, very crisp in her dark-blue suit—who was an expert in such matters. For people who take pleasure in killing, she told me, there's a pattern, a signature. Often the signatures are apparent, the same thing with every victim: dismemberment, a bashed head, a staged accident, suffocation, poison, a knife in the heart. Other times, the cause of death is dissimilar, at least on the surface. The killer varies the modus operandi, either deliberately or because something situational demands improvisation. The detectives look for hidden similarities, connections, motivations. An accomplice, maybe, who takes secret pleasure in things she pretends not to know. Or a professional working for pay. Even when everything falls into place—when all the clues align—the investigation sometimes fails. Like anyone, the detective admitted, we police have blind spots. We are susceptible to certain influences, pressures. We see what is convenient to see.

# 7.

THE NIGHT EVAPORATED, SLIPPING AWAY. Across the room, Orsini mingled with his guests. I watched him, how he moved, how he talked, and he watched me back. There wasn't much pretense about it. He watched the way I sat myself down in an overstuffed chair, folding my legs up beneath my skirt. Isabella had vanished from the party. Frank lingered in the adjoining room, caught up in conversation about the Palio, about the betting odds and the horses.

My brother sat next to me. He was high. He toyed with my hair like he sometimes did, and I tilted my head against his shoulder. I still stung from my encounter with Isabella, but I took comfort in the champagne and in my blouse from Biagiotti, the feel of it, the sheer material. I liked how the fabric caught the light. I caught a glimpse of Frank in the next room talking with some redhead in a green dress, and I caught, too, fragments of a conversation closer by, between Orsini and his hangers-on. The men lobbied for a card game to take place upstairs.

My brother nodded toward the redhead.

"Frank's quite popular with the ladies."

"I see that."

"A dowager."

"She doesn't look like a dowager to me."

"She has money, at least. See her jewelry."

"Maybe it's not her money."

"She seems to like your husband."

The redhead was older than me, though not too much older. She wore pumps to match her dress. I'd seen her earlier with the grandson of the American mobster.

Orsini moved to the landing above.

"Your face is red," said my brother.

"No."

"Beet red. Why do you suppose?"

"I've no idea."

My brother motioned again toward the redhead flirting with my husband. "Perhaps you have emotions you don't admit to. Your jealousy rises to your face."

"Stop it."

"I've hit something tender."

"Don't be silly."

If my face was red, it was on account of the champagne. That's what I told myself. Or the warmth of the room. Or because Orsini watched from the landing above.

"You shouldn't be too angry with your husband, though. He's taken up this strategy on my advice."

"What strategy is that?"

"You notice he hasn't been hanging by your side."

"We had words."

"I reassured him. And made a few suggestions."

"You've been tutoring him."

"Sometimes men need reminding. It's in the nature of women to want what they can't have."

"Not just women."

"No. Senators, too."

"And yourself?" I asked. "What do you want?"

My brother made no answer, but I knew him well enough. When we were younger he had arranged dates for me with his friends, boys several years older than me. I liked the attention. For Johnny, it was a way of moving in circles wealthier than our own and receiving small favors in return. A car for the evening. A jacket. A weekend house on Galveston Island. I rarely found these boys amusing for long, and to be honest my brother took pleasure in that. In stringing the boys along after I had broken it off, watching them become more and more morose, entangled in their obsession, until finally he, too, would walk away, leaving them with no avenue back. It had been something similar with that boy in Dallas.

"I told Frank he should stay here tonight. Play late at cards."

"And me?"

My brother leaned close.

"The senator . . ."

"Yes?"

"Come with me."

He winked at me again—and smiled in a way I remembered from when we were young and alone together in our house, and my mother was out with one of her men. Frank saw us get up. We went down the hall, away from him—and away from Orsini, too. My brother took me by the arm in his confidential way, speaking in half whispers and innuendos, saying that the senator could only play cards for so long. When he was done, he'd leave the guests to continue without him. And the senator himself . . .

"The palazzo is full of rooms. Guest rooms, of course. Also rooms for lingering. Rooms with velvet couches. It's easy enough to find privacy, even with a house full of guests."

"And Isabella?"

"She's gone for the evening."

Something about that didn't seem right to me—vanishing from your own party. Then Frank appeared at the other end of the hall. It was a long hall, not very well lit. I let my brother pull me along the corridor, around the corner and into a parlor. He took me by the shoulders. He had an expression I'd seen before— boyish, insistent. His eyes glowed.

"What is it?" I asked. "What are you trying to say?"

We heard Frank, closer now.

In a fit of silliness—a giddy moment, as if we were children again—I let Johnny push me into the parlor closet with the visitors' coats: the synthetic furs and the leather and the erotic smell of perfumed silk. He closed the door and left me alone, hunched in the dark. I felt dizzy from the champagne. I reached for the handle but then heard Frank's voice:

"Where is she?"

"Who?"

"My wife."

"She went to freshen up," said my brother. "And to call a taxi."

Whether he had thought the story up that minute or planned it out in advance, I had no idea—but my brother enjoyed this kind of thing. To play the go-between, to improvise.

"She's jealous," said Johnny.

"But why?"

"She expects to be the center of attention. You know how she is."

"They invited me to cards."

"Then play. And let my sister pout."

I considered coming out of the closet to end the whole business, but our apartment back on the Campo was so small and hot, claustrophobic in the Italian style, cluttered with bric-a-brac. The walls were lined with books. Musty books, falling apart in their jackets. Moravia and Camus and the *Confessions of Saint Augustine*. I had read them, or parts of them, but the thought of lying in that bed, in that room of ancient books with their deteriorating spines . . .

"You know how it is," Johnny said.

"I'm afraid I don't."

"The secret, I tell you, is to lock yourself from her. Only then will she spread herself open."

"But for who?"

Frank was drunk. The way the sound carried, it seemed the voices came from within the closet itself. Then there was a thump at the door. I jumped, but it was only my brother, thumping for emphasis as he spoke.

"Take my advice," he said. "And you will lie in a bed stuffed with turtle feathers."

My brother raised his voice, waxing poetic. When he was a boy, my mother had imprisoned him in theater classes. He had talent as a mimic—affecting an archaic tone.

"Who are you quoting?"

"No one but myself."

"You're lying"

"Listen to me, and your love will come to you. You will swoon in perfumed linen like a goose smothered in roses."

"*Ha, ha.*"

"Like a pig smothered in oil."

"I like the first better. But are you talking to me, or to the closet?"

"What do you mean?"

"The way you're standing, so close to the door."

"I'm speaking to the coats," he said. "Would you like to see?"

I feared my brother might pull the door open and leave me exposed, hunched absurdly in the closet. It was the type of thing he might do just for the spectacle.

"Don't weaken."

"No."

"Don't worry," my brother said. "These are rich men. With money to burn. Play, if that's what you want. Vicki will get over it."

I understood, I thought, the general intent of my brother's plan. He meant to separate Frank and me—to give me time with Orsini. I could have stopped it simply by stepping out of the closet, but I thought of Paolo's dark eyes, watching from the landing above. I stayed tucked away until my brother and Frank Paris finished talking and only then walked down the long hall back into the central room. Orsini and the remaining guests observed my entrance. Before I could get close, my brother caught me by the arm, speaking under his breath, something about a gate, a wooden gate, down the Vicolo del Gallo. *Go there and I'll let you in.* He spoke as a ventriloquist might. His lips barely moved. *The gate on Vicolo del Gallo.* Then he spoke more openly, for all to hear.

"Your taxi is here," Johnny said to me.

I scrutinized Frank.

"The taxi," Johnny repeated.

Frank stood with his wry smile, his battered nose, a glass of whiskey in his hand.

"Are you coming?" I asked.

Frank bowed his head, scrutinizing his glass. I saw how it was. He wanted to come home with me, but the cards tempted him, and the whiskey, and maybe the redhead, too. More than that, he'd already promised, and he had no choice but to play it out. The redhead smiled, and Jimmy Luciano, the grandson of the American gangster—he smiled, too. No doubt her jewels had come from him. And no doubt the man had no intention of losing anything that belonged to him.

I kissed Frank good-bye.

Outside, there was no taxi. Nor could I find the gate my brother had mentioned.

# 8.

I SHOULDN'T HAVE LEFT THE party alone. It's easy for a foreigner to get turned around in Rome, especially at night, in the old part of the city. Mount Giordano, where Orsini lived, was a maze of narrow alleys and gray walls atop an old hill that had been mounded up by hand around the time of the Crucifixion. The area had been built over many times since. During the day, specialty shops were open along here, but these stood shuttered now. The walls of old palazzos and their aging tenements slouched one against the other.

I still couldn't find the gate.

I might have tried retracing my steps back to the main entrance of the palazzo, back to the party—but I didn't want to appear foolish. So I decided to find my way to the Corso Vittorio, where I might hail a taxi home.

The street narrowed to an alley, then narrowed again. Something skittered in the shadows. Rome was notorious for its feral cats living in the old ruins and the alleys, under bushes, inside gutter pipes, and tucked between walls. This was different. The animal let out a small yelp, not very catlike, and presented itself in a patch of gray light. It was one of those small dogs that had been popular for a while, a toy dog tiny enough to fit in your purse: a bug-eyed creature, hungry and without a collar. Lost, maybe, or abandoned by one of the street peddlers who hawked the ones without pedigrees. I cooed at the little beast, trying to make friends, but that only agitated him. I tried to walk by. He kept at it, yelping and nipping. Finally I lunged toward him and he scuttled back, teeth bared, barking, his chest puffed and his feet clattering on the stones. I hurried by. He followed, darting at my heels—then suddenly fell silent, his attention distracted by some bit of offal.

The alley darkened ahead.

I was lost.

I walked until I came to a small piazza, dimly lit, where I heard people talking. Voices fell silent. Two men lingered at a table. I hesitated because I know how men regard women alone in such situations, especially a woman dressed as I was dressed, stuttering along the cobblestones in her heels.

There was a church in this small piazza—and, as it happened, another dog, a bit larger than my little friend, nosing behind the pillars.

I asked for directions.

The men looked at me stupidly.

"I just came from a party. At Senator Orsini's."

I emphasized the name, thinking it might offer some security. But as soon as I spoke, I realized my mistake. Something in the way the men shifted, their change of posture. The moonlight stark against their faces. The one closest to me was a lanky marionette of a man, unnaturally thin. The second man, the one in the back, with his chair tilted precariously against the wall . . . the high forehead . . . the slicked hair . . . the slack-jawed smile that wasn't really a smile at all . . .

I recognized him even in this light.

I laughed awkwardly. It was because I was afraid, that laugh, and because I hoped somehow I was mistaken. The coincidence of it—of running into Lodovico, Isabella's bodyguard . . .

My little dog reappeared, scampering onto the church steps. He paid me no mind but rather greeted the other dog, putting his nose up its private parts. The two of them continued snuffling along the church wall.

"So you've left the party?"

His tone was menacing, and the other man shifted in his chair, the metal legs grinding against the stone. A door lay open behind them, a dim light tumbling out. I had thought it might be a café, but I saw from the clutter it was one of those ground-floor apartments in which building managers sometimes live, together with the furnace and the brooms.

"Do you have a rendezvous?"

I didn't answer. Stumbling on him like this made me uncomfortable, and I wondered about the circumstances. Maybe he lived here, in this quarter. Or he had come here to drink with his friend, to have a bite to eat. There could be no explanation other than happenstance, but that didn't reassure me. The other man, his companion—the lanky one, the marionette, with his shirt buttoned to the collar—had seemed at first the less threatening of the two. But the way he looked at me now, up and down, in the lascivious way of Italian men, didn't give me a lot of comfort. They spoke in a southern dialect I couldn't follow entirely, though I gathered they talked about me: I was all but certain I heard my name, spoken in the language of the gutter, my name and Paolo Orsini's, uttered in a drunken chuckle; and the name of my brother, who was being called a faggot and a pimp.

"I understand everything you say," I said. The men fell silent. I was lying, but they didn't know that. "And I know who you are."

I heard the Corso in the distance. The dogs, closer by, snuffled against the church wall.

"Come here," the guard said.

"You are Lodovico."

He called me a name, in Italian first. Then English.

"You are a cunt," he said. "You and your brother, you are both cunts."

I responded in English with a common vulgarity.

Lodovico started to his feet, and I slipped on my heels. It could be that my clumsiness saved me. The dogs began barking and the men stopped in their tracks. They laughed. I scampered to my feet and they laughed even more, calling to me obscenely, and the dogs laughed in their own way—yowling and nipping, snapping at my heels—until a man bellowed from an upstairs window. Like that, the noise let off.

I hurried up the alley. I paused to listen for footsteps, but I heard only my heart in my chest. I had no idea where I was. I recognized nothing. Then I came on a street name, carved in brick, on a corner illuminated by a small lamp:

### Vicolo del Gallo

I had come full circle. Here was the palazzo, there the narrow alley, and in this direction the foot passage that led around to the gate. I found it unlocked, just as my brother had promised. Johnny waited on a garden bench not far from where I'd stood earlier with Isabella. Up above, the men were playing cards, and their voices echoed down. I hadn't been gone as long as I'd thought.

"Dogs," I spat.

"The men upstairs?"

"Them, too. But that's not what I meant."

I told him about my encounter with Lodovico. My brother tried to reassure me. The man lived nearby with his cronies, but he wouldn't be around much longer. There would be charges against him soon, on an old matter recently come to light. "He'll deny involvement . . . he'll cast blame elsewhere," Johnny said, "but it doesn't matter . . . Italy is so corrupt . . . the people who hired him . . . My guess, with their assistance, he'll escape the country rather than face charges"

"What did he do?"

"He murdered his former employer," Johnny said, "a powerful man, in his bedroom in Palermo . . . he was paid by the man's enemies . . . to infiltrate security . . ."

"Orsini knew about this?"

"Not at first."

"And Isabella . . . ?"

"Don't worry about her. She takes care of herself," Johnny said. He hesitated. "Would you like to see her where she sleeps?"

I didn't understand. Upstairs there was the sound of laughter, the men at their game. My husband's laugh was louder than the others. It wasn't a happy laugh.

"He must be losing," I said.

"You are shivering."

"The street . . . those men . . ."

Johnny put his arm around my shoulders, comforting me, full of sympathy, taking me under the arbor to a stone building on the other side of the garden.

# 9.

YEARS BEFORE, THE COTTAGE HAD been the palazzo's kitchen. There'd been fewer buildings inside the walls then, and the pigs and chickens had wandered where the flower garden was now and been slaughtered on stone slabs inside. Some time after that, the slaughter kitchen had been remade into a servants' house, and later remade again, into quarters for an illegitimate daughter of one of the Renaissance popes. Despite its history, the interior was nice enough, a bedroom with slatted shades and windows opening onto the garden. We could still hear the men at cards, though more faintly. My brother lowered the shades.

He had a bottle of champagne. And some cocaine as well.

"Are you trying to seduce me?"

It was a joke, one my brother understood. He put his head on my shoulder. We'd grown up in close quarters as children, often sleeping in the same room. With my mother gone so much—forever with a different man—we'd learned to take comfort in each other's presence.

"This is Isabella's room?"

"When she's in Rome. Sometimes."

"They don't sleep together?"

My brother shrugged. "Who knows what people do? She also keeps a suite at the hotel. As it happens, the British director is staying there, too."

"She's too old for the Brit."

"That doesn't stop anyone."

"She's hoping for a role herself. That's why she was so unkind to me." I examined the room. "This must be hers?"

I'd picked up a case by a wicker chair. Inside, I found jeweled containers filled with expensive makeup. My brother shrugged again, in his loose-jointed way. "It doesn't matter to her. She's got more waiting wherever she goes. And people to send fetch."

The closet here held only part of her wardrobe, my brother explained. She had more upstairs in the main house. And more in Florence.

"A woman like her—every day is a photo shoot, whether she likes it or not. She's flying to New York in a few days to help with the marketing of some perfume."

A blouse hung from a hook nearby, along with a pair of velveteen pants. I recognized this as the outfit she'd had on at the party. I imagined her looking in the mirror as she changed: a body like my mother's at the same age. I picked up her blouse, examining the delicate stitching, and then buried my nose in the expensive cloth, taking in the smell of her.

Isabella had fine taste in clothes and spent considerable time in Milan, judging from the labels. One piece caught my attention more than the others: a rather simple dress, a shift all but identical to the one she'd worn in one of her early films—the movie everyone remembered—in which she'd played an artistically inclined young vagabond wandering the countryside, taken in by this man and that, the dress growing more tattered with each adventure until eventually she was found frozen in a ditch.

"This can't be the original."

"There was more than one. You know movie people. The scenes were shot out of order—there were multiple copies of that dress. That one hung in mothballs down in Studio Cinecittà."

"For how long?"

"They gave it to her recently. In a ceremony promoting the rerelease. But her body, you know, has changed."

"More pear-shaped."

"The dress wouldn't quite zip in the back."

I stood before the mirror and held the dress in front of me. I could see it would fit me fine. That it would hang on me as it had hung on Isabella all those years ago.

"Put it on."

"No."

"Why not?"

"I should go. If I can get a taxi . . ."

"You'd look good in that dress."

"It's Isabella's."

"She wasn't so pretty as you at the same age. When she tried it on recently, it looked a bit vulgar. But on you . . ."

"I should go home."

"It's very late—and getting a taxi, well, as you know . . ."

"If she should return . . ."

There are moments in every life, I guess . . . moments when you can turn this way or that . . . Whether the direction one turns is determined by inner substance or by circumstance, by fate, I don't pretend to know . . . Though it's true, I suppose, that if Isabella had been more gracious with me at the party . . . if Frank

Paris hadn't behaved in such a way . . . if there'd been no yelping dogs on the street that night . . . no strangers casting surly remarks in the piazza . . .

My brother touched my arm.

"Try it on."

The dress would look good on me, it was true. I undid my blouse and stood a moment in my bra, my brother watching. Then I slipped the dress over my head. Johnny poured some champagne.

I regarded myself in the mirror. It was a modest shift, very simple, that tapered at the waist. I looked a little younger in it, more innocent, boyish.

He took out his jar and laid two crystalline lines by the lamp.

"For you."

"I don't want to set a bad example."

"Then I'll set one for myself. And I'll be the bad example." He did what people do with cocaine.

"Adjust the light," he said.

I liked the dress. It was a soft material, very thin, and I enjoyed watching myself in the mirror. My brother enjoyed watching me, too. He had used to do the same thing when I dressed in my mother's outfits. Now he studied me from the door as I sat on the edge of the bed, legs crossed, posing in the famous dress. I bent over some fresh lines by the lamp and took them up my nose. I lay back on the bed, feeling my body, electric in the warm light. The champagne and the cocaine together made a nice sensation. I felt both inside the moment and outside it at the same time. I felt as if I were glowing there on top of the bed.

My brother came toward me and we sat together, close by, shoulders touching, our backs against the headboard.

"We are orphans," he said.

"Yes."

"It's not an enviable position."

"There are worse."

"We have to look out for ourselves."

"I'll be okay."

"With Frank Paris?" my brother scoffed. "What makes you think he'll have anything left in his accounts after he dies?"

"There's his inheritance."

"How much do you think will pass to you?"

My brother's cell buzzed. He glanced at the message screen. "Orsini?" I asked. Johnny didn't answer. We remained on the bed and listened to the echo of the men above the garden, laughing at cards.

"We can't allow ourselves to be bullied."

I didn't quite know who he meant, but this was something he said on occasion, and I understood the sentiment. We'd grown up in the same household.

"We're all trapped, one way or the other."

"You can accept it if you want, but I . . ." He engaged me with those dark eyes of his. "We need to secure ourselves a higher position."

"How's that possible?"

"Orsini is obsessed with you."

"He's married. And so am I."

"Marriage doesn't last forever."

My brother's phone chimed again. This time I didn't ask who it might be—I knew. He left. I lay down on the bed after he was gone, in the dim light. The drug was wearing off, and I was crashing and felt that small gnawing inside, the kind that comes with cocaine. But it wasn't simply that. There was another kind of hunger, as well. The kind you get when you've been to a party, and the events play through your head, and there's something in you yet to be satisfied. I lay in that fitful way, for how long I wasn't sure, slipping for a while into a state that was almost like a dream. It wasn't an altogether unpleasant sensation, and I was still lying there in that sort of half state when the cottage door opened and Paolo came in. I wasn't surprised to see him, and he didn't seem surprised that I was lying there in Isabella's dress.

We didn't speak.

He put his hand under the dress and lifted it up, just partway at first, then farther up, so that the shift was over my head. He kissed me on the mouth through the thin, gauzy fabric. I closed my eyes and arched my back. Frank Paris was upstairs somewhere, but I pushed him from my thoughts, pushed everything away so that it was just Paolo and me and Isabella's dress. Then, for a little while, it was like we were figures on a canvas, a white screen, suspended in the dark.

# 10.

WHEN IT WAS OVER I lay with my legs and arms spread, and he lay with an arm draped over my waist. The dress lay on the floor by the bed.

"*Mi ami?*"

I didn't answer.

Italian men were always asking such foolishness.

Lying there, I dreamed of home. I dreamed of strip malls and wide streets flooded with light. Of tables stacked high with blue jeans. Of endless prairies and giant yellow cups filled with soda.

I cried out.

Or I must have, because Paolo took me in his arms. We slept like that until morning, when there was the sound of keys at the door. There was no reason to be surprised, really. There was her makeup case on the wicker chair, and her overnight bag in the closet. She stepped inside. The shades were drawn, the room still in shadow. Paolo sat up in bed, and I lay stupidly against the pillow.

"Isabella," Paolo said.

Isabella said nothing. She picked up the case and went into the closet. She rummaged around. Then I remembered the other part of the dream. A pair of hands. Reaching up from the ground, pulling me by the legs, grabbing, pulling me under, back into the land of the yellow cups.

Isabella emerged from the closet.

I held Paolo's hand under the covers. He started to speak, but I squeezed his fingers, afraid of what might happen. There was a sharp intake of breath, and Isabella paused. She didn't look at us. She stepped over the dress and went out the door.

"She'll tell my husband."

"She doesn't know he's here."

"She'll ruin me."

"No," he said. "It's me she wants to ruin."

He kissed me then. I kissed him back.

"But first there's this business in New York. The perfume shoot. And an article in *Vanity Fair*."

"Are you going?"

"It's expected."

I told him about my dream then. About the hands pulling me under.

"Don't worry," he said. "About your husband. Or Isabella."

"No?"

"No," he said. "I'll protect you."

We made love again, more fiercely than before.

THAT MORNING, I WALKED HOME through the square where I'd gotten lost last night: past a woman selling bread, children kicking a rag ball. It seemed remote now, my fear from the night before, of Lodovico, of the silly dogs. At my building the landlady saw me return up the stairs alone, disheveled. Frank Paris was still at Orsini's, probably in one of the guest rooms, sleeping off his evening.

He came home later, sheepish and embarrassed.

He expected me to upbraid him, but instead I was more attentive to him, and a bit submissive, as if delivering on my brother's promise that I would become more dedicated if only he would assert himself.

That same evening, Frank went out with Johnny again. It was my brother's idea—and had something to do with the changing odds on one of the races leading up to the Palio. Not too long after they had gone, someone knocked on my door.

It was Orsini.

He fell to his knees and buried his head in my skirt, there in the open doorway. He kissed me between the legs

"My jewel," he said.

I heard footsteps on the staircase below and got a glimpse of my landlady's head as she climbed. I tried to shush Paolo, but he kept muttering over and over, kissing me as he muttered. Telling me how he had to leave the next morning with his wife for New York but needed to see me first. To touch me. To feel my body against his.

I let him in.

Three days later, Isabella was dead.

# PART TWO

# 11.

MY BROTHER AND I TEND to attract attention. This has been true ever since we were young. Partly it's because of our resemblance, though it might also have to do with the similarity of our gestures or the intimate way we arrange ourselves in public, sitting close. When we were young our mother dressed us in matching outfits and posed us as kissing cousins. We didn't continue this habit as we got older, but our tastes were similar enough. "People enjoy looking at you," my mother used to say. "At how handsome you are together, how cozy." Maybe this was the case now as we sat under the rustic awning at Il Volpe, but I felt anxious, given Isabella's death and the rumors going around. And the waiter knew my brother, since Johnny had been here often with Orsini.

"You didn't tell me your sister was a twin."

"In more ways than one."

"We're not twins," I said.

Most of the waiters at Il Volpe were professionals of the old-world sort, practiced in the trade, who looked after you but didn't pry. This man was younger.

"You were in a little film, your brother tells me."

"A little one, yes."

"And you model?"

"On occasion."

"I believe I saw you on a bus shelter."

"No," I said. "I don't do bus shelters."

This wasn't true. I had been on several bus shelters, with my eyes heavily made up, in the campaign for La Marche, the one that showed me as a poet. I lit a cigarette now and blew smoke in his direction. Unlike in the States, you could still smoke here. You could still blow smoke in the face of someone who irritated you—or whom you wanted to seduce. This man, I only wanted him to go away.

I had never been a been a big smoker, as I said before, but begun craving it more since that evening at the palazzo.

"It's too bad, this tragedy with Isabella."

"I didn't know her so well."

"You were at that party at her house," he smirked. "Before she left Rome."

"Maybe you should mind your own affairs."

The waiter was taken aback. It was possible he had only been trying to flirt, or ingratiate himself in some way. I worried I had spoken too sharply, but at the same time I wondered how the waiter knew about the party. I suspected my brother had told him. Johnny sometimes talked too much.

"I didn't mean anything," the waiter said.

"Of course not."

"Your friendship with Paolo Orsini, I'm sure it's all very innocent."

The innuendo was clear. I would have snapped at him again if not for the chill that ran through me. I thought about how Isabella had discovered Paolo and me in bed, and I wondered who else might know, and to what conclusion this all might lead. I held these concerns from my face and instead looked over the menu, glancing over the top of the card as I ordered—meeting the waiter's eyes without seeing him, smiling in the icy way I'd seen my mother smile at men who'd overstepped their bounds.

"*Melone con prosciutto*," I said. "*E vino bianco.*"

I took away my gaze and didn't look at him anymore. After he left, I turned to my brother.

"Can't you keep your mouth shut?"

"I'm not the only source of rumors in this town."

"Things are difficult enough," I said. "You don't need to aggravate the situation by talking to waiters."

"You're the reckless one."

"That's not fair."

"It's the point of meeting me here, isn't it? To make arrangements," my brother snapped. "Do you think I enjoy playing your pander?" We weren't usually like this with each other. "I'm sorry," he said. "I know how difficult things are." His eyes went tender. Johnny was like that. He could be charming and sweet, but there was darkness beneath that charm, and he could switch on a dime. Most everyone is like that sometimes. Even so, I had an unpleasant thought about the kinds of things my brother was capable of. I pushed the idea away. Isabella had been almost five thousand miles away when she died, on another continent, across the Atlantic Ocean.

"Paolo's making arrangements," my brother said, "to have her body flown back to Rome. And in between dealing with that—talking to the police in New York. And the carabinieri here"

"Some of the things people are saying. About how she died."

"No one takes those seriously."

"Still."

"Never mind," he said. "Paolo wants to see you."

The waiter brought my melon wrapped in prosciutto. He brought some bruschetta and a nice glass of wine. And ceviche fresh from the Adriatic coast. He seemed chastened and served us without speaking. After a while some new people came in, and there was a small buzz on the patio around us. I heard Paolo's name in the same breath as Isabella's. It wasn't surprising. Her face was in all the media. And the coroner's photos were trending, too.

Isabella in her lingerie, on the bathroom floor. Her hair ruffled up, all a mess. You could see her mottled face and heart-shaped lips and long lashes. There was something provocative in the way she lay there. In how her legs were spread, and in the arch of her back.

"It's a pity."

"Yes."

"Such a beautiful woman."

"Though a little matronly."

"It's a shame."

"In the last photo, even. Her weight. You can see it in her hips."

Isabella had died in a hotel overlooking Central Park, and her body had not yet been released for return to Rome. The original reports said she had spent the night alone, that she had taken some sleeping medication, too much, apparently. She had a problem in that regard, it seemed, a history. Only this time, there'd been no one to help her. So she'd slipped and cracked her head on the tile, and the hotel maid found her in the morning. The fact she'd been alone had caused some confusion—since she and Orsini had checked in together. Now it seemed Orsini had left New York the afternoon before her death, and after he left she'd been seen drinking with a man in the hotel bar until late. The man with her had been quite a bit younger, according to the waitress; but the waitress had since contradicted herself. The hotel security video turned up blank. People wondered why.

"Isabella was no angel," said Johnny.

"What do you mean?"

"She didn't like getting old. And, well, you know, she loved attention."

"The young man at the bar?"

"It's just a rumor. But I wouldn't doubt it."

"You wouldn't?"

"Everyone blames Paolo for the trouble in the marriage—but sometimes it's not the husband. As you know."

"As I know."

Initial toxicology reports showed Ambien in her blood, and Vicodin, and alcohol, as well. Even so, it wasn't the drugs that had killed her but the fall. A peculiar tumble, a bad angle. According to some reports she had numerous bruises on her body, contusions on her face, and a cracked jaw, and these were not necessarily consistent with the injuries someone might receive from such a fall.

All this information had come out helter-skelter over the last several days. It was hard to tell what was accurate and what the tabloids had invented as a way of making the story more enticing.

"You're right," I continued. "There's no point being reckless."

"You don't want to see Paolo?"

"I do. But I can't. Not this afternoon, anyway—"

My brother interrupted with a wave of the hand. "I know," he said. "You have to go with Frank to see his uncle. Cardinal Whiting. But that's not for several hours."

How Johnny knew about this . . . well, I suppose Frank had told him . . . These visits to Frank's uncle, they weren't something I liked to talk about much, nor did Frank. We dreaded them, but we had to go. Like my husband, Whiting was a writer, though of an entirely different nature: he wrote about religious issues and the crisis confronting the Catholic Church. The reason we went . . . Though the clergy was not allowed personal possessions, it wasn't uncommon in certain circumstances for them to administer the inheritance of their relatives' heirs, particularly—as in Frank's situation—if the principal would revert to the Church. This was the case with Whiting. He controlled Frank's stipend, his only real income: a dwindling inheritance his parents had left years before and placed under the uncle's control.

"So . . ." my brother said.

How my brother looked at me then, I can't explain. The way we are with each other, he knows things a brother might not usually know. The day before—to avoid prying eyes: the press, the palazzo staff-—he'd taken me on his Vespa down the Appian Way to where Paolo waited in his car, just outside the Aurelian Wall. It was the boundary of the old city, beyond which the ancients had buried their dead. Paolo and I went off behind the graves. All the while, my brother waited on his scooter.

"He wants to see you again," my brother insisted. "Especially since tomorrow he's going to Florence, to meet with Isabella's family about the estate. He might be in Florence for a while . . . If we go now, you'll have time . . ."

"I don't know."

I was conscious of how the light filtered through the flowers on the trellis, and of the sounds of a fountain bubbling nearby, the people muttering their gossip at the table. I heard the passersby on the street, the buses, all the noisy mess of Rome. I closed my eyes. He reached across the table. I should have resisted, but I didn't. I was already with him, on the back of his scooter, darting through the shadows. I felt the dampness between my legs. I saw myself disappear behind the stones. I heard myself moan, and later I brushed the grass stains from my skirt.

# 12.

CARDINAL WHITING WAS SO ANCIENT, IT was impossible to guess how old he might be. He didn't leave his apartment often but spent a great deal of time in front of the television. Frank and I found ourselves in front of the set, too, eating warmed leftovers from a tray. A crucifix hung on the wall nearby, and the shelves were filled with very old, very dusty books: the works of church philosophers and the ancients. Some of these Whiting regarded as blasphemy, but he hoarded them all the same, along with rows of religious journals of varying stripes, in the margins of which he wrote—in fine blue ink—his objections and qualifications to the views expressed therein. Along with these publications were stacks of tabloids he read assiduously—not for pleasure, he insisted, but in order to keep track of the moral decay of the world.

When we visited, I took care to dress modestly. I wore no makeup and made myself dowdy: my hair in a bun, my face pale.

"It's so kind of you to have us over, Uncle."

"I know why you are here."

"It's not the only reason," Frank Paris said. "But it's true. The cost of living . . ."

These monthly visits were always something of a humiliation, but unavoidable. Cardinal Whiting held tight to the purse strings he'd been entrusted with decades ago by his nephew's mother.

"Oh, it's always so pleasant here," I said. "So contemplative."

His quarters stood adjacent to Quirinal Hill, in a building run by the clergy. Though they were communal facilities, many of the apartments were quite elaborate. I asked about the origins of a fresco in the coffered space at the top of walls.

"Franceschini?"

"No." Whiting puffed up a little. "Baldassare Franceschini did no work here. That's the Virgin as rendered by one of Rafael's students, before Rafael himself died. He'd been too dissolute to finish."

"Well, she's as buxom as the last time we visited," Frank laughed. "Like all of Rafael's women."

His uncle didn't see the humor.

"Rafael died of debauchery," he insisted.

I started to perspire. Though I had scrubbed myself before we came here, I could still smell the sex on my body.

"That's true," I said.


THE ROOM WAS FILLED WITH ORNATE paraphernalia—a processional cross, a ciborium, a chip of bone from Saint Teresa's tomb, and other relics Whiting had collected over the years. The apartment had a cloistered smell redolent of the man himself, of the clothes that hung in an open armoire, of urine, of holy water, of paper and dust. He had a desk on which he wrote out his diatribes in a small, tedious script. He was fluent in Latin, Italian, English, French, and had an influential column in *Avvenire*, the

Catholic daily. There was a balcony off to the side where he lingered on occasion, ruminating, stepping forward toward the black railing, glancing over the edge, down to the traffic, as if getting ready to address the gathered masses in his imagination.

"The world is profligate," he said.

He held a remote control in his hand and flicked through the stations. He paused at EWTN, the Catholic station, where some bishops were debating what the Church could do to appeal to modern Europeans.

"It's not the Church's job to appeal," said the old man. "Jesus is not a soft drink."

"No."

"He's not a hamburger."

"Of course not."

"He's not something to be put into a package and consumed."

He clicked some more.

Past *The Powerpuff Girls* dubbed in Italian. Past Mick Jagger and Shakira. Past *World News Today.* Away from the typhoon in Thailand and a drone attack on the Gaza Strip.

Eventually he ended back on the BBC, a reporter in front of a Manhattan hotel. It was the hotel in which Isabella had died, and the reporter was saying that some people believed that Isabella's death might not have been the accident the New York officials seemed willing to believe. As evidence, these skeptics cited certain irregularities: alleged gaps in the hotel's security tape, in witnesses' memories; a lapse in passport protocol; inconsistencies in a passenger list showing who had been on the chartered jet that carried Orsini and his party across the Atlantic. All this suggested to some a sinister hand, a cover-up. The reporter went on to discuss the events preceding Isabella's death, including the parties she'd been to recently and the celebrities in attendance.

"They don't mention you, I notice," said Cardinal Whiting.

"Why would they?" Frank said. "I'm not so well-known."

"But you were there, at one of those parties."

Despite the old man's isolation, he had ways of knowing things. Maybe from one of those aging politicians who'd been at Orsini's. Even the crooks—those the cardinal condemned—had been known to crawl up these stairs and drop to one knee. I worried what other rumors might have reached him. Frank, so far as I knew, was ignorant of the affair. Or feigning ignorance.

"And you were there, too, at Orsini's," he said to me.

I glanced down at my shoes. They were black and plain and functional, of the type nuns wear. I wore a checkered dress of very little shape, and stockings that bagged. The cardinal gave me a look. Not a pretty look. I felt him peering inside me, as if at something particularly unpleasant only he could see.

"Beware the glamour of evil," he said.

After dinner the cardinal hobbled onto the balcony and stood teetering with one hand on the rail. You could see he yearned for the lectern. He looked as if he was on the verge of calling out to the passersby, the woman in the too-short skirt, the man on the Vespa, the kid with the cigarette in one hand and a slice of pizza in the other. Telling them things they might not want to hear but which were his job to say. How the world had fallen to apostasy and sin.

"The truth will out," he said, smiling at his cleverness. "Paolo Orsini used his wife's name to get elected—and certain members of society, even priests and bishops, were taken in by his celebrity. Never mind that he consorts with criminals. Even Isabella's bodyguard—one wonders why he was dismissed shortly before her murder?"

"No one has called it murder," I said.

"You are naive."

We sat on the balcony eating Italian cookies, drinking espresso, and watching the light fade from the Roman sky. It might have been pleasant but for the cardinal, who kept going on about how the senator benefited financially from Isabella's death. Killing her was much simpler than divorce. After he was done maligning Orsini, the cardinal expounded on the weaknesses of the current pope, who was quite ill. He praised the virtues of the German cardinal he hoped would replace him.

Eventually he turned his attention to his nephew.

"Have you been to confession?"

The old man often raised this question. He regarded it as part of the charge given to him by Frank's mother: to look after Frank's spirit as well as his material concerns. Frank would have been wise to say yes, but he couldn't bring himself to bow to his uncle.

"And you, my dear . . . ?"

I felt his eyes boring into me again. I turned my cheek, but I still didn't like it, the feeling of him tunneling about inside, sifting through the debris, all those things about me I couldn't see myself or didn't want to see. As if he'd been perched there on the Aurelian Wall, watching as my body clenched and trembled, one hand in the dirt and the other clutching my lover's head. I was sweating again. The scent of the cemetery, this room, the relics, myself, the exhaust of the Roman streets . . .

Frank Paris intervened.

"Uncle," he said, "I need to talk with you alone."

I WAITED BELOW, MY PURSE cradled between my legs, while Frank petitioned him about our finances. I took out some eyeliner and blush and examined my face in my compact. I regarded myself dispassionately. I regarded my virtues, my flaws. I have large pupils, unusually so, that give me a distracted look, as if I am too intensely in the moment and can't see what is in front of me. When I was young, I'd been referred to the school psychologist. There'd been a death in the neighborhood, a boy I'd known—whom I'd kissed once, while Johnny watched from the closet. The school called a number of us in for trauma counseling after they'd found the body. Me, because of my eyes, that distracted look—I was asked to come back. The psychologist called in my mother.

"I can't get under her," the woman said.

"My daughter's very beautiful," said my mother.

"Yes, she's very striking," the psychologist agreed, "but that's not what I mean." The woman had questions about our family life, the men my mother dated, my relationship with my brother. My mother didn't like these questions, but the psychologist persisted. The shrink was concerned about certain blank spots, emptinesses, memories I skittered around, dissociative tendencies typical of certain kinds of trauma. My mother sat with her purse. Not too long after this meeting, she transferred me to another school and sent Johnny abroad.

# 13.

W E WERE IN THE THICK of summer. Anyone with any sense had left for the ocean or the lake country. It was just Frank and I who remained, and the tourists sweltering in the ruins. Isabella's body, meanwhile, remained in New York. There were delays—technicalities at the coroner's office and other problems, too, having to do with the transportation of human remains across the Atlantic.

Frank wanted to go to the Palio.

"It'll be awfully hot on the trains," I said. "And crowded. And Siena—this time of year . . ."

"The heat's worse in Rome."

Frank had written about the Palio in his novel, and it held a special place in his imagination. It was an old festival with colorful parades. On the last day there was a horse race: jockeys riding bareback in a wild scamper through the center of the old city. There was a frenzy of wagering and drinking. The streets filled with wood smoke, the smell of spiced meat soaked in oil, wine spilled on old stones. Those things attracted him just as they had attracted the hero of his novel: a young man, in the flush of his early success, who'd visited the city with his wife and daughter.

That young man had gambled it all away. It wasn't the lost money that haunted him but rather the memory of those horses, thundering down—and then the feeling of emptiness the next morning, something unfulfilled, the desire to go riding out into the warm countryside, in all those golden hills.

"There's something I've been meaning to tell you . . ."

I had an idea of what he was going to say. Or I thought I did. Just yesterday the landlady had been by.

"Do you remember Jim Swinson?"

"No," I said.

I hadn't expected this. Then the memory came: a wiry man Frank had gone hunting with a few times in the quail country of south Texas. They were buddies from a long time back, a million years ago. The man had recently taken a job as dean of a college in Little Rock.

"I've had a couple of conversations with him these last weeks* . . . There's a position . . ."

I sat with my legs crossed, sweating.

"Arkansas?"

"We'll need to be there by the end of August . . . So we have a little time . . . after Siena we could go to Lake Como . . . Or maybe the beach, in Cadaqués . . ."

He went on. The money from his uncle wasn't enough to live on, but if he had a salary we could travel over the summer. And there was a repertory program at the college . . . with a bit of a reputation . . . Doris Day had gone there . . . or maybe Lana Turner . . . Sally Field . . . One of those, all of them, maybe none* . . . I wasn't paying strict attention but imagining the place Frank would rent for us . . . coeds and faculty dinners . . . the Piggly Wiggly out on the strip . . .

"My brother—"

"He has his own life here," Frank said. "But you . . . As far as that business in Dallas . . . no one's thinking about that anymore. There never were any charges."

"Why do you bring that up?"

"I don't want you to worry, that's all."

*He knows,* I thought. *He knows about Orsini and me. He might not admit his suspicions, even to himself, but he knows.*

I looked out at the Campo. It had been a flower meadow once, then an encampment. The Roman priests had laid offerings to the statue of Venus down in the caves, and centuries later the clergy and the nobility had met their mistresses here before taking them up to the papal orgies in the gardens above the Forum. Now it was midday and the stalls were shuttered. The Campo was empty of people, except for the hooded statue of the heretic and an old woman who sat at the base of the statue, hanging her head in the heat. Closer by, I could see a couple sitting at the fringe, on a restaurant patio. The woman swung her leg idly, and the man next to her tapped his fingers on the table. There was something beautiful about them, something illicit. They didn't touch each other. It was too hot. It was that long, slow time of day when even the tourists seemed to flag—when it was easy to imagine the world had always been like this and always would be—and the waiters were at any rate in no hurry to bring anyone a drink.

# 14.

THE NEXT DAY I TALKED with Johnny. We were at his apartment, eight stories up. Rome was outside the window, all cluttered and dirty. The apartment had air-conditioning, but the building was old and the unit couldn't keep up with the weather. I stripped down then took a shower. I sat in in my panties and T-shirt with the balcony door open and the fan spinning overhead. Johnny sat bare-chested in his shorts.

We had done the same as kids, in Houston, when it got too hot and the air-conditioning failed. We talked about our mother's men—Johnny and I, hanging around in our flimsies, under the fan—and usually we didn't find much good in them. The more we talked, the more black-and-white things became. That was how it was with families.

*There's me and you. And then everybody else.*

It was the same talking about Frank. Johnny sat close to me on the bed.

"You don't have to go with him."

"What choice do I have?"

"You could stay in Italy."

"And how would I survive?"

"There are ways."

"Divorce in Italy isn't so open-and-shut."

"I hate to see you like this. Orsini would be willing to help."

"I'm not a whore."

"His intentions—"

"How will that look? With Isabella not even in the grave. People will talk."

"They will talk, yes. For a while. Then, later, they'll talk about something else."

Johnny ran cool water over some washcloths. I leaned my head back and he placed the cloth over my brow.

"You're looking a little pale," he said.

"It's just the heat."

"A fever coming on, maybe." He reached out and put a hand on my forehead, feeling my temperature. "And the world spins a bit when you walk."

"Don't be silly."

It was true, though—the heat was wearing me down. I suffered flashes. Things shifted inside.

"Frank mentioned Dallas," I said.

I saw the hard set of my brother's jaw. I remembered that hardness from when Johnny was young, whenever one of my mother's men had questioned something he had done. He had a temper.

"Give yourself a couple of days. You owe that to yourself."

"We're going to Siena."

"Tell Frank you aren't feeling well but you'll meet him in Siena two days from now. In time for the spectacle."

Johnny brushed back a bit of my hair. "At Orsini's stables," Johnny said, "there's the stallion who ran the Palio a few years back. I know Frank wants to ride that horse."

My brother's eyes were dark, like my own. Our faces were like mirrors, one of the other, and in those mirrors we saw ourselves, our thin lips, our chestnut hair, the black eyes that seemed to be looking at something far away. I felt something well up inside. I buried my head in the crease of his shoulder.

"I can see your feelings are torn."

He kissed me on the neck.

"Frank's been good to me."

"You need time to think."

"I guess so."

"A couple of days alone, you'd be surprised. Things have a way of solving themselves."

I FELL ASLEEP ON JOHNNY'S bed there in the heat, on the white sheets, with the fan spinning overhead. The grogginess stayed with me later on the way to the Campo, as Johnny throttled his scooter through the streets. Johnny didn't want me to leave Rome. I was his sister and he wanted me close, but he had selfish reasons, too. He'd done well with Orsini. He made money as a go-between, off the record, in a situation where his status as an out-sider—whose actions could be disavowed—was of particular ad-vantage. If I left, Paolo's interest in Johnny might soon disappear.

"Out on the trail alone, beyond those stables, just Frank and I . . . we'll have a chance to talk."

"What will you tell him?"

"I'll just soften the ground a little bit. So he has some idea how you feel."

"This is really for me to do."

"But you won't."

It was true. I'd never been good at such things.

"I depend on you too much."

"You do."

"You'll be delicate?"

"Of course."

We were at the Campo now, the scooter idling. The look he gave me, I didn't know what to say. I tasted something black at the back of my throat. He leaned toward me. He put his fingers on my lips, shushing me. He smiled in that way of his, so I couldn't help but smile back.

His keys hung from the ignition.

The key chain was a plastic lamination stenciled with the skyline of Manhattan. I was surprised I hadn't noticed it before, but there it was, shaped like an apple, bright red and engraved with the initials:

## NYC

He was on the scooter, straddling the seat.

"You were in New York?"

"It's just a souvenir."


I LINGERED IN THE CAMPO, watching the tourists. I envied them, but I knew how it was. You looked down some alley and imagined yourself walking into some other life. But it didn't happen. You were still yourself, standing in the same heat, restless, a little bored, damp under the arms, with that same sticky feeling between your legs. The heat rose up from the pavement, up under my skirt. I went inside to get away from the heat, but it was worse. I climbed the stairs and found Frank, his shirt off. He was on the phone, talking to Johnny. And I remembered those hands in my dream, pulling me under.

THEY ARRIVED AT THE STABLES later than intended and headed up along the ridge overlooking the stone villas and the yellowing fields. The heat was rising, and Johnny rode the stallion. It wasn't what Frank had wanted, but Johnny insisted. He had experience with the animal, and the stallion was always high-strung first thing out of the barn.

"I'll give you a shot at him later," Johnny said. "Farther along."

"I can handle him."

They took it easy, stopping every now and again to get a look at San Gimignano, the old hill town across the ridge, sandstone towers and medieval walls off in the jagged distance.

How I know all this . . . how the hills looked, and what happened that afternoon . . . How I know . . . I came up from Rome after the accident and walked the trail along with Johnny and two Italian men. The Italians thought it might be hard for me, but I walked it anyway, so I could see what Frank had seen: the landscape with its gridded fields, its wild reserves and gravel roads.

I saw Frank swaying in the saddle, peering out at Tuscany, woozy in the awful heat, sensing as he always did the blackness at the center of everything, just as he sensed it in me. He was hungover, needing sleep. The insects buzzed like crazy. It induced amnesia, that noise. It made it seem like you were an insect yourself, a million insects, voracious in the grass. Tuscany spread out front of us, beautiful, ancient. The landscape had a runic quality, like a puzzle waiting to be solved.

"It was pretty hellish," Johnny said.

The older of the two Italians was a local rancher who'd brought us up here in his four-wheel drive via the gravel road. The younger one was an officer in the local Carabinieri who had a report to file. They both knew Paolo Orsini. Everyone up this way did, and many were indebted in some manner.

I suppose that played in our favor.

"The heat is more worse in the canyons," said the rancher. His Italian was thick and his English sometimes hard to understand. "You water the horses?"

"Wherever we could. Some of the troughs were dry."

"A day like this heat, no water, a horse gets lathered. A man, too . . . a woman."

The rancher spoke as if he'd seen it before, inexperienced riders wearing out themselves and their animals in the heat. When that happened, well, all you could do was shrug. He held his palms out flat in front of him, shoulders hunched. Johnny shook his head.

"It's my fault . . ." Johnny said.

No one corrected him.

The sun bore down, not just hot but brutal. The trail got pretty steep in places. Johnny explained how it had been. How, farther on, he and Frank had gotten off their horses and scrabbled up the rock. They made it okay. It was on the return loop, traveling through shadier country, when things went wrong.

We were approaching that spot now.

"You were drinking?" asked the cop.

"He had a flask . . ."

Johnny stopped.

It was a harmless-seeming stretch of trail that wound its way around the edges of a grove, then through a copse of those tall, wig-headed cypress trees that grow in the Italian countryside.

Oaks huddled down at the bottom, a stone building, open fields.

"Here?"

"No, farther on . . ." He nudged his chin toward the oaks. His eyes clouded. For once, Johnny wasn't smiling. "But here, this spot, we changed mounts . . . I can show you . . ."

Johnny took out his phone and passed it around. Frank sat high in the saddle, bridle in hand, posing for the grainy photo. He didn't wear a riding helmet but a wide-brimmed hat, like that of an Argentinean gaucho. He looked sweaty, tired, old as dirt. There were large sweat stains underneath his arms, and his brow was damp. The wry expression was gone. He looked punch-drunk.

Probably it wasn't just alcohol.

Johnny carried all kinds of things in his pouch.

"I should have said no," Johnny said. "But he was pretty insistent. You know how he could be . . ."

I glanced toward the oaks and the outbuilding farther along. I imagined Frank spurring the stallion down the trail.

"Old man they do foolish things," the rancher said. He looked at me in my bright blouse and capris, my sunglasses, my head-band and designer mules. The carabiniere looked me over, too.

"Not that I blame your husband," the rancher said. "That stallion, he was not some easy beast . . ."

We kept walking. The heat grew worse, the insects louder. It was true that Frank knew horses, but it had been a while. And he hadn't known this horse at all. Johnny had handed him the reins anyway. The irony being the ride was almost over, the hard part done. Four kilometers to the stables. Just this gentle slope, barely a slope at all. They remounted . . . Frank struggled with the stallion . . . It wanted to run . . . That's how it had seemed to Johnny then, watching from behind . . . That's how he described it . . . Frank taking the horse to a cantor, reining him back just past the bend at the bottom of the hill, holding off the gallop . . . The cluster of oaks looming at the bend . . . a small stone building . . . a line of cypress hedging the dirt road, winding through the yellow fields toward the stables.

We stood under an oak.

"It spooked," Johnny said. "That's the way it looked . . . or maybe, I don't know, the horse wanted water . . ."

There was a trough by the building. Maybe that was it. Or there'd been something unexpected on the path, right here, slithering across the gravel.

The stallion had reared. At the edge of the path stood a live oak, a majestic tree whose branches spread over the trail. One of these branches caught Frank in the back, and Frank sidewheeled over the stallion, head down, his foot caught in the stirrup. The stallion went wild, trying to shake the man loose. He dragged Frank around the corner, kicking and trampling, until finally the body fell free. The horse ran all the way back to the stables.

The Italians watched me as if they expected me to weep, but I was numb. The policeman knelt in the dust. There were hoof marks, footprints, tire tracks. He stared up at the tree, walked to the trough, to the edge of the field. If he had doubts, he didn't say anything. His department was small, just an outpost. His job was to file an accident report.

There'd been men in the field nearby, two of them, Algerians, and the officer had talked to them the day before.

Migrant workers—illegals.

Who were already gone, no doubt. Who could not afford entanglement with the law. This would cause problems later, when Johnny's story fell into doubt: suggestions the Algerians had been not field hands but accomplices. That the death had not been accidental but that Frank had been attacked and beaten, trampled after the fact, his corpse dragged through the dirt. Just as there were rumors that Isabella had not died from slipping on the tile but had been knocked about, her head smashed against the sink.

The young carabiniere, whatever he thought, kept his mouth shut. We walked down through the heat and drove to Volterra so I could identify the corpse. A ancient town, narrow streets, new construction on the outskirts, cheap and modern—but in the older part of town buildings from the dark ages held most of the town's officialdom, including the police office and the morgue. Inside, Frank lay uncovered on a slab: neck broken, head swollen, beaten out of round. Face abraded, eyelids torn, eyes that did not look like eyes. Crooked nose more crooked, mouth smeared wide and bloody. It was still him, though—I could tell by the slope of the shoulders, the shape of him, the mole on his neck, the curled left foot with the yellowing nails.

"*Si*," I said.

The morgue attendant and the carabiniere talked in the hall. I heard Orsini's name. He was influential around here. After a while they made a phone call. A different carabiniere appeared, this one of higher rank. He expedited the matter. They released Frank's body and sent us to the mortuary down the road.

THEY BURNED FRANK'S BODY IN Tuscany, and I rode back in a private car, with my husband's ashes on the seat beside me. In Rome people had begun to gather around the gate at the old entrance to the city, but I didn't think too much about this. People often gathered there, tourists and pilgrims, coming as in the old days to tuck notes between the stones, messages to be carried along to the dead.

"She has returned," said the driver.

"Who?"

"Isabella."

I didn't understand. Alone, back at the apartment, I folded Frank's shirts and slacks and books into the black steamer trunk he'd been packing for Arkansas. Then something broke inside me, or maybe it was broken already, I don't know. I felt tears on my cheeks, but they weren't the kind of tears they were supposed to be, I don't think. Maybe that's how it is for everyone. I wept anyway. I took up the urn and headed toward the river. The streets were more crowded than usual. I pushed through them to Ponte Sisto, where Frank and I used to stroll, only here the crowds were thicker, the people carrying on as if my grief were their own. I still didn't understand. Then I saw a vendor working his way from the other side, selling photographs of Isabella, and I realized that the crowds were for her. Isabella's body had returned to Rome. I pushed through the Italians to the river wall and gazed at the black water. I opened the box and shook Frank's ashes into the Tiber.

I watched the ashes fall.

I tried to think about Frank, but I couldn't see him. Instead I saw that boy who'd kissed me in the closet when I was little.

They'd found his bruised body at the bottom of a well.

# 15.

I SABELLA'S BODY HAD ARRIVED IN Rome in a casket too plain for words, the sight of which, rolling down the cargo conveyor at Fiumicino Airport, was captured on a cell phone camera by a baggage handler, then republished in *Corriere della Sera.*

The image stirred a call for something more fitting, a public ceremony and a procession through the streets. People gathered in piazzas throughout the city, as Italians did at the passing of beloved figures—movie stars and popes. The same had happened after the death of Pietra Trista, the sad-eyed little dog who'd had his own show on Italian TV.

In this context, the death of an American writer on a horse trail in Tuscany didn't attract much attention.

The crowds grew, and I mingled with them. It was impossible to do much else. People gathered not just in the piazzas but also in the streets and at locations from her films. They carried their little devices. They peered over one another's shoulders, watching news clips and films, bleary-eyed and sentimental, laughing, carrying on.

*Oh Isabella!*

*Oh regina bella!*

*Non seppellirla senza noi, Paolo!*

*La vediamo un più tempo!*

Suspicions persisted as to what had happened in New York. These suspicions grew uglier and more ornate, encouraged by a rumor that Paolo had refused a public procession. Then an army of young men and women appeared on motor scooters, circulars bundled on racks behind them. Soon these handbills littered the streets.

They announced a public memorial.

Day after tomorrow.

At the end, Isabella would be interred in Verano Cemetery.

The great cemetery at the heart of Rome.

The posters carried only the barest information. People extrapolated. She would be on public display in a glass case . . . The ailing pope himself would be in attendance . . . Francis Ford Coppola, the famous director, would crawl on his knees behind the coffin . . . When the procession reached the gates of the Verano, an American fighter jet would appear, and tens of thousands of roses would fall from the sky . . . wild roses, of the type Isabella had grown in her garden . . .

The crowd grew enormously.

It surged and I surged with them, pushing to the front, hands outstretched, reaching toward her coffin as she passed.

# 16.

I F I'D VISITED CARDINAL WHITING after Frank's death . . . if I'd spent time in widows' clothing . . . if I'd posted, as was the local custom, notices of his death in the cafés he used to frequent . . . But I didn't do any of that. I kept to myself, and in my solitude I grew reckless. I slept during the day and danced at night at the clubs in the Testaccio. I went alone. Something shifted inside me—about to reveal itself—but I pushed it away and went out again, to a crowded room where I could throw my arms in the air and feel my body pulse. The men crowded close in the blue light. When the clubs closed, I walked alone in the morning heat, in the early dawn when there was no one else out but the drunks and the nuns. I walked all the way to Roma Termini. I studied the train schedules—to Paris, Prague, anywhere—but I never got on. Back at the apartment, Frank's boxes lay in crooked stacks and the landlady awaited her rent.

"What's the matter?" my brother asked.

"I don't want to talk about it."

"Let me hold you."

I could have left Rome then, but I didn't. Johnny was my brother. I have certain loyalties. "This will pass," he said, "things will settle." Maybe they would have, if not for the photograph that appeared in *Il Foglio*. The picture showed Paolo and me emerging from Emilio's, a five-star restaurant in the Testaccio. It wasn't a new picture but had been taken several weeks back, not long after Frank and Isabella died, in one of our careless moments.

GRIEVING SPOUSES: Spotted together at Emilio's: Paolo Orsini, husband of Isabella, and Vittoria Paris, wife of slain novelist Frank Paris.

That was all there was to it, just the caption and picture. But one thing triggered another. The tabloids competed in such matters, but the biggest purveyors were the readers themselves. They posted photos that then found their way everywhere, and the news blogs began to take an unexpected interest in the details of Frank's passing. All this might have passed, too, if Cardinal Whiting hadn't taken up the drum in his column for *Avvenire*, the Catholic daily.

He complained of the cursory investigation into his nephew's death. Of witnesses who had disappeared and evidence suppressed. He found his way onto television.

"Who lay behind the suppression?" he demanded. "Who's pulling the strings?"

He didn't answer these questions himself, but everyone could see where he was leading. They could see where his finger pointed. At Paolo Orsini, the senator from Lazio. Whose own wife had died not long before, under suspicious circumstances. And who had been flaunting himself with Frank Paris's widow through the streets of Rome.

# PART THREE

# 17.

I WAITED UPSTAIRS AT MOUNT Giordano. The lawyers and the wardrobe specialist had just left. It was getting late, and I was due to testify at Palazzo Madama the next morning. I was trying on a jacket they had chosen for me: a pale color, to go with the skirt.

Paolo was downstairs, showing my brother to the door. Time had passed. The investigation had been going on for almost a year.

The room had been Isabella's once, before she'd moved into the cottage. And before that, a long time before, it had been the province of a Renaissance queen. There was a frieze along the upper wall, somewhat faded, painted with animals and mythological beasts. The panels told a story with some significance, but the fading made it hard to tell what the significance might be.

I went to the closet. It had been Isabella's main closet—much larger than the one in the cottage—and her things still hung there. She had worn a lot of it only once or twice, or perhaps not at all.

I started to undress.

TECHNICALLY THE MATTER BEFORE THE Senate wasn't an investigation but an inquiry, one that promised to end but never did. It had moved without resolution from the police department to the Department of Justice, only to emerge by circuitous route in the Chamber of Deputies, where it had taken on a political dimension. Officially, the question at hand was no longer the alleged murders—since the evidence couldn't be found—but whether Paolo had used his office to suppress the initial investigations. My testimony couldn't shed any light on this, but it didn't matter. It was all spectacle now, and the senators wanted me on the stand.

"Your testimony tomorrow should be the end of it," Paolo said to me. "Then we can move on."

Johnny interrupted. "I don't trust this."

"I've been assured."

Paolo held one of those little Italian cigars between his fingers, and the room filled with blue smoke. He had grown heavier over the last months and smoked incessantly. My brother was anxious. It was a hard situation, and the investigators were doing their best to pit us against one another.

"This is about money," my brother said.

He was referring to Isabella's family. They were fighting the will, and for this reason they had aligned themselves with the political opposition.

"It's not just money," insisted Paolo. "Some on the committee, in my own party—they'd like to force me from the Senate."

My brother cut me a glance. Though I didn't usually pay much attention to politics, everything was intertwined. Orsini was under pressure to abandon us, to cut loose his mistress and her troublesome brother and let them fend for themselves.

"The pope," Orsini said. "He's dying."

"The pope is always dying," my brother said. "This is the primary occupation of popes. To die. And to take a long time about it . . . But I don't see what that has to do with us."

"There are political implications."

"Such is the requirement for popes, to be half-dead. So that the cardinals might immediately begin lobbying as to who should replace him. But still—"

"As I said, there are political implications."

"You mean Cardinal Whiting and his New Piety?"

My brother scoffed, but we all knew the situation. La Nuova Pietà, as it was called, decried the unwholesome links between politicians and the criminal element and sought a new activism among Church leaders. Such pleas were nothing new, but Orsini's party was worried that the opposition might use the renewed fervor to launch further investigations. Fortunately, the opposition had its own secrets to hide. So they'd reached a compromise of sorts, with me at the center.

I would testify to satisfy the public sentiment, but it was to be pro forma only, nothing rigorous, and afterward the investigation would close.

"I don't know if I trust this agreement," said Johnny.

"It's not for you to worry about."

"It might be a trap."

Such uneasiness was inevitable. The air frayed. I found my own loyalties torn back and forth, but we were bound, the three of us, at least for now.

"It'll be all right," I said.

"Are you sure?"

My brother lingered. He didn't want the conversation to end. He wanted to be alone with me for just a little while, like we often used to be.

I STOOD IN THE CLOSET, half dressed. The cabinets smelled of cedar—a sweet-smelling cedar, scented with rose petals—and the bottom few drawers overflowed with antique scarves and silks and intimate attire. Among these I found a lace nightgown, handmade. Isabella had owned many items like this, pretty things, very fine and delicate. I put the gown on—meaning only to look at myself—but then Paolo called me to bed. He dimmed the overhead lamp. Because of the nature of the filament, how it glowed, the room was cast in shadows that seemed to move along the wall, on up to the animals in the frieze.

"When the investigation's over, we'll go someplace. We'll get away."

"That would be nice."

"We'll have our honeymoon," he said.

"Where will we go?"

"Someplace away, out of the public stir."

We'd discussed this before, but marriage hadn't seemed wise with the investigation pending. And though we didn't speak of it, there were suspicions between us, given the scandals and the rumors. Paolo touched me. The light quavered. For a moment it seemed I could see the shadows of those beasts, up there in the frieze, moving along the wall.

# 18.

O
N THE DAIS, ON THE FLOOR OF THE OLD chamber, stood a
small, lachrymose man who worked for the Italian Department of Justice. He was a midlevel official of no particular distinction but of no particular loyalties either, and for
this reason he had been assigned special investigator in the case.

"This committee shall come to order," said the special investigator. No one seemed to be paying attention.

The special investigator didn't have a mellifluous voice, nor
was he pleasant to look at. He resembled the sort of slump-
shouldered man who might stand too close behind you on the
bus. Below him, on the floor, the press inhabited its own area,
with mongers from all the important outlets. A small group of
special witnesses were gathered in a nearby box. These included
Cardinal Whiting and my ex-landlady, a small woman dressed in
polka dots.

I wondered why she was here.

The special investigator didn't yet turn his attention to me
but suffered the audience with various matters of protocol.
Then—without explanation or transition—he began to read, in

his dry shion, a letter of petition from Isabella's banished body-guard.

I felt a chill.

I remembered Ernesto Lodovico: his raked hair, the odd twist of his smile, and how he'd behaved toward me that night when I'd gotten myself lost in the streets below the Palazzo. Lodovico had fled the country and was under extradition back to Italy, facing charges in the case of a former employer, the cabinet minister who'd been stabbed to death in his pajamas.

Lodovico's letter claimed the charges against him had been arranged through a corrupt judge in the Florentine district. The letter petitioned the committee to examine the mechanism of this corruption and dismiss the charges. Furthermore, the letter insisted, the timing of Lodovico's dismissal as Isabella's bodyguard was by no means accidental but had been deliberately arranged so that she would be vulnerable and alone. He would testify to all this if given immunity.

The committee debated how to react to the letter but in the end tabled the matter, as they tabled everything. I told myself not to think about this, that the reading of the letter was just another part of the spectacle.

GRAY WAS POPULAR THAT SEASON with Italian politicians. Gray with a slash of red. A crimson tie, maybe. A handkerchief exposed in a breast pocket. The committee members wore different shades, some more muted and others more shiny, sharkskin gray, lung-cancer gray, gray the color of old clouds and cigarette smoke. The faction leaders were difficult to tell apart, friend from foe. By prior arrangement, so the opposition might have its moment, Senator Anthony Secca led the questioning: a small, thick man, dressed in gray like all the rest. He had yellow teeth and a detestable manner. He focused with the most intensity on the nature of my preparations: the clothes I had worn and the makeup I'd put on that day, before the party at Palazzo Orsini.

"And do you remember what lipstick you wore that evening?"

I glanced at my lawyer to see whether he might protest this line of questioning, but he seemed to have fallen into a trance. He gazed at me as if he, too, was curious.

"No, I don't remember," I said.

Cardinal Whiting flustered up from his seat, but only as far as his infirmities allowed, hunched and absurd, flapping like some withered crow.

"I would beg otherwise," he said. "Vittoria was quite obsessed with her lipsticks."

One might expect such outbursts wouldn't be tolerated, but the committee operated by its own protocol. "She took elaborate care of her lips," said Whiting. "And she always knew the names of her lipsticks."

Secca then read into the record the names of the lipsticks discovered when the police had searched and inventoried my apartment on the Campo.

> *Cherry Lush.*
> *Roman Tart.*
> *Pale Desire.*

"You spent all day, prior to this party, out shopping?"

"What does that matter?"

"And you purchased a blouse that you charged to your husband's credit card?"

The projector displayed pictures from that evening. They weren't unflattering. It had been a long evening, though, and the camera caught me in a slatternly moment. My blouse hung off my shoulder, and I was smiling, a sloppy smile, a little too much light in my eyes.

"And this was the outfit you wore that evening?"

"Apparently."

"But you left early?"

"My husband stayed late at cards."

"You left separately?"

"We did."

"And you went home?"

Before my appearance, Paolo's lawyers had stressed one thing: not to perjure myself, no matter how trivial the matter. I scrutinized my former landlady down in the witness area alongside Whiting. She didn't appear particularly happy in her polka dots.

"No," I said. "I tried to leave, but there were no taxis available." I explained how I had gotten lost on the streets and ended up back at the Palazzo. "My brother let me back in."

"And you stayed the night?"

"I did."

I waited for the next question—and at the same time wondered how I should answer, not knowing whether some servant had witnessed Orsini enter the cottage. Or if Isabella, before she died, had told someone how she'd caught Paolo and me together.

Secca did not ask the question.

I realized the committee had nothing. If they'd had evidence regarding the deaths of Isabella and Frank Paris, it would have emerged long before. So they focused on innuendo instead.

"Your husband went out the next day?"

"He did."

"Did you receive any visitors while he was out?"

My landlady wouldn't meet my eyes. I understood now why she was here and where this was going. I understood the arrangement the party had made. I was to give up my dignity and play the trollop. In exchange, the committee would abandon their inquest into Paolo Orsini.

"I don't see what this has to do with anything."

"I think you do," said Senator Secca.

He turned his sights on my landlady, the poor woman in the blue gauze with the big white polka dots. Such a small woman, aging, with such thin shoulders. Those shoulders twitched now and again, as if she possessed a nervous condition.

Secca asked her for a description of the visitor.

"I was a flight below," she replied. "From my angle, I couldn't see very well."

"What could you see?"

She nodded her chin in my direction. "Her," she said.

"You mean Mrs. Paris?"

"Yes."

The woman's discomfort was plain.

"Could you describe what you saw?"

"I saw Vittoria Paris standing in front of her apartment door."

"Is that all?"

"No."

"What else?"

"There was a man on his knees in front of her. With his head in her skirt."

She delivered this line with some pleasure, and a touch of disgust. She seemed glad to spit it out. The chamber came alive, rattling with noise.

"Could you make out the identity of the man?"

"I didn't try. It wasn't my business. But later I heard footsteps coming down the stairs. My husband heard them, too."

"You got a look at the man then, as he came down the stairs?"

The woman looked frail and lonely and afraid. She didn't glance my way, but it wasn't me she was afraid of, I knew—because it was one thing to impugn my character, but another to mention the name of Paolo Orsini, a powerful man, after all.

"I didn't see anyone," she said. "I didn't look."

I thought Secca might pursue her, but he grew sly. He let the moment linger. He let the chamber see the fear on the woman's face, up on the big monitor. He turned to me.

"This fellow on his knees," he asked, "who was this person?"

The senator gloated, thinking he had me, no matter my answer. Because if I was not with Paolo, then I was with someone else, and I was a whore either way. I saw more clearly the bargain that had been made. It wasn't justice these men wanted. They wanted a devil to blame. A whore, a slut. I wondered if Paolo had sold me out.

"There was no one."

"Mrs. Paris, it's quite obvious you are lying. This woman and her husband will both testify to the fact that there were footsteps on the stairs that evening."

"Footsteps?"

"Yes, footsteps."

"What is it you want me to say—that I spread my legs and by this power bewitched Isabella to her death? And likewise knocked my husband from his horse?"

The chamber rattled again, filling with hoots and cackles and a noise like the Italian boys' hissing on a street corner.

"I ask you not to defile these proceedings with such crudity," said Secca.

"Yet it's fine for you to defile me."

"I'll hold you in contempt."

"And I'll hold you the same way."

"Mrs. Paris—" One of the other senators tried to intervene, maybe a member of Orsini's party, or even Il Primo himself, the faction leader, hoping to get things under control. The men were indistinguishable in their gray suits. I challenged him as well.

"Is this the bargain you have settled on?"

"Mrs. Paris—"

"If you could have this bit of spectacle at my expense, then whatever corruption lies beneath the surface—"

"Mrs. Paris—"

The special investigator snapped the gavel . . . but something had been unleashed inside me. They were hypocrites . . . they were fools . . . they engaged in every petty vice imaginable, and some not so petty . . . Their country was going down the drain . . . and all they could focus on was whether some young woman . . . a nobody . . . an orphan . . . a widow . . . All they could focus on was whether she had lifted her skirts in an apartment hallway . . .

The audience whistled and stomped. The gavel snapped again. I heard catcalls, I heard applause. My lawyer put his hand on my shoulder, urging me down, and somewhere inside me a curtain fluttered, and I watched shadows move on that curtain.

"Order!" cried the special investigator. "Order!"

No one paid him any mind. The committee was divided. While they debated among themselves, the chamber grew more restless. Things were getting out of control. One of the senators took the microphone—a friend of Orsini's or one of the opposition trying to save face, I couldn't tell. He scolded my outburst but at the same time asked the committee to withhold, for the time being, an order of contempt. "I think, given the hour of the day and the emotional nature of the proceedings, it might be wise to recon-vene—and allow the witness counsel with her attorney in this difficult matter." The crowd hooted.

The bailiff led me out. I felt flushed and dizzy. It was a warm day, and perhaps the warmth got to me. A car backfired.

The ground rushed at my head.

It happened in slow motion, outside, with the television cam-eras looking on, there in front of the Palazzo Madama, which had been the residence of the princess of Austria before it was gutted and remodeled on behalf of the Italian democracy. My knees gave way. My hand grazed the shoulder of the guard at my side.

"I'm falling," I said.

I fainted. Though some thought the moment had been staged, I hit the cobblestones hard enough. I heard the fuss around me. I lay on the ground with my purse open and my stockings split. I tried to get up, but things went black again, and in that black-ness the news went out:

#### VITTORIA SWOONS IN FRONT OF PALAZZO MADAMA

They rushed me to the hospital. Two days later, on the doc-tor's advice—and that of the party leaders—I was taken to a Catholic retreat, a place of convalescence. Around this time, I

have been told, my picture first appeared for sale in the vendors'
booths outside the Forum.

# 19.

I L SANGUE WAS IN THE heart of Rome at the top of Aventine Hill. Just outside the walls stood a medieval church with a statue of Pope Pius elevated in an outdoor vestibule. The good pope bowed his head, smiling in a way designed to evoke one of the beatitudes, I believe; but instead it had a punishing effect. A path led past the pope to a vista over the city. That first evening, I saw the nuns at the vista at sunset, gathered like birds in their winged habits.

My admittance had been arranged by the higher-ups in Orsini's party. The idea, or so I was told, was to remove me from the scene in a way that would shame the committee from taking further action. The party had influence with the nuns' confessor, Father Angiosti, and the priest had helped persuade the sisters to allow me in.

They gave me a small room, simply furnished, with a window overlooking the garden. I heard the sounds of birds in the morning and the nuns at matins. Though it wasn't a place I would have chosen, I enjoyed the stiff bed and the bitter coffee. The convent wasn't a place of escape, though, not really. Whatever intrigues I faced on the outside soon followed me in.

# 20.

I NSIDE THE CONVENT I HAD a mentor of sorts, Valentina Marie, an aspiring novitiate not too much older than me. Valentina was somehow related to the Lamborghini family—not on the automotive but on the textile side—and her father controlled a good portion of the fashion industry in Milan. She was a nervous girl with dark, glittering eyes. She knew my situation. The nunnery wasn't as cut off from the outside world as it pretended. The convent library carried the daily papers, and a number of the sisters had Internet devices in their rooms.

"I'd think those would be discouraged."

"They are," said Valentina. "Except for purposes of contemplation."

"Not gossip?"

"Gossip can be holy, too."

On the surface Valentina seemed to be a wholesome young woman, an impression enhanced by her wardrobe—a simple linen robe and a little cross about her neck—but this impression proved misleading. Out in the world she'd had troubles with OxyContin and alcohol and been to the abortionist twice. There were also charges pending on another matter. She didn't tell me this right away but only gradually, between matins.

"Of course I'm grateful to have escaped it all." Her voice held a winsome note. "But at any rate, like you, I have no choice."

"What do you mean?"

"Either I stay here, or I must face the judge."

"I imagine, though, that with your changed character and the testimony of the sisters you might expect leniency."

"There's only so much anyone can do. Unless I'm accepted to the novitiate—as a missionary. To Africa, maybe, or South America. Then the court might show leniency."

"Africa? That seems extreme."

"You don't know the specifics. Or how much my father had to pay to get me here. And how little he wants me home."

The specifics were ugly—involving her lover, a gigolo of sorts, who had been stabbed to death with a pair of scissors—but I didn't know that yet. Valentina was friendly, and I had my own concerns. She was my source of news via her electronic tablet, even if this news was erratic and contradictory, indicating in one moment that the committee had gone into indefinite adjournment and in the next that Paolo had decided to abandon me in order to save his political career.

"You should speak to the priest," said Valentina. "He might let you talk to your lawyer, at least. It's not uncommon once you've reached a certain point in your rehabilitation."

"I will."

"But you must have your epiphany."

"My epiphany?"

"Yes," she said. Her eyes shone. "It's in the brochure. The one they gave you when you checked in."

## The White Devil

I WENT TO SEE FATHER Scirocco, the younger of the two priests.
I went to him rather than Father Angiosti because the latter was
connected to the party, and that connection made me leery. I had
no reason to trust Father Scirocco any better, but he was younger, at least. He had blue eyes and blond hair but a mottled face,
pocked with small white scars. I felt disappointed at how soon he
turned the conversation toward the sacraments.

"Have you availed yourself of the confessional?"

"On occasion."

"Since your admittance?"

"To be honest, Father, since arriving here I've had little opportunity to sin."

I caught the vaguest smile.

"But there's a reason you are here."

"I collapsed."

"In return for being sheltered, you've agreed to commit yourself to this program. There's the lay component, the group counseling, together with the tending to the body. But there's also the
spiritual."

"I meditate. In the garden. Working alongside the others."

"In the group counseling session, from what I hear, you say
little."

"I listen."

"You find those sessions instructive?"

"Yes."

"And this?"

"Pardon?"

"I have a degree in psychology. We don't have to do this in the booth, in the dark. We can be more modern, if you like."

"God is everywhere, I suppose."

"Yes," he said. "And just so you know, inside the booth or outside, the same rules of confidentiality apply."

I understood the sanctity of the confessional, beyond which nothing could be repeated. But people were human, after all. The priests spoke to one another, no doubt. And there were pressures, I imagined, from within the institution and from without. From Orsini's party, perhaps, or the likes of Cardinal Whiting. The situation was not immune to intrigue. Nor to a code of ethics that might allow certain exceptions in this circumstance or that.

"I haven't had a chance to talk with anyone, not even my lawyers, regarding my legal situation. It might make it easier for me here if I could know what's going on."

"Are you afraid?"

He studied me hard with those blue eyes, and I felt my lips tremble. Maybe I was acting, I don't know. I trusted him, almost.

"Sometimes," I said.

"Of Paolo Orsini?"

They were full of sympathy, those eyes of his, and kindness, but also an eagerness. Maybe he was good, as he appeared, but often good people are the ones you can trust the least.

"I'm not sure, really, who to be afraid of."

"That's the worst kind of fear," he said. "The one we can't identify."

Then he spoke to me of the moment of death; of the infinite nature of time; of how certain individuals—like Saint Augustine himself, while writing his journals—experience a premonition of death: the moment in which the individual, confronted with eternal darkness, must fall in submission before God. Confession was not just a preparation for that ultimate submission, not just a foreshadowing, but a way of entering into the moment of death itself, since all time was one time, all moments one moment, and we were, all of us, forever caught in that single moment. As he spoke, I couldn't help but feel that blackness closing in. And maybe I experienced something of what he was talking about. Maybe I was in that eternal moment then—outside myself, looking down—no longer in that one place but the many, here, too, on the Avenida, on the balcony, listening to the footsteps rushing up from below . . .

*Lodovico.*

The man's face, the leering mouth . . .

I startled up.

The priest looked at me expectantly.

"What?"

I shook my head. The image left as quickly as it had come. Or maybe I had no such premonition and only imagine it now, after the fact, and it was simply the priest's droning that had gotten to me.

"Nothing," I said. "I was only wondering if I might make a phone call. To my lawyer, maybe. Or my brother."

The priest lowered his eyes.

"Sometimes it's best to let things settle within. To ignore the churning of the world. Of the mind." His smile was too gentle, his voice too calm—and I could tell he wasn't going to give me permission. "I'm here to talk with you," he said. "Whenever you'd like." But I didn't trust him that far, no matter his pockmarks or his blue eyes.

"I GOT MY DISPENSATION," SAID Valentina.

"From the court?"

"I'll be spared prosecution. Arrangements are being made."

We were bent over in the garden there by the Romano beans, sweating, with our hands in the dirt. Some sisters labored farther down the hill in the tomatoes and the corn, but none was so close they could hear what we said. "I've been accepted as a novitiate. At the mission in Sierra Leone."

"Africa?"

"It isn't where I'd choose, but I'll be in a city, at least. For a while I thought they'd refuse me."

"Why?"

"Well, it's only—sometimes the novitiates are insincere. They don't have a true vocation but only use it as a way out. They disappear after a few months in the mission, maybe a year. Never to be seen again. Particularly if they have money."

"Oh."

"It's a way to escape the law. Of course, I wouldn't do that."

"Of course not."

"Some women, they even return to Italy. Under a new identity. Or even their old one, depending on the arrangements."

"On the money?"

"Yes. Though sometimes it isn't just the money."

"No?"

"There are other ways to achieve indulgence." She paused then, regarding me. "It might only be some information they want. Some small cooperation."

VALENTINA DIDN'T LEAVE THE CONVENT right away. They kept her waiting. Meanwhile, she kept me up to date with the news. There came a new flurry of stories, contradictory as always. About my supposed conversion here in the nunnery. How the committee had me locked up against my will and Orsini was raging at the convent gates in his senatorial limousine, half-mad, desperate to get me out.

Then another letter.

It was a favorite trick of the tabloids, these letters.

This one was supposedly written by Francesco, Isabella's brother, who through some tortured and sensational logic confessed his secret love for me. He deplored my persecution, or so the letter said. He didn't blame me for his sister's death but suspected my brother, acting as Orsini's agent, the two of them conspiring, with me caught between. While he had suspected this all along, the depth of his feelings for me hadn't become clear until he'd glimpsed me on the cobblestones in front of Palazzo Madama.

"Paolo is jealous," said Valentina. She never showed me her tablet but kept it hidden in her room—as she didn't want it taken. "That's what they say. Publicly, he scoffs—but privately, he doesn't know what to believe."

"He knows it is nonsense."

"They mean to turn you against each other."

"It's only the tabloids."

"This man Lodovico . . ."

"What about him?"

"He seems to have a special hatred for you and your brother. And for Orsini."

"He was dismissed."

"They say he was an assassin."

"This is nothing new," I said. "Why do you bring this up unless to frighten me?"

"I'm sorry."

She put her arm around me and cooed and petted me, telling me not to worry. I leaned against her just a little. I was afraid, that was true. I felt trapped between Paolo's enemies on one side and his friends on the other. "You think I'm foolish to go to the novitiate," she said, "but I'm not. Father Angiosti can help you. If you want to escape your situation."

"I don't know if that's possible."

"South America," she said. "It's more modern than people think—the cities there, the missions."

"I don't know."

"There are other places. But you must be sincere in your confession. Sometimes the authorities want some kind of restitution. In my case, for the family of the victim . . . In yours it might be something else. But if there is sincerity and underlying innocence . . ." She smiled then, almost. "Father Angiosti—he'll find you a mission."

"I am here voluntarily," I said, though this wasn't exactly true. "Besides, all my contact has been with Father Scirocco."

She balked.

"I can't trust him?"

"It's just that Father Angiosti has more sway in these matters. He's much more acquainted with the practical aspects."

I imagined then how she had been in her wild days. Those dark eyes of hers, the pouting lips. Sitting in an expensive dress on a bed in the Hotel Roma with the foil spread on the night table, and her lover across from her, looking into those eyes.

"Do you love him?"

"Who?"

"Paolo," she said. "Isabella's husband."

It occurred to me I should be careful. Some small thing in her manner, maybe. Or just my fear the answer might be carried away to other ears. I hesitated—wondering what bargain she had made, with whom, in order to win her freedom—and then I gave her the answer I thought might protect me more than the other.

"Yes," I said.

She gave me a kiss—a little too fervent—and clutched me close. The next morning, at matins, she was gone.

LATER I WENT DOWN TO the chapel and knelt in the shadows with the penitents. Father Angiosti came along, an old man with a large head and bowed legs, hobbling toward his duties in the confessional. He wore a black robe, the sacramental scarf about his neck. He didn't look up as he hobbled but smiled at the floor, a smile not unlike that of the statue of the Holy Father in the outdoor vestibule. He went inside the confessional and one of the nuns followed; the light above the door turned red. Father Scirocco was in the other box, waiting for a penitent.

I wondered if could trust either priest, or if, no matter whom I talked to, my words would travel somewhere else.

I crossed myself and left.

The nunnery hovered on a bluff overlooking the river. On the other side of the garden, down the slope, stood a tower that had been on the grounds since medieval times. The interior staircase twisted sharply, very narrow and dark, with high steps and low ceilings, so I had to walk in a crouch, lifting my knees as I climbed. At the top, the staircase opened to a view of the old part of the city. Sometimes the old nuns wandered up here to pray, but there wouldn't be anyone this time of day.

Supposedly visitors such as myself, the convalescents, could end their stays at Il Sangue any time. All we had to do was stroll out back into the world. No one would stop us. In reality, leaving wasn't so easy. There was the matter of clothing. There was the matter of money. There was also the matter of the front gate and talking to those who held the keys, and also the fine print, the fact that upon entry you had signed a psychological release entitling the convent to detain you in certain circumstances, or to have you transferred to another facility.

It was a beautiful view. The old cathedrals and the monuments and the Tiber were streaked with evening color, while below me the terrace sloped over some ruins down to Via della Lungara and the rushing cars.

I'm not suicidal, at least not in the ordinary ways, but I grew vertiginous then, looking over the side to the rocks below.

I considered the matter of the priests and saw myself in the confessional, in the darkness, seeking mercy. But what would I say? That I was not the instigator. Rather, it was my brother, the panderer. Who ingratiated himself to other men—and found favor in the world—by promising them his sister. Then, when these men were no longer useful . . .

I stopped myself.

What they seemed to want was humility, an admission of complicity, guilt. It was only then you could be forgiven. I didn't know that I believed this. What they really wanted—whether it be one faction or the other—was something to hold over Orsini. That's what Valentina had been implying, I think. Though at the same time, I wondered the opposite—whether it was a test on Orsini's behalf, to see if I'd betray him under pressure.

I didn't go to the confessional.

Maybe that was wise.

Because later, as I came into the main hall, headed to my room, there stood Paolo.

"I have gone through hell," he said.

He looked grizzly, unshaven. Several of his security men accompanied him, and also a lawyer. We stood watching each other.

"Come," he said.

Whatever my reservations, I showed no hesitation. I went and threw my arms around him.

# 21.

WE WERE OFF THE BEACH near Piran, on the Slovenian coast. It was our honeymoon, and we had taken the boat out onto the Adriatic. Rilke's castle was visible somewhere on the other side of the inlet, and so was Trieste, the old port city, which had been given back to Italy after the Second World War. A vital place once but an outpost now, out of the mainstream, stodgy and forgotten. Frank Paris had taken me there when we first came to Italy. I didn't speak of that now, just as we didn't speak of my time in Il Sangue or whatever suspicions we might have of each other.

"Put some lotion on my back."

"My pleasure."

I was naked. We were both naked. We had moored about a hundred yards off the coast and then swam to the beach. Closer to shore, the sea was quite shallow, the bottom covered with rocks, so we'd had to stand and hobble the last bit, bowlegged, until we reached the sand. Paolo put his hands on my shoulders, clenching, massaging, loosening the muscles in my neck. He walked his knuckles down my spine. It felt good, even while it frightened me.

"Everything will be okay," he said.

"Everything will be fine."

"I adore you."

"And I adore you."

"I love to run my hands down your body."

"I love the feel of your hands."

"You are the most beautiful."

"No, you."

This whole while I lay on the sand, belly down. I could feel his breath in my ear. He leaned with his weight against me. Over the last month we had been all over the Mediterranean. We had been to the Riviera and to Capri, and also to Sicily; now we were staying in a small villa on a large island off the Croatian coast, and we had taken the boat out for the day.

Back in Rome, the committee had dropped its investigation in a deal brokered behind the scenes by those gray men and women in their gray suits with the splashes of red. It all had to do with government contracts and appropriations. The press had pursued us on our honeymoon and found us in Monte Carlo. Soon after that, we left the Riviera, but our departure didn't stop the stories.

NEWLYWEDS SEEK REFUGE IN CORSICA
VITTORIA VISITED BY ISABELLA'S GHOST
FRANCESCO HIRES MAFIA ASSASSIN
HAPPY LOVERS THUMB NOSE AT CARDINAL WHITING

The villa on the island where we were staying had been the property of Isabella's family, but at least it was remote. We pulled anchor and returned there now. Though the family still wanted it back, the property had passed to Paolo by virtue of Italian law.

"Why have you brought me here?"

"Because it's a beautiful place."

"It was hers."

"Not really. Such beauty can't belong to a single person."

"But you used to come here with her."

"That doesn't matter."

"I feel her presence."

Later he walked me out from the villa to the shore. It was a longer shore, a stretch of gray sand along the water. Isabella's father, a director, had shot scenes from several movies here—and eventually Isabella had been filmed here, too, in her greatest movie, the one in which she wore the famous dress.

"I know what you're thinking."

"Of course you do."

"Say it."

"It's not the kind of thing I should say."

"Then let it go."

"My brother—"

"Shh . . ."

"And you—"

"Some people are very jealous. They see what they want to see. The press, every accident, every coincidence . . . Don't let them poison your mind."

"The timing, though, of their deaths."

"There's such a thing as fate. Things happen."

"That's true."

"Anyway, you can't say you didn't wish it."

"I could."

"But you'd be lying."

The sky was red now, the sea calm. You could smell the salt and see the boats out on the water way out there. It was an isolated island. There was a Croatian couple farther along, out on the sea wall. I wondered whether we might be recognized, but the people in the village were fishermen and goatherds who lived in their stone-colored houses and cared nothing for us either way.

"No matter—the investigation is over," he said. "And the police cases, those are even further behind us."

"Are you sure?"

"There's no reason to think about it anymore."

I felt her presence everywhere. I felt it when I looked out at the sea. In the breeze. In the sweater I had wrapped around my shoulders and the scarf about my throat. I felt it when he touched me.

"No," I whispered. "Please."

Then he kissed me.

And his hands strayed underneath my skirt.

And he pushed me back in the sand, in a little culvert between the stones.

"I'd never hurt you."

"No?"

"Never."

"You'll protect me?."

"Of course."

My breathing became wilder, and in that instant, pulling him close to me, I realized I didn't believe him, no, not for an instant. I smelled Isabella, her perfume, her hair, and Frank Paris, too, poor Frank, stupid Frank—the smell of him rose high in my nostrils.

I cried out, my legs in the air, and pulled him closer.

I shuddered.

In the morning it was as if they had never existed, the pair of them.

I made Paolo breakfast in the scorched white light. We were a simple couple, on the edge of the earth. We lived three weeks like that, and then we went back to Rome. Things settled down. We went to the opera. People came to dinner. I had a small role in that American television series set here in Rome, and my picture appeared in the celebrity magazines and on the cover of *Vogue Italia.* My brother and I were featured on a layout inside.

Then one day, the dark smoke came rising from the Vatican.

The pope was dead.

And Lodovico, by some sleight of hand, had been given leave to reenter the country.

## 22.

WE LOST A NUMBER OF STAFF MEMBERS in the days following the pope's death. The laundress abandoned us midshift, leaving delicates to fester in the basement sink. A cook disappeared. There were defections among security and administrative staff. The reasons weren't clear. There had been some ugliness in the press lately, old rumors circling back, and new ones, too.

Outside, the black smoke continued to leak heavenward from the chimney of the Vatican.

The tradition went back.

The smoke burned black upon the death of the pontiff and kept burning, streaking the sky, while inside, the College of Cardinals convened to decide who would be the next pope. When the decision was made, the smoke would turn white. It would billow forth in its whiteness to fill the Roman sky. This would be the sign that the new pope would appear soon on the balcony at Saint Peter's. The crowds were already gathering in anticipation, much as they had in the old days, coming down through the Porto Populo amassing along the Tiber and in the square in front of the Basilica.

From our place on Mount Giordano, we saw the dark smoke smudging the horizon.

"These zealots," said Paolo. "They undermine everything."

He was in a black mood, weary of the New Piety and suspicious of his colleagues in the Senate. At the same time, new issues were arising, new people to contend with. Paolo was having problems with his own family, his sister and brother-in-law, the man Johnny had replaced as a go-between at Uzio Station. The man had always been a brute, but lately, more and more, had taken his resentment out on his stepson, Dazio.

So Paolo's sister had sent Dazio to live with us.

Paolo was fond of his nephew, and I was fond of Dazio, too. The press had gotten a hold of this new story and made it into a show, playing up the familial split, the rivalry between the two brothers-in-law, Johnny and Dazio's stepfather.

"Poor Dazio," I said. "The press makes everything into a circus."

"This business with the pope—it's a circus, too," my brother said. "Whoever the cardinals choose, it changes nothing."

Paolo shook his head.

He had thickened since our marriage, and suffered recently from pains the doctors couldn't diagnose.

"You're wrong," he told Johnny.

Paolo touched his stomach. He was worried. The Italian cardinals attacked him regularly. They spoke out against the government's failure to go after organized crime. They spoke against the general atmosphere of degeneracy in which a prominent official could marry his concubine, both of their spouses still warm in the grave. Behind the scenes these same critics lobbied for Cardinal Ratzinger, the German papalist who had coined the phrase

Nuova Pietà and for whom Whiting himself carried on a public campaign in the pages of *Avvenire*.

"This is only noise," my brother said.

"I fear otherwise."

"Ratzinger is German. What does he care about Italian politics?"

"If he becomes pope, it will be because of the Italian cardinals—and because of Cardinal Whiting. He'll be indebted to them. And support my undoing"

The smoke kept rising.

I went inside, and my brother followed.

Johnny took me by the hand.

The tabloids wrote things about Johnny and me, what went on between us. And about Paolo, too. There was a devil's bond, secrets we had to keep. Not everything the tabloids said was true, but Paolo had lost his lean look. He had stomach complaints and his feet swelled without reason. He sat for hours in his chair, mulling the shadows.

My brother touched my face.

"Not now," I said.

Soon it was dark, and Paolo came upstairs. I took off my clothes and lay naked on the bed, and he lay naked, too, but we didn't touch each other. We slept. We nestled our heads in the pillows. Outside, the sky was black. And sometime in the middle of the night, the smoke from the Basilica turned white.

IN THE MORNING, THE STREETS were jammed with people headed toward the great square at the Basilica. According to tradition, the identity of the new pope wouldn't be revealed until he stepped out onto the balcony. In reality, the identity was revealed through feints and rumors, deliberately so, so that the name of the chosen would run like a whisper through the streets.

This whisper hadn't yet reached us at Palazzo Orsini.

Because of the traffic, our staff was running late. One of these was relatively new, Zanche Alessandra, a dark-skinned, Moorish-looking woman who'd been hired as a political secretary. In the current situation, though—given all the defections—her job was to assist with the itinerary and the domestic staff. If she resented this, she didn't mention it. Though striking in her looks, she could be officious, prim. I'd never known her to be late, but that morning—while the white smoke streamed from the Basilica—she'd been approached near the Corso. The man was affable enough, at least at first, and seemed to know her. At least, this is what she told me. A man with black hair thinning on top, skin the color of putty. Sharply dressed, with a familiar manner.

"You work with Senator Orsini?" he asked.

"Yes."

"How about a favor?"

He sidled closer, and she backed away.

"You misinterpret me."

"I hope so."

"The favor isn't for me but for yourself."

"I don't understand."

"It would be wise for you to quit your position with the senator."

"Why?"

He grabbed her arm. From the way he moved, the man seemed accomplished at such intrusions. He moved without seeming to move, communicating by the way he held her and by the expression in his eyes, the turn of his mouth, that he had the ability to snap the bone if that's what it came to, or run her through with a knife, and to do so in such a casual way that the crowd on the street wouldn't notice and might even stand aside for him as he left the scene. He stuck his chin into her face.

"Before too long, Orsini and his slut will pay for their crimes. So if you want to live, my suggestion—find another employer."

Then he let her loose.


THE MAN WAS LODOVICO.

I took Zanche upstairs to tell Paolo.

I burst in, but my brother was already there, along with my husband's security chief: Antonio Gasparo De Lucca. If I have not mentioned Gasparo before, it was because he worked in the background, unseen, but was becoming more visible now. Although Johnny did not trust him, the two of them had been on the street together all morning, listening for news from the crowd. Now everything was happening at once.

Gasparo and Zanche exchanged a fluttering glance.

"It's the German," my brother said. "They chose the German. Ratzinger is pope."

"All right," Paulo said.

His face grew more pale. His skin took on an unhealthy pallor in the morning light.

"But I am still high in the party . . . these desertions in my staff . . . the attacks . . . this must be stopped . . ."

He asked for Zanche's story then, realizing before she spoke, I, suppose, that Lodovico—despite his desire for vindication, his alleged devotion to Isabella—would not risk coming after us alone.



THE STREETS WERE CLOTTED WITH pilgrims. They massed about the arch at the city's old entrance and overflowed onto the cobblestones. They streamed along the ancient wailing wall, in whose crevices they tucked handwritten messages for the dead pope. The carabinieri put up barriers blocking passage, redirecting traffic into alleys that led back the way we had come. Drivers abandoned their cars.

Gasparo rolled down the window.

"We are on state business."

The officer peered inside. I had my shades on and my hair up so that the crowd wouldn't recognize me. I heard crying along the ancient wall. According to legend, the spirits of the dead remained trapped here until their grievances were settled, and the sound of the wind whistling in the crevices at night was not the wind at all but the voices of those dead.

"Let me see the papers."

Gasparo handed the identification papers through. Paolo was not with us. He had kept Johnny with him at the palazzo, meaning to confront the evolving situation in Rome: to protect his own position and get rid of Lodovico as well. Meanwhile Paolo had sent his nephew, Dazio, and me north, toward Salò. He'd assigned Gasparo to drive, to keep us safe, with Zanche in attendance.

"I can move the barriers," said the cop. "But the crowd is thick and stubborn. Without a siren it might be difficult. And even then."

"The other way will take hours," said Gasparo.

"You might want to roll up your windows."

The officer winked at me. It was a lascivious wink. Then he patted the car's fender in the same way you might pat an animal on the rump. We edged past the barrier into the crowd. The stream of people became more dense. The crowd didn't part easily. They were devout but surly, solemn-eyed, nervous in the heat, at being herded together like cows. We came to a standstill. A child pressed his nose against the glass and put his hands on the window. Soon another child did the same, and a curious old gypsy, too.

"Do something," said Zanche.

Gasparo leaned on the horn and gunned the engine. The crowd surged away, but the mass behind pushed back. They thumped their fists on the trunk and kicked at the sides, and a young man threw himself over the hood, rolling and laughing, and Gasparo gunned it again. The car rolled over something. There was another thump, a cry, and the people fell away. Dazio turned to look back but I took him by the hand. We reached the A1 headed north. We drove through the sprawling Roman suburbs up into the middle of the country, toward Tuscany and Bologna and the mountains beyond. The traffic on the Autostrade was thinner than usual, maybe because by this time the Italians had gathered around their televisions to see the new pope when he appeared on the balcony.

"Mussolini," said Zanche. "He had a place in Salò."

I knew what Zanche was talking about. Everyone knew. When Mussolini fled Rome, he had lived up by Lake Garda in the northern part of the country.

The Republic of Salò, it was called.

Eventually, fleeing the oncoming Americans, he'd been caught by the partisans and executed.

Italians loved to retell the story.

Of the partisans who'd captured him, and how they'd pumped the bald dictator and his mistress full of bullets.

I didn't want to hear about Mussolini and his dead mistress.

"I need to stretch out."

"Should I ride in the front?"

We pulled over then so Zanche could ride with Gasparo in the front, and it was just me and Dazio on facing seats in the back. The glass divider was drawn to give everyone their privacy, and I unbuckled my seat belt, slid off my heels, and stretched my feet.

Dazio laid his head in my lap.

He was a young boy, barely seventeen. He was somewhat naive for his age and thought of me as a sister. I comforted him for a moment, brushing my fingertips along the hair on his brow. Then I sent him back to the other side, where he put his head against the window and slumped into sleep.

# PART FOUR

# 23.

WE DIDN'T STAY LONG IN SALÒ. Three days after our arrival, a tourist snapped a photo of Dazio and me at a restaurant down by the water. In the photo I was wearing a scarf and sunglasses, and you could see Dazio's good looks. I'd applied gloss to my lips, and Dazio was leaning toward me. It was, I suppose, possible to mistake the nature of the moment—to infer an intimacy where none existed. But I was just his aunt. He was just a child in my keeping.

The tourist sold the photo.

It was bad timing, given the sudden realignment of political allegiances taken place in the Senate, under religious guise. Paulo's enemies saw opportunity. Worse, the photo attracted the press to Salò.

It prompted a threat painted in red on the garage door: a giant heart, a dagger driven through.

*Cazzo assassino di Isabella nel cuore!*

We left, pursued by photographers on motorcycles. We lost them in a mountain pass at the border, when Gasparo maneuvered the limousine in a way that sent the paparazzi spinning toward the tunnel wall.

## 24.

ANCHE REMAINED A MYSTERY TO me. I can't say I trusted her, but that was her fate, not to be trusted—at least, not in Italy, not with her dark skin and Muslim cast. She carried herself with an air of privilege. Her family had immigrated to Italy when she was young, escaping Tehran. They'd been upper-class merchants who'd fallen from grace and lost everything when the winds shifted back home. She spoke several languages, all with a British accent. Maybe this last explained her reserve, and her tidy looks.

She aspired to go into the diplomatic service, so I wondered why she stayed with us. I thought it might have to do with Gasparo. There were more looks between them, fervent glances.

Zanche's employment had been screened by Italian intelligence. Meanwhile, Gasparo had started his career within the intelligence ministry and knew the head deputy. The Agency for the Security of the Republic held no party affiliation, at least officially, and screened employees for all sides of the political spectrum. Still, I sometimes wondered whether Zanche's loyalty, and Gasparo's, too, might ultimately be more to the head deputy than to us.

"I'd suggest—if you want to stay out of the limelight—Canada, as opposed to the United States," said Zanche.

"Along those same lines, I suppose you'd suggest Finland over France?"

"Yes, I would."

"The cold weather makes people less inclined to murder me?"

"There would be less media to seek you out, at least. And fewer people to care."

She had a point, but it was not her decision. Though my departure would be sudden, Paolo had arranged for certain contingencies. These plans didn't include the Canadians.

# 25.

W E WENT TO MALIBU. It might not seem, given the colony's reputation, the best place to escape the public glare—but the colony maintained its own security, versed at keeping gawkers at bay, and the house we rented was unapproachable from the street. It stood on pillars above the sand, security cameras on all sides.

"No one will bother us here."

"But if the press finds us—"

"The press doesn't bother the colony."

"The beach—it's public access."

"Only the part down there, along the surf."

Zanche and I lingered at dusk on the deck overlooking the Pacific. The air smelled of jasmine and smoke. Bonfires burned along the beach. There was a pair of rooms below for her and Gasparo, steps to the sand. Though she said nothing, I knew it appealed to her. I'd seen her and Gasparo together and had a good idea of what went on between them.

The original plan had been to stay away only until things calmed down in Italy, but the situation there kept worsening. The murder rumors persisted—revisited by conspiracy theorists, for the hell of it, for political slander—and the New Piety entangled Paolo in other issues: irregularities with the online casino where Paulo had a stake; influence peddling; the discovery of kickbacks from the construction contract at Uzio—with my brother involved. This latter was their main focus, as the alleged corruption affected the new pavilion in Milan.

In Malibu, we fell into a kind of limbo in which our primary occupation was to keep from being recognized. I spent a good deal of time with my nephew, Dazio. He was lonely and got a bit of a crush on me. Sometimes as we walked along the beach, I let him take me by the hand—but it meant nothing. We had developed a routine and would lie out in the sun at a particular time each morning. A man who lived up the beach came almost every day to swim in the ocean in front of our house. I watched him take off his shirt and wade into the water.

"Why does he come down here?"

"To swim. It's too rocky on the point."

Dazio slouched forward, his long arms over his knees. The morning fog had burned away, and the surface of the ocean was bright. The man was a strong swimmer and before long he was pretty far out, bobbing along in the gray water.

"I'm thirsty," I told Dazio.

"Then let's go inside," he said.

"I'd rather have something out here."

"You'll burn."

"I'm okay."

"You need some lotion."

"Not now."

I put a shirt over my shoulders and squinted out toward the swimmer. His head remained visible, though at this distance it might have been a seal, or a log, or some other bit of flotsam. The small spot grew smaller, and before long it would disappear altogether. I knew because I'd watched him before and had nothing else to think about out there on the sand. He would disappear for a time, long enough that I'd start to wonder if something had happened to him; or my mind would wander, forgetting him altogether—but then I'd see something: a tiny blackness, some small dot, a disruption way out on the horizon.

"Go make some lemonade for us. Fresh squeezed," I said. "Wouldn't that be nice? And bring it down in a pitcher."

Dazio hesitated.

"It would be lovely of you," I said.

"All right."

The swimmer reappeared. He worked his way back, vanishing and reappearing, looping through the swells. Slowly his form grew larger, and he emerged from the water. His chest glistened in the sun. I sat close to the tide line, not far from where he'd dropped his shirt before wading in.

"You're new?" he asked.

I had my sunglasses on and my hair in a bandanna. I wore a yellow two-piece, with the white shirt draped over my shoulders. I was glad of the shirt because it hid my long arms, my gangliness. All this time, Gasparo and Zanche watched from the deck. No doubt they'd have preferred I mind my own business— that I talk to no one—but the swimmer looked at me without a trace of recognition. I was just a woman in a bathing suit, sitting on the sand, her long legs splayed clumsily in front of her.

Lodovico back in Rome seemed a distant threat.

"We're vacationing," I said.

"For how long?"

"Just a little while."

Our house was not the only one on this stretch leased out during high season to wealthy tourists from abroad. Though I'd only lived there a few years, I liked to think I'd been in Italy long enough that I spoke English with an Italian accent. I could tell the swimmer anything, I supposed. I didn't have my wedding ring on. I hadn't worn it since arriving in Malibu—since I didn't want to lose it in the sand. The man didn't wear one, either.

"I've seen you walking," he said. "With the boy."

"My nephew."

"That explains the resemblance. You are built alike."

There was no blood relation between me and Dazio, but I didn't bother to explain. He glanced up toward Gasparo and Zanche on the deck as if wondering about their connection to me.

"This Friday, some friends and I are having a get-together." He gestured at his house. "The one with the fire circle, out on the point."

"I notice that you build a fire most every night."

"Most nights, it's just me."

He was nice-looking, almost too nice, and his eyes held a pleasant vacancy. He looked back toward our house. I followed his gaze and saw Zanche, with her beautiful black skin and her bright suit, coming toward us through the sand. She'd been carrying herself more loosely these last days, especially around Gasparo, but when the stranger tried his smile on her, she went cold.

"You're needed back at the house," she said to me.

"No, I'm not."

"You are."

The swimmer understood her drift.

"I'd better go," he said.

Zanche and I watched him head down the sand toward his place on the point. She had come to drive him off—to make sure I didn't give our situation away. Gasparo observed from the deck, leaning there on his elbows, in his swimming trunks and a khaki shirt worn loose to conceal his holster.

"You could be more subtle," I said.

"So could you."

"Don't be so judgmental."

"I judge nothing."

"Meanwhile, Gasparo and you—you do as you please."

"Only you are allowed pleasure?"

I pursed my lips. I could feel the sun beating down through the haze.

"You hurt my feelings when you say things like that," I said.

My voice cracked a little, but I don't know whether Zanche believed me. I was curious about her—to see whether her features might soften. I suspected her coldness might be a mask. If it was, that mask didn't crack. She went back to her Gasparo.

Dazio returned with a thermos and some ice.

"Lemonade?"

"I don't care for any," I said.

I saw the disappointment in his face. I felt badly. He was just a boy, trapped here through no fault of his own. I took off my shirt then to get some sun. The swimmer was gone, and I didn't mind if Dazio saw me for the bony, disjointed creature I happen to be.

"I need some lotion, please."

He spread it on my back, sullenly at first, but after a while his sullenness turned to pleasure. He enjoyed touching me, and something about his touch reminded me of my brother when he'd been younger and sweeter. I pushed this thought away and lay down with my face in the towel.

PAOLO AND JOHNNY ARRIVED ALL of a sudden. Their appearance took me by surprise. We'd been in Malibu awhile. Sometimes it seemed as if the outside world didn't exist. There was just this moment, and the next, a long stream of moments held together by a sense of anticipation. In the morning when I stood in front of the mirror, I didn't necessarily see Vicki Wilson, or Vittoria Paris, or Mrs. Paolo Orsini. I didn't see the woman from the tabloid sites, or the doll-eyed girl from Texas, or any of the other people I have been reported to be. I just saw a woman regarding herself in the glass, posing in her white shorts—lips pursed, not entirely pleased with her looks but at the same time possessing a hint of vanity, of surreptitious pleasure, as she turned her heel and admired the curve of her body. She had a nice tan, after all. She lay down on the bed, admiring herself in a different way, indulging herself in the way people sometimes do. She put a hand on her stomach, then lower, sliding beneath the tan line. Maybe she thought about the swimmer then, or someone else, or no one in particular. Maybe she thought only of herself. It was only an interlude. Already Paolo and Johnny climbed from the limo, arriving with their bags from LAX.

PAOLO'S EYES HELD AN UNUSUAL luminosity. He'd always possessed a light in his eyes—but the light had grown feverish. His illness had worsened since I left Italy, and he'd been consulting with a Chinese herbalist in Rome. He measured a honey-colored

liquid from an amber bottle into a cup of tea, and soon the feverish look gave way to something glossier.

"Have you missed me?"

"Too much," I said.

"The investigation— it's in recess."

"I thought this was all over."

"It's never over," he said. "They have a new angle."

I wondered why he'd come to Malibu when there was so much
at stake in Rome. Something crossed his face, a raw glimmer.

"Your brother—" Whatever he'd been about to say, he
changed his mind. Or else it got lost in the glossiness from that
amber bottle. "I came to be with you, and to rest. There's a regimen, certain herbs . . . but it can be very taxing. I started it, but
then . . . I thought, all in all . . . I thought it might be better to go
through the regimen here. Rather than in Rome . . . surrounded
by people I can't trust . . ."

The old committee had reconstituted itself—bolstered by the
new religious cast to the senate—and been meeting behind the
scenes with people who had once been close to him, former employees and associates, including his sister's husband, Dazio's
stepfather, who'd lost his role at Uzio Station to Johnny.

"Your pain?"

"It's not so bad."

"You look tired."

"Close the curtain," he said. "It's past midnight in Rome. I'll
never sleep, all this light."


MY BROTHER WAS RESTLESS. WE stood on the deck together and
watched Dazio head down the beach with his headphones on,

plowing sullenly through the sand. Young people, close to his own age, gathered in groups along the shore this time of day. He longed to mingle with them, but our situation didn't permit much interaction.

"This medicine helps Paolo?"

"He only has a limited supply, on account of customs."

"It helps him?"

"Sometimes, without it, his will weakens. He has moments of despair."

"He has those anyway."

"And moments of rage."

"He blames me for his situation?"

"Me, more likely," my brother shrugged. "You he holds tender. You and Dazio both." Johnny spoke the boy's name with a touch of mockery. "Just before leaving Rome, Paolo was on the phone with his estate attorney. Some amendment to the bequest."

"What was it about?"

"I don't know exactly. He didn't confide in me."

"It's likely some small thing."

"Likely," my brother said, though his tone suggested otherwise. "You know Paolo has left you everything. The irony is that the longer he lives, the less there'll be to give. The committee means to strip him bare—to take everything and divide it among themselves."

"And you?"

"They want a goat. A little animal with horns—and a throat to slit."

I reached up and brushed a curl from Johnny's face. The wind had picked up, blowing in over the tide. I made out Dazio farther down the beach, slumping along on his way back. I saw boredom and loneliness in his shuffle.

"The way you look at him."

"He's just a boy."

"There are plenty of boys in the world."

"He's so innocent."

Johnny whispered a vulgarity. It might not seem so, but Johnny was fragile, and much of what he did, he did for me. That fragility could make him ugly sometimes. He could be envious, unreasonable.

Dazio clumped up the steps.

"Where have you been?" Johnny demanded.

"Just walking," said Dazio.

"Where?"

"Just down the sand."

"Don't."

"Why not?"

"You know why," Johnny said. "You put us all at risk."

"I was just walking on the beach."

"Stay where we can see you."

"I did," he said. "You could see me fine."

"He was just getting some air," I said. "Someone his age . . . he can't sit in one place all day and night."

Johnny shot me a glance.

Dazio had some height on Johnny. He looked at Johnny down his nose, a haughty look, and I feared the boy might say something foolish. My brother was in such a mood, I worried what might happen. Then Paolo appeared from inside and embraced his nephew. This rankled Johnny. He leaned over the deck toward the ocean—but the view offered little solace.

Gasparo and Zanche lingered by the water.

"And I wouldn't trust those two, either," he said. "They come from the intelligence ministry."

"The head deputy is an old friend, I thought."

"They are all friends," said my brother. "Lodovico, if you remember—he worked for the ministry, too."


THAT EVENING, PAOLO AND I went down to the ocean. The gulls swooped low, scavenging in the fading light. People tended fires along the beach. We strolled down the retreating shoreline toward the far rocks. Not too far away stood the house of the swimmer who had invited me to his party. I caught a glimpse of him mingling with his guests in front of the fire ring.

"I've been offered a deal," Paolo said.

I stopped then, not wanting to go any closer. The swimmer had seen me, I thought, standing in my white shorts alongside Paolo by the darkening shore.

"What do the senators want?"

"A bit of everything."

"What do you get in return?"

"My capitulation to their demands will be announced as a reform. I'm not only cooperating but even leading the way."

"It's blackmail. You're being forced."

"I'll hold onto my seat. I won't go to jail. For kickbacks—how the contracts were assigned."

"And your money?"

"It's not the assets they want—or not all of them—so much as control."

"This will satisfy them?"

"The moralists still need to be appeased."

"How?"

"Someone must go to jail."

"Who?"

Paolo said nothing. I pretended ignorance in these matters, but I understood. Half the members of the Italian Senate were lawyers, and the various committees they served upon awarded contracts. The beneficiaries changed, the owners, the go-betweens, even the rules. Who was corrupt, what was legal—these definitions changed, too, especially when it came to the control of assets, the trickling of government money through private channels. The legislature, Orsini's colleagues, might honk and holler, but underneath they were loath to punish one another. What they wanted more was their own private deals. In the meantime, someone had to pay the price.

"Johnny?"

"The laborers—Trenitalia, the housing hub—and some of the supplies . . . they came through outside channels."

"He worked for you."

"Your brother was taking money—from the laborers, and from the contractors. He did it without my knowledge. He did a lot of things without my knowledge."

I didn't believe this last part. My brother was no saint, but whatever he had done, I doubted Paolo had been unaware.

"Why are you telling me this?"

"I can't protect him anymore. You know how it is with Johnny. He says something, he smiles. You're not sure what he means, quite, and then the next thing—well, something happens . . ."

Overhead, the clouds moved, shifting shape, and the fog roiled in a white mass against the blackness. There were bonfires up and down the shore.

"What am I supposed to do?"

"Come back to Italy with me. And make sure he comes, too."

"You overestimate my influence."

"You can reassure him."

"If he suspects—"

"He doesn't need to know. He shouldn't know. Not until we are back in Rome. There, if he pleads, it will go easier for him."

"It's safe to return?"

"There's no choice."

"None?"

"I could defy the Chamber. I could refuse to cooperate. But the U. S. and Italy have an extradition treaty, so that means we'd have to go elsewhere. It would be difficult. I've moved some assets already, it's true. But still . . . I would do anything for you."

"And I for you," I said. I looked back at the swimmer's house. "They want Johnny and me both?"

"No . . . only him."

# 26.

THE CHINESE HERBALIST IN ROME went by the name of the Yellow Emperor. He had an elite clientele whom he relieved in the ancient ways—with acupuncture needles and suction cups and tinctures of various elaborate mixture. Dandelion and monkshood. Astragalus and ginseng and concentrated aconite. He practiced by the homeopathic method, treating the malady with compounds that invoked symptoms similar to those of the illness, thus agitating the disease out of the body. He worked in the old Jewish ghetto, not far from the crumbling Portico of Octavia, and carried in his stock herbs and exotic compounds—elephant's tusk and shark's fin and tongue of the Bengal tiger—any one of which might have brought charges of illegal trade if it hadn't been for the elevated nature of his clientele, whose influence kept him protected. It was rumored he tinctured his compounds with other substances, as well—including the extracts of certain Afghan poppies, and the coca leaf—as some of his most devoted clients possessed a glossiness of expression that implied other reasons, aside from mere loyalty, that necessitated their frequent return.

THE NEXT MORNING PAOLO SUFFERED an episode, alone, while walking on the beach. I learned later he'd had a number of these episodes since I'd left Rome: severe attacks, dizziness, cramping in the gut—but they could be relieved with assistance from the amber bottle. This time he didn't have the bottle with him and had to struggle up the sand while the white gulls circled overhead. I was lying on my beach towel, eyes closed. I heard the gulls squawking but didn't think anything of it. They always squawked. Then Paolo loomed over me, drenched in sweat.

"What's happened?"

"My tea . . ."

I got him inside. I mixed it for him, and he seemed better. The little amber bottle was all but empty.

"It needs filling," I said.

He'd been trying to decide whether to take the herbalist's full regimen here or wait until we were back in Italy.

The regimen was quite strenuous.

Meanwhile, there remained the unfinished business with my brother.

Either way, he needed the amber bottle.

"Here," he said.

He gave me the name of an herbalist down in Hollywood— highly recommended by the Yellow Emperor—who could provide the highest quality of this element, and other essentials in his regimen. He handed me a list of ingredients the Emperor had written out on blue paper.

"Do me a favor?"

"What's that?"

"Go alone," he said. "Just you. I don't want Johnny involved."

MY BROTHER CAUGHT ME ON the way out, my purse in hand, and when the taxi came, he slid into the backseat alongside me. I could have told him no, or made some excuse. I could have said I was going shopping and would be hours in the dressing rooms. Or that I needed, after all these weeks, please, a few hours alone. I could have told him something like that—but I don't know that he would have believed me. I had a choice to make. It was the same old choice.

I gave the address to the cabbie.

"The apothecary?" asked Johnny.

"You know everything."

"I know his medicine cabinet. In Rome, I ran these errands."

"He wanted me to go."

"You're his wife. He trusts you."

The taxi took us up the canyon through the careening scrubland and rock-scuttled hills toward Route 101. We didn't sit next to the car windows but more in the center of the seat, like we used to do when we were kids. Johnny took my hand, trying to make up for his peevishness the evening before. It was pleasant sitting next to him, enjoyable in a thoughtless, family kind of way. There was an undercurrent of the sort there always was with Johnny. The taxi clattered over the pass through Calabasas, then plundered down 101 through the Hollywood Hills. The herbalist's place was off Hollywood Boulevard, down in the used-up part of town, in a little yellow bungalow with a yucca out front and bars on the windows. My brother leaned up toward the cabbie.

"Next corner," he said. "Take a right."

He had the cabbie take another turn after this, then stop in the middle of the block. I didn't understand. It was a beat-up part of the boulevard with nothing much to recommend it, empty except for a middle-aged couple in shorts and an old man on his knees holding a rag and a can of polish.

"It's the Walk of Fame," Johnny said. "The stars. Their handprints."

"No handprints along here. Just stars," said the cabbie. "The handprints are over at Grauman's."

"That's fine," said Johnny. "This is exactly where we want to be. Just keep the meter running. In the meantime, here."

Johnny handed the cabbie some cash.

"Isabella," he said. "She's over there."

"I thought. . . . "

"It would be a more glamorous? . . . That's what everybody thinks . . . It's just a piece of cement on a sidewalk."

"That's not why we're here."

"I thought you might want to take a look while I'm in the apothecary. There's no need for you to come. Just give me the list."

"I promised Paolo."

"I can make sure of the ingredients in a way you can't. You'll have your part to play, don't worry."

"What part?"

Johnny spoke with his eyes, speaking without saying. Paolo was right about Johnny in that way. All this time, Johnny held on to my wrist. He held it gently and didn't say anything, but I understood. He knew everything, the same way he always knew everything. He knew what was going on behind the scenes in Rome.

"Sister?"

I didn't really want to go in. Such places were alien to me. The smells were unfamiliar, the rows of containers: animals ground to power, organs suspended in vitreous fluid, tiny capsules filled with gels packaged halfway around the world, little bottles wrapped in discolored paper.

I gave Johnny the blue piece of paper with the exotic names written in the Emperor's exotic script.

He let go of my hand.

He kissed me on the lips.

I waited, with the meter running. I stepped outside the car and smoked a cigarette. I was tempted to leave my brother then. To get away, from him and Paolo both. I'd had such chances before, but I didn't know if I'd have one again. All I had to do was get back in and tell the driver. He'd take me anywhere I wanted. Out to Palm Springs. All the way to Phoenix, if I gave him the money. Across the ocean to Sierra Leone. Instead I walked across the street to look at Isabella's pink star in the concrete.

MY HUSBAND'S REGIMEN HAD SEVERAL aspects. There were the herbs and powders he mixed at mealtimes. The exact proportions of these didn't stay the same but changed from day to day, from dose to dose, in a manner that had been prescribed beforehand by his practitioner in Rome. As to the exact nature of these ingredients, it was difficult for me to tell. The correspondence between the outer packaging and the lettering on the bottles wasn't clear. Some containers were hand lettered in Chinese script; others not labeled at all. Of all these various tinctures and powders, the amber bottle concerned Paolo most, because it induced the euphoric effect that eased the pain and made the rest of the regime tolerable.

Orsini held it to the light.

"The color," he said.

"Is something wrong?"

"No," he said. "I was just admiring."

He mixed it with his dandelion tea and a drop of royal cornflower. This latter possessed traces of aconite, an herb poisonous in some forms and some doses. Orsini knew this and measured it carefully. The mixture seemed to have the desired effect: it put him in a delightful mood, and shortly after he fell asleep. The next morning he was drowsy and complained of stuffiness in his ear—and then he slept for the rest of the day.

That evening he developed a low-grade fever accompanied by chills and bouts of nausea. It was part of the process, triggered by the herbs, through which the body was encouraged to expel the underlying illness. Toward this end, the agitating compounds were to be added in greater proportions until the end of the third day. At that point the fever would break—at least in theory— since the underlying imbalance would have been addressed. Then the regimen would change, commencing with a restorative tea.

A sullenness fell over the household.

"I can't stand being cooped up," Dazio said.

"It won't be much longer."

"I thought it would be better after my uncle arrived. But your brother . . ."

"Don't be jealous."

"How much longer will he be here?"

"I don't know."

"Are we going back to Italy?"

"Maybe."

"Zanche says you'll abandon us."

"Zanche said that?"

"She says you'll do what suits you and leave us to fend for ourselves."

"I wouldn't abandon you."

"You'll send me back to my stepfather."

"No, that isn't true," I said. "You and I, we are birds of a feather."

His stepfather had turned against Paolo and my brother. Not only that, he was a brutish man, and Dazio's mother pretended not to see. I knew something of how that felt, and I could see Dazio had no desire to return to them.

"We can go for a walk."

"All right," he said.

"I'll get my sweater."

Inside, Paolo had just taken some concoction, a mix of herbs stirred like some kind of curry into a cup of rice. He leaned at the counter, head between his hands, sweating. He sweated like a pig. He jittered. I took him into the bedroom and brewed his tea. He spoke of his enemies in Rome and of the trumped-up nature of the charges against him, then drifted into a stupor.

"It looks like it's going to be a long night," Johnny said.

"Yes."

"Come to my room."

Dazio watched from the deck. Paolo moaned.

"He'll be all night," my brother said.

My husband let out an ugly noise that carried through the wall. I found him on his knees, retching into a trash can, in full fever, mumbling inchoately. He thumped about as I tried to help him back into bed. The noise brought Dazio and Zanche.

"This regimen . . . ?" she wondered.

"It has to do with the humors of the body. The mixture— Li Lu curry, he calls it, mixed with pepper—it brings out the heat."

"There's more in there than pepper."

"The goal is to bring out the imbalances and sweat the toxins from the body."

"Maybe we should call a doctor."

"I suggested that earlier," said my brother, though he'd said nothing of the kind. "But Paolo won't have anything to do with traditional medicine."

"The herbalist, then."

My brother wandered onto the deck with his cell, as if to have the conversation in private, or to get better reception.

"Is he dying?" Dazio asked.

"I don't think so."

I heard Johnny on the deck, making a show of it. I had no idea who he might be talking to: it was Sunday in Rome—the Emperor would not be in his office—and I knew Johnny well enough to know he might not be talking to anyone at all. By the time he returned, Paolo had fallen still.

"What do we do?" I asked.

"Let him sweat out the night. There'll be more fits, but let him sweat."

"Those were the instructions?"

"Then in the morning be sure, by all means, that he takes the restorative."

# 27.

PAOLO LAY QUIETLY FOR SOME time, and I climbed into bed beside him. Later he began raving. It's difficult for me to describe his behavior. He seemed both unable to move, as if held down by a horrible weight, and at the same time possessed by an irrepressible energy. He threw the compress on the floor. "Off!" he cried, then grabbed himself by the scalp, twisting and pulling. "Oh, it burns so! How can this be!" He stared wild-eyed into the shadows, addressing the darkness with a laugh—carrying on like some figure in a play, a king gone mad. "And who is this? What clever disguise?" He peered at me suspiciously. He spoke my name sweetly, then not so sweetly. "You've brought them here. You've let them in," he ranted. His enemies had some-how entered his room, using me as a vehicle—issuing forth from my nose, for all I could tell—and fastened to his head a cap whose lining had been dipped in poison. "Remove it from me, please," he begged. He bargained with the unseen, pleading his innocence. Apparently it did no good. He was going to hell. His entire being was on fire, his skull burning from within. Then he lunged at me as if I were not his wife but one of those demons, those ghosts, who had conspired against him and stood mockingly over his bedside.

I backed onto the bedroom balcony. I stood on the threshold with the moonlight falling all over me and the sound of the black waves crashing against the rocks.

He fell quiet.

Just before dawn the fever broke, though I didn't realize at first. I thought he was dead, he was so quiet, his breathing so shallow, and I myself so tired, so exhausted, it hardly seemed to matter, and I fell asleep beside him on the bed.

For how long, I couldn't be sure.

Hours.

Minutes.

A gull crept along the balcony railing, and a watery light filled the room. Orsini awoke. He seemed to have very little memory of what had happened during his fever. He regarded me fondly.

"You were here all night."

"Mostly."

"The others betrayed me at every turn. But you—"

"Rest," I said. "Don't worry about anything."

"I'm feeling better."

He touched the collar of my robe, a silk garment I'd brought from Rome. It was Isabella's. I know how that makes me look, but Isabella's things and mine—they'd hung all intermingled in that closet. And she had so many things just hanging there, collecting dust.

"We'll go shopping tomorrow," he said.

"Yes."

"Down in Beverly Hills. Then we'll leave."

"Where?"

"Mexico, Buenos—what does it matter, *mia bella*."

He smiled wanly. This had been his nickname for her.

"I'll buy us an island," he said.

He wasn't a good man—I knew that. But he'd been strong, I thought. He possessed things. He knew what he wanted. Now I realized that wasn't true. None of what he'd possessed had actually belonged to him. It had come from Isabella. Once, he'd wanted her more than anything. But he'd never gotten her, not really. Or maybe he'd just changed his mind. Things change. I knew this as well as anyone. You want something for a little while. Then you want something else.

Sooner or later he'd be done with me, too.

"Don't be afraid."

"I'm not afraid."

"We'll get a car," he said. "A silver Mercedes. And drive down the beach."

"That will be nice."

"I'll buy you a new dress."

He made plans then, quite animated. We could do anything we pleased, he explained. There'd been plenty of people who'd done similar things. Exceptional artists, thinkers. Dante Alighieri, for example. Roman Polanski, the filmmaker. The great American poet, what's his name, who'd spoken on the radio for Mussolini. Exceptionally talented people who didn't play by the ordinary rules. We were the same, he and I. We didn't need to go back to Italy. There were ways to protect his money, to escape extradition. To live in our own private kingdom.

"I need my tea."

"Of course."

I HEATED THE WATER AND took out the restorative. For the past several days he'd been adding royal cornflower to his dandelion tea, along with the amber potion. That changed now. This new ingredient was the inverse of the cornflower, and—according to Paulo—was to be added in modest amounts at first, increased, then tapered down. The outer packaging reflected those inverse qualities, the colors reversed and the flower itself not yet in bloom.

My brother had explained some of this to me that day in Hollywood, after he finished in the apothecary. He told me to ignore Paulo on the dosage.

"How much?"

"You may have to administer it yourself."

"Why?"

"He'll be weak. And the new ingredients, the proportions, they may confuse him."

"He'll want to know."

"These items come in different proportions, different mixtures, varying according to the supplier. Just explain to him: this is what the apothecary in Hollywood advised. Paolo might resist. So I'll leave it to you whether to persuade him or simply administer it yourself, to his tea."

"How much?"

"All of it," he said.


I SHUT THE CABINET DOOR. I didn't look in the mirror but only at my hands. It struck me then how odd my hands were, how unnatural—how much they resembled my brother's, though it was also true that my brother's hands in turn were oddly delicate for a man's, slender and refined. He kept care of his hands the way women do—with lotions and creams. I watched my own hands now as if they were his. I watched my hands work out the little cork and empty the contents of the vial. I stirred, mixing in some honey.

I glanced at the packaging. At the brightly colored box and the bottle. The labels didn't match. I'd be lying if I said I didn't notice that. If I said that after close examination I'd not suspected the contents were not an inverse at all but rather a concentrated version of the cornflower.

But I am not an expert on such things.

I snuck a glance at the woman in the mirror. We were handsome people. I smiled just like my brother had smiled, leaning toward me in the taxi, over that shopping bag nestled in my lap, whispering into my ear.

*All of it.*

Orsini was on his feet by the bedroom's sliding door, looking out at the morning, at the intense light already breaking up the fog and the seals hollering in the distance. He appeared oddly invigorated. It seemed the regimen had been good for him, after all. He looked like a man just emerged from a fever, ready for health. He stood in his colorful robe, and I remembered the heat in the air when I'd first met him, how he'd looked me over with those black eyes.

He sipped the tea.

"I feel odd," he said.

He put his hand to his chest.

"Are you hungry?"

"Perhaps. Yes."

He smiled then. Only there was something off. It wasn't a smile, really. More a twitch. The muscles gone rigid in the face. He tried to speak, but something burst inside him. His shoulders tightened, hunching inward, and his arm went up, as if hailing a taxi. He buckled at the knees.

I called for Zanche.

He lay there, eyes open. He wasn't dead yet, I don't think. He was still conscious—and what he saw wasn't the demons of the evening before, come to seek their vengeance. It was me. His eyes locked onto mine. Then his pupils clouded and turned to milk.

"Zanche!"

The house was silent.

I pounded him on the chest, like I have seen done, and put my mouth to his, trying to force the air in, but his lips tasted foul and his breath stank. I pulled away reflexively. At this point Zanche walked in. I sat straddled over my dead husband—hand raised up to my face, as if wiping the taste of him from my lips.

# PART FIVE

# 28.

ORSINI'S DEATH LIFTED A CLOUD, but it created a dilemma, as well. Once the story broke, we wouldn't be able to stay long in California. It might raise suspicions to leave so soon after his death, but I knew the nature of Paolo's enemies—and of his friends—and how they might use the opportunity to move against us.

I called 911, and the paramedics came. They went through the motions, attempting to resuscitate Paolo as I stood out on the deck listening to the surf pound the beach, glancing every now and again at the house on the point.

They declared Orsini dead at the scene.

A massive coronary.

"He was so young," I said.

"Any history?"

"He'd lost weight, he'd been ill, but the doctors in Rome, they couldn't find anything."

"Medications?"

"Some Chinese herbs. For his stomach."

A police officer arrived after the medics, and he, too, examined the scene. At my brother's insistence, I'd left the teacup on the floor—and the herbs and bottles in the cabinet. It would have been foolish to do otherwise, Johnny insisted. Everyone in the household knew about Orsini's regimen and how he followed it religiously, under his own volition. We all knew the stress he'd been under.

The cop took my name without reacting. I didn't know if that was because this was Malibu and they had been trained in nonchalance, or if in fact the name meant nothing to him.

Maybe I felt a small bit snubbed. But the tabloids, this side of the Atlantic . . .

They had no idea.

The paramedics covered Paolo and strapped him to a gurney. Then they wheeled him out to the front of the house—to the ambulance that waited in front of the long line of garages that clung to the sand along the edges of the Pacific Coast Highway.

AS A MATTER OF ROUTINE, the coroner performed an autopsy at the hospital, slitting open the chest to get a look. That glance confirmed that the heart muscle had seized up: death by cardiac infarction. The examiner took some fluids for chemical analysis, also a matter of routine. The results weren't back yet, but in the meantime the hospital released the body to the Malibu Funeral Home.

"YOU CAN'T BLAME YOURSELF FOR this," Johnny said. He put his arm around me, and the funeral director rose discreetly to her feet. "It isn't your fault," he whispered, "no, no," and he continued murmuring to me in this tender, gentle way even after she was gone. We'd been talking about burial options, and at the mention of cremation I'd broken down. "We tried to talk to him," Johnny said. "We both did. Those concoctions from China, those dosages—there's no quality control. I understand how you feel. But he was devoted to this particular agenda. Quite stubborn."

I dabbed my eyes.

"He was insistent," I agreed.

"Maybe the ingredients were impure. Or mislabeled. I blame myself, too. Though how were we to know?"

I'd heard my brother talking about this to the police, telling them we had no idea where Paolo had bought his medication. He'd simply gone out on his own one morning. Then three days later, he was dead.

It wasn't exactly true, of course.

"You can't blame yourself for this," he repeated. "There's no way you could have known."

I pulled myself together.

"What about the chemical analysis?" I asked.

My voice was different.

"What about it?"

"At the morgue? What will it show?"

The mask dropped.

We looked at each other.

"It doesn't matter," he said. "He poisoned himself, unintentionally or otherwise. No one can prove differently."

"Are you sure?"

"Yes."

I sobbed.

"Poor sister," he said. "You have such bad luck with men."

# 29.

THE NEXT DAY I SPOKE with my husband's estate lawyer, Romeo Ferragamo, whom I'd first met not too long after I married Paolo, when my name replaced Isabella's on documents related to the estate. Ferragamo was a dry little man, very thin, who wore a black suit tailored too short at the extremities. He spoke to me now by phone from his office along the Via di Ripetta. He was fluent in both English and Italian, but in either language his voice was very droll and overly precise, like the small print in a very long contract.

The news wasn't good.

On account of the government's pending action, Orsini's financial matters were in disarray.

And his bequest to me was in danger.

That was the essence, though there were other issues. Isabella's family had an outstanding claim against the estate, as yet unsettled—and more recently, Dazio's stepfather had moved to have himself named executor of his stepson's portion of the estate.

"It's a tangled situation. The government—if you fight them, it will be costly. And you will lose."

"So what should I do?"

"Your husband was in the midst of negotiation with certain committee members, in their unofficial capacity. He had made agreements, in principle. I would capitulate on those quickly and gracefully. And as for Isabella's family . . . their claim has moral legitimacy."

"Moral?"

"They are Italian, you are not."

"Oh."

"What I am trying to tell you is that they have the public sentiment on their side. Give them what they want. You'll still be a wealthy woman, just not as wealthy as you might have been. But you'll have fewer enemies."

"Only fewer?"

"I can't eliminate them all . . . Meanwhile there's one other change your husband wanted to address before he died . . . It needs your approval."

"Yes?"

"In regards to Dazio."

"What is it?

"In the event of his own death, Paulo wanted you to take on guardianship of Dazio's trust . . . However . . . if you too should die before Dazio is of age, that duty would pass to me."

"As opposed to the boy's mother?"

"He distrusted the stepfather."

"He should be distrusted," I said. "But as to the rest of it, how do I know the others will be satisfied? The senators in particular."

"I can talk to them."

"All right."

"You would like me to proceed?"

"I'll speak with my brother."

A silence followed, and I guessed that Johnny wasn't welcome in the bargain.

"I'll see what can be done," said Ferragamo.

AFTER THE CONVERSATION, I WALKED on the beach alone. I continued down the sand, past the houses with their enormous windows. We had been here long enough to know something of the people who lived nearby. Of the man who had starred many years ago in a television show of some repute, and whose wife had committed suicide on the beach. Of the aging actress—she lived in the blue A-frame with the cantilever windows—who'd had her lips enlarged in order to play the role of a famous magazine editor. Of the director who'd made it rich by creating aliens that resembled little children on steroids. I walked down Carbon Beach to the ocean, turned my back on the houses, and let the waves run up against my feet. I felt the wet sand between my toes. A couple approached. I could tell they weren't Malibuites by the careful way they straddled the tide line along the narrow strip of public access, in the damp sand between the beach and the waves. They glanced at me shyly—as if wondering who I might be.

I watched the tide come in. It came in raggedly, uneven along the beach; but farther down, near the point, it had already begun to obliterate that space where the public could walk, swooping up toward the rocks, under the pillars, beneath the houses where the stars lived.

I hurried back along the ribbon of dry sand prohibited to the public. The couple, caught in the water, scrambled up the rocks in their wet shoes—headed for the highway beyond.

FERRAGAMO GOT BACK IN TOUCH sooner than I expected, with news that the various parties would be amenable, as he put it, to such solutions as had been suggested. There were technicalities with regard to the transfer of property, he explained, and because of these it was preferred—in fact, all but imperative—that I be present at the signing of the various declarations back in Italy. There were other ways to proceed, but none simple, and all involved a substantial delay.

That was how the lawyer expressed it, proceeding then in likewise manner—in similar language—to assure me that there was nothing to worry about with regard to my returning to Rome: that, in fact, there had been several developments of late that made any hesitation on my part unwarranted. Indeed, he insisted, my return to Italy and attendance at the memorial would be welcome: the powers that be had been sobered by Paolo's sudden death—especially his former allies, who felt remorse over their aggressive posturing, fearing it had caused strain on his heart and a premature expiration. Meanwhile, on the other side, among those who had despised Senator Orsini, there was little profit in going after me, his widow, since there had been slim evidence to suggest my involvement in the alleged murders, and it was clearer yet I had no connection whatsoever with the broader criminal issues haunting Uzio Station. Furthermore, there were people in the government, not to mention the prime minister himself, who wanted to see a proper burial for Paolo

Orsini of Rome, whose parental heritage, or so it was believed, went back to the sucklings at the city's gates on one side of the family, while on the other side could be found ancestors to the Huns, who had reinvigorated the Roman blood. His family had served in the days of the Renaissance alongside the Colonna family, in defense of the Vatican, and had stood ground in the catacombs against the Nazis (or alongside them—Ferragamo's choice of words was such that it was hard for me to tell), but regardless, the attorney concluded, it would be neither wise nor prudent for even the most vociferous of enemies to continue the harassment and persecution of Paolo Orsini's widow, especially as she had been generous to the extreme, forsaking the majority of her fortune in order to make amends with Isabella's heirs. At no point did Ferragamo make any insinuation that either I or Johnny might be suspected in Orsini's demise. No doubt there was such talk—or would be soon, in the tabloids or elsewhere—but he did not repeat it.

"And my brother?"

"If he comes, if he submits . . . it will go easier for him. On the corruption charges."

"How much easier?"

"I can't make any guarantees."

"I don't know if I'll be able to persuade him."

"Then he'll be extradited. And punished more severely. You should make this clear to him. Consider, too, the consequences for yourself."

"WHAT?"

Johnny wasn't pleased. I'd waited until evening to tell him. We were in the living room overlooking the sea. The sky still held a trace of red, but it was darkening fast. The sun was already gone, collapsed under the horizon.

Johnny didn't like this. He didn't like it at all.

I tried to explain what Ferragamo had told me on the phone, how it would be best to settle the issue and move on; that I wouldn't win against the government in a fight over the estate; and that if I returned to Italy, having made this gesture, the criminal charges against him—regarding diversion of government funds—would be treated more kindly.

"Do you think they are suddenly going to welcome you with open arms?"

"I have no illusions."

"Cardinal Whiting—you know how much he despises you. He's got the pope by the ear—and the prime minister, too."

"This may be, but . . ."

"They mean to split you open. They will take everything."

"If we run, they'll track us down. We'll get nothing."

"You're well provided for. For me, there's nothing."

"I won't abandon you."

"This is exactly what you are doing."

"What would you have me do instead?"

My brother had no real answer. He hadn't imagined the estate would be tied up in this way. He was getting worked up now. I had seen this before, when things didn't turn in his direction. He'd done everything for me, he said. He'd given up his own life. He'd licked ass and sucked dick and put up with those vainglorious Italians—not to mention Frank Paris—and he'd listened to their talk, shuffling his feet all the while, running every fool's errands. And all for what? So his sister could dress up like some housewife on holiday, with her legs spread open and the Prince of Egypt on his knees, peering in.

"Don't speak to me that way."

"What?"

"Don't make a spectacle."

It was the wrong thing to say. He kicked at the table. He swept an ashtray onto the floor. Johnny didn't usually act this way, not with me, but the veneer cracked and the charm gave way to rage. Dazio rushed from the deck.

"Stop it!"

Dazio's chest was out, his face all red. It was a brave moment, but he was just a child.

"No, Johnny. Leave him alone."

"This one, too, then. You're fucking him, as well."

"Johnny."

"You've always liked little boys."

"You shouldn't talk to her like that," Dazio said.

"I shouldn't?"

"No, it's rude."

Johnny struck him in the face. Dazio raised his arm in self-defense and cowered toward the wall. This infuriated Johnny even more. He kicked the boy. He threw him to the carpet. Then kicked him again.

"Johnny!"

"Shut up."

Gasparo came up from below. Bigger than my brother and stronger, carrying that sidearm in the holster underneath his shirt. If it hadn't been for the sidearm, Johnny might have gone after him, too—but I don't think Gasparo would have minded. Gasparo didn't care much for Johnny. He felt cooped up, too.

"What's going on here?"

Dazio lay curled and moaning on the floor.

"Come," my brother said.

I ignored him.

I tended to Dazio. There was no dealing with Johnny when he was like this. I was angry, and the boy was hurt. Later, Zanche and I took Dazio down to Santa Monica to walk along the Palisades and look at the lights and the ocean and the young people gathered on the pier.

By the time we returned, Johnny was gone.

# 30.

I DIDN'T GET ON THE plane to Rome. Part of the reason was that not long after the fight with my brother, we were visited by a Los Angeles homicide detective. She was an Asian woman, plainclothes, who told me the autopsy had found aconite in Paolo's system, as well as a Chinese herb called Li Lu. Both of these were used in Eastern medicine. The problem was that in combination, they could be quite calamitous to the heart.

I was very cooperative.

I told her the treatment had been prescribed in Rome and then continued here, though Paolo had gone through some difficulty to find the herbs. When she asked where he'd gotten them, I told her I didn't know. Someplace out in Pasadena or Long Beach, I wasn't sure.

"He was a believer in alternative medicine," I said. "My brother and I, both of us, we expressed our concerns. That last morning, Paolo seemed to be getting better. Then all of a sudden . . ."

She asked about Johnny, and I told her he'd gone off to Tahoe for a few days. I could see her mind clicking, but whatever her suspicions, those doubts would take time to follow up, to check out every Chinese pharmacy in greater Los Angeles, and it would be harder yet to prove Paolo hadn't fallen victim to an error in his own judgment, or to the general quackery and misinformation that permeated the field.

"Do you know the name of the hotel?"

"No," I said. "But I can have him call you."

"Please."

I didn't tell her about the fight. That Johnny had rummaged through my room before he left and taken an envelope with a good deal of cash, emergency money I'd been carrying since Rome. So I'd been forced to arrange an international wire transfer, moving quickly, as I feared access to my husband's accounts might be in jeopardy.

I HADN'T GIVEN UP THE idea of returning to Rome, but after seeing the detective I had second thoughts. I wasn't worried about the evidence so much as the publicity. Leaving here all of a sudden, off to Italy, might deepen suspicions. On the other hand, I was his wife. I should attend the service in Rome. Not doing so might cause even more doubts.

Then there was the matter of the will, the various settlements, and the consequences if I delayed signing too long.

I hesitated.

Maybe it was because I didn't entirely trust Ferragamo's arrangements. I knew how fickle Italians could be. At the same time, the circumstances surrounding Paolo's death in Malibu were attracting scrutiny here and it might not be safe to linger.

I did nothing.

One day passed, then the next. I didn't get on the plane. Ferragamo sent papers by courier so I might get the process started, but I let the papers sit. More days passed. They passed in a haze. I fell into a kind of lethargy, suspended in inaction, caught between going and coming. Looking back, my behavior—my lack of decisiveness—seems inexplicable, but I had fallen prey to a kind of inertia. Maybe that inertia had something to do with my brother. With his absence. That inertia was made palpable by the expanse of the ocean in front of our house. It was easy, in the face of that great emptiness, to imagine there was no outside world. There was just this strip of sand, sun blaring down through the fog.

I spread my blanket and lay down in my colorful two-piece.

Dazio lay beside me.

Gasparo and Zanche lounged on the deck. Whether they stayed out of loyalty or for some other reason, I didn't contemplate. They existed in the same suspended state as I did.

This place lulled you.

Others might dream of coming here, but they couldn't.

They were stuck in that other world.

Meanwhile we were safe, away from the clamor, anonymous as the sand. I sighed. I closed my eyes.

I felt a horrible dread.

# 31.

THAT NIGHT I WENT ALONE to the house of the swimmer who lived on the jetty overlooking the rocks. Though I hadn't talked to him since that day on the beach, I'd seen him at a distance and watched through my shades as he emerged from his swim. He'd linger at the edge of the surf, drying himself, and at the last minute he'd glance toward where I lay on the chaise, up on the deck.

He was a nice-looking man.

I had learned his name since then and looked him up in the online gossips, and read about his career and a little about his life. None of that interested me so much. Maybe it was his looks that drew me. Or the vacancy in his eyes. Or because what I knew about him didn't add up to much, and I could imagine anything I wanted. It didn't take him long to answer the door. He wore a white shirt rolled at the sleeves, a little bit rumpled.

"I hope I'm not disturbing anything."

"No. I'm glad you stopped by."

"I'm sorry I missed your party. I'd hoped to come."

"Well, that's nice."

What I wanted from him, I don't know. Maybe I hoped he would somehow be able to lead me from this place. Or perhaps I am disingenuous with such statements. Perhaps what I wanted was a different kind of escape. Something simple and quick.

"And your husband?"

He'd seen Paolo and me together on the beach that evening when we'd gone walking. Apparently he was not aware that Paulo was the man who had died, or had not heard of the death at all. Our place was a ways down the beach.

"I'm not married."

"Oh. I had just assumed."

I could've told him something else. The truth, I suppose. That while the man he'd seen on the beach some days ago was lying on his deathbed in the midst of hallucinations, I'd stepped out onto the balcony and gazed toward this house and the small fire out front. We sat down, and he poured me some wine.

"Divorced?"

I shook my head.

He poured the glass full, and we sat watching the sun go down. The sky was scarlet and gold, and the birds were sliding through it, and the ocean was a wave of black spreading out to the horizon. *So beautiful*, I thought. In a little while the colors started to fade, and it was just the darkness.

"Yourself?"

"Divorced twice. My current—we're on pause."

He told me the names of the women. One of those names I'd heard before; the other two, no. They'd all been involved in film at one time or another, and the third—the one from whom he'd just separated—had been on a television sitcom.

"Actresses?"

"Of course."

"What were they like underneath?"

He shrugged.

"What's anyone like? I don't even know that about myself."
He paused then, as if contemplating this mystery. His eyes grew
pale. "I'm going to the Caribbean next week. A friend of mine has
a private jet."

"How wonderful."

He told me his friend's name. It was the name of a man well-
known in the business.

"Do you act?"

"A little."

He moved closer on the couch. He was a good-looking man, as
I've said, though a little too ruddy from all the sun.

"Maybe you could take me with you."

"Where?"

"On the jet."

He smiled.

"Why don't you sit next to me?"

He wasn't subtle. I appreciated that, because in certain things
there is no point in subtlety.

"Do you ever want to run away?" I asked.

"I already have."

"Sometimes I'd like to be someone else."

He kissed me then. I sipped at my wine. It was a good wine.
The darkness had rubbed all the color out of the sky, and the
waves slapped noisily on the rocks in the cove.

"The tide's coming in."

"I think I should leave."

"I'd rather you didn't."

I thought about this. It would be nice to stay here, away from the others, and for a minute I imagined it might be possible. Of course it wasn't, but I allowed myself to think it.

He asked me about myself.

The story I told him was pretty much true. I told him I'd gotten married when I was very young, and that I'd lived in Italy—and then my second husband had died, too. And now I was trying to decide what to do with my life. I didn't give him all the details. There was no reason to. But there was nothing I said that wasn't true, and I could see, just for an instant, he was imagining things about me that maybe had nothing to do with who I was.

And I imagined I might vanish into some other kind of life.

He walked me out to the deck. I lingered, staring into the blackness. The light was all but gone from the sky. I felt chilly and clutched myself as I leaned over the railing. He lingered beside me.

"I'm looking for someone to make me good."

It was a line, the worst kind of line, but I didn't mind.

"Me, too," I said.

He kissed me again, and in that kiss there was the taste of something large and empty and thoughtless. The waves rolled, full of darkness, and I wanted to taste it some more. I remembered how he'd disappeared, swimming out there in the water. I remembered Orsini as he died.

"Have you eaten?"

"No."

"We could go out."

"I'm not dressed for it."

"You're fine."

"It's chilly. I need a sweater, at least."

"I'll walk down with you."

I thought of Zanche and the others. I didn't want them to see us together.

"I'll run down. And be back in a minute."

"You promise?"

"I promise."

I left then, going down the sand, and as I did, I allowed myself to get carried away. I felt a lightheartedness I hadn't felt for some time. The distance from his house to our place wasn't far, but it seemed longer in the dark as I trudged through the sand. I was maybe a hundred yards from our place when I saw a figure lurching toward me in the darkness. It was Zanche.

"We have to go."

"What?"

"They are here. In Los Angeles."

"Who?"

"Lodovico and two others, from Rome. They've come to murder us all."

"What are you saying?"

"They've come to kill you. And Dazio. So long as you are alive, the estate . . . it can't be settled . . ."

She was quite worked up, and very earnest, and nervous in a way I hadn't seen before. The tide rushed in more quickly. I glanced back toward the man's house with its seductive light—and I knew then I wouldn't be going back.

"I'll do what they want. I'll sign the papers."

"It's too late."

"How do you know?"

Zanche had no answer. I wondered where Johnny was. I remembered him saying we couldn't trust Zanche, or Gasparo, either. They came from the head deputy, *il vice capo*, who provided security for all parties, with loyalty to none.

"We must go," she said.

"We'll make arrangements."

"No. It must be immediate."

"Why?"

"They are here in Los Angeles."

"How do you know this?"

"Gasparo," she said. "He got a warning. He has gone now to meet them—to play decoy. So we have time to escape."

# 32.

THE FLIGHTS TO THIS PART of the world are by nature long, via indirect routes, with interminable delays. Zanche accompanied Dazio and me not so much out of duty, I don't think, as fear for her life. Since our arrival here, she has been sullen. Partly this has to do with Gasparo, from whom she has heard nothing. They were much in love, it seems now, though in my opinion she was the more smitten of the two.

"We are without protection. "

"It's not Gasparo's fault."

"No," I said. "I'm grateful to him."

"If he hadn't made arrangements. . ."

"Yes—I realize we owe him our lives."

I'm not convinced we are safely delivered. We found this apartment through a name Gasparo gave Zanche—but the city has inherent dangers, to say nothing of the neighborhood. The owner of the apartment, a small man of German descent, told us that it wasn't uncommon in this city for women like us, of our class, to carry small revolvers in their purses. On his advice we'd already visited a certain shop along the Avenida.

"You've still heard nothing from Gasparo?"

"What are you suggesting?"

"I only think we must maintain our vigilance. Be careful who you contact."

"You can do any fool thing—and I must show caution."

"All I'm saying, don't hold out false hope."

She began to weep, and it became clear to me that she, too, had realized the most likely possibilities. Either Gasparo had met an unhappy fate back in Los Angeles, or he'd abandoned us and didn't intend to jeopardize himself for our safety. Or, worse yet, he intended to betray us altogether. Regardless, I held my tongue.

"I don't see why I should be killed for you," she said.

"We won't be killed, any of us."

"You have Dazio."

"I don't know what you mean."

"You know exactly."

"Dazio's my nephew."

"Not by blood. Besides, that kind of thing—I wouldn't think it would matter to you . . . You and your brother, after all . . ."

"I don't like your implication."

"I've seen you run your fingers through his hair."

"Dazio's a boy," I said.

"My point exactly."

She left me sitting on the balcony overlooking the Avenida. She was a dark-eyed one and ever prim, even now, in her lovelorn state. I didn't like the way she had spoken to me, but she had no one. Though I resented her suspicions, I understood them. Dazio was a good-looking boy who acted foolishly at times, but his company was pleasant. Partly it was his looks: his jet-black hair and his dark eyes and the lanky, youthful body that—in slacks and a white shirt just a hint too large for him—drew the glances of women both young and old, and of men, too. He had large, feminine lips, not unlike my brother's. But unlike my brother, he had no guile. He followed me like a puppy. Or at least he often did—though he was growing more aloof lately. I noticed this the next morning, when he went with me on my errands down to the market.

"What will we do?"

"We'll have lunch."

"I don't mean that. I mean, how will we live?"

"There are beaches to the south."

"Like Malibu?"

"Better than Malibu."

I didn't know if this was true, but I said it anyway. I ordered him some coffee and a pastry, and then went around the corner to my errand at the bank. Before the accounts had been shuttered, I had managed to wire money to myself under an assumed name, and then I'd put it in a cashbox, registered under yet a different name, where I would be able to access it without electronic scrutiny if I needed to make a quick exit. The teller took the box down and left me alone in the room. It was a fair amount of money but by no means infinite. It wouldn't last forever. As I stood looking at the cash, my fears came over me: that I couldn't trust Zanche, that I would be better off alone—and I felt tempted to take all the cash at once. But I didn't. I took only enough for the next several weeks. I returned to the little plaza. Dazio sat as I had left him, smoking.

You wouldn't know, looking at him, that he was as hopeless as he was. He looked older, a little glamorous, almost, with that cigarette hanging from his lip.

"I'm sorry to have kept you so long."

"It's all right."

"Did you get bored?"

"No."

"Did you read the paper?"

"No. I just sat here."

"That's nice."

"A man talked to me."

He was often approached by men. As I said, both genders found him attractive. Given the circumstances, I feared who the stranger might be—and that there might have been some other, more sinister intent.

"A man?"

"Yes."

"What language did he speak?"

"Italian."

This wasn't entirely out of the ordinary. The city had long been a refuge for Italians, so much so that the Spanish tongue here—especially along the port—sounded more of Calabria than of Castile.

"What did you speak about?"

"He wanted to know of any good hotels in the area."

"Did you tell him where we are staying?"

"I'm not that stupid."

"I didn't say you were."

"I'd like to go back to America."

"I thought you didn't like Los Angeles."

"At least there, a person can go out at night."

"The streets here aren't safe," I admitted.

"I can't stay cooped up forever, you know."

## The White Devil

Even in the wealthiest neighborhoods, the windows stood barred and the streets smelled of mold. The financial district was under private patrol. Tin shacks stood in the shadows of the high-rises; shanties sprawled forever. The police didn't venture into the neighborhoods below the Avenida, and along the Avenida itself beggars and bash artists and gypsy kids roamed without license. Our neighborhood stood a bit off the beaten path, on higher ground: an older neighborhood, houses built the century before, in the distant twenties; a neighborhood past its prime, smelling of urine and damp stucco, but with its own small plaza and failed urban renewal farther up the hill. One heard gunshots at night. There were stabbings and robberies in broad daylight— but not so many as on the lower boulevards, or in the club district, where gangs of sexed-up boys and prostitutes prowled about with their knives and their genitalia, wandering among the dolled-up *ricos* on the slum and the chauffeured limos that trundled the little *niñas* down from the heights. The clubs interested Dazio. I'd seen him studying the fliers plastered and peeling on every corner. Those dangers were not my primary concern now. I wanted to know more about the man who'd approached him in the square.

"It was nothing," he said. "Don't worry about it."

"The man was alone?"

"No."

"Who else?"

"Another man."

"They both walked up to you."

"No. The other one stood over there. By the fountain."

"What did they look like?"

"He saw I was smoking. He wanted a light."

"Then you started talking?"

"Only for a moment. Please."

"What?"

"You're making me upset."

We went to the counter and paid. The waitress checked Dazio up and down, then checked me over, too—and gave me an approving wink.

"He's my nephew."

"Of course."

She winked again, this time at Dazio. Her manner made me uneasy. I didn't care what she thought, but I didn't want the attention.

"About those men . . ."

"Don't worry," he said. "Those ones—they were only faggots."

"How do you know?"

"I know a faggot when I see one. Besides, not everything's about you."

We caught a taxi to El Viejo Centro—the city's aging downtown, all but fashionable—and went shopping. Dazio got a leather jacket—tightly tailored, in the style of the *ricos*—and I bought shoes. At Dazio's suggestion we bought a colored blouse for Zanche, to help cheer her up. We needed to conserve our money, but I could only be so cautious. We stopped again, lingering over some coffee and rum. Dazio skimmed the local girls, and they skimmed back. A chime sounded on my cell. I pushed the device farther into my purse.

"Who is it?"

"No one."

"Then why did it ring?"

"Just a reminder, a little alarm I forgot to turn off."

Dazio regarded me skeptically—and I saw he wasn't so naive as I sometimes thought. Then his attention was drawn again to the passing girls, little *chicas*, brazen in their laughter.

AFTER LEAVING MALIBU, MY BROTHER had gone to Vegas. That world wasn't new to him. Like Frank, my brother liked to gamble. He liked cards, he liked dice rattling on felt, he liked the drinks at the table—but more than that he liked the private game, the one that started at the bar, with the smiling and the chatting up, and ended in a hotel room, late at night, with the taking of the money. He did well n that world, or did well for a while, but then something happened and he retreated to New Orleans. Recently, he'd left the States altogether. He was out of money. He didn't mention this last detail in his texts, but I knew him well enough to put it together.

Both of us faced extradition now. The cop in Los Angeles had checked our history—working backward from Rome to that young man in Dallas, even to the boy in the well—and later found her way to the Chinese medicine shop in Hollywood. The practitioner had identified my brother. The evidence was circumstantial, but it didn't matter. We were wanted on suspicion of murder. Meanwhile, the estate deadlines had all but expired in Italy. I couldn't return while I was facing extradition for murder—but if I wasn't there to claim the bequest, the distribution of the assets would fall to the state. The pending government seizure endangered the agreements Orsini had made privately with the senators on the committee. Because I'd never enacted Ferragamo's suggestions with regard to Dazio's trust, that would still fall to Orsini's sister upon my death. Meanwhile the pending

government action drained everything away bit by bit, to lawyers, to taxes, to fines. This infuriated Isabella's family on the
one side and Dazio's stepfather on the other. It didn't make certain senators happy, either. There were only two things that
could end this situation. One was my returning to Italy before the
deadline, so that the estate might be processed. The other solu-
tion was a certificate of my death.

# 33.

I SPEND MY NIGHTS OUT on the balcony. The Avenida glows, the city is full of noise. Inside, Dazio has grown bored. He watches television and lies indolently on the couch, but his eyes don't follow me as they once did. He sneaks out at night to visit the clubs, then wakes up in the morning rumpled and smelling of whiskey. This morning I heard the giggling of some vamp returning with him, climbing in by the back way. I should intervene for his own good and for the sake of our security—but I'm not heartless. Meanwhile Zanche, in need of distraction—with little to do and nothing to manage—studies the globe for a place of future retreat.

Bangkok, maybe, or Hong Kong. Or one of the foreign emirates.

She knows as well as I do that none of these will be safe. She is on the computer constantly, scanning in a half dozen languages, reading the gossip, the posts and tweets, still hoping for news from Gasparo. She ignores the obvious.

Not so long ago, I found this in the Los Angeles coroner's reports:

## Domenic Stansberry

A body, male, late thirties, unidentified, was found with his face mutilated and hands removed after having washed ashore on the beach below Pacific Palisades.

I don't ask if she has seen it but leave her be, staring into the computer.

So I end up alone, drinking on the balcony.

The evening has a sullen beauty. The smog. The clattering televisions. The rusted wires hung with frayed laundry. I hear the rituals of the couple on the vista, out for their nightly paseo, edgy and bickering as they wander up the cobbled way to the stone bench.

They do not see me. They do not care about me.

It's just the night.

I drink it in. Or it drinks me.

I turn off my cell so as not to read what new things people are saying online, the thousand rumors since my husband died, since the autopsy reports. I'm curious, I admit. I can't keep it off for long. Though I yearn for anonymity, I fear it, too.

The stars a white smear on the black horizon.

# 34.

I N THE MORNING THE SUN whitens the haze, and the worries of
the night seem unfounded. Whatever goes on in that vague,
twittering darkness no longer matters. I frequent a café
where no one recognizes me. I enjoy this. I eat a pastry with my
black coffee and read the local paper. I'm not proficient in the
language, but I imagine a day when I might be. I read the articles
with something like concern, as if I am someone other than a visitor, as if it might be of interest to me, the widening of the port
and the effect this will have on local traffic, on the old part of the
city that many regret to see modernized, and on the factory
workers whose jobs will be lost to telecommunications. I read
such things over my coffee, things I never cared about before,
and think about them as I walk back, forgetting for a while what
pursues me.

So I didn't notice at first the man who had taken up position
across from my apartment, on the terrace overlooking the Avenida. He leaned against the white brick, smoking a cigarette. He
watched me as I unlocked the gate, in the unabashed way a Latin
man watches a woman. That wasn't what unnerved me. I was
used to the stubborn lechery of Latin men. It was his looks—

hawk-nosed, puppet thin: a lanky, slope-shouldered man whose clothes hung loosely about his body. His shirt, like that of Lodovico's companion that night in Rome, was buttoned up to the neck. The world brims with men of similar appearance, but I felt the chill of recognition nonetheless.

I checked on Dazio and found him asleep, lying with a young girl curled sweetly around him.

I felt a pang in my heart. I had at once the impulse to tear her from his arms and at the same time the desire to bend over her, to cover them both with the white sheet that had fallen to the floor. I lingered by the door, watching them. I might have lingered longer if it hadn't been for the sound of footsteps in the hall behind me.

I feared at first that I had left the gate open and the man outside had somehow found his way in. The German landlord had warned us of the dangers facing women who became careless in the city.

The intruder was Johnny.

However mixed my emotions had been about Johnny before, they were more so now. It was my own doing, my own mistake. A few evenings before, out on the balcony with a glass of wine in my hand, in a fit of loneliness, I'd weakened. I'd texted where we were. I allowed myself to believe afterward that he wouldn't come. Even to imagine—to forget, to push the memory into darkness—that I hadn't responded at all. I dismissed it, as one does drunken behavior. But there he stood, my brother, Johnny, in front of me in the hall. I wondered if the appearance of the man outside was coincidental.

"Your boy, he sleeps quite prettily."

"I asked you to wait."

"I didn't see the sense of a hotel."

"You could've told me you'd arrived. So I could prepare the others."

"Zanche wasn't particularly happy to see me, I admit."

"She let you in?"

"Reluctantly."

"Where is she?"

"Off to the market. She blends in quite well. Before long, I suspect she'll be able to walk with a basket of fruit balanced on her head."

I went to the balcony doors and peered through the slats. The man had migrated up the street. His appearance was yet more disconcerting from a distance, the way the clothes hung about his body, so long and thin, almost skeletal.

"Come here, Johnny. That man—"

"Aren't you glad to see me?"

"Just come here."

"Let me finish what I have to do."

He was in the bathroom, taking a shit.

Outside, the man seated himself with his back to the building, on the steps at the top of the terrace, looking down over the little park and the rooftops toward the gulley below. The Avenida ran in that gulley. It was full of noise, of honking horns, an endless, slow-moving road that dwindled forever toward the pampas. I wished I had taken the rest of the money from the bank.

Johnny emerged.

I nodded toward the balcony.

"Do you know that man?"

"Which man?"

"Outside. On the steps."

My brother went to the blinds. He peered through the slats, then opened the doors and stepped out forthrightly, standing there like he owned the balcony and the world it looked over.

"It's quite the view," he said.

I stayed sitting on the bed.

"Do you recognize him?"

"Who?"

I went to the balcony. The man was gone. Then I saw him on the lawn below the terrace: his long body, how he moved his arms and legs, as if jerked about by a string. He turned a corner and vanished altogether. It was possible I was mistaken. Men leaned against the wall all the time, to smoke and look at the view. When I glanced at my brother, I couldn't help but remember that night at Palazzo Orsini, and the little dog who had chased me down the streets of Mount Giordano toward Lodovico and his gangly friend.

WE HAD TWO GUNS IN the flat, *pistolas para mujeres*, as the clerk had called them, pocket revolvers Zanche and I had picked up at the gun shop on the Avenida not long after our arrival. One of these Zanche carried in her purse. The other I kept behind a planter at the top of the stairs.

Late the next morning I was sitting at the desk in the hall when the doorbell rang. I heard a man's voice below, on the other side of the locked gate, speaking with Zanche.

"Cuántas personas están aquí?"

"Por qué?"

"Hay un problema con la electricidad en este barrio. Puedo entrar, por favor?"

"Esto es una residencia privada."

"Lo entiendo. Pero, los circuitos eléctricos . . ."

The stranger wanted access to the property—I understood that much. He spoke in a jovial, flattering way. Zanche wasn't the kind to succumb to flattery, but something about the situation and the man's tone got me to my feet.

I took my gun from its place behind the planter. It held a wax plant with red flowers.

I went to the bottom of the stairwell and leaned against the dirty wall, the gun tucked close against my skirt. It felt warm and small in my hands. I couldn't hear them as well as I had from above, but I gathered the man was a workman of sorts. Or posing as such. Their conversation fell into a lull, and the lull went on. I stepped around the corner into the foyer. I stood in the shadows, holding the pistol so it couldn't be seen.

"What's the issue?"

"This man says there's an electrical problem in the neighborhood," said Zanche. "The issue is in the side alley—on a pole there."

"Our electricity is fine."

"He wonders if we would unlock the gate to the alley so he can investigate."

A cyclone gate stood alongside the building, concertina wire strung overhead. The landlord kept the gate padlocked to avoid hoodlums using the alley as a throughway.

"Tell him no."

"I've already done so."

The man lurked opposite Zanche on the other side of the iron mesh, peering in. He was a burly man in gray work clothes, official looking, and he carried a clipboard. The outfit didn't mean anything to me. Maybe the city had sent him, but everybody knew the city was corrupt and bribery was required to get service of any kind. Zanche repeated to him what I had just said. The man kept his face pushed to the mesh.

"Tell him to leave," I said.

I stepped out of sight. The conversation went on, more animated than before, though too rapidly for me to understand. I didn't think Zanche would let him in, but she hadn't been herself

lately. The conversation grew more subdued, the man more solic-
itous and friendly, as if trying to find some other means to get his
way. There was another lull—and the gun grew sweaty in my
hand. Just as my patience broke, Zanche came to me at the bottom of the stairs.

"He's gone."

"What did he want?"

"To know if there was another entrance around back, so he
could address the problem without bothering us."

"What did you tell him?"

She glanced at the gun.

"I told him no."

"Good."

"Do you think I'm so foolish, to let in a stranger?"

"There's been another man lately lingering out in the park."

"I know," she said.

She started up the steps, haughty as ever but with no fewer
suspicions about Johnny than I had, wondering too if the appearance of these new men had something to do with my brother.
Johnny had just woken. He sat at the table, crumbling bread into
soft-boiled eggs and drinking black coffee. He was in a jovial
mood, whistling the refrain from a song called "El Perro Negro."
I peered through the balcony slats into the street. The two men
loitered by the terrace, the gangly one and the workman in the
gray clothes. They engaged in a brief conversation. Then the
burly one went on his way, pressing his nose against this gate and
that, testing the handles, poking around for a passage through.

THERE WAS A BACK WAY out, not easily discerned from the street. Dazio's window overlooked a storage shed. A ladder leaned against the shed, heading downward to an enclosed court-yard shared by the buildings on all sides. This courtyard offered entry into an adjoining building through a laundry room, which in turn entered onto the alley whose entrance was blocked by the cyclone gate. If you left that way, you would be within sight of the gate, though only for a moment, because the alley twisted and led by roundabout means onto The Avenue of the Sacred Queen. I hadn't discovered this by myself—it was the path by which Dazio came and went with his young waif from the clubs.

The pair lay in Dazio's room even now, curled up against each other, dead to the world. She was as beautiful as he and just as naive, with her oversize eyes and her big, pouting lips.

I was envious of them both.


THAT AFTERNOON WE SLEPT. It was the local custom, because of the heat. After the morning business, the shop doors shuttered. In this respect the city resembled Europe before the days of the new currency, back when the great dictators and the Church were still in charge. We had fallen into the local habit and lay down to rest, despite the men lurking outside. Zanche's room got the brunt of the sun, so she lay on the daybed in the front room, under the ceiling fan. Dazio was at the back of the house with his little princess. My brother loitered on the bed beside me. We had done the same as children often enough—and occasionally as adults, when circumstances conspired—and I lay there now, looking at him, at his open lips and the lock of hair that fell over his forehead. I probably shouldn't have told him where we were.

But he was my brother, and when I looked at him, I had a hard time looking away.

It might not have been wise to sleep, but it was afternoon—nothing ever happened in the afternoon, everyone slept, even the criminals. The fan spinning overhead, together with the heat, and the faint breeze stirring through the window slats, the breathing of my brother so close, my lack of sleep these nights before—given all this, I felt myself drifting. I heard giggling, footsteps out in the hall, rushing water, more giggling, Dazio and his girl lathering each other in the shower. I should have warned them of the danger outside, but it was still light, they wouldn't be going out, not so soon, and perhaps it would be wiser to worry about my own escape. I saw myself as in a dream, wandering down into the barrios. The streets grew narrow, full of litter. I kept walking, drowsing as I walked. The people knew my face. It appeared on rags, on old newspapers tacked as insulation against shanty walls. The young men watched me, hands in pockets, cradling their dicks, eyes alive with a steel glint. A boy smiled at me, back in the land of blue jeans and soda, and a hand grabbed my thigh, reaching up from down below.

I was awake now. Or half-awake.

It was my brother's hand on my leg. His fingers on my thigh, up under my skirt.

He pulled me under.

Call it a dream if you want. A dream I'd had many times and forgotten as soon as it was over.


IT WAS LATER NOW. The heat hadn't broken, and I was coated with a film of sweat. My closet had been rifled, my things disarranged, and my brother no longer lay in bed beside me. I heard rummaging down the hall, drawers opening and closing. I peered outside. Men often loitered in the plaza below the terrace wall, whistling and catcalling, more as evening drew on. Through the slats I saw the thin one, the marionette, his crooked shadow sketched like graffiti along the cobbled wall. Another man loitered farther below, sitting on a porch stoop, a sharp-looking man, smoking a cigarette, studying his shoes as he smoked. He could have been any one of the rakish men who wander the streets here. But I recognized him. The way he moved, how he flicked his ash into the street, glancing at a passing mulatto girl.

The man was Lodovico.

I went down the hall. Zanche lay as before, under the ceiling fan in the central room. Her bedroom had been disarranged. Johnny's doing, I guessed. At her window, nearer the street, I got a closer look at Lodovico. He sat on the stoop, watching the mouth of the alley that led by twists and turns from our building to the Avenue of the Sacred Queen. But he didn't have access. The cyclone gate was locked and strung with concertina wire.

I wondered where the third man had gone, the burly one in the gray work clothes. I wondered if he'd found the back way. Then I saw him farther down, urinating against a stucco wall.

I found my brother standing at my desk in the alcove at the end of the hall. My valise lay on the desk: the zippered bag where I kept the money I'd taken from the bank. Zanche's purse was there, too. Johnny had taken her revolver out of its little holster and was examining it. He knew something about guns, having grown up in Texas. So did I. It was a snub nose, with a five barrel chamber, and a light action trigger.

"What are you doing?"

"I found this in Zanche's purse."

"For protection," I said.

I didn't mention my own *pistola* some half-dozen steps away, stashed behind the exotic wax plant with the red flowers.

"You went through my closet, too," I said. "My valise . . ."

"She has her bag packed—ready to go."

This didn't surprise me. She was a meticulous person and had kept a bag containing her most vital possessions at the ready ever since Salò.

"Lodovico is out there. With two others."

"I've seen."

"There's a back way."

"I know. I've seen your little friend come and go. Your Dazio. We can't take him with us. None of them."

Zanche was up now, down the hall. I heard her footsteps approaching on the wooden floor.

"You went through my things," she said. "You were in my room."

"Just to open the shutters," my brother said. "To get some cross breeze. You'd think, having lived in Rome, you'd know something about managing the heat."

His explanation was nonsense. He had her purse on the desk, her gun in his hand.

She gave me a beseeching glance.

"You trust this woman too much," my brother said to me. "For all you know, she has been in touch with the murderers outside."

"You're the one who led them here," said Zanche.

"They were lying in wait. I suspected as much. But I came anyway, to help my sister."

Her eyes slanted from one of us to the other. At the picture we made. Myself in this thin skirt, with a damp film all over me, my hair mussed. My brother covered in the same must, his shirt out, his belt hanging loose. I guessed what she was thinking. I thought she might spit out the accusation, or part of it, anyway: *Murderers, the pair of you.* Her lip trembled and there were tears in her eyes, but this welling of emotion wasn't on behalf of Isabella, or Frank, or even Paolo Orsini. It was because she was afraid. For herself, and her lost Gasparo.

"Aw," mocked my brother. "Such crocodile tears."

"Leave her be," I said. "She suffers."

"That's because her man, her lover, has sold her down the river."

"No," she said.

"He was reporting to the head deputy all along, to intelligence ministry. Our every move. Isn't that right?"

Zanche said nothing.

"It's on account of the estate, dear sister. Because on your death, as it now sits, with the papers unexecuted, the money will fall to Dazio's mother. And the stepfather takes control. Meanwhile Isabella's heirs . . . "

"So the head deputy sends these men to kill me. But why?"

"For his own share. With a nickel to the senators. And a penny for the pope."

"No," said Zanche. "Gasparo knew nothing of this."

"You lie."

"No."

"Then you were deceived. Gasparo betrayed you. He obeyed the head deputy's instructions and sent you here, so my sister would be murdered in this country. Because here there'll be no investigation. And as Gasparo's reward, they chopped off his hands and dumped them in the ocean for the fish to chew away the prints."

She called Johnny a name in Italian. It was a foul name, for a man who makes his living by lying facedown and letting a rich man fuck him up the ass.

My brother didn't say anything.

He smiled that sweet smile of his. He held the revolver in his palm. Zanche's lip trembled, but she still had that haughty look. Johnny stepped forward and struck her head with the butt end of the gun.

I cried out.

"Hush," said Johnny.

Zanche lay bleeding. She moaned. I couldn't tell whether she was conscious, but the way she looked up at me—with that wide, black face of hers—some part of me, down in my own darkness, took satisfaction in seeing her humbled. But it was only part of me. Johnny went to the desk and gathered up the valise. Then Dazio and his girl appeared at the other end of the hall. At the sight of us the girl tugged at Dazio's hand, trying to pull him back. Her instincts were right, but Dazio ignored her. *No*, I thought. *Run.* But Dazio wouldn't run, I knew that, or he wouldn't run fast enough, and Johnny would beat him the way he had just beaten Zanche, only more. He would break Dazio's face into pieces, shattering it like so much fine glass.

I reached behind the clay planter and turned to face my brother.

I held the gun in my hand, my *pistola para mujer.*

"Sister," he said.

His eyes sparkled in the way I'd seen a million times. He had that hunger in his eyes, that debonair glint, as if he could persuade me to do anything.

It was true, maybe, but only if I let him speak.

He lowered his hand, imploring me—a funny gesture I remembered from when I was a kid.

I was damp with sweat, and the film was all over me.

I fired.

It was a small-caliber gun, with small-bore bullets. He raised his hand, the one with valise, eyes wide, too wide, and reached with the valise to the spot, below the gut, where the bullet entered. He clutched the valise in one hand and Zanche's gun in the other, and there was an instant in which he could have fired back. The instant passed. I fired again. Then twice more. The bullet holes made a tufted pattern on his chest. He dropped the gun and fell.

"Go," I told Dazio. "Go now. Both of you. The back way."

"You must come, too."

My brother was still alive, facedown, panting into the floor. Zanche's gun lay on the carpet next to him. I picked up her purse and put the gun inside, and the money from the valise. It wasn't all the money. The rest was still in the bank.

"Just go."

"Where?"

"Far away."

"Where?" he asked again.

I gave him the name of a city somewhere along the coast.

"There's a beach there. A long beach. It goes on forever."

"You'll meet us?"

I glanced at my brother, on his side now, curled painfully on the floor. I thought about the men on the street, watching the front of the house and the alley alongside. They needed distracting.

"Are you coming?"

My brother's eyes beseeched me. His hand opened and closed.

"Don't wait for me," I told Dazio. "Just go."


THE LANKY ONE, THE MARIONETTE, leaned as before, standing in the same spot, as if he were a permanent fixture, a lamppost, his long shadow etched forever onto the walk. Lodovico remained at the stoop, hunched and smoking, talking to the burly man who'd done with his urinating but had failed to negotiate his way behind the cyclone gate. From the looks of things, Lodovico was put out with the man. He gestured, spinning his finger in a circle, as if to send him around the block one more time. The marionette raised his fingers to his teeth and whistled.

They came toward me, all three. They came with their sly grins and their cocked heads. I stayed as I was, on the balcony looking down, despite the risk. The front door below was still locked and barred, so they couldn't get in that way. Meanwhile I wanted them away from the stoop so they wouldn't catch a glimpse of Dazio and his girl on the other side of that gate, headed down the alley toward the Avenue of the Sacred Queen.

I had the revolver with me but held it low. In the five chambers, I had one bullet remaining. No doubt they had guns more accurate and deadly than the *pistola para mujer*.

"Ah," said Lodovico. "*Mia bella.*"

Likely they had an assortment of weapons. Lodovico could have shot me from where he stood if that's what he wanted. But no. He might be a hired hand, but he hadn't come all this way to gun a woman down. He wanted something more intimate.

He made a gesture, a hand to his lips, blowing me a kiss.

Then he showed me the blade.

I stepped back through the balcony doors.

INSIDE, MY BROTHER LAY AS before. Zanche was on her hands and knees, struggling to get up. Whether or not she'd betrayed us, it didn't matter. She would never make it. She had lost her love, her Gasparo. I felt sorry for her, but the truth was she needed kindness, not pity. I put the gun to her temple.

I pulled the trigger.

I got on the floor and curled myself around my dying brother.

MY BROTHER DID NOT DIE quickly. I had shot him three times in the chest and once just below the stomach. Since it was a small-caliber weapon, the bullets didn't pass through his body. I felt with my fingers for the entry points: the little frayed holes in his shirt. The wounds were sealed at the surface, cauterized from the heat of the slug but still seeping, and the slugs lay lodged underneath. It seemed one of the bullets had penetrated his lung somewhere near his heart, in the chest cavity. I guessed this because there was blood in his sputum. It hurt for him to breathe, let alone speak. I didn't know what else to do, so I wrapped myself around him and cooed and petted and tried to keep him calm. He moaned and swore softly, over and over, my name mixed into his obscenities, and as the hour grew later and he grew weaker, his voice grew more incoherent until it was just the sound of him rasping into the floor. I thought of Dazio and his girl out there in the streets. If I meant to join them I should go soon, before Lodovico and his cronies found the back entrance—but whenever I moved, my brother tightened his grip on my hand. Outside, the light drained from the sky, not all at once but slowly, until finally it was dark and the sound of my brother's muttering grew so faint it was indecipherable from the vibrations of the surrounding apartments, from the televisions and the white noise of the Avenida and the catcalls in the park. His body coiled and spasmed, and his hand tightened more fiercely around mine. He voided himself and his skin grew cold. Something came over me then. It had happened before. I could have left, but something held me, and I lay for a long time in the stink of him, cooing and petting. Finally I separated myself. Outside, Lodovico's companions lingered—one by the terrace wall, the other by the stoop—but Lodovico himself had disappeared. I went to Dazio's room to study the courtyard below. There was no light other than that which fell from the upper floors, from behind the curtains and slatted window shades of the adjoining flats.

Then, in the slumping shadows, the sudden glow of a cigarette.

IT IS LATE. THE SITUATION outside hasn't changed. The two men maintain their stations across the way. Meanwhile, below, in the courtyard, the smoker remains. The ash glows faint, then bright. After a while he extinguishes the cigarette. Then he lights another, holding the flame longer than necessary, so the flare of the lighter illuminates his features. His head tilts upward, toward me.

Then the flame goes out.

I RETURN TO MY DESK—to the words on this screen, the glittering type—though I stop now and again to pour myself some wine and peer through the slatted blinds toward the Avenida. I check the Internet for rumors of myself. It is a nervous habit, but it gives me some comfort, all those pictures, the speculation, my infinite selves out there in the dark.

The stories multiply.

I have rejoined the nunnery. I am murdered. I have ascended into heaven on a miraculous cloud.

People see whatever they want. So do I.

The night is filled with noise.

The sound of a shadow. The scrape of a ladder. A rattling gate. All three men converge at once. The neighbors sleep, the police, too. On the other side of the world, the head deputy awakens. The pope blows his nose. A key turns in the lock below. Passed along by the German landlord, maybe, gotten by intimidation or money. Or given to them, as my brother suggested, by Zanche herself.

I hear a rush of footsteps.

They are in the house by whatever means, and I see myself as if from above—rising to my feet, headed toward the nearer balcony, where I might make my way over the wall and drop into the street.

Then they are upon me. I'm grabbed from behind, roughly treated, hurled to the tile floor. They hold me, a man on either side, while Lodovico watches. The metal glints in his hand. I try to squirm away, biting and scratching, but the burly one ends this with a fist into my stomach. Then I'm on the bed, the gangly one clamping me on one side, the brutish one on the other, heavy and corporeal, his cheek bristling against my neck. Lodovico looms over me. He holds the tip of the blade beneath my breast. It's a longish blade, flat and thin, with an intricate handle. "Stop wiggling," he says. He pauses. The gray brute makes the sign of the cross. They are superstitious, these assassins, giving me my moment with the divine. I know what comes next, steeling myself. But I don't close my eyes. My lips tremble, searching for something noble, something defiant—at least to spit in Lodovico's face—when all of a sudden he pushes the rapier between my ribs.

*Confess.*

He turns his hand, twisting the blade in my heart, like a man skilled in such maneuvers. The others hold me tight, but I don't see them anymore. It is just me and Lodovico and the blade in my chest. I look into his eyes. They are infinite and black. I feel a great wooziness, a great silence—and in that silence a presence, an emptiness waiting, now, in the moment of death, for me to fall at last upon my knees, to succumb.

But no . . .

I won't succumb. None of this has happened, I tell myself, not yet. I'm still at my chair, at the desk. I raise the glass to my lips and take a drink. I hear the noise below and walk toward the balcony. I make note but ignore the sound out in the hall, the crescendo of rushing feet. The moonlight falls over me, and the men fall into a hush. I am beautiful, I am ugly. I am anything you want. But I am not contrite. The moment collapses into itself, and somewhere in the depths of that instant, I tell myself I will not die. I see my escape. I wander past the terrace wall to the Avenida. And from there to the empty pampas beyond.

## AUTHOR'S NOTE

THOUGH CONTEMPORARY IN ITS SETTING, this novel borrows many elements from John Webster's older play (1612) of the same title, which itself was a reimagination of the true story of a young woman and her brother implicated in a notorious double murder in Rome.

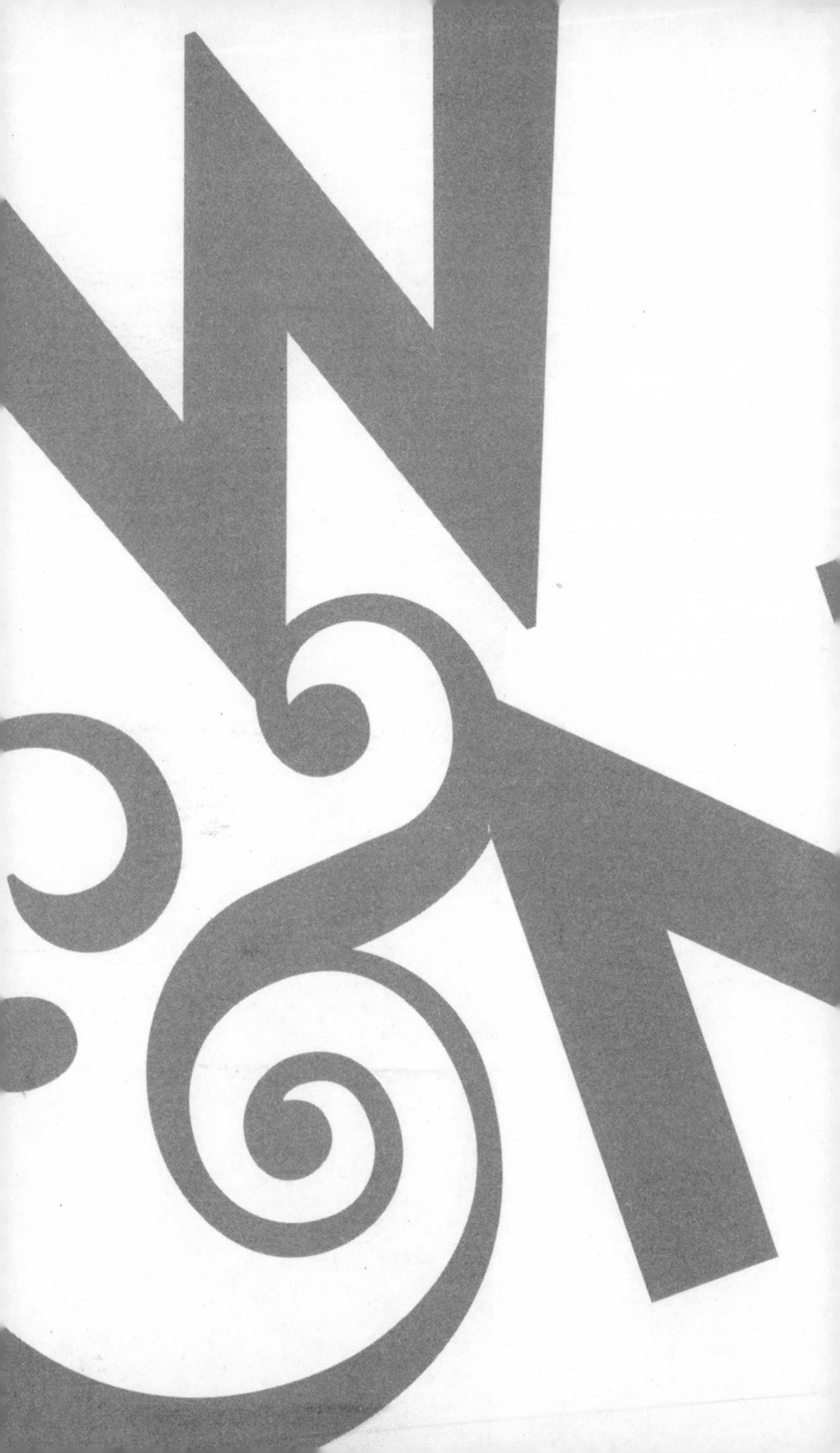